SELECTING EUROPE'S JUDGES

Selecting Europe's Judges

A Critical Review of the Appointment Procedures to the European Courts

Edited by

MICHAL BOBEK

OXFORD
UNIVERSITY PRESS

OXFORD
UNIVERSITY PRESS

Great Clarendon Street, Oxford, OX2 6DP,
United Kingdom

Oxford University Press is a department of the University of Oxford.
It furthers the University's objective of excellence in research, scholarship,
and education by publishing worldwide. Oxford is a registered trade mark of
Oxford University Press in the UK and in certain other countries

Published in the United States of America by Oxford University Press
198 Madison Avenue, New York, NY 10016, United States of America

British Library Cataloguing in Publication Data
Data available

Library of Congress Control Number: 2014958060

ISBN 978–0–19–872778–1

Printed and bound by
CPI Group (UK) Ltd, Croydon, CR0 4YY

Cover image: *Hercules at the Crossroads between Virtue and Pleasure*
(Vice), 1750, by Pompeo Girolamo Batoni.Sabauda Gallery, Turin.
Mondadori Portfolio/Electa/Sergio Anelli/Bridgeman Images

Contents

List of Contributors

Alberto Alemanno is Jean Monnet Professor of Law at HEC Paris and Global Clinical Professor at NYU School of Law.

Michal Bobek is Professor of European Law at the College of Europe, Bruges, and Research Fellow at the Oxford University Institute of European and Comparative Law.

Armin von Bogdandy is Director at the Max Planck Institute for Comparative Public Law and International Law in Heidelberg and President of the OECD Nuclear Energy Tribunal.

Damian Chalmers is Professor of EU Law at the London School of Economics and Political Science.

Henri de Waele is Professor of International and European Law at Radboud University Nijmegen and Guest Professor of European Institutional Law at the University of Antwerp.

R. Daniel Kelemen is Professor of Political Science, Rutgers University and Visiting Fellow, Program in Law & Public Affairs, Princeton University.

David Kosař is Assistant Professor at the Law Faculty Masaryk University in Brno.

Christoph Krenn is Research Fellow at the Max Planck Institute for Comparative Public Law and International Law in Heidelberg.

Koen Lemmens is Associate Professor of Human Rights Law at the University of Leuven and Director of the Leuven Institute for Human Rights and Critical Studies.

Mikael Rask Madsen is Professor of Law and the Director of iCourts-Centre of Excellence for International Courts at the Faculty of Law, University of Copenhagen.

Bilyana Petkova is a Postdoctoral Emile Noël Fellow at the New York University School of Law and a graduate from the Yale Law School.

Aida Torres Pérez is Professor of Constitutional Law at Pompeu Fabra University in Barcelona.

Jean-Marc Sauvé is Vice-president of the French Council of State and the President of the Panel provided for in Article 255 of the Treaty on the Functioning of the European Union.

Georges Vandersanden is Professor Emeritus at the law faculty of the Université Libre de Bruxelles and honorary lawyer at the Brussels bar. Between 2009 and 2013, he was a member of the Civil Service Tribunal Selection Committee.

List of Abbreviations

255 Panel	Panel provided for in Article 255 of the Treaty on the Functioning of the European Union
Advisory Panel	Advisory Panel of Experts on Candidates for Election as a Judge to the European Court of Human Rights
AG	Advocate General
BVerfG	Federal Constitutional Court (Germany)
CDDH	Steering Committee for Human Rights
CFI	Court of First Instance
CJEU	Court of Justice of the European Union
CM	Committee of Ministers
CoE	Council of Europe
Convention	European Convention on Human Rights
COREPER	Committee of Permanent Representatives
CST	Civil Service Tribunal
ECJ	(European) Court of Justice
ECHR	European Convention on Human Rights
ECtHR	European Court of Human Rights
ECSC	European Coal and Steel Community
EFTA	European Free Trade Area
EP	European Parliament
EU	European Union
EUI	European University Institute
GC	General Court of the European Union
IACtHR	Inter-American Court of Human Rights
ICC	International Criminal Court
ICJ	International Court of Justice
ICTY	International Criminal Court for the Former Yugoslavia
OJ	Official Journal of the European Union
PACE	Parliamentary Assembly of the Council of Europe
TEC	Treaty Establishing the European Community
TEU	Treaty on the European Union
TFEU	Treaty on the Functioning of the European Union
UDHR	Universal Declaration of Human Rights
UNTS	United Nations Treaty Series
USSC	United States Supreme Court
WTO	World Trade Organization

Prologue

The Changing Nature of Selection Procedures to the European Courts

Michal Bobek

1. The Topic

Legal realism claims that positivist legal methodology is not genuinely able to control or to constrain judicial decision-making. The modernist idea of a proper legal 'methodology' is just the proverbial façade (*bruxelloise*) behind which the judges will do as they please anyway. Therefore, the only way in which one may perhaps influence what judges will do when they are on the bench, and also to some extent control the judicial quality, is through judicial selection.[1] Metaphorically speaking, once the *how* bastion is declared to be lost, the *who* bastion gains renewed importance. Both are joint vessels: if guards believe they are able to control internal circulation within a town, they might be more relaxed in terms of who is allowed to enter the town. In contrast, if they realize that the policing of all the streets and dark corners at all times is impossible, they are bound to become much more vigilant at entry.

In the course of the past decade, the selection procedures to the European courts, ie the Court of Justice of the European Union (CJEU) and the European Court of Human Rights (ECtHR), have been undergoing significant changes at both the European and national levels. Within the EU, although frequently overlooked, the first practical steps in terms of selection reforms have been taken already with the creation of the first Civil Service Tribunal (CST) Selection Committee in 2005.[2] The evaluation panel established pursuant to Article 255 of the Treaty on

---

[1] Within the European realist tradition, see eg E Ehrlich, *Freie Rechtsfindung und freie Rechtswissenschaft* (Scientia 1973, reprint of the 1903 edn) 28–32. See also eg F Gény, *Méthodes d'interprétation et sources en droit privé positif: Essai critique* (2nd edn, LGDJ 1919); J Esser, 'Motivation und Begründung richterlicher Entscheidungen' in Ch Perelman and P Foriers (eds), *La motivation des décisions de justice* (Bruylant 1978); or generally J Esser, *Vorverständnis und Methodenwahl in der Rechtsfindung* (Athenäum 1970).

[2] There has naturally been previous academic debate on how to reform judicial selection to the EU courts, as well as political proposals. Further see eg A Arnull, *The European Union and its Court*

Functioning of the European Union (TFEU) (the 255 Panel) was created only in 2010 following the changes made by the Treaty of Lisbon, in spite of being already discussed in the Convention on the Future of Europe and later introduced in the stillborn Constitutional Treaty (Article III-357). The task of the 255 Panel is to give opinions on candidates' suitability to perform the duties of judge and advocate general of the Court of Justice and the General Court (GC) before the governments of the member states make the appointment by common accord. Within the Council of Europe, the continuous attention which the Parliamentary Assembly of the Council of Europe (the PACE) has been paying to the quality of the selection process of judges to the ECtHR was boosted by the Interlaken and Izmir conferences in 2010 and 2011. In 2010, the Committee of Ministers established a panel of experts to advise the high contracting parties whether candidates to the ECtHR meet the criteria set by the European Convention (the Advisory Panel). Finally, these changes occurring within both European systems have been influencing corresponding reforms on the national levels. More states have started to openly advertise judicial positions in European courts, making national nominations subject to (at least some) competition.

In sum, the permeating *leitmotif* of the day has become greater professional quality of European judges, with 'judicial comitology' on various levels being identified as the suitable means for achieving this aim. Expert advisory panels in both European systems and advisory or selection committees in a number of states have been set up. The majority of these new expert panels on the European level are composed of sitting or former judges from higher national or European courts. This choice appears logical and natural. Who else should be giving the 'seal' of quality, the *imprimatur*, if not another experienced and esteemed professional? Thus, a distinct element of *de facto* professional co-optation was added to both systems.

Presumably, Europe has always wanted quality judges to sit on its courts. But only recently did it actually start doing something tangible about it. This raises the question: why now? Why the sudden quality concerns? Why the spree of expert advisory bodies for judicial selections some 50 or so years since both European jurisdictions handed down their first decisions? Has the quality of incoming judges all of a sudden dropped? Or, even worse, has Europe realized that the quality was not stellar even in the past, but only now ventured to address the problem?

The described institutional changes are perhaps not as sudden as they may appear. They can hardly be attributed to a renaissance of *legal realism* in the corridors of European institutions or in the breaks of intergovernmental conferences.[3] They may, however, be traced back to a changed *legal reality* in both European jurisdictions of the past decade or two. There was no one single cause in either of

---

of Justice (2nd edn, Oxford University Press 2006) 19–25 or the various contributions and documents in A Dashwood and A Johnston (eds), *The Future of the Judicial System of the European Union* (Hart 2001).

[3] Although imagining diplomats or officials secretly circulating the writings of Ehrlich, Gény, or Esser (n 1) among themselves at an intergovernmental conference, under the desk in a 'samizdat'-like fashion, is certainly intriguing.

the two jurisdictions that could be said to have brought about the changes on its own. Rather, a number of influences can be identified that have been gradually bubbling up within both systems over the past two decades. Their timely convergence or intersection pushed the entire issue to the surface and towards institutional change.

First, both European jurisdictions have witnessed exponential growth in their dockets in the past years. This came, in the case of the ECtHR, rather suddenly after 1998, with the establishment of the permanent Court and, with the benefit of hindsight, the somewhat short-sighted abolishment of the European Commission of Human Rights that previously operated as a filter for the Court. In the case of the CJEU the change was more gradual, but led to similar results. New areas of jurisdiction were added. The number of cases kept increasing, both at the ECJ and in particular at the GC. This in turn began to require much more professional and managerial skills on the part of the sitting judges. Still, this institutional metamorphosis was particularly visible at the ECtHR: no more cosy meetings of wise old men and diplomats who are to travel to Strasbourg every so often, but avalanches of tens of thousands of cases to be dealt with in a factory-like style. All this naturally requires a different type of judging and judges.

Second, the eastern enlargements of both systems brought in not only the increased number of cases just referred to, but also internal diversity within both European jurisdictions. In the span of a few years, both courts almost doubled their membership.[4] The fact that such diverse membership also brought in diverse ideas about who is qualified to sit as a judge at these courts is perhaps no secret. This is certainly not to say that there had not been questionable cases before, with appointees from the 'old' member states raising eyebrows;[5] all is, however, a question of scale and scope. Moreover, it is only natural that in any enlarged institution, the informal, diplomatic understanding about the dos and don'ts is the first thing that is likely to disappear, and will have to be replaced with written, formalized rules.[6]

Third, there has been a change in the academic as well as the political environment in Europe. On the academic side, courts, both national but also European

---

[4] According to the Council of Europe Treaty Office (http://conventions.coe.int), the European Convention was ratified in 1992 by Bulgaria, Hungary, the Czech Republic, and Slovakia (in 1992 still Czechoslovakia, but from 1993 the two independent successor states); in 1993 by Poland; in 1994 by Romania and Slovenia; in 1995 by Lithuania; in 1996 by Estonia, and in 1997 by Latvia. Furthermore, a number of post-Soviet and Balkan countries ratified the European Convention in the second half of the 1990s, namely Albania (1996), Croatia (1997), Georgia (1999), Moldova (1997), Russia (1998), the Former Yugoslav Republic of Macedonia (1997), and Ukraine (1997).

In the case of the European Union, the 15 old member states were joined by ten new member states in 2004 (all, with the exception of Malta and Cyprus, from the former 'Eastern Bloc') and by a further two (Bulgaria and Romania) in 2007.

[5] Moreover, the qualifications required and professional biographies of judges have also changed significantly over time. See eg A Cohen, 'Sous la robe du juge. Le recrutement social de la Cour' in P Mbongo and A Vauchez (eds), *Dans la fabrique du droit européen: scenes, acteurs et publics de la Cour de justice des Communautés européénnes* (Bruylant 2009); N Brown and T Kennedy, *The Court of Justice of the European Communities* (5th edn, Sweet & Maxwell 2000) 58–63.

[6] An illustrative example confirming this suggestion: the Court of Justice of the EU felt the need to enact its first ever Code of Conduct only in 2007. See OJ [2007] C 223/01.

and international, have become the subject of more critical and intense analysis and questioning than before.[7] The discussions among legal scholars have been complemented by contributions from political scientists who, in no minimalist fashion, do not hesitate to talk of 'judicialization of politics', 'judicial governance', or even 'juristocracy'.[8] Both types of academic discourse naturally interact with and are fuelled by the political debates. Within the political realm, the on-going Euro-fatigue and omnipresent Euro-crisis that gradually turned into Euro-scepticism started to create a different political climate than before—a climate in which the European institutions may feel a greater need to justify what and how they are doing. Consequently, the European courts might encounter increased resistance today, both with respect to individual judgments that displease one or more member states[9] and also in terms of full-scale institutional contestation.[10] Occasional Euro-resistance is certainly nothing new. What is striking today is the scope of the wholescale contestation of Europe, no longer limited to a few ministerial corridors or courtrooms in one member state.[11]

Within such a climate, who sits on a European court and how s/he got there matters much more than before. As with any human activity, disagreement *ad rem* might quickly spill over into attacks *ad hominem*. Sadly, it tends to be much easier to shoot down the messenger than to honestly engage with the message. Thus, judicial authority and credibility have become more important than ever.

In sum, the dual enlargement (jurisdictional and geographical), coupled with changes in both the political and discursive spheres in recent years, prodded both systems into revisiting their institutional arrangements with regard to judicial selections at the next opportune moment, when larger institutional changes were being discussed. However, even with the European side of the process enhanced following the infusion of 'judicial comitology', the primary responsibility for nominating quality candidate(s) to the European courts no doubt remains with the states, with the notable exception of the CST. It now, however, goes hand-in-hand with European quality-based supervision.

---

[7] Further M Bobek, 'Legal Reasoning of the Court of Justice of the EU' (2014) 39 *EL Rev.* 418, 427–8.

[8] For an introduction see eg R Hirschl, 'The Judicialization of Politics', in K Whittington, RD Kelemen, and G Caldeira (eds), *The Oxford Handbook of Law & Politics* (Oxford University Press 2008).

[9] Suffice it perhaps to mention just two cases as keywords: *Hirst v UK (No. 2)* App no 74025/01 (ECtHR, 6 October 2005) and Case C-144/04 *Mangold* [2005] ECR I-9981.

[10] Culminating recently in, for example, the Czech *Ústavní soud* flatly refusing to follow a decision of the ECJ and declaring it to be *ultra vires* (ÚS, plenary judgment of 31 January 2012, Pl ÚS 5/12, available in English at <www.usoud.cz>) or the Polish *Trybunał Konstytucyjny* in the judgment of 16 Nov 2011, SK 45/09, in English translation at <http://trybunal.gov.pl/en/case-list/judicial-decisions>, stopping perhaps one step before that and 'just' subjecting Council Regulation (EC) No 44/2001 of 22 December 2000 on jurisdiction and enforcement of judgments (the Brussels I Regulation) to direct judicial review as to its compatibility with the Polish Constitution. Furthermore, the German *Bundesverfassungsgericht* has recently decided to 'join the conversation' by not sending requests for preliminary rulings to the ECJ, but rather issuing 'preliminary threats' (BVerfG of 14 January 2014, 2 BvR 2728/13, online at <www.bverfg.de>).

[11] See eg B Davies, *Resisting the European Court of Justice: West Germany's Confrontation with European Law, 1949–1979* (Cambridge University Press 2012).

These changes open up an array of fascinating questions, both empirical and normative. Have these institutional reforms been successful in securing a greater quality of the judicial appointees? Which of the European systems generates 'better' results and why? What are the persisting problems? How do the two levels of selection, national and European, influence each other? Has the creation of advisory panels shifted the institutional balance in any way—either horizontally, among the various institutions of the respective international organization, or vertically, between the organization and its member states? Do the new selection mechanisms have any positive impact on the legitimacy of the European courts? On the whole, what should be the guiding principles for selecting Europe's judges—Expertise only? Social representativeness? Is the move towards expert selection panels to be welcomed, or should political considerations (still) matter?

These and a number of other questions are addressed in this volume from a comparative and interdisciplinary perspective. This book has two principal aims: first, to describe in depth, for the first time,[12] the operation of the new selection mechanisms from different vantage points, including contributions not just by (academic) external observers but also by insiders, practitioners engaged in the judicial selections in each of the systems discussed. Second, having mapped the ground, the aim is to critically engage with selected common themes in a comparative way, analysing the new mechanisms with respect to values and principles such as democracy, judicial independence, transparency, representativeness, and legitimacy.

Neither of these two aims is an easy one, given the confidentiality of the selection processes. However, it is precisely the information barrier that may give rise to the wildest academic speculations or even accusations as to what precisely the selection panels are doing and why. It is therefore essential to lift the veil at least a little bit, allowing for a reasonable exchange between 'insiders' and 'outsiders'. Once such an exchange takes place, it becomes apparent that even if confidential, the selection panels are not the (sometimes imagined) bloodthirsty secret judicial fraternities that, following esoteric and arcane rituals, are admitting new acolytes into the ranks of the transnational judicial priesthood. They are, rather, a group of professionals who, faced with a delicate task, are trying to do the job they have been asked to do, within the confines of the mandate that came with it. This naturally does not mean that all of the decisions taken by them are irreproachable or that none of the standards set are open to further debate. Quite to the contrary: such a debate must be happening and must be seen to be happening, even more so in a procedural setup in which the operation as well as the results of the panels' work are confidential and, as a matter of fact, final. Absent such visible debate and exchange, even a panel composed of the most illustrious judicial experts will lose

---

[12] For notable recent articles on the topic see NP Engel, 'More Transparency and Governmental Loyalty for Maintaining Professional Quality in the Election of Judges to the European Court of Human Rights' (2012) 32 *Human Rights Law Journal* 448 and T Dumbrovský, B Petkova, and M Van der Sluis, 'Judicial Appointments: the Article 255 TFEU Advisory Panel and Selection Procedures in the Member States' (2014) 51 *Common Market Law Review* 460.

the only source of legitimacy it really has: the trust and support of the professional community, which is in real terms more important than the formal mandate given by the institutions that established the panel in question.

2. The Structure

The book is divided into three parts. The first part consists of Chapters 1–4. It focuses on the Court of Justice of the EU, the operation of the 255 Panel and the CST Selection Committee, and their relationship with other institutions and bodies of the EU. The second part is composed of Chapters 5 and 6. It carries out a similar exercise with respect to the European Court of Human Rights and the system of the Council of Europe, introducing in particular the work of the (Committee of Ministers') Advisory Panel and the Parliamentary Assembly's Sub-Committee on the election of judges to the European Court of Human Rights (the Sub-Committee). The third part, consisting of Chapters 7–12, is transversal and more theoretical in its approach. Chapters in this part focus on a more specific issue or element, which is then examined more deeply and comparatively with respect to both European systems as well as other international or national regimes. Finally, the Epilogue wraps up the discussions by revisiting some of the recurring arguments and ideas.

In Chapter 1, Henri de Waele sets the scene with respect to the selection mechanisms to the CJEU: *who* selects (who are the selectors and how are they themselves chosen); *how* (according to what procedures); and *what* are the results in terms of figures and raw data (how many are approved, how many rejected). The meticulously researched chapter provides, however, more than just an introduction to facts and procedures relating to both the selecting bodies to the CJEU: the 255 Panel and the CST Committee. First, the introduction given is comparative. It explains not only what both bodies do, but also what their counterparts might be in the national legal systems or other international regimes. Although EU lawyers like to think of their system as a *unique, sui generis* creature, in terms of selection of judges they should rather conclude that 'we are not alone'. Second, the author has the gift of making otherwise fairly uninteresting facts and figures talk, or certainly to prod the reader's curiosity: how in fact were the selectors, ie the members of the individual committees, selected? Did it make a difference in the criteria coined and employed by the 255 Panel that its first members were predominantly senior male national judges?

De Waele's chapter also articulates for the first time several themes that continue to resound in following chapters, approached from different angles. First, there is the question of (dis)continuity. In general, one might be tempted to believe that a certain degree of continuity with regard to both selectors as well as selectees might be beneficial. By way of illustration, the high turnover at the GC is sometimes identified as one of the vices that contribute to its not performing well. Yet, as the author puts it, in crude terms of numbers and statistics, both the CST Committee and the CST membership itself appear to be dominated by considerations other than the desire for any continuity. The consideration of geographical representativeness is certainly understandable; however, should it be allowed to dominate the entire process as well as its results so completely as to leave no stone unturned at every renewal of the CST as well as its Selection Committee? Is it wise to renew the membership of the entire CST Committee completely every four years? Is it reasonable not to renew the terms of sitting judges where one has apparently no doubt that they have performed well? Even if the answer to these questions is yes, why then should such considerations be applicable only to the CST Committee and not to the 255 Panel, where it was (luckily) decided to keep a fair degree of personal continuity? With tongue in cheek, it would appear that the issue with regard to the iron bed that Procrustes built and which makes its appearance in the title of the chapter is not necessarily one of size, but one of time: every guest is allowed to spend one night only. Each morning, however, heads will roll.

De Waele's chapter also raises the issue of the mutual influence between the European and the national levels. Not only can the European level through the 255 Panel effectively block the national nomination. It also starts projecting itself back on the national level with respect to the procedure required as well as, very likely, the criteria employed. At the same time, the overview of the national selection mechanisms offered by the author reveals a variety of the procedures employed on the domestic level: from the open national competitions that might—but might not—have been adopted in view of the changed European requirements down to the nominally closed nominations, where, essentially, the sitting government of the day choses a candidate.

Chapter 2, authored by Damian Chalmers, suggests that there is a correlation between the professional backgrounds of the judges at the Court of Justice and the values and visions that are translated into the decisions rendered by the institution. The fact that there is likely to be a connection, perhaps in the form of correlation rather than causation, between these two elements may appear to be common sense. That common sense is, however, notoriously difficult to quantify in any empirical research. The classical Weberian conundrum relating to sociology of institutions arises quickly: how far can an individual and her background really shape an established institution, or is it rather the institution that will decisively form the individual, quickly diluting her personal characteristics and imposing the institutional culture and spirit?

To substantiate the central argument, the chapter divides the history of the Court of Justice into four periods. For each of the periods, a correlation is suggested between the composition of the Court of Justice in that period and the prevailing judicial mentality translated into the decisions it produced back then. Thus, a distinctly political early Court of Justice (up until 1969) composed chiefly of university professors and national civil servants with previous negotiation and diplomatic experience perhaps had different ideas and institutional dynamics than the subsequent Court of Justice (1970–93), in which the judicial element, albeit with a strong disposition towards academia, was more strongly represented.

The internal balance might have changed again between 1994 and 2009, when it appears that former civil servants acquired a much more prominent role in the Court of Justice.

The divisions and classifications set out by Chalmers might be contested in a number of ways. Equally, there is no doubt that some of the judicial 'objects' observed and evaluated by the author in a certain way might challenge their classification. Especially those judges or advocates general from diverse backgrounds might feel that they belong in a different box. Be that as it may, by connecting judicial output with judicial background, Chalmers' chapter makes a strong indirect claim for the realist vision introduced in the opening paragraph of this prologue: judicial selections and the background of the individual appointees matter to the way in which a court will be deciding.

Chalmers goes even a bit further and claims that selection and appointment to the Court of Justice should be informed by the function that the Court of Justice is supposed to exercise. In other words, the traditional sequence ought to be reversed. Instead of waiting until after appointments have taken place to find out what judicial skills and expertise will be present in the institution, and consequently wondering which course the new Court of Justice is likely to take, the required judicial skill set needed ought to be defined first and judges should be selected on its basis. Chalmers concludes that this is even more important today, since the Court of Justice finds itself at a crossroads between acting as a quasi-constitutional court for Europe and as a mere guardian and interpreter of more technical secondary EU legislation. Each direction requires a different skill-set from the judicial appointees. If the declared direction is out of sync with the skill-set present at the Court of Justice in question, this will only lead to judicial dogmatism and all kinds of negative effects, with the overall level of authority and legitimacy naturally diminishing.

Chapters 3 and 4 are authored by notable practitioners who have been involved in the work of the respective selection panels for the CJEU. In the third chapter, Jean-Marc Sauvé sets out the aims and the operational mode of the 255 Panel, coupled with an evaluation of the first four years of the work of the 255 Panel over which he has presided. It is suggested that the key objective of the 255 Panel has been achieved: to evaluate, in all independence and impartiality, the ability and competence of a candidate and thereby to contribute to the safeguarding and increased legitimacy of the EU judiciary.

There are at least three significant observations in the chapter that merit highlighting. First, as Sauvé rightly reminds us, the 255 Panel can only block a nomination made by a member state. Although it wields a powerful veto, which could be overridden only by a unanimous decision of all member states, this still remains just a blocking veto. Thus, the frequently raised academic suggestions that the 255 Panel should prefer this type or that type of candidate might be slightly misplaced since the 255 Panel cannot exercise a positive choice between more options, at least not directly. On the other hand, it is fair to admit that by repetitively rejecting certain types of candidates and formulating certain sets of criteria, the 255 Panel can exert considerable indirect influence over the type of nominations made.

Second, distrust is voiced towards the election of judges. Although discussing only the potential elections by the Council (of the EU) or by the European Parliament, the reservation could be perceived as a somewhat hidden thorn aimed at the way in which the judges are selected to the ECtHR. After all, it is only the Parliamentary Assembly of the Council of Europe that provides a notable exception to the overall European dislike for judicial elections.

Third, and perhaps most important, it is suggested that the 255 Panel could be seen 'as a germ of a council of judiciary within the Union'. This is an intriguing proposition. If embraced, it would have, among other things, implications for the future composition of the 255 Panel. It could be interpreted as suggesting that the majority of the 255 Panel members ought to be appointed from within (national) judiciaries. This is certainly possible, but it ought to be recalled that such a specific composition of the 255 Panel is not the sole possibility. Art 255 TFEU foresees three different sets from which members of the 255 Panel might be drawn. 'Members of national supreme courts' is just one of them, standing alongside 'former members of the Court of Justice and the General Court' and 'lawyers of recognised competence'. This is not to suggest that the proposal made by the president of the CJEU and endorsed by the Council nominating four and, later, five senior national judges to the seven-member 255 Panel was not a good one, beneficial for the CJEU's legitimacy in the eyes of national judiciaries today. To identify the 255 Panel as a germ of a council of judiciary within the Union nonetheless goes a bit further. It establishes a narrative that seeks to petrify a *certain* composition of the 255 Panel also for its future embodiments.

Chapter 4, by Georges Vandersanden, deals with the practical experience of the CST selection committees. The wisdom with which the chapter acknowledges that no selection process is in fact able to guarantee the selection of a good judge, and that all that members of a selection panel can do is to place a 'qualified bet', is in many ways remarkable—certainly within a volume that is otherwise permeated with a process-driven optimism, labouring under the modernist belief that sound, fair, and transparent processes must be able to deliver good results.

Vandersanden reminds the reader of the often neglected fact that within the Union structure, the first testing of the new ways in which Union judges are to be selected started as early as 2005, with the first CST Committee starting its work and selecting the first seven judges for the CST. In spite of being perhaps less in the limelight than its by now better known companion, the 255 Panel, the work of the CST Committee(s) is truly revolutionary in terms of principle: no more one state – one judge convention, no more state-based nominations, no more backstage diplomatic dances detrimental to the professional quality. Instead, there are Europe-wide open competitions to which any EU citizen can directly apply and the decisive criterion is merit.

That ought to be the case, at least in theory. The first ten years of practice as analysed by Vandersanden offer, however, a slightly more nuanced and sobering picture: nominally open, nationality-blind competitions generate a court composed almost exclusively of former CJEU legal secretaries, with seats carefully distributed amongst the individual nationalities. Six out of seven CST judges are former legal secretaries, all seven are of different nationalities. The latter consideration, disguised under the heading of the requirement of a 'broad geographical basis', apparently even leads to a Council policy of non-renewal of outgoing judges. Some sort of representativeness of different legal systems within the Union is certainly understandable—should it, however, lead to considerations of merit and continuity being superseded by an uncompromising 'every state must have a go' principle that seems to be more important than the proper operation of the CST? Equally, experienced legal secretaries from the Court of Justice or the GC will typically have a mastery of EU law and EU civil service law like that of few other candidates. Is this nonetheless true to the extent as to make the CST, as Vandersanden puts it, the exclusive 'end-of-career station' for senior legal secretaries? The devil is, as always, in the detail, and in the execution of generally laudable ideas. Vandersanden's chapter shows how such details may amount to a problem eventually undermining the very foundations of an otherwise progressive model.

In the following chapters, our attention turns to Strasbourg. Chapter 5, authored by Koen Lemmens, introduces the current (s)election mechanism to the ECtHR and its evolution. We see a complex institutional landscape emerging, at the level of the Council of Europe as well as in the contracting parties. At the level of the Council of Europe, a multitude of institutions are engaged in the process: they include the Committee of Ministers and its Advisory Panel as well as the PACE and its Sub-Committee. Even in such a bifurcated system, it remains clear that the PACE is the key player eventually electing the judges. Over the years, the institutions of the Council of Europe have issued a rich array of various guidelines and recommendations. In contrast to the EU, European 'projection' onto the national levels is stronger. There is an explicit (soft law) framework regarding how the contracting parties ought to carry out national selections of the three candidates to be forwarded to the Council of Europe, what criteria the candidates should meet and what the gender balance should be, all the way down to rather detailed issues such as to how candidates' CVs ought to be structured, and so on.

But still, even with (or perhaps because of?) all these explicit and detailed rules, it would appear from the chapter and the sources quoted therein that the more recent practice of judicial selections to the ECtHR has not been entirely satisfactory. More and more 'incidents' have recently occurred in the process, or there is certainly a more critical debate about them going on. The mechanism is not working properly: the opinions of the Advisory Panel are neglected or even blatantly disregarded; the position of the the PACE Sub-Committee is not that strong in the process either; and the ultimate decision-maker, the Parliamentary Assembly, seems to be nonchalantly disinterested in the democratic act of electing the judges to the ECtHR, at least judging from the low numbers of the PACE members present at the recent elections.

The moderately better news emerging from Lemmens' chapter is that at least some contracting parties take the national part of the selection process seriously. The three samples chosen, namely the UK, France, and Belgium, may show some deficiencies, but on the whole the competition for nominations is indeed open. Finally, the issue of 'de-politicization' of the judicial selections to the European courts first takes the stage in this chapter. Lemmens' simple but very pertinent statement in this regard merits underlining: 'As long as the Convention hallows the idea of democratically elected judges, we have to accept the flip side of this coin: lobbying, political games, international wheeling and dealing'.

David Kosař's Chapter 6 is rich and thought-provoking. If, in Lemmens' chapter, the shortcomings of the current selection mechanism of judges for the ECtHR were rather diplomatically flashing through the assorted facts and figures, Kosař's chapter dissects them in full light. The gloves are off. Building on a recent empirical study, Kosař suggests that the optimistic and diplomatic tone taken in talking of success, with perhaps occasional 'mishaps' or 'incidents', in judicial elections to the Strasbourg Court is no longer warranted. Instead, the inadequate qualifications, experience, and stature of some of the Strasbourg judges pose a threat to the institutional legitimacy of the ECtHR, which is already being perceived in some states. In other words, 'mishaps' are perceived as more of a rule than the odd exception and spill over into the (lack of) institutional legitimacy of the ECtHR.

What went wrong? Kosař's analysis proceeds in two parts. First, he critically discusses the individual criteria currently set by Strasbourg for the judicial candidates: gender; language requirements; age; knowledge of national law and public international law. Second, he outlines the recent individual 'mishaps' from the procedural point of view, pinpointing what precisely the problem might have been. The example of the election of a Czech judge in 2012 features prominently in the discussion. It offers the example of a contracting party pushing through—and the PACE, after heavy lobbying, eventually electing—a candidate who had been apparently declared unsuitable for the office by the Advisory Panel and who was not recommended by the Sub-Committee.

How can one trust a system that allows for such results? The picture arising from detailed discussion of both of these types of shortcomings, ie with regard to substantive criteria as well as the procedure, is troubling. A more pessimistic reader pondering on the chapter and also seeking to interpret other recent cases might gain the impression that the ECtHR is being staffed with '30-something judges' of questionable competence, who became judges at the Strasbourg Court only because they were put on the candidate list in order to provide a third name, but then miraculously (or after heavy political lobbying with the PACE, with merit replaced by political behind-the-scenes deals) were elected, or only because they happened to be a woman, or in fact because of both. A more optimistic reader might perhaps not be that disheartened (yet), pointing out that the cases discussed are the odd exceptions and that the system is still able to elect stellar candidates.

Finally, apart from providing extremely rich food for thought with respect to the substantive criteria as well as the procedure, there is one common theme that is continually raised in Kosař's chapter and merits highlighting: namely the sad fact of the PACE disregarding its own criteria and conditions. As both Kosař and, previously, Lemmens show, the PACE is not shy in formulating recommendations or guidelines as to how the contracting parties ought to behave when selecting candidates for the ECtHR at the national level. The same requirements seem, however, to be nonchalantly disregarded when it comes to individual elections by the

PACE. In some cases requirements relating to gender or age are applied; in others they are not. This fact, coupled with secrecy and non-transparency as far as (s)elections on the level of the Council of Europe are concerned, may generate a bitter aftertaste for some contracting parties and academic observers. Fair, foreseeable, and transparent procedures are required, but apparently only as long as they apply to somebody else—ideally to the contracting parties only. However, the rule of law is something other than 'the rule of the Assembly'. Even a sovereign, if it wishes to be respected, is bound by the rules it enacts in future individual cases. Thus, in the popular sport of blame-shifting between the European and the national levels, Kosař places the blame back at the Strasbourg doors. He concludes that when observing such a state of affairs, potential top candidates for judicial office in Strasbourg may be discouraged from applying as the PACE is unpredictable and unprincipled, whereas less-than-stellar candidates will apply precisely because the PACE is unpredictable and unprincipled.

Chapter 7 opens the transversal and comparative part of the volume. In their argument, Armin von Bogdandy and Christoph Krenn may be believed, at first sight, to swim against the tide of the previous chapters. When introducing and analysing the operation of the individual selection mechanism, the authors of the previous chapters appeared to be largely satisfied with the technocratic selection process of the EU that is, however, able to generate quality selection 'output', and dissatisfied with the Council of Europe, in particular in the case of the PACE, that follow democratic processes leading nonetheless to questionable output. This may be labelled as pragmatic, results-oriented thinking. Von Bogdandy and Krenn reverse this way of thinking, by putting a principle first, and only then looking at the respective selection mechanisms.

The principle guiding their analysis is democracy, which is a legal commitment common to both international organizations. It can be subdivided into further requirements of transparency, participation, and deliberation. The authors are certainly not suggesting that respect for the democratic principles would require election of judges. Their approach is more nuanced, distinguishing between two stages: the elaboration of rules and criteria that will be applied in judicial selections, and then the application of these criteria in the individual selections. The principle of democracy requires a different type of involvement for experts and expert panels at both stages. As a rule, it is not the task of experts to define the general criteria by themselves. They may advise and inform the decision-maker with regard to the criteria, but the ultimate decision on those ought to be democratic.

If judged against such a yardstick, it is the Council of Europe and in particular the PACE that perform better than the EU and the 255 Panel. Von Bogdandy and Krenn suggest that when devising the criteria for selections to the ECtHR, the PACE engaged in a communicative and democratic exchange with other institutions. Its stance on the matter was subject to open contestation and reconsideration, including an advisory opinion from the ECtHR and exchanges with the Committee of Ministers. This co-operative, multilevel, and deliberative outlook is convincing in the light of democratic principles. Conversely, the unilateral 'decreeing' of both conditions as well as their application in individual cases by the 255 Panel, without there being any exchange with other institutions and any possibility of review of individual cases, fails to convince in the light of the principle of democracy.

If approached on the level of an ideal, the analysis is compelling. As the authors remind us at the very end of their chapter, there might nonetheless often be a gap between the level of ideals and their practical application. Thus, whereas the Council of Europe and the PACE might be regarded as leaders in the way they elaborate the rules for selecting judges to the ECtHR, they can hardly claim the same status as far as the actual application of these rules is concerned. For that, they would have to respect their own rules first. Thus, consonant with the conclusions of the previous chapters, the authors acknowledge the huge problems encountered in the Strasbourg practice. Their previous ideal-driven analysis presents, however, an important reminder: ideals and symbols do matter, not just pragmatic results.

Chapter 8, written by Aida Torrez Pérez, analyses judicial selections to European courts as well as other international courts in the light of the principle of judicial independence. More specifically, the question asked is how to constrain state governments in their nominations to the European courts, in order to safeguard independence of the judicial appointees. Torrez Pérez notes that with respect to judicial selections to international courts, the traditional scenario well evidenced in a number of other areas of international co-operation is present: self-empowerment of the national executives through the international plane. With regard to judicial appointments to international courts, the whole process is dominated by the national executive(s). With the exception of the election of judges by the PACE, it is the government that selects the candidate at the national level, and then the same government that appoints the candidate in the company of similarly minded and mutually sympathetic governments at the international level.

This creates the risk of governments nominating 'loyal' judges who will defend governmental interests and endangers the judicial independence of international courts. Torrez Pérez' concern is, however, not with politics. She acknowledges that a national government might express some political preferences as to what candidate they wish to nominate. The objective is thus not to completely depoliticize the nomination processes, which would most likely not even be feasible, but to constraint the government as to the range of choices it can make. In other words, there ought to be incentives for governments to seek and appoint the most suitable candidates in terms of merit, without denying the role that politics inevitably play.

In the remainder of her chapter, the author outlines four mechanisms that may constrain governments in this regard: parliamentary bodies, expert panels, transparency, and tenure. All four mechanisms are discussed in detail, with special attention being paid to their operation with respect to the CJEU and the ECtHR. The chapter concludes that in spite of all their (current) flaws in terms of transparency, expert advisory bodies may represent the most suitable means available to improve the chances of selecting independent judges in terms of merit and quality, untainted by party politics.

Alberto Alemanno's Chapter 9 challenges on many levels the conventional statement that both panels—the 255 Panel as well as the Advisory Panel—are bound to operate within an enhanced level of confidentiality in order to protect the privacy and reputation of the judicial candidates they are called to evaluate. In terms of transparency, which is the key principle discussed in Alemanno's chapter, both panels operate as a sort of 'black box'. Neither their input nor their output are known, with the 255 Panel's regular general activity reports providing some dim light into the EU box. With respect to the level of transparency required by the European actors, the same paradox is identified as in previous chapters: neither of the two panels operates in a context of transparency equal to what they require from the member states when selecting their judicial candidates.

Alemanno argues that such a secretive approach is flawed on many levels. How can opinions have any pedagogical effect if they are kept secret? Coupled with a lack of oversight of the activity of the panels, and no judicial or other control of individual decisions, can this be in fact beneficial for the legitimacy of European courts—that judges are vetted by a secret committee and, on the basis on undisclosed reasons, are declared (un)fit for judicial office? Additionally, as Alemanno points out, since there is difficulty in drawing the line between expertise-checking and opinion-checking in any form of suitability assessment, what prevents the advisory panels taking considerations other than those officially stated into account? Certainly, such prophylactic suggestions might be considered completely misplaced. The problem with secrecy is, however, precisely that: nobody can know in fact whether or not they are misplaced.

In the remainder of his chapter, Alemanno takes apart one by one the most commonly used objections against the disclosure of individual opinions of the advisory panels: duty of confidentiality; data protection; reputational costs; and the potential chilling effect on future candidatures. His objections to the argument based on the threat to the reputation of an unsuccessful candidate are particularly convincing. If the name of the candidate put forward to the advisory panels' assessment is publicly known, and then the result inevitably becomes known as well (since the candidate will not be appointed), not knowing the reasons for which a particular candidate was rejected is only bound to give rise to the wildest speculation and gossip. That might be more harmful to the candidate in question than the (diplomatically put) truth. As Alemanno concludes, one may be tempted to believe that the current confidentiality policy seems more effective in protecting the panels' operation from public scrutiny than the candidates' reputation.

In Chapter 10, Bilyana Petkova demonstrates that the elaboration of criteria and procedures for judicial selections on the European level is not taking place in isolation from the national ones. Mutual influences and inspiration—or spill-overs, as the author calls them—are occurring in both directions: vertically, ie between the European systems and Europe's member states, but also horizontally, ie between the European systems, the EU, and the Council of Europe. Moreover, in all of these directions, the inspirational traffic flows in both ways. This means, in its vertical dimension, that the exchange between the European and the national levels includes not just top-down impositions, but also bottom-up inspiration.

For discussion of horizontal spill-overs, Petkova uses the example of gender equality. At the outset, the readers are reminded of the dynamic nature of criteria for judicial selections in the past, even the definition of merit. The chapter shows how the requirement of gender equality, originally neglected or flatly rejected in the early 1990s, made its way into the mainstream some 20 years later and is likely to become accepted as a criterion in selecting judges in Europe. It became the norm with respect to nominations to the Strasbourg Court, albeit with mixed success. Will the EU, in view of the looming accession to the ECHR, be able to resist a vertical spill-over of the same requirement being imported from Strasbourg to Luxembourg?

Lastly, Petkova also gives examples of vertical spill-overs, in terms of procedure as well as the elaboration of substantive criteria for judicial selections to the European courts. There is a clear engagement between the European and the national. As far as selection procedures are concerned, there are four member states that have modified their national selection procedures under a distinct lead emanating from the 255 Panel; there are, however, more states that organize some sort of national competition or selection—although this pre-dates the establishment of both European advisory panels. Thus, any sweeping statements about the 'Europeanization' of the national selection procedures following the European lead would be precarious. As far as the time-line is concerned, it would be difficult to say who in fact 'Europeanized' whom: whether Europe its members or, more likely on the basis of the evidence presented, member states their Europe.

The two closing chapters take a broader, explicitly multidisciplinary approach to judicial selections. Chapter 11, written by Daniel Kelemen, starts by soberly reminding any reader potentially too excited about the freshly carved novelty of selection procedures to the European courts that Europe has in the past experimented with a wide array of ways of selecting and appointing judges, reflecting different convictions as to how a legitimate judicial power ought to be properly constituted. Today, it would appear that in the name of enhancing the legitimacy of both European courts, the newly established selection procedures wish to get rid of politics, to 'depoliticize' the selection process. This might be, Kelemen feels, slightly short-sighted. In order to maintain legitimacy, democratically elected officials must continue to play a central role in the process of judicial selection and appointment.

This lies at the centre of the paradox discussed by Kelemen: 'depoliticized' judges, cut loose from any democratic/political processes in the name of enhancing their legitimacy and submitted to the scrutiny of only expert panels of their peers, are bound to lose the only (democratic) legitimacy they ever had. In the second part of his chapter, Kelemen focuses more specifically on the cases of the ECJ and ECtHR, showing why the use of 'a bit of politics' in selecting their judges may not be harmful. Even when the appointment of judges becomes more politicized, this is not necessarily bad, provided that political influence over judicial appointments is not concentrated in a narrow set of hands or in one period of time. As long as such danger of 'court-packing' is excluded, which is in fact the case with respect to both European courts by default, the various potential political preferences expressed by the nominating governments will eventually create a judicial 'median', democratically representative of the various views present in Europe.

This, in turn, is certainly bound to bolster the legitimacy of the European courts, not to threaten it.

An important point made by Kelemen concerns the conviction that the involvement of supranational legislative bodies, such as the PACE or the European Parliament, will confer the much desired democratic legitimacy onto supranational courts. This may, however, not be the case, since the legitimacy of international courts tends to reflect the legitimacy of the international institution of which it is a part. To put it in a metaphor, a person drowning in a river can hardly ask another person drowning next to her in the same stream to pull the former out. Within such a context, it might be better to rely again on national institutions instead.

In sum, the chapter offers a refreshing view from the other side of the Atlantic. In Europe, we tend to automatically ban the word 'politics' from the realm of judicial selection, shying away from putting the two even within the same sentence. Kelemen suggests that, first, the wisdom of this may not be entirely true, even with regard to seemingly 'expert' advice, and second, 'a bit of politics' in selecting judges might not be entirely bad either.

In Chapter 12, Mikael Rask Madsen offers a multilayered reflection on legitimacy of international courts, in particular with regard to the ECtHR. On the first, basic level, with regard to the case study of the ECtHR, Madsen suggests that over the years, the composition of the ECtHR has undergone a deep transformation. Before the creation of the permanent ECtHR, the Strasbourg Court was essentially composed of (elderly, male) law professors with significant connections to both politics and legal practice, who were actively engaged in legal diplomacy. In contrast, the post-1998 permanent ECtHR has witnessed a greater 'legalization' and technicalization in its composition, seeing relatively younger persons with a predominantly human rights profile being appointed to the Strasbourg bench, but plagued by a lack of certain *auctoritas* and *gravitas*. This increased technicalization can be attributed in large part to the current processes of selection to the ECtHR. It generates a structural weakness in the current ECtHR: the inability to address the political challenges ahead by the means of renewed legal diplomacy, acknowledging the fact that international human rights law is as much 'technical law' as it is, in fact, international relations and diplomacy.

In this dimension, Madsen's analysis neatly complements the second chapter by Damian Chalmers, this time focusing on the diachronic mutations of the professional background of the ECtHR judges. On its deeper level, however, Madsen's chapter challenges the mainstream legitimacy discussion. It suggests that in order to properly comprehend the notion of legitimacy, there is a need for change in the analytical focus: from the dominant normative idea of the legitimacy defined by discussions about representativeness or notions of transparency and accountability, to a more dynamic understanding of legitimacy. Moreover, legitimating strategies of international courts are multilayered, including more levels of external interface: legal and political as well as societal. Lastly, if viewed in such interaction, conflicts and controversies that are commonly perceived as threating the legitimacy of international courts might, in fact, operate in precisely the opposite direction. They might very well serve as moments of crystallization and legitimization in which international courts develop a certain institutional robustness vis-à-vis their critics and even transform their originally more fragile roles into new, more powerful ones.

3. The Themes

As is apparent from the previously offered chapter summaries, the volume displays a rich diversity of opinions. This may not necessarily mean that the authors disagree, although even that naturally happens at some stages. It rather means that they analyse the same theme from a different angle, with divergent starting assumptions and against different values.

It is not the role of an editor to make all the authors sing *unisono* the same tune in perfect harmony, but rather to tease out different variations on the same theme and thereby open the door to a good argument within the volume. It is only natural that when capturing such complex, multilevel, and multi-actor processes as the selection mechanisms to the European courts, inevitably a number of tensions will be present. Instead of downplaying these tensions or sweeping them under the carpet, they ought to be brought to light.

What will therefore be offered in this section, by way of an introduction to discussions that follow in subsequent chapters, is a concise identification of the key themes that recur throughout the volume in one way or another. Their highlighting may help readers to start structuring their own thinking about these issues. In a way, legislating and giving a concrete shape to a judicial selection process is nothing other than placing the balance somewhere, making a personal choice between such abstract principles or values that will inform the institutional design. There are seven such overreaching themes that, given the richness of thought, had to be arbitrarily selected by the editor. They shall be introduced in a binary, dichotomic format with the help of a series of questions.

3.1. Democracy *v* technocracy

How are judges to be selected and what type of legitimacy do we want to generate for them? In the newer European, in particular continental, tradition, there is a historical distrust towards the election of judges. It is expertise and knowledge that should count, not politics. At the same time, however, it is still believed that judges ought to be appointed with at least some participation of democratically elected officials. Thus, in practice, it will be the head of state, the head of the government, or other officials that will be called to appoint new judges. Moreover, for higher or constitutional courts, national parliaments are likely to be involved in the selections in the form of confirmation hearings, assent procedures, or otherwise. Thus, similar to the saying about having our cake and eating it, we would ideally love our judges to have both types of legitimacy at the same time. They should not only be excellent professionals, but also come with some democratic mandate. The eternal question that remains is how precisely these two are to be balanced in one and the same selection procedure.

Projected to the European level, these classic and unsettled questions become outright vexing. On the level of principles, there is the ECtHR, whose judges are said to be democratically legitimized since they are elected by the PACE. Conversely, there is the technocratic operation of the 255 Panel within the EU, which cannot be said to be endowed with any democratic legitimacy—or, at best, has only very, very remote democratic legitimacy. When looking at the results that these different systems have been able to deliver recently, however, the EU technocratic style has in fact been able to guarantee a better quality of judicial candidates eventually appointed than the democratic and more open Council of Europe system.

Is this an example of the eternal tension between democratic (process-based) and technocratic (outcome-based) legitimacy? Is the decision to strive for one or the other inevitably Sophie's choice—to have to choose between shiny democratic procedures with questionable outcomes, or less shiny technocratic procedures with better outcomes? Or is the difference in outcome due only to a few wrongly set elements of procedure in the ECtHR selections which, if remedied, will redeem democratic decision-making in the European judicial selections? Even more importantly: is this perceived dichotomy and putative choice between them mistaken, since axiomatically, in any democratic system worth the name, the democratic principle must prevail, even if it may lead to sub-optimal results?

3.2. Politics *v* expertise

Connected to the previous dichotomy, but focusing more on one element of the selection procedure which finds its reflection also in the qualities required from a candidate: can political convictions be a relevant criterion for judicial selections? Should political preferences play any role in the process of selections? If so, how and at what level? European? National? Both? Moreover, what kind of politics? Open and acknowledged ideas and convictions or only the much despised but hardly dissociable process of political trade-offs, politicking, and wheeling and dealing in the backrooms? It is possible to distinguish at all between 'good' politics and 'bad' politics, like there is apparently 'good' and 'bad' cholesterol in our bodies?

Views clearly differ. Normatively, is it inherently wrong if politicians, democratically elected officials, seek to select judges whom they believe will share their political views and are likely to interpret the law as they would wish it? Most people might agree that this is wrong if sharing certain political convictions becomes *the only* detectable merit in a judicial candidate. But what if it is used as the tiebreaker criterion for choosing within a group of comparably qualified individuals? Or what if it is used as an additional criterion within a group of plausible candidates? If all the candidates pass certain common thresholds, it may become difficult to judge on professional merits only. It makes little difference if one of the university professors competing for judicial office has published 15 books and the other only 12, if all of them are quality publications. Thus, once a certain 'minimal threshold' has been passed by all of the candidates, other considerations will inevitably come into play.

Empirically, as long as judges are elected, as they are in the Council of Europe—ie their selection is made subject to some type of democratic process—politics in the process are inevitable. Calls for 'depoliticized' elections in a system where the ultimate choice is made by a representative, by definition political, assembly, sound odd—a bit like preaching to a tiger on the merits of vegetarianism.

However, even in systems that declare themselves to be purely 'expert-based', such as the 255 Panel within the EU, may we safely claim that expert decision-making is genuinely free of any political choices? Or will these choices still play a role, disguised under the heading of the candidate's 'independence and impartiality [not] being beyond reasonable doubt', since she might be too close to a given government—or in the assessment of other criteria, such as 'legal expertise'?

3.3. 'Merit' only *v* other considerations

In order to be legitimate, the bench (and, by extension, the selectors themselves) ought to be socially representative. A representative bench is more likely to produce more socially responsive decisions, reflecting the diversity of the given society. Whatever particular reason we choose, making an abstract claim for diversity at the European courts will perhaps be easier, although certainly not automatically accepted, than implementing the same diversity in practice.

In the debates surrounding the diversity in procedures of selection to the European courts, the issue of gender has found itself in the limelight in past years. In the ECtHR context, the rejection of all-male lists of candidates submitted to the PACE generated considerable controversy. It opened up the traditional, more general debates about permissible criteria and the definition of merit. How far can/ should one go with the diversity agenda? At which stage does it start threating the legitimacy of a court, especially since some appointees might be perceived as not having sufficient (mainstream) merit, only the right gender? For whom precisely should such measures be introduced? On the one hand, the top candidates within the given disadvantaged group are typically the first ones to vehemently object to such measures, since it undermines their own merit, which they arduously acquired independently, and which might be comparable or much better than that of the extant majority. On the other hand, it will not help the weaker candidates within the same group either, unless we redefine what constitutes merit altogether. If we do, however, gender will no longer be a tiebreaker or one of the criteria, but *the* criterion overriding any other.

Again, addressing these issues in the multilayered European environment further enhances their complexity. First, it may be suggested that composite European jurisdictions are actually already quite diverse in terms of professional backgrounds; nationalities; languages; religions, cultural, or social backgrounds; and so on. Are, therefore, the debates and concerns articulated and discussed in relation to the desired degree of diversity in the often homogeneous national jurisdictions fully transferable to such European jurisdictions? Second, if so, how are the diversity requirements—presumably those primarily relating to gender, ethnic origin, and/ or sexual orientation, since they are the only ones left—to be implemented practically in the specific context of multi-actor selections, in particular in the EU context?

3.4. Independence *v* accountability

Another classic tension that surfaces with respect to the operation of the expert advisory panels concerns accountability. On the one hand, in order to fulfil their mission correctly, the experts must be free of any external guidance or pressure. On the other hand, can/should they be held accountable as regards their work and output? What does 'accountability' mean in practical terms in the case of an international expert panel, freely floating in the European diplomatic space? Accountable to whom and for what precisely?

The search for a reasonable balance between these two values imposes itself in particular with respect to the 255 Panel. On the one hand, and on the more formal level, it could be maintained that this Panel is clearly the agent of the governments of the member states (and institutionally an emanation of the Council). The member states have created it pursuant to the Lisbon Treaty. The Council has adopted its operating rules and appointed its members. Moreover, it is again the member states that interact with and control the Panel, by following (or potentially by not following) its legally non-binding opinion.

When assessing the role of the 255 Panel more critically and functionally, it nonetheless soon becomes apparent that the control exercised by the member states' governments is more hypothetical than real. On the general level, the 255 Panel has itself established a list of criteria the judicial candidates must meet in order to obtain its *nihil obstat*. The criteria just 'materialized', without the approval or sanction of anybody else. In the individual case, to reverse the opinion of the 255 Panel, unanimity amongst the member states would be required. More importantly, however, since the opinion of the 255 Panel most likely cannot be subject to judicial review—and the same goes for the decision of the member states (which additionally will not even exist, since no 'common accord' has been reached)— nobody can challenge the Panel's opinion.

Can this state of affairs be said to represent the right balance between independence and accountability, further amplified by the fact that everything in and around the 255 Panel's work is confidential? Should the wielding of genuine power not be accompanied by genuine accountability? If yes, where precisely should the balance between power and responsibility lie in the case of European/international panels of experts? Could more be done within the confines of these bodies remaining advisory panels of experts?

3.5. Transparency *v* confidentiality

The tension between transparency and confidentiality in the work of the advisory panels is a logical subset of the previous point. It focuses more, however, on the position of a concrete candidate and her rights. On the side of confidentiality, primarily functional, pragmatic arguments relating to the type of work carried out by the expert panels are made. The panels are said to be only able to assess in depth the competence and motivation of a candidate if they are allowed to proceed in a calm, discreet way. Thus, hearings of candidates ought to be taking place behind closed doors. With respect to the candidates' personality rights and data protection, it is suggested that candidates face high reputational stakes, which justify the confidential nature of the report and its non-disclosure to the public. Both of these arguments combined account for the possible chilling effect that disclosure of the process of 'grilling' or its results might have on potential future candidates, especially from the ranks of senior national judiciaries.

The dual reply by proponents of transparency not only challenges the functional arguments, but adds normative, value-based objections to confidentiality, pointing out the lack of legitimacy of secret, *in camera* interviews with judicial candidates. Moreover, how can the activity of such a secretive panel fulfil its more general pedagogical mission of informing the public what the criteria are, and how they are applied? In addition, not only does confidentiality potentially lead to arbitrariness, but the arguments concerning the protection of the individual reputation and data are said to be more hypothetical than real. How precisely is the reputation of a candidate protected if, following her rejection by an advisory panel—which will be a known fact, for which, however, no reasons are given—the wildest speculation and gossip is likely to start circulating?

Two unresolved issues lurk beneath these debates. First, a number of essentially factual claims tend to be made, without there being much empirical evidence for them. What impact a decision or practice X will have on the behaviour and preferences of the respondent group Y in few years' time in a member state Z may give rise to intriguing speculations at the present point in time, but hardly much more. Second, it might be useful to distinguish which of the transparency-enhancing suggestions, if embraced, could in fact be implemented within the institutional settings of an expert advisory panel, and which of them would require a more complex institutional overhaul. It is fair to admit that some of the critique relating to the lack of transparency ought to be aiming more at the 'principals', ie the institutions that established the system of advisory expert panels, than the 'agents' themselves. There is naturally only that much that one can do within the confines of a given mandate.

3.6. The European *v* the national

Another major theme surfacing in a number of chapters is the interaction between the European and the national levels in both individual selections and their outcomes, as well as the elaboration of standards and procedures for those selections. Is there a distinct process of Europeanization of selection procedures to the European courts going on at the national levels? The overall picture painted tends to be a positive one (aka 'shared responsibility and best practices for a qualified and legitimate European bench'), but on occasion more negative tunes also surface (aka 'it is not us but the other level that is to blame for this particular embarrassing outcome'). Analysing the same phenomenon more critically, however, how much exchange or inspiration is genuinely occurring? Does the system of shared responsibility for the European judicial selections work, or is it bound to degenerate, as in any system of unclear responsibility, into a system of collective irresponsibility, when one level keeps blaming the other and nobody is ready to assume responsibility for the ultimate result?

Apart from the quantitative level, ie how much mutual inspiration and exchange is really occurring, it is certainly rewarding to focus on its quality as well. In particular, when looking at some of the choices and institutional adaptations made following the model or practice taken over from somewhere else in Europe, it might be worth examining closely how far it really does follow the putative or real model. Did the invoked model serve as a genuine inspiration, or is the invoked model really more of a convenient multilevel fig-leaf, a hollow incantation of the other level to introduce something one wants, but might not have that much actual support for. On the national level, domestic opposition might be silenced with the ultimate argument that 'Brussels wills it', even though Brussels or Strasbourg demand nothing of the kind. Conversely, on the European level, a solution or design is introduced with reference to the 'national traditions' or 'principles common to the member states', followed by a conspicuous silence as to which specific member states are precisely being invoked.

3.7. The chameleons of legitimacy

Finally, the overreaching theme that runs like the proverbial *fil rouge* in one way or another through all the chapters is the question of legitimacy. It is the master-theme of the volume that keeps coming back in different contexts and guises. At the same time, however, the notion of legitimacy remains hopelessly vague. What type of legitimacy? Sociological? Political? Normative? Or a combination of these that is, however, bound to render the notion all-embracing, and impossible to analyse in any meaningful way? Moreover, who assesses what exactly, with respect to what constituency or respondents? What precisely is being looked at? Against what criteria is the output of the institution measured?

A consensus appears to exist on the fact that the expert panels have been put in place in order to guarantee greater professional quality of the judicial appointees, and thusly enhance the legitimacy of both European courts. However, beyond that, views already differ as to whether some of the recent, perhaps less fortunate appointments to the European courts have already eroded the legitimacy of these courts. At what stage do 'less-than-optimal' appointments translate into a perceptible decrease in the legitimacy of a European or international court? Do they necessarily have to? With tongue in cheek and somewhat cynically put, if the quality of the support apparatus is kept, ie there are good legal secretaries and support staff, the quality of the decisions might remain the same. In the European jurisdictions, as well as in a number of the highest jurisdictions in the member states today, a judgment is a collective enterprise.

Even if, at the end of the day, it will be the person of the judge and not necessarily her jurisprudential output that will be evaluated, by whom will it be evaluated? By the 'European professional community'? By the general public? Is there even a 'European professional community' that could make up its mind, or is it rather a loose association of different national professional 'tribes', each of them making up their own mind with respect to their own tribal standards and as to whether or not their tribal envoy in Europe meets those standards, and is therefore worthy of their trust? Later on, the conglomerate of such tribal opinions (or the opinion of the tribe that is most vocal in its articulation and loudest in its trumpeting) morphs into the 'European opinion'?

4. Acknowledgements

This book is the fruit of a conference which was held at the College of Europe in Bruges on 4 November 2013.[13] Many thanks are due to the College of Europe for generously funding the conference, and in particular to Professor Inge Govaere, director of the Department of European Legal Studies, and Rector Jörg Monar. Editorial assistance from Emmanuel Robberecht, Athena Christofi, Valérie Hauspie, and Angela O'Neill from the College of Europe in preparing this volume is also gratefully acknowledged.

The authors attempted to capture the law (and practice) as it stood in May 2014.

---

[13] See J-V Louis, 'La nomination des juges de la Cour de justice: quelques observations à la suite d'une Conférence' (2013) 49 *Cahiers de droit européen* 567.

1

Not Quite the Bed that Procrustes Built

Dissecting the System for Selecting Judges at the Court of Justice of the European Union

Henri de Waele

1. Introduction

Petrus Josephus Servatius Serrarens lived a rich and varied life. Born in 1888 in Dordrecht, the Netherlands, he started his professional career in 1907 as a secondary school teacher. He subsequently joined the Catholic Socialist Movement as a librarian, moving on to become secretary general of the International Federation of Christian Trade Unions and a member of the Dutch Senate and, later on, the House of Representatives. Among many other side jobs, Serrarens served on the editorial board of several journals, as president of the European Movement in the Netherlands, member of the Parliamentary Assembly of the Council of Europe, and special advisor to the European Economic and Social Committee. By way of final act, on 4 December 1952, he was appointed judge in the Court of Justice of the European Coal and Steel Community (ECSC)—despite never having completed any legal training. The latter handicap posed no formal obstacle, though, for the Treaty of Paris merely stated that judges were to be chosen 'from persons of recognised independence and competence'.[1] Serrarens's term of office expired after three years, yet it was happily renewed in 1955. Had he not reached the age of 70 in 1958, signalling statutory retirement under Dutch law, he might well have been reappointed that same year to the ECSC institution's successor, the Court of Justice of the European Communities. His much younger colleague, the French judge Jacques Rueff, did indeed make such a transfer, holding out until 1962, when he was replaced by Robert Lecourt. Rueff, incidentally, was an economist by training, who had until then spent most of his career as a civil servant. In the words of one deft *chroniqueur* of integration history, 'if the first nominations sometimes appeared to be quite far from, if not the legal realm, then at least

---

[1] Art 32 of the Treaty establishing the European Coal and Steel Community.

the judicial function, the professional qualifications of the Court's members were heterogeneous, to say the least'.[2]

Meanwhile, times have changed. The number of judges has greatly expanded from the original humble 7 to a staggering 61, distributed across three different tiers. The entry criteria for taking up office have also been beefed up substantially, with the Treaty on the Functioning of the European Union (TFEU) nowadays ordaining that 'only persons who possess the qualifications required for appointment to the highest judicial offices in their respective countries, or who are jurisconsults of recognised competence' are eligible to accede to the Court of Justice, while for the General Court, only persons 'who possess the ability required for appointment to high judicial office' are considered fit for purpose.[3] The provisions moreover reiterate that the independence of any candidate members should stand above doubt. Consequently, the seconding of colourful figures like Serrarens and Rueff to the Kirchberg has not merely become unthinkable, but legally impossible; such candidates would not make the grade *ab initio*, notwithstanding an illustrious track record in their personal field of expertise.

As the appointment criteria have evolved, so has the relevant procedure, though only much more recently. In particular, the novel Article 255 TFEU, introduced by the Treaty of Lisbon in December 2009, led to the setting up of a panel tasked to produce an opinion on the suitability of candidates proposed by the governments of the member states to perform the duties of judge and advocate general of the Court of Justice and the General Court (hereinafter 'the 255 Panel'). This innovation is said to have sprung from the widely shared idea that objective criteria should be applied for assessing the suitability of members of the judiciary, and that an independent body can assist in such an assessment process.[4] Since the procedure did not undergo modifications in the previous 50 years, it has taken quite some time for this thought to become entrenched at the EU level. Nevertheless, the underlying principle remains completely sound, as the risks of putting less qualified persons in office are obvious and manifold. A lack of the proper case-management skills can, for instance, lead to undue delays in the administration of justice.[5] It has therefore rightly been posited that the quality of the rule of law is dependent upon the quality of the judiciary charged with upholding it.[6] And indeed, the credibility of the appointment, as well as the authority and integrity

---

[2] A Cohen, '"Ten Majestic Figures in Long Amaranth Robes": The Formation of the Court of Justice of the European Communities' in A Vauchez and B de Witte (eds), *Lawyering Europe* (Hart Publishing 2013) 30.

[3] Respectively Arts 253 and 254 TFEU; cf Art 19 TEU.

[4] J-M Sauvé, 'Le rôle du comité 255 dans le sélection du juge de l'Union', in A Rosas, E Levits, and Y Bot (eds), *The Court of Justice and the Construction of Europe: Analyses and Perspectives on Sixty Years of Case-law—La Cour de Justice et la Construction de l'Europe: Analyses et Perspectives de Soixante Ans de Jurisprudence* (Asser Press/Springer 2013) 102–3.

[5] cf Case C-58/12 P *Groupe Gascogne SA v European Commission* [2013] ECR I-0000, Opinion of AG Sharpston, para 89.

[6] Lord Woolf, 'Foreword', in R Mackenzie, K Malleson, P Martin, and P Sands, *Selecting International Judges: Principles, Process and Politics* (Oxford University Press 2010) vii.

of the tribunal concerned, may be said to depend on the process by which judicial appointment takes place.[7]

In the EU, that process continues to be dominated all the same by the governments of the member states. As Articles 253 and 254 TFEU stipulate, the new Panel is only to be consulted before the member state governments may proceed to the appointment phase. During negotiations on the creation of the Coal and Steel Community in 1951, the French delegation strongly pushed for maintaining their sovereign prerogative, insisting on appointment by common accord (essentially a simple intergovernmental agreement), despite objections from the German representatives who argued that this approach would compromise judicial independence.[8] The European Parliament has through the years experienced comparably little success in its repeated calls to increase democratic scrutiny of the nomination procedure.[9] Ultimately then, the system today is still one based on mutual trust. Thereby, at the highest political plane, ordinarily no member state will venture to question another member state's candidate, at the risk of having to face a similar (future) confrontation itself.[10] In contrast, owing to the introduction of the 255 Panel, of late it has finally become possible to assess in a more objective and independent manner whether the nominated candidates truly meet the criteria laid down by the TFEU, whereas in the past, a variety of considerations unrelated to judicial aptitude seem to have played an undue role.[11]

The creation of a judicial selection panel was first mooted in the Due Report of 2000.[12] After further deliberation in the discussion circle on the Court of Justice at the Convention on the Future of Europe (2002–3), the suggestion was taken over in Article III-357 of the abortive Constitutional Treaty, and subsequently ended up in the Treaty of Lisbon that entered into force on 1 December 2009. The Panel was officially established on 1 March 2010, pursuant to a decision of the Council of 25 February 2010.[13] The decision laying down the Panel's operating rules was adopted simultaneously.[14] In line with the terms of Article 255 TFEU, both decisions were taken on the initiative of the president of the Court of Justice.[15]

The 255 Panel comprises seven persons chosen from among former members of the Court of Justice and the General Court, members of national supreme courts, and lawyers of recognized competence—one of whom has been proposed

---

[7] Ibid, viii.

[8] A Boerger-De Smedt, 'La Cour de justice dans les négociations du traité de Paris instituant la CECA' (2008) 14(2) *Journal of European Integration History* 7.

[9] A Arnull, *The European Union and Its Court of Justice* (Oxford University Press 2006) 21.

[10] cf Sauvé (n 4) 101.

[11] KJ Alter, *The European Court's Political Power* (Oxford University Press 2010) 126.

[12] O Due et al, 'Report by the Working Party on the Future of the European Communities' Court System', January 2000, <http://ec.europa.eu/dgs/legal_service/pdf/due_en.pdf> accessed 15 April 2014, p 56.

[13] Council Decision 2010/125/EU of 25 February 2010 appointing the members of the panel provided for in Article 255 TFEU [2010] OJ L50/20.

[14] Council Decision 2010/124/EU of 25 February 2010 relating to the operating rules of the panel provided for in Article 255 TFEU [2010] OJ L50/18.

[15] V Skouris, Recommendation concerning the composition of the panel provided for in Article 255 TFEU, Brussels, 2 February 2010, 5932/10 JUR 57 INST 26 COUR 13.

by the European Parliament. After conducting the necessary investigations (possibly including an interview), they draft a collective opinion on the merits of the proposed candidate. Blazing a trail for this new creation, a similar body has in fact been up and running since 2005, in order to facilitate the selection of judges for the European Union's Civil Service Tribunal (CST).[16] This so-called Evaluation Committee (hereinafter 'the CST Committee') consists of seven members of reputable provenance, but does not vet candidates that are put forward by member state governments. Instead, after a publicly advertised vacancy notice, it chooses among all applications submitted by those who desire to be appointed to the CST, invites the selected individuals to an interview, and then draws up a list of most suitable candidates. While the two forums resemble one another in composition, they thus differ in their *modus operandi*.[17]

In the sections that follow, this new system for selecting judges to the EU courts, comprising both the 255 Panel and the CST Committee, will be examined in closer detail. Thereby, we shall first inquire into staffing issues, reviewing the 'selection of selectors' (section 2). Next, we take a look at the varying methods for pre-selecting (potential) candidates for appointment to the EU courts at the national level (section 3). Hereafter, we proceed to analyse the system's ordinary functioning (section 4), after which we turn the focus on its place within the broader institutional architecture (section 5). Lastly, we highlight the experiences of its first years of operation (section 6), before we wrap up with some concluding reflections (section 7).

While the EU system may be regarded as original, it certainly is not entirely unique.[18] Therefore, where useful, it seems apt to draw comparisons with relevant domestic and international mechanisms.[19] Of course, one may argue about the most appropriate *tertium comparationis*—for can the Union judiciary itself be equated with anything at all or does it belong in a league of its own? This essentially harks back to the classic, interminable discussion on the exact nature of the EU legal order and the validity of its *sui generis* claim.[20] Without taking sides in this

---

[16] Its creation was set out in the Annex to Council Decision 2004/752/EC, Euratom, of 2 November 2004 establishing the European Union Civil Service Tribunal [2004] OJ L333/7; its operating rules were laid down in the Annex to Council Decision 2005/49/EC concerning the operating rules of the committee provided for in Article 3(3) of Annex I to the Protocol to the Statute of the Court of Justice [2005] OJ L21/13.

[17] Slightly odd is the remark by L Sevón, in 'The Procedure for Selection of Members of the Civil Service Tribunal: A Pioneer Experience', paper available at <http://curia.europa.eu/jcms/upload/docs/application/pdf/2010-10/5anstfp_sevon_en.pdf> accessed 15 April 2014, p 7, that the 255 Panel would probably not have been set up if the work of the CST Committee had been deemed a disaster. After all, the former's creation was legally required, and as remarked above, already foreseen much earlier (*viz* in the Constitutional Treaty of 2003). Further on the operation of the CST Committee see also ch 4 below.

[18] cf Sauvé (n 4) 107.

[19] For general reference, see respectively J Bell, *Judiciaries within Europe: A Comparative Review* (Cambridge University Press 2006), and Mackenzie et al (n 6).

[20] The two opposing views are magisterially advanced in, respectively, R Schütze, *From Dual to Cooperative Federalism: The Changing Structure of European Law* (Oxford University Press 2009) and B de Witte, 'The European Union as an International Legal Experiment', in JHH Weiler and Gráinne de Búrca (eds), *The Worlds of European Constitutionalism* (Cambridge University Press 2012) 19–56.

debate, occasional analogies will be attempted with both national and international counterparts. The system in use at the Council of Europe for selecting judges to the European Court of Human Rights shall however be largely left aside, as it forms the central topic of dedicated contributions in a different part of this volume.[21]

2. Staffing the System: The Selection of Selectors

As remarked, both the 255 Panel and the CST Committee are meant to be staffed by persons chosen from among former members of the Court of Justice and the General Court, members of national supreme courts, and lawyers of recognized competence. The Council is in the hot seat with regard to their appointment, also deciding who shall chair the Panel and the Committee, thereby acting on the initiative of the president of the Court of Justice. Neither Article 255 TFEU nor the Council Decision that established the CST contain specific rules on gender balance, geographic criteria, or other factors that should be taken into account. How the potential selectors are actually recruited also remains shrouded in secrecy. Rumours suggest that this, in all likelihood, calls for extensive lobbying with the CJEU president.[22] A singular, crystal-clear additional principle with regard to the composition of the 255 Panel is that one member shall be proposed by the European Parliament.[23] For the CST Committee, no such rule exists. We now briefly zoom in on the *équipes* that have been put to task in the respective forums and take stock of their lineage.

2.1. The 255 Panel

On 25 February 2010, the following seven persons were appointed to serve on the 255 Panel for a period of four years: Jean-Marc Sauvé, vice president of the French Council of State; Peter Jann, former judge at the Court of Justice (1995–2009) and before that judge at the Austrian Constitutional Court (1976–95); Lord Mance, judge of the Supreme Court of the United Kingdom; Torben Melchior, former president of the Danish Supreme Court; Péter Paczolay, president of the Hungarian Constitutional Court; Ana Palacio Vallelersundi, member of the Spanish Council of State, former Spanish minister, and former member of the European Parliament (1994–2002); and Virpi Tilli, former judge at the Court of First Instance of the European Union (1995–2009). Mr Sauvé was designated president.[24]

---

[21] Below Chs 5 and 6 of this volume.

[22] T Dumbrovský, B Petkova, and M Van der Sluis, 'Judicial Appointments: The Article 255 TFEU Advisory Panel and Selection Procedures in the Member States', (2014) 51(2) *Common Market Law Review* 460.

[23] Since the parliament addresses its proposal to the President of the Court (at least according to the practice in 2010), the latter is in theory capable of rejecting the proposed candidate; cf Dumbrovský, Petkova, and Van der Sluis (n 22) 460.

[24] Council Decision 2010/125/EU of 25 February 2010 appointing the members of the panel provided for in Article 255 TFEU [2010] OJ L50/20, Art 1.

With the expiry of the first *équipe*'s mandate close at hand, on 11 February 2014, the following persons were appointed to the second incarnation of the 255 Panel: Jean-Marc Sauvé, Lord Mance, and Péter Paczolay, as before; Luigi Berlinguer, member of the European Parliament and former Italian minister; Pauliine Koskelo, president of the Finnish Supreme Court; Christiaan Timmermans, former judge at the Court of Justice (2000–10); and Andreas Voßkuhle, president of the German Federal Constitutional Court. Mr Sauvé was once again designated the Panel's president.[25]

Obviously, the gender balance in both groups could be considered skewed, as only two women have been included—Ms Ana Palacio (the candidate proposed by the European Parliament, succeeded in 2014 by Mr Berlinguer) and Ms Pauliine Koskelo. A second critique may be that both selections tilt a bit too heavily towards senior members of national judiciaries, to the detriment of their junior colleagues and/or lawyers of recognized competence who might also have been considered.[26] Nevertheless, at both counts, all official recruitment criteria were met. On top of this, with roughly all corners of the EU being covered, a neat geographic equilibrium was attained in 2010 as well as 2014. Equally sensible was the decision to reappoint no less than four Panel members in 2014, in order to preserve continuity.[27] As expounded below, that interest was not taken to heart so scrupulously when it came to the repeated (re)composition of the Panel's sibling.

2.2. The CST Committee

On 18 January 2005, the following seven persons were appointed to serve on the CST Committee for a period of four years: Leif Sevón, former judge at the Court of Justice (1995–2002), former president of the Court of the European Free Trade Association (1994–5), and former president of the Finnish Supreme Court (2002–5); Sir Christopher Bellamy, former judge at the Court of First Instance (1992–9) and former president of the UK Competition Appeals Tribunal (1999–2007); Yves Galmot, former judge at the Court of Justice (1982–8) and former member of the French Council of State (1981–2); Peter Grilc, professor of law at the University of Ljubljana; Gabriele Kucsko-Stadlmayer, substitute judge at the Austrian Constitutional Court and professor at the University of Vienna; Giuseppe Tesauro, judge at the Italian Constitutional Court, former advocate general at the Court of Justice (1988–98), and president of the Italian Competition Authority (1998–2005); and Miroslaw Wyrzykowski, professor of law at the University of Warsaw and former judge at the Polish Constitutional Court (2001–10). Mr Sevón was designated president.[28]

[25] Council Decision 2014/76/EU of 11 February 2014 appointing the members of the panel provided for in Article 255 TFEU [2014] OJ L41/18, Art 1.

[26] Conversely, too many former members of the EU Courts and the Panel's Legitimacy might have been compromised more severely.

[27] Council Decision 2010/124/EU of 25 February 2010 relating to the operating rules of the panel provided for in Article 255 TFEU [2010] OJ L50/18, Annex, pt 3, allows for members to be reappointed once.

[28] Council Decision 2005/151/EC, Euratom, of 18 January 2005 appointing members of the committee provided for in Article 3(3) of Annex I to the Protocol on the Statute of the Court of Justice [2005] OJ L50/9, Art 1.

Here too, the presence of only one female may have formed an easy target for criticism. At the same time, the official criteria were fully met, and the collected expertise of this first assembly stood beyond question.

From a gender-balance perspective, progress was made with the second *équipe*, appointed on 18 December 2008 for a period of four years: it consisted of Günther Hirsch, former judge at the Court of Justice (1994–2000) and former president of the German Federal Court of Justice (2000–8); Rafael García-Valdecasas y Fernández, former judge at the Court of First Instance (1989–2007); Csilla Kollonay Lehoczky, member of the European Committee of Social Rights and professor of law at Central European University; Fidelma O'Kelly Macken, former judge at the Court of Justice (1999–2004) and the Irish Supreme Court (2005–12); Romain Schintgen, former judge at the Court of Justice (1996–2008) and the Court of First Instance (1989–96); Kateřina Šimáčková, judge at the Czech Constitutional Court and former judge at the Czech Supreme Administrative Court (2009–13); and Georges Vandersanden, lawyer at the Brussels bar and former professor at the Université Libre de Bruxelles. Mr Hirsch was elected president.[29]

In its third incarnation, the number of women was reduced from three to two. Perhaps more striking at this point is the complete lack of continuity; for on 22 April 2013, seven entirely new members were put in place: Pernilla Lindh, former judge at the Court of Justice (2006–11) and the Court of First Instance (1995–2006); Pranas Kūris, judge at the Court of Justice, former president of the Lithuanian Supreme Court (1994–8), and judge in the European Court of Human Rights (1998–2004); Ján Mazák, former advocate general at the Court of Justice (2006–12) and former president of the Slovak Constitutional Court (2000–6); Jörg Pirrung, former judge at the Court of First Instance (1997–2007); Mihalis Vilaras, former judge at the Court of First Instance (1998–2010); Roel Bekker, a former Dutch civil servant; and Elena Simina Tănăsescu, professor of law at the University of Bucarest. Ms Lindh was appointed president.[30]

On the one hand, the integral replenishments in both 2004 and 2008 come across as very drastic when, in the interest of continuity, it might have been advisable to keep in place even the barest minimum of Committee members. On the other hand, as emerges from the preceding overview, it thankfully did prove possible to ensure a continuously rich variety of professional and geographic backgrounds.

2.3. Observations from comparative law

Judicial selection panels and committees are no standard feature in national legal systems, at least where the highest jurisdictions are concerned. In various countries,

---

[29] Council Decision 2009/69/EC, Euratom, of 18 December 2008 appointing members of the committee provided for in Article 3(3) of Annex I to the Protocol on the Statute of the Court of Justice [2009] OJ L24/11, Art 1.
[30] Council Decision 2013/180/EU, Euratom, of 22 April 2013 appointing members of the committee provided for in Article 3(3) of Annex I to the Protocol on the Statute of the Court of Justice [2013] OJ L111/48, Art 1.

one nevertheless stumbles upon many kindred bodies, all with their very own particular compositions. In the United Kingdom, for instance, judges of the Supreme Court are appointed by the Queen on the advice of the prime minister, to whom a name is recommended by a special selection commission.[31] This commission is made up of the president and the deputy president of the Court, and a member each from the Judicial Appointments Commission, the Judicial Appointments Board for Scotland, and the Northern Ireland Judicial Appointment Commission. The members of the latter are either recruited through open competition or appointed on the basis of holding a specific function, and originate from the judiciary, the legal profession, or even the wider public.[32] The trial judges in the French *Cour de Cassation* are appointed by a decree of the president of the French Republic, acting on a proposal from the *Conseil Supérieur de la Magistrature*. The latter has a total of 16 members, encompassing a special judicial subcommittee composed of one administrative judge chosen by the *Conseil d'Etat*; three individuals chosen by the president, the Senate, and the *Assemblée Nationale* each; five judges; and one prosecutor. In contrast, the French *Conseil Constitutionnel* consists of 12 members appointed by the French president, the president of the *Sénat*, and the president of the *Assemblée Nationale*, subject to parliamentary approval.[33] The judges of the German *Bundesverfassungsgericht* are elected by the *Bundestag* and the *Bundesrat*. The *Bundestag* has delegated this task to a special body composed of 12 *Bundestag* members, called the *Richterwahlausschuss*. Judges of the Federal Court of Justice, however, are selected by an electoral committee, which consists of the secretaries of justice of 16 German *Bundesländer* and 16 *Bundestag* representatives; once a judge has been selected by this committee, he is appointed by the German *Bundespresident*.[34] In the United States, the construction is again much more straightforward, with the Justices of the US Supreme Court being appointed by the president, conditional upon the approval of (a majority in) the Senate.[35]

Intricate systems for judicial selection have also been set up in multiple international organizations. Potential members of the World Trade Organization (WTO) Appellate Body are, for example, vetted by a committee composed of members elected by the Dispute Settlement Body (which in turn consists of representatives of WTO members).[36] Candidates for appointment as members of the International Court of Justice are nominated from each member state by a national group that is 'recommended to consult its highest court of justice, its legal faculties and schools of law, and its national academies and national sections of international academies devoted to the study of law'.[37] Judges at the International Criminal Court (ICC)

[31] See Constitutional Reform Act 2005, ss 23(2), 26(2), and 26(3).
[32] Eg the case for the Judicial Appointments Committee of England and Wales.
[33] See further M Balandier, *Le Conseil supérieur de la magistrature—De la révision constitutionnelle du 27 Juillet 1993 aux enjeux actuels* (Editions Le Manuscrit 2006); P Avril and J Gicquel, *Le Conseil constitutionnel* (Montchrestien 2005). It should be noted that the former presidents of the French Republic also hold the right to sit on the *Conseil Constitutionnel*, but not all of them have opted to exercise this right.
[34] German Basic Law, Arts 94 and 95(2).   [35] US Constitution, Art II, s 2, cl 2.
[36] Understanding on Rules and Procedures Governing the Settlement of Disputes, Art 17.
[37] Statute of the International Court of Justice, Arts 4–6.

are nominated by states party to the Rome Statute, either following the procedure for the nomination of candidates for appointment to the highest judicial offices in the state in question or through the procedure provided for the nomination of candidates for the International Court of Justice. The ICC judges are elected by secret ballot at a meeting of the Assembly of States Parties.[38] Since 2010, the Council of Europe has been equipped with an evaluation panel composed of seven eminent lawyers, appointed by the Committee of Ministers. It may be applauded that the resolution that led to its establishment calls for the panel to be balanced both geographically and in gender—but then just as justifiably critiqued that it currently counts only two women among its members.[39]

One common inference that can be drawn from this very brief overview is that the eligibility rules for acceding to domestic judicial selection bodies are notably vague, even more so than those applicable to membership of the 255 Panel and the CST Committee. Quite frequently it looks as if no criteria have been set down at all. This does not hold as strongly, though, with regard to the mechanisms for selecting members of the courts and tribunals of some international organizations. With some notable exceptions, rules related to gender balance would appear to be more ubiquitously absent, and across domestic and international forums, a relatively small size would seem to constitute another broadly shared characteristic.

To be sure, these assertions are not meant to censure any of the highlighted regimes, since no benchmarks for such 'selection of selectors' regimes exist to begin with. All the same, praise is due for those systems that endeavour to set down detailed guidelines in this delicate matter, especially when it comes to gender and diversity aspects. For, such ground rules ought to guarantee at least some measure of popular representation, and help to avoid potential self-duplication (ie panellists wittingly or unwittingly composing a court in their own image).

3. Preparing Nominations to the EU Courts: National Pre-selection Procedures

Upon publication of vacancies in the Civil Service Tribunal, those interested in taking up position in the CST may tender their application without further ado. Subsequently, it is for the CST Committee to separate the sheep from the goats. Before the names of candidates for membership of the Court of Justice and the General Court are conveyed to the 255 Panel, however, more or less extensive pre-selections are undertaken at the national level.

---

[38] Rome Statute on the International Criminal Court, Art 34(4) and (6).

[39] Resolution on the establishment of an Advisory Panel of Experts on Candidates for Election as judge to the European Court of Human Rights, CM/Res (2010) 26, para 2. See further NP Engel, 'More Transparency and Governmental Loyalty for Maintaining Professional Quality in the Election of Judges to the European Court of Human Rights', (2008) 32(7–12) *Human Rights Law Journal* 448.

In acts establishing international courts, one seldom comes across provisions that stipulate how candidates should be nominated at the national plane.[40] This also holds for the acts founding the three EU courts. Equally, in domestic legal systems, provisions outlining how candidates for positions at international courts should be nominated are no common feature. Yet in many of those systems, such provisions do exist with regard to nominations for the EU courts. In this respect, it appears a distinction can be made between countries in which the pre-selection procedure is somewhat hazy and largely dominated by the executive, and countries in which advisory committees have been installed as intermediaries, commanding varying degrees of influence over the eventual appointment.[41] Hereby, multistage trajectories occur as well, whereby, for instance, a pre-selection panel engages in a first scrutiny, a further sifting or ranking exercise is undertaken at a higher level, and then the executive takes the final decision.

Greece is a noteworthy example of the executive-dominated category. Whenever a pertinent vacancy at the EU courts arises, the Greek government comes up with a nominee, without there existing clear legal ground rules on how or on which basis the individuals in question are to be chosen. The Ministry of Justice and the Ministry of Foreign Affairs traditionally forward a combined shortlist to the Cabinet of the Prime Minister and ultimately the latter takes its pick in an entirely autonomous manner, thereby occasionally deviating from said shortlist. Matters are no less opaque in Spain, where the government autonomously determines its favoured candidate on the basis of a joint proposal of the Minister of Justice and the Minister of Foreign Affairs. Practices in Italy rest on a similar footing, and are hardly more transparent. The Polish system stands out slightly, with the Minister of Foreign Affairs publishing a call for applications that outlines the relevant criteria and setting up a special team entrusted with assessment of the applicants' suitability. If the Polish Council of Ministers accepts the ensuing proposal, it may authorize the Ministry of Foreign Affairs to officially put forward the successful applicant, after consultation with the Committee on European Affairs of the Polish Parliament.

At the other end of the scale, Germany offers a fine illustration of how national pre-selection procedures can be solidly entrenched. For starters, section 1 part 3 of the Act on the selection of federal judges (*Richterwahlgesetz*) stipulates that nominations by the Federal Government to the CJEU under Articles 253 and 254 TFEU are to be made in agreement with the Judicial Selection Committee (*Richterwahlausschuss*).[42] Candidates can be proposed by both the Committee members and the Federal Minister of Justice. The latter chairs the Committee and

---

[40] With the Council of Europe regime belonging to the few exceptions; for further details see Chapter 5 of this volume, section 3.

[41] Dumbrovský, Petkova, and Van der Sluis (n 22) 466. They also distinguish a third category of 'judicial self-government', yet fail to indicate a country in which the judiciary is exclusively or predominantly in charge of the whole process.

[42] This body consists of ministers of *Bundesländer* and members chosen by the *Bundestag*. The latter are required to be seasoned lawyers who themselves meet the conditions for election to the *Bundestag*.

ultimately has to approve the candidate, but does not possess voting rights.[43] For academic purposes it is unfortunate that the Committee operates behind closed doors and does not disclose further information on its workings. In the United Kingdom, the above-mentioned Judicial Appointments Commission decides on the most suitable nominee after a broadly advertised announcement of a vacancy at the CJEU.[44] This leads to a recommendation by the Lord Chancellor to the Foreign Secretary, who subsequently takes his pick on this basis. The recommendation itself is not published, and the exact proceedings remain classified. In similar fashion, in the Netherlands, a public call is issued for candidates to submit their application to an advisory committee consisting of representatives of the Dutch Supreme Court, the Council of State, and a reputable expert on EU law.[45] The committee reviews the applications and shortlists three candidates. On the basis of this confidential shortlist, the Minister of Justice and the Minister of Foreign Affairs propose a candidate to the Dutch Council of Ministers, where the ultimate decision is taken. Comparatively more convoluted is the contemporary practice in the Czech Republic. There, the Ministry of Justice has been rendered responsible for the first step, the launching of a public competition in order to find suitable candidates for appointment to the EU courts. Hereafter, a special committee is convened chaired by the Minister of Justice, further composed of the Foreign Affairs Minister; Presidents of the Constitutional Court, Supreme Court, and Supreme Administrative Court; the Agent representing the Czech Republic before the CJEU; and three members appointed by, respectively, the Minister of Justice, the President of the Czech Bar, and the deans of the Czech public law schools.[46] This committee conducts oral interviews with applicants in order to evaluate their suitability, and recommends the best candidate to the Czech government. Next, the Ministry requests the (non-binding) opinion of the Committee for European Affairs of the House of Representatives, before it forwards its decision to the Czech government for a final decision. If the latter does not approve of the candidate, the entire procedure begins anew.[47]

Whatever approach is taken at national level, the past and present methods of selection have certainly ensured the nomination of many a colourful figure for appointment to the Court of Justice and the General Court. Simultaneously, the varying methods applied have many a time resulted in a remarkably heterogeneous judiciary, while proper checks on whether the nominees possessed the necessary professional qualifications were not always carried out.[48] Occasionally, this is still the case today; yet since 2010, the 255 Panel has functioned as a felicitous,

---

[43] *Richterwahlgesetz*, ss 10–13.   [44] Constitutional Reform Act, Art 98.

[45] 'Procedure for nominations to the European Courts', agreement between the Minister of Justice and the Minister of Foreign Affairs, *Kamerstukken I*, parliamentary year 1999/2000, appendix to the minutes, No 7.

[46] Annex to Government Resolution No 525, 13 July 2011, Arts 2–9.

[47] For the previous practice in the 2004–11 period, as well as recent controversies surrounding nominations, see Dumbrovský, Petkova, and Van der Sluis (n 22) 475–6.

[48] Cohen (n 2) 30.

invaluable safety valve, which has even induced a number of member states to adjust or overhaul their domestic evaluation procedures.[49]

4. Practical Dynamics: The *Modus Operandi* of the 255 Panel and the CST Committee

The practical operations of the 255 Panel and the CST Committee resemble one another to a considerable extent. Details of both are set out in the relevant Council decisions, which shed a useful (though not overly generous) light on their *modus operandi*.[50]

4.1. The 255 Panel

The first two points of the 255 Panel's operating rules merely rehearse the content of said TFEU provision. The third point adds that Panel members are appointed for four years, and that they may be reappointed once.[51] The fourth point charges the general secretariat of the Council with providing administrative support, including translation services.[52] The fifth fixes a quorum, determining that meetings of the panel are only valid if at least five of its members are present. Interestingly, nothing is stipulated for situations of deadlock, eg in a scenario where five members show up, one of them abstains, and consequently the votes in favour of and against the proposed candidate turn out to be equally divided. Naturally, this could be perceived as a rejection, since the candidate did not garner a majority. At the same time, the vote cast by the president might be attributed a double weight, wherewith the ayes could outnumber the nays (or vice versa); yet this fails to resolve the matter if the president himself were to be the person who chose to abstain. Another conundrum arises in the case that six members show up, one of them abstains, and three turn out to favour the proposed candidate, while the other two reject him. Though in this scenario, once again, the basic quorum has been attained, it may seem awkward that the person elected did not obtain an overall majority. In practice such situations are probably very rare, but the system could nevertheless benefit from some additional guidance here. In contrast, the operating rules of

[49] Dumbrovský, Petkova, and Van der Sluis (n 22) 457.

[50] Council Decision 2010/124/EU of 25 February 2010 relating to the operating rules of the panel provided for in Article 255 of the Treaty on the Functioning of the European Union [2010] OJ L50/18, respectively Council Decision 2005/49/EC concerning the operating rules of the committee provided for in Article 3(3) of Annex I to the Protocol to the Statute of the Court of Justice [2005] OJ L21/13. Further see also ch 4 and ch 5 below.

[51] A person who is to replace a member before the expiry of that period shall be appointed for the remainder of his predecessor's term.

[52] The Third Activity Report of the Panel provided for by Article 255 of the Treaty on the Functioning of the European Union, <http://curia.europa.eu/jcms/upload/docs/application/pdf/2014-02/rapport-c-255-en.pdf> accessed 15 April 2014, p 4 (hereinafter: Third Activity Report) indicates that such tasks have been carried out from 1 March 2010 to 1 October 2012 by Ms Csilla Fekete, and since 1 October 2012 by Mr Anthony Bisch.

the CST Committee leave much less room for doubt by stipulating that meetings are valid if at least five members are present, that decisions are adopted by simple majority, and that the president's vote is decisive if votes are tied.[53]

Point 6 of the operating rules indicates that member state governments, once they have selected their nominee, are to send their proposal to the general secretariat of the Council. The general secretariat then forwards this proposal to the president of the Panel. If it wishes, the 255 Panel can request the government to submit extra information or other materials, but it possesses no self-standing powers of investigation, and is thus dependent on their cooperation. Where it concerned candidatures for a first term of office, the Panel members have so far taken particular account of:

1) the essential reasons which led the government to propose the candidate;
2) the letter from the candidate explaining the reasons for the application;
3) a bibliographic list of works (if any) published by the candidate;
4) the text of recent publications of which the candidate is the author, written in or translated into English or French;
5) information on the national procedure that led to the candidate being selected;
6) other works published by the candidate, if publicly available.[54]

Whenever any of these elements, bar the last one, are not included in the dossier submitted, the standard practice of the Panel has become to ask the government of the member state concerned to supplement it.[55] Should any unfavourable or potentially damaging facts come to the Panel members' attention, these are never taken for granted, but always discussed with the member state government and/or the candidate himself.[56]

Unless the procedure pertains to the reappointment of a judge or advocate general, an interview constitutes the centrepiece of the entire *parcours*. Point 7 of the Panel's operating rules cements this key feature, adding that the hearing takes place in private. Suggestions to open up these sessions to the broader public have been mooted during the deliberations of the Discussion Circle on the Court of Justice at the European Convention, but were ultimately rejected in order to protect candidates' privacy.[57] The interview lasts one hour. The first ten minutes are reserved

---

[53] Council Decision 2005/49/EC concerning the operating rules of the committee provided for in Article 3(3) of Annex I to the Protocol to the Statute of the Court of Justice [2005] OJ L21/13, Annex, pt 5.

[54] The Second Activity Report states that '[t]his information can help the panel shed light on the candidate's interests and above all on his/her reflections on judicial challenges and issues, and thus on the candidate's suitability for performing the duties of Judge or Advocate-General', but that '[t]he lack of published works or the inability to produce older works cannot however in itself penalise a candidate'—Second Activity Report of the Panel provided for by Article 255 of the Treaty on the Functioning of the European Union, Brussels, 26 December 2012, 5091/13, COUR 2 JUR 5, pp 9–10 (hereinafter: Second Activity Report).

[55] Ibid, p 8.   [56] Sauvé (n 4) 109; further also in this volume, ch 3 s 2.

[57] Final report of the discussion circle on the Court of Justice at the European Convention, Brussels, 25 March 2003, CONV 636/03, pt 6. Further see also below ch 9.

for a short presentation by the nominee, either in English, French, or another official EU language. Next, the Panel members pose questions on various aspects related to the nominee's candidacy, either in English or in French. Thereby, the interviewee is expressly invited to respond in the language in which the question was asked, but may still resort to answering in any other official EU language.[58] When the procedure concerns a candidate for renewal, the nomination is only considered on paper at a Panel meeting.[59]

The operating rules do not elaborate on the criteria that are to be used in order to assess a candidate's suitability for taking up office at the CJEU. In this respect, one therefore has to fall back on the benchmarks spelled out in the Treaties. As regards the Court of Justice, Article 253 TFEU currently demands that judges and advocates general are chosen from persons whose independence is beyond doubt and who possess the qualifications required for appointment to the highest judicial offices in their respective countries, or who are jurisconsults of recognized competence.[60] In line with Article 254 TFEU, members of the General Court need to be chosen from among persons whose independence is beyond doubt and who possess the ability required for appointment to high judicial office.[61] Concerning the nationality of the persons concerned, as has been noted more often, anything goes: startlingly, nothing in the Treaties prevents a future Court exclusively composed of, for example, Chinese.[62] In practice, there have been no surprises in this regard, and the Panel has concentrated on the following six aspects when evaluating a candidate's suitability:

1) his legal expertise, demonstrating a real capacity for analysis and reflection upon the conditions and mechanisms of the application of EU law;

2) having acquired professional experience at the appropriate level of at least 20 years for appointment to the Court of Justice, and at least 12–15 years for appointment to the General Court;

3) possessing the general ability to perform the duties of a judge;

4) the presence of solid guarantees of independence and impartiality;

5) knowledge of languages;

6) aptitude for working as part of a team in an international environment in which several legal systems are represented.[63]

---

[58] Activity Report of the Panel provided for in Article 255 of the Treaty on the Functioning of the European Union, Brussels, 11 February 2011, 6509/11, COUR 3 JUR 57, p 4 (hereinafter: First Activity Report).

[59] Lord Mance, 'The Composition of the European Court of Justice', talk given to the United Kingdom Association for European Law on 19 October 2011, <http://www.supremecourt.gov.uk/docs/speech_111019.pdf> accessed 15 April 2014, 18.

[60] These requirements were originally derived from the Statute of the International Court of Justice; see Cohen (n 2) 29.

[61] The Lisbon Treaty newly inserted the adjective 'high'. Most remarkable here is the (continuing) omission of the phrase 'in their respective countries'.

[62] cf T Kennedy, 'Thirteen Russians! The Composition of the European Court of Justice', in AIL Campbell and M Voyatzi (eds), *Legal Reasoning and Judicial Interpretation of European Law. Essays in Honour of Lord Mackenzie-Stuart* (Trenton Publishing, 1996) 69.

[63] Above (n 58) 6–9. In the margins of the Third Activity Report (above n 52), p 7, a substantial adaptability factor is stressed as well: all candidates are expected to show that they possess the capacity

One would perhaps expect a mastery of French to be of critical importance, given that it is the CJEU's internal working language. The 255 Panel has however stated that the linguistic skills of the nominee are of themselves not considered decisive for a favourable decision.[64] Conversely, though, if a candidate displays a manifest deficiency on any one of the aforementioned elements, this may trigger a negative outcome. Not taken into account at all are gender considerations, a desire to strike a balance between different professional backgrounds, or the need to secure the presence of a specific legal expertise at the EU courts, for these elements allegedly go beyond the limits of the mandate conferred upon the 255 Panel.[65]

In accordance with point 5 of the operating rules, all deliberations take place *in camera*. Once the Panel members have formulated their reasoned opinion on the candidate's suitability, it is communicated to the representatives of the member state governments. On the basis of point 8, if so desired, the Presidency of the Council may call upon the Panel's president to elaborate on the decision before the member states' representatives. From a combined reading of points 5 and 8, it has been inferred that for the rest, the opinion ought to remain confidential.[66] Moreover, the opinion would seem to constitute a third party document under the Union's general transparency rules and, under Article 4 of Regulation 1049/2001, the Council is bound to refuse access to a document where disclosure would undermine the privacy and integrity of individuals, in particular concerning the protection of personal data.[67] Indeed, the 255 Panel has concluded from this provision, in conjunction with the judgment of the Court in the *Bavarian Lager* case,[68] that its opinions on individual candidates could be principally qualified as personal data, so that their content therefore ought not to be disseminated to a wider audience.[69] The overriding rationale forms the desire to protect the candidates' reputation; equally, it is thought that more openness here might discourage potential candidates from allowing their name to be put forward.[70] By way of compensation, the 255 Panel has moved to publish periodic reports on its activities.[71]

'to make an effective personal contribution, after a period of adjustment of a number of months, rather than a number of years, to the judicial role for which they are being considered'.

[64] First Activity Report (n 58), p 9.

[65] Sauvé (n 4) 117: '[L]*e comité n'a pas été conçu comme un organe responsable de la composition de la Cour, mais comme une entité permettant d'alerter les États sur l'absence d'adéquation entre une candidate et les fonctions juridictionnelles à exercer.*' One may wonder, though, whether, in the laying down of its main evaluation criteria and their application, said limits have not already been surpassed; cf Dumbrovský, Petkova, and Van der Sluis (n 22) 466, but contrast J-V Louis, 'La nomination des juges de la Cour de justice', (2013) 48(3) *Cahiers de droit européen* 574.

[66] Above (n 58) 5.

[67] Regulation 1049/2001 of the European Parliament and of the Council of 30 May 2001 regarding public access to European Parliament, Council and Commission documents [2001] OJ L145/43.

[68] Case C-28/08 P *European Commission v The Bavarian Lager Co. Ltd* [2010] ECR I-6055.

[69] Mance (n 59) 19–20.

[70] Sauvé (n 4) 116. Compare B Vesterdorf, 'La nomination des juges de la Cour de Justice de l'Union européenne' (2012) 47(3) *Cahiers de droit européen* 610, who contends that the procedure as it is already threatens to put off prospective candidates, who may either fear a negative result or believe the whole scheme violates their dignity.

[71] Above (n 52, n 54, and n 58). These published documents reflect in general terms on the nature of the opinions the Panel has issued. Mance (n 59, at 19) reveals however that more specific versions are issued to the member state governments.

The various talks and publications by its members are thought to offer sufficient additional insight on its working methods and ordinary proceedings.[72] It should not be forgotten either that no secrecy surrounds governments' nominations to the Panel, so whenever a second candidate is put forward, everyone will understand that the first candidate did not make the grade.

One final aspect worthy of note with regard to the operation of the 255 Panel concerns financial arrangements. Point 9 of the operating rules determines that members who are required to travel away from their place of residence in order to carry out their duties are entitled to reimbursement of their expenses. Hereby reference is made to Article 6 of Regulation 422/67/EEC, 5/67/Euratom of 25 July 1967, and the Council is singled out as the entity that covers the corresponding expenditure.[73] The amusing outcome is that travellers are entitled to a paltry daily allowance of 750 Belgian francs, or 1,250 Belgian francs in case of journeys outside Europe. Crucially omitted here are the words 'as amended', which would properly redirect us to Regulation 904/2012/EU.[74] In practice, however, the sums have no doubt been paid out in the corresponding amounts in today's money, corrected for inflation.

4.2. The CST Committee

Article 3(3) of the Annex to the decision establishing the Civil Service Tribunal foresees that a Committee shall be set up comprising seven persons chosen from among former members of the Court of Justice and the Court of First Instance and lawyers of recognized competence. The Council, acting by a qualified majority on a recommendation by the President of the Court of Justice, shall determine the Committee's membership and operating rules.[75] These operating rules, adopted on 18 January 2005, barely fill half a page. With a marked feeling for understatement, the Committee's first president characterized them as 'fairly rudimentary'.[76] In several respects, they mirror the principles that guide the operation of the 255 Panel, though the latter are twice as long. For what it is worth, the CST Committee commands greater seniority nevertheless, since it was already established in 2005, long before its sibling saw the light of day.

---

[72] See eg the overview in the First Activity Report (n 58), p 14.

[73] Council Regulation 422/67/EEC, 5/67/Euratom of 25 July 1967 determining the emoluments of the President and members of the Commission and of the President, Judges, Advocates-General and Registrar of the Court of Justice [1967] OJ 187/1.

[74] Council Regulation 904/2012/EU of 24 September 2012 amending Regulation 422/67/EEC, 5/67/Euratom determining the emoluments of the President and Members of the Commission, of the President, Judges, Advocates-General and Registrar of the Court of Justice of the Communities, of the President, Members and Registrar of the Court of First Instance and of the President, Members and Registrar of the European Union Civil Service Tribunal [2012] OJ L269/1.

[75] Council Decision 2004/752/EC of 2 November 2004 establishing the European Union Civil Service Tribunal [2004] OJ L333/7, Annex.

[76] Council Decision 2005/49/EC concerning the operating rules of the committee provided for in Article 3(3) of Annex I to the Protocol to the Statute of the Court of Justice [2005] OJ L21/13, Annex; Sevón (n 17) 2.

In familiar fashion, the rules first of all rehearse the terms of Article 3(3) of the Annex to the decision establishing the CST, adding that the persons concerned are to be appointed for a period of four years, that they may be reappointed once, and that the Council designates the president. The general secretariat of the Council is once again tasked with providing administrative support. A quorum of five is fixed in order for meetings to be valid, decisions are adopted by qualified majority, and, as noted, the president's vote counts for two in the case that no majority exists either way. In practice, all CST Committee members were present at the meetings, and all decisions were taken unanimously.[77]

As indicated above, when vacancies arise at the CST, the Council publishes an open call for applications for appointment to the Tribunal.[78] These applications are to be sent by registered mail to the general secretariat of the Council, accompanied by a curriculum vitae and a letter setting out reasons for the application, as well as photocopies of supporting documents. Subsequently, in accordance with Article 3(4) of the Annex to the decision establishing the Civil Service Tribunal, the Committee is meant to produce an opinion on the applicants' suitability for office, and append to its opinion a list of candidates having the most suitable high-level experience. This list needs to contain the names of (at least) twice as many candidates as there are judges to be appointed. While the rules did not explicitly intend for a ranking in order of preference to be made, the CST Committee naughtily decided to pursue this strategy in 2005.

The rules also do not make clear what working methods the CST Committee was supposed to adhere to. In 2005, after a first discussion, it opted to proceed by letting all members fill in a form for each applicant, assessing the suitability of the applicants on various counts and attributing points relative to the fulfilment of each element.[79] Next, it decided to organize interviews with the most appropriate candidates. Each of these took 30 minutes, wherein the applicants were quizzed on their motives, tested on their judicial capabilities, and sometimes asked to provide supplementary information.[80] These methods have become the standard ever since; no new interviews are deemed necessary if judges apply for reappointment.

With regard to the criteria for assessing an applicant's suitability for taking up office at the CST, the very first call published by the Council pointed out that candidates had to be Union citizens of unquestionable independence, possessing the ability required for appointment to judicial office.[81] In the forms mentioned above, these requirements were broken down into the following aspects: knowledge of general EU law; European civil service law; international and national civil service law; and professional experience acquired in use of this knowledge, either through

---

[77] Sevón (n 17) 6. See also Chapter 4 in this volume.

[78] The modalities are governed by Council Decision 2005/150/EC, Euratom, concerning the conditions and arrangements governing the submission and processing of applications for appointment as a judge of the European Union Civil Service Tribunal [2005] OJ 50/7.

[79] Sevón (n 17) 5.   [80] ibid.

[81] Council Decision 2005/150/EC, Euratom, concerning the conditions and arrangements governing the submission and processing of applications for appointment as a judge of the European Union Civil Service Tribunal [2005] OJ 50/7, Annex, pt 6.

judicial or quasi-judicial activities, or through legislative, academic, or administrative activities, or through work of a legal nature in international organizations in a multinational or multilingual environment.[82] During the first interviews, the CST Committee members particularly focused on the nature, significance, and duration of the candidates' experience, their aptitude for team work, linguistic skills, ability to maintain independence, and ability to work in a multinational and multilingual environment.[83] Because the CST only consists of seven judges, Article 3(1) of the Annex to the decision establishing the Tribunal instructs the Council to ensure a balanced composition on as broad a geographical basis as possible from among nationals of the member states, and with respect to the national legal systems represented. The CST Committee duly recognized the need to strike a fair geographical balance when compiling its first opinion in 2005, which prompted it to avoid proposing more than one candidate from the same member state, and influenced the order of presentation of the first seven names on the list.[84]

As is the case with opinions of the 255 Panel, the eventual advice of the CST Committee remains principally confidential. Moreover, it does not compile and disseminate periodic activity reports. It would seem therefore that any transparency here, apart from the judicial appointment decisions, mainly has to flow from the public speeches and writings of current and former members. That this is far from ideal from a good governance and, more particularly, an accountability point of view goes without saying.

Lastly, point 6 of the CST Committee's operating rules outlines an identical arrangement for the reimbursement of travel expenses as applies at the 255 Panel, albeit that, upon referring to Article 6 of Regulation 422/67/EEC and 5/67/Euratom, the footnote proffering the location in the Official Journal places it beyond doubt that claimants may rely on the latest amended version of that provision.

4.3. Observations from comparative law

Where kindred systems for selecting judges exist at national level, the panel or committee is almost as compact as the bodies serving the EU courts. By way of example, the 15 members of the English Judicial Appointments Committee, the nine of the Swedish Judicial Committee, and the 11 of the Slovenian Judicial Council may be mentioned. For the supreme jurisdictions, as described above, deviating systems may be used, such as the five-member selection commission for the UK Supreme Court, or the 12 members of the German *Richterwahlausschuss* that scrutinize prospective *Bundesverfassungsgericht* judges. The quorums and voting rules are not always evident but appear to vary, with majority decisions presumably being a possibility as well as a recurring feature. For regular judicial

---

[82] Sevón (n 17) 5.
[83] ibid. Sevón notes that during the interviews, the Committee members were unable to gauge the personality of the candidates, nor their capacity to decide cases efficiently in an adequate manner.
[84] Ibid, 6. But see this volume, ch 4 s 2.2.

functions, they ordinarily invite applications, go through the files, stage interviews with prospective candidates, and draw up a list of suitable candidates. Gender balance considerations are taken into account, and the proceedings mostly remain confidential. When parliamentary assemblies are involved and no separate panel or committee has been installed, as is for instance the case with regard to the Supreme Court in the United States, the nominee's dossier may be generally accessible, and the hearings public.

For international courts and tribunals, a study group of the International Law Association issued the so-called Burgh House Principles on the Independence of the International Judiciary.[85] These call for judges to be chosen from among persons of high moral character, integrity, and conscientiousness who possess the appropriate professional qualifications, competence, and experience required for the court concerned. While procedures for nomination, election, and appointment should consider fair representation of different geographic regions and the principal legal systems, as appropriate—as well as of female and male judges—appropriate personal and professional qualifications must be the overriding consideration in the nomination, election, and appointment of judges. Moreover, procedures for the nomination, election, and appointment of judges should be transparent and provide appropriate safeguards against nominations, elections, and appointments motivated by improper considerations. Another request is that information regarding the nomination, election, and appointment process and information about candidates for judicial office is made public, in due time and in an effective manner, by the international organization or other body responsible for the nomination, election, and appointment process.

While the Burgh House Principles do command wide support, not all international organizations abide strictly by these terms. Apart from the ECHR—discussed elsewhere in this volume[86]—screening mechanisms that resemble those installed for the EU courts have only been put in place for the WTO Appellate Body and the International Criminal Court. The six members of the screening committee of the WTO Appellate Body consult with the states party on the names of the most suitable and geographically representative candidates, engage in a written examination, and hold an interview with the nominees, before submitting the names for appointment to the WTO Dispute Settlement Body.[87] Since 2013, an Advisory Committee on Nomination of Judges has been up and running for selection of new members of the International Criminal Court. Article 36 of the Rome Statute declares that judges are to be chosen from among persons of high moral character, impartiality, and integrity who possess the qualifications required in their respective states for appointment to the highest judicial offices. They need to possess the necessary legal experience, as well as an excellent grasp of the ICC's working languages. The Advisory Committee thus needs to assess candidates on the basis

---

[85] Study Group of the International Law Association on the Practice and Procedure of International Court and Tribunals, *The Burgh House Principles on the Independence of the International Judiciary*, <http://www.ucl.ac.uk/laws/cict/docs/burgh_final_21204.pdf> accessed 15 April 2014.
[86] See this volume, ch 5 s 3.   [87] Mackenzie et al (n 6) 157–8.

of these criteria, and thereby also takes aspects of geographical and gender balance into account. On the basis of nominations by the states that are party to the Statute, it draws up two shortlists; the Assembly of States Parties subsequently elects the judges by secret ballot. That the Committee makes available reports of its activities underlines that the transparency offered by the 255 Panel is definitely not a unique phenomenon.[88]

5. Position Within the Union's Institutional Architecture

The formal legal position of the 255 Panel and the CST Committee within the Union's institutional architecture is not very strong, and at least on paper, the weight their decisions carry is not formidable. Whenever a vacancy arises at the EU courts, there incontestably exists a duty to *involve* both bodies: bypassing them and following the old-fashioned route instead, ie a member state proposing its candidate for appointment directly to the Council, would represent an egregious violation of Article 253 TFEU, Article 254 TFEU, and Article 3(1) of the Annex to the decision establishing the Civil Service Tribunal, for a candidate cannot be validly appointed if the 255 Panel or the CST Committee were not consulted beforehand to assess his suitability.

Nevertheless, the opinion that the Panel and Committee deliver to the Council is not officially legally *binding*. In theory, it may thus be ignored or brushed aside without consequence. Conversely, nominees or member states that disapprove of the Panel or Committee decision are unable to turn to the General Court seeking the annulment thereof. After all, pursuant to Article 263 TFEU, that action requires a Union measure intended to produce legal effects vis-à-vis third parties, which is lacking here.[89] Besides, ostensibly we are dealing with Union 'bodies' here, since the Panel and the Committee obviously qualify as neither Union institutions, nor offices, nor agencies—yet this view would first need to be confirmed by the Court, to place the *légitimation passive* of the prospective defendant beyond dispute.[90]

Naturally, the Panel and the Committee would serve little purpose if their advice were to be regularly disregarded, but the fact remains that the Council is not formally bound to heed it.[91] At the same time, if an individual member state ventures to ignore or downplay a negative opinion on the suitability of its own candidate, in reality the chances may be slim that the required 'common accord of the governments' can be procured; among that company, the predominant feeling will probably be that the appointment of an unqualified person is bound to damage the credibility and effective functioning of the EU courts.[92] What is

---

[88] See eg Assembly of States Parties, 12th session, Report of the Advisory Committee on Nominations of Judges on the work of its first meeting, The Hague, 20–28 November 2013, ICC-ASP/12/23.

[89] Case 22/70 *Commission v Council* (ERTA) [1971] ECR 263; Case 60/81 *International Business Machines Corporation v Commission* [1981] ECR 2639.

[90] Further see K Lenaerts et al, *EU Procedural Law* (Oxford University Press 2014) ch 7.

[91] cf Mance (n 59) 14.

[92] Sauvé (n 4) 116; Vesterdorf (n 70) 607.

more, having happily 'outsourced' a share of their own responsibilities to the Panel, they are likely to be ill-disposed to erode the whole arrangement in that way. While theoretically the 255 Panel and the CST Committee therefore find themselves in a weak and potentially most ungrateful institutional position, they may be said to exert significant political influence nevertheless, and their input carries a notable moral weight. Arguably, the 255 Panel even holds a *de facto* veto power, since its negative assessments can only be overturned through unanimity. Similar situations seem to prevail in other domestic and international systems, where the selectors' opinions wield sizeable persuasive authority, without these necessarily being legally binding.

6. The System in Action—Experiences So Far

In the first years since their inception, both the 255 Panel and the CST Committee have been actively discharging themselves of their entrusted tasks. In particular, the annual activity reports generated by the former provide useful insight with regard to the number of meetings, opinions delivered, and the favourable or unfavourable nature thereof. The CST Committee releases no such reports, so that, apart from the official decisions appointing judges to that Tribunal, information has to be pieced together on the basis of secondary sources. The compiled data and statistics may immediately be gleaned from Table 1.1 and Table 1.2.

Table 1.1 Statistics on the activities of the Article 255 Panel[1]

Year	Meetings	Candidatures examined	New mandates	Renewals	Favourable	Unfavourable	Unsuitable candidate(s) withdrawn?
2010	8	18	CJ: 2	CJ: 0	15	3	
			GC: 5	GC: 11		(CJ: 0; GC 3)	Yes
2011	2	3	CJ: 1	CJ: 0	1	2	
			GC: 2	GC: 0		(CJ: 0; GC 2)	Yes
2012	6	22	CJ: 4	CJ: 14	21	1	
			GC: 4	GC: 0		(CJ: 0; GC 1)	Yes
2013	8	24	CJ: 4	CJ: 0	23	1	
			GC: 10	GC: 10		(CJ: 0; GC 1)	Yes
Total	24	67	42	25	60	7	
			(CJ: 11	(CJ: 14			
			GC: 21)	GC: 21)			

[1] Data derived from the three activity reports issued by the 255 Panel (n 52, n 54, and n 58). 'CJ' denotes Court of Justice; 'GC' General Court.

Table 1.2 Statistics on the activities of the CST Evaluation Panel[1]

Year	Meetings	Vacancies	New mandates	Renewals	Nationality of judges elected
2005	Unknown[2]	7	7	n/a	BE, FI, FR, GE, GR, PL, UK
2008	4	3	0	3	BE, GE, PL
2009	4	1	1	0	SP
2011	5	3	3	0	IR, IT, NL
2013	4	1	1	0	DE
Total	17+	15	12	3	

[1] Data derived from the Council decisions referenced above.
[2] Recital 6 to Council Decision 2005/577/EC appointing judges of the European Union Civil Service Tribunal states that the Committee met 'on several occasions in May and June 2005'. Secondary sources provide no exact number.

6.1. The 255 Panel

In 2010, the 255 Panel was convened eight times. It examined 18 candidatures: two for appointment to the Court of Justice (all nominated for a first mandate) and 16 for the General Court (five nominated for a first mandate, 11 renewals).[93] Of these nominees, 15 were eventually considered qualified to take up office, with the remaining three being deemed unsuitable. These unsuccessful candidates envisaged to join the General Court originated from Greece, Italy, and Belgium.[94] Pursuant to the Panel's negative advice they were withdrawn and replaced by three others, all of whom managed to secure a favourable opinion.

In 2011, the 255 Panel was convened two times. It examined three candidatures, one for appointment to the Court of Justice and two for the General Court (all nominated for a first mandate).[95] The latter two, nominated by Malta and Sweden, were deemed unsuitable, withdrawn, and replaced.[96]

In 2012, six meetings took place, at which 22 candidatures were reviewed; 18 for appointment to the Court of Justice (four new, 14 renewals) and four for the General Court (all new).[97] One candidate, nominated by Lithuania to take up office at the General Court, met with an unfavourable opinion and was subsequently withdrawn and replaced.[98]

[93] The First Activity Report (n 58), p. 3, lists a total of 16 opinions (two for the Court of Justice and 14 for the General Court), but this is contradicted by both the interim total provided in the Second Activity Report and the grand total provided in the Third Activity Report (67, not 65—see Table 1.1).
[94] Engel (n 39) 454; Vesterdorf (n 70) 608.
[95] The Second Activity Report (n 54), p 7, suggests that three meetings took place, but this is forcibly contradicted by a table in the latest report indicating that only two meetings took place that year; see Third Activity Report (n 52), p. 7.
[96] Vesterdorf (n 70) 608; Engel (n 39) 454.   [97] Second Activity Report (n 54), p. 7.
[98] Dumbrovský, Petkova, and Van der Sluis (n 22) 459.

In 2013, the 255 Panel held eight meetings and examined 24 candidatures. Of these, four pertained to the Court of Justice (all newcomers) and 20 to the General Court (ten renewals, ten first terms of office).[99] All of these nominations received the green light bar one—the Czech candidate for a position at the General Court, whose candidacy was ultimately retracted in favour of the sitting judge.[100]

At first sight, the frequency of 255 Panel gatherings might appear almost random. Yet its work actually follows a natural cycle, corresponding to the periodic replacement of Judges at the Court of Justice and the General Court as dictated by Article 253 and Article 254 TFEU (ie every three years). Surplus meetings only need to be organized whenever judicial mandates are terminated prematurely (ie in case of voluntary retirement, compulsory dismissal, or death), which did not occur in the 2010–12 period. In the first exceptions to the natural cycle, however, following the resignations of the Luxembourgish and Estonian judges in early 2013, the Panel came together in order to examine the suitability of the persons proposed to serve out the remainder of these terms.

As noted above, the 255 Panel is entitled to request a member state government to submit additional information if the candidate's file displays lacunae, or other points arise that call for clarification. In 2010 it has not availed itself of this competence; for 2011, 2012, and 2013, the activity reports fail to pronounce themselves clearly on the issue. We are equally kept in the dark on whether the Panel's president was so far ever summoned before the Council to elaborate upon the content of an opinion rendered.[101]

In total, seven out of the total of 67 nominees met with an unfavourable opinion in the 2010–13 period. With regard to the motives underpinning the negative verdicts, the principle of confidentiality holds sway. Still, some cryptic discussion is provided in the 2012 and 2013 reports, wherein the Panel points to an instance in which a candidate's length of high-level professional experience was found to be uncomfortably short—a drawback that was not (but apparently could have been) compensated for by exceptional or extraordinary legal expertise.[102] On another occasion, a nominee displayed a complete absence of any professional experience relevant to EU law.[103] The Panel also issued negative advice where it had the impression that the legal abilities of the candidate were inadequate, which prompted it to stress in its report that that all candidates ought to be capable of demonstrating that they have sufficient knowledge of the Union's legal system and a sufficient grasp of the broad issues relating to the application of EU law as well as the relationships between legal systems.[104] It is easy to overlook the positive side to these outcomes, namely that they could spur on member states to create or reform

---

[99] Third Activity Report (n 52), p. 8.

[100] Dumbrovský, Petkova, and Van der Sluis (n 22) 476.

[101] Lord Mance stated that 'this course could well be taken' in his 2011 lecture on 'The Composition of the European Court of Justice' (n 59) 14. The Third Activity Report (above n 52), p 21, does point out that Mr Sauvé was heard by COREPER on 3 October 2012 and, together with Ms Palacio, by the Parliament on 28 February 2011 and 30 May 2013.

[102] Second Activity Report (n 54), p 14.

[103] Ibid.   [104] Third Activity Report (n 52), p 20.

the (apparently not infallible) pre-selection mechanisms at domestic level. In some quarters they already have.[105]

On the opinions' delivery speed, conclusions can be drawn with mathematical precision. Whereas there exists no fixed time frame within which the 255 Panel is bound to come up with its advice, between 2010 and 2013 it has managed to do so within a reasonable period that averages 64 days. Roughly 61 per cent of the assessments were wrapped up within a span of 45 to 90 days, and in roughly 30 per cent of cases within a span of less than 45 days. The remaining 9 per cent took more than 90 days, a blemish mainly attributed to inertia from the side of the governments concerned.[106] This has resulted, inter alia, in a protracted period in which the General Court has had to function without a sitting judge from Malta and Italy. It also prompted calls for the member state governments to adapt to a more proactive and responsive judicial appointments strategy.[107]

6.2. The CST Committee

Since its establishing Decision determined that the Civil Service Tribunal was to consist of seven judges, in 2005 the CST Committee was charged with nominating candidates for seven vacancies. As noted above, Article 3(4) of the Annex to the Decision requires the Committee to compile a list that contains (at least) twice as many candidates as could be appointed, ie the names of (at least) 14 persons. The Council issued a public call which attracted 243 applications.[108] After examination of the files, and through the form-based method canvassed above, the CST Committee narrowed down the number of potential candidates to 31, all of whom were invited to interviews in Brussels. At this point, five of them withdrew their application, meaning 26 interviews were conducted. The Committee proceeded to deliver an opinion listing the names of the 14 candidates it considered most suitable, in order of quality, thereby striving to strike a proper geographical balance. According to its former president, no major difficulties were encountered in the internal decision-making process, and consensus was easily achieved.[109] Next, the Council appointed the judges according to the proposed order of preference.[110] Afterwards, though, it complained in writing that the Committee had strayed beyond its mandate, since assurance of an adequate geographical balance was an exclusive prerogative of the Council.[111]

---

[105] Dumbrovský, Petkova, and Van der Sluis (n 22) 457.

[106] Second Activity Report (n 54), p 7. An alternative, more diplomatic explanation is provided in the Third Activity Report (n 52), p 10: 'The longest periods were caused by the early proposal of candidates by some countries, well before the end of an ongoing term of office.'

[107] M van der Woude, 'Het Gerecht van de Europese Unie—Een bestuursrechter onder druk', (2013) 87(14) *Nederlands Juristen Blad* 879. See also the remarks of AG Sharpston in her Opinion in Case C-58/12 P *Groupe Gascogne SA v Commission* [2013] ECR I-0000, par 89.

[108] Sevón (n 17) 5.

[109] Ibid, 6.

[110] Council Decision 2005/577/EC appointing Judges of the European Union Civil Service Tribunal [2005] L197/28.

[111] Ibid. See also this volume, ch 4 s 2.2.

Pursuant to Article 2 of the Decision establishing the Civil Service Tribunal, three of the CST judges were to sit only for a period of three years. Following a choice by lot carried out by the President of the Council in October 2005, the duties of Judges Irena Boruta, Horstpeter Kreppel, and Sean van Raepenbusch were to expire on 30 September 2008.[112] A public call for applications was published on 7 December 2007 and 53 applications were received, including those of the three retiring judges.[113] The number of applications and interviews conducted has, unfortunately, not been disclosed. Curiously, after meeting four times, the CST Committee ultimately came up with two lists—one containing the names of the three Judges of the Tribunal that could be reappointed, and the other containing the names of three other candidates (despite the Council's earlier remonstrations, once again with visible consideration of maintaining an equal spread across the different member states). The Council chose to reappoint the three judges whose term had expired, giving vent to its dissatisfaction with the fact that two lists had been compiled instead of the one prescribed by Article 3(4) of the Annex.[114]

Upon the expiry of the CST Committee's own term of office, at the end of 2008 a fresh *équipe* was put in place. At the beginning of 2009, a vacancy in the CST arose, pursuant to the intended transfer of the Finnish member Heikki Kanninen to the General Court. A public call for applications was published on 6 March 2009, but no figures have been released on the number of reactions or interviews conducted. The Committee reached agreement on a list after meeting four times. The procedure led to the Council's appointment of the Spanish judge Maria Isabel Rofes i Pujol.[115]

The terms of office of CST judges Stéphane Gervasoni, Paul Mahoney, and Harissios Tagaras expired in September 2011.[116] A public call for applications had been issued months before, in June 2010. Again, no information has been disclosed on the number of reactions or interviews conducted. After meeting five times, the Committee delivered its opinion, eventually resulting in the Council's appointment of the Dutch René Barents, Irish Kieran Bradley, and Italian Ezio Perillo.[117]

---

[112] Drawing of lots concerning judges of the European Union Civil Service Tribunal [2005] OJ C262/1.

[113] Council Decision 2008/569/EC of 27 June 2008 appointing three Judges of the European Union Civil Service Tribunal [2008] L183/31.

[114] The aforementioned Decision refers to a list containing six candidates; it makes no mention of the division into two, nor of the discontentment of the Council described in Sevón (n 17) 6. The tenth recital does stress that in its decision to reappoint the three retiring judges, the Council took into account 'the exceptional fact that their effective term of office has been two years', adding that this shall '[u]nder no circumstances constitute a precedent'.

[115] Council Decision 2009/474/EC of 9 June 2009 appointing a Judge to the European Union Civil Service Tribunal [2009] L156/56.

[116] On the proposal of the President of the Court of Justice, Mr Tagaras was later placed on the list of temporary CST judges per Council Decision 2013/181/EU of 22 April 2013 drawing up a list of three temporary Judges for the Civil Service Tribunal [2013] OJ L111/49. Mr Gervasoni was appointed Judge at the General Court per Decision 2013/337/EU of the Representatives of the Governments of the Member States of 26 June 2013 appointing Judges to the General Court [2013] OJ 179/93.

[117] Council Decision 2011/459/EU of 18 July 2011 appointing Judges to the European Union Civil Service Tribunal [2011] L194/31.

In early 2013 Judge Irena Boruta made known her intention to resign, sparking off a public call for applications on 21 March 2013. One month later, seven new members took seats in the CST Evaluation Committee. They convened four times to fashion their shortlist, from which the Council picked the Dane Jesper Svenningsen.[118]

7. Conclusion

Before the introduction of the novel selection mechanisms, as far as we know, no candidate for appointment to any of the EU courts was ever rejected.[119] At the same time, with no system of prior screening in place, that it was possible for a Petrus Serrarens to get elected—someone who would be considered patently unsuitable by today's standards—should not raise many eyebrows. After all, in the old, straightforward approach, member states had a powerful hold on one another: whoever objected to someone else's nominee risked equally negative reactions vis-à-vis their own nominee at the next instance, so 'live and let live' was probably the wiser course of action. Allegedly, the quality of judges at the CJEU has nevertheless been high for a long time, meaning there was little cause for dissatisfaction with the classic approach.[120] This did not obviate the desire for a wholesale refurbishment emerging in the mid-2000s. The novel system, up and running for barely five years now, has already led to the rejection of more than ten per cent (and counting) of the nominees. However, when renewals of sitting judges' mandates are excluded and only Panel opinions on first-term candidatures considered, the rejection rate virtually doubles, rising to over 20 per cent. This figure may be seen as both alarming and reassuring. On the one hand, it would seem that the member state governments can in fact not always (or can no longer) be trusted to come forward with the most qualified person. On the other, the felicitous new selection mechanisms now guarantee that candidates who lack the right credentials are barred from taking up office.

That none of the candidates rejected by the 255 Panel has become a judge so far underscores that the forum exerts a tangible impact, even when its views are not officially legally binding.[121] Technically, a member state could stick with a candidate repudiated by the Panel, and diplomatically withdrawing him might be a much more humiliating tactic than maintaining him. At this stage, just as in the Council of Europe, the government concerned is likely to experience peer pressure to justify itself, but if it refuses to present an alternative, it may yet have its cake

---

[118] Council Decision 2013/457/EC of 16 September 2013 appointing a Judge to the European Union Civil Service Tribunal [2013] L247/37.

[119] See this volume, ch 3 s 1.

[120] cf Vesterdorf (n 70) 602–3: '*La flexibilité et la liberté laissées au États members ont, en général, été bien appliqués et ont permis à la Cour et au Tribunal de bénéficier d'un excellent mélange de personnalités hautement compétentes.*'

[121] So far, it has not delivered an unfavourable opinion on any candidate pursuing a renewal of his term of office.

and eat it.[122] Here, the confidentiality of the 255 Panel's advice—while *in se* perfectly justifiable—plays right into its hands, and minimizes the political collateral damage. Nevertheless, such scenarios have not materialized so far; on the contrary, faithful compliance has proven to be the rule.[123] Still, the 255 Panel—just like the CST Committee—does not mean to usurp the member states' prerogative, merely to facilitate their decision-making. The member states retain full sovereignty in this respect, and can thus be held responsible for their actions. Moreover, if the Panel and the Committee were ever to be confronted with a persistent string of unconvincing candidates, they could ultimately only acquiesce; for, unlike the bed that Procrustes built, their standards cannot be adjusted in accordance with the capacities of the persons who come before them.

Whereas in the past, a variety of factors has influenced member states' choices when selecting future judges, the novel system has evidently made a more objective review possible.[124] The importance of its continuing smooth operation therefore almost goes without saying. The Panel and Committee members are bound to have their work cut out for them, though, if the progressive expansion of the General Court goes through—let alone if, at some point in the future, additional first instance tribunals are established.[125] It would at that point significantly relieve their workload if the member states were to refrain from needlessly replacing well-functioning judges eligible for reappointment. Simultaneously, in order to secure the most efficient task management, their operating rules will be in need of revision.[126]

If the quality of judges at the CJEU has been high in times past—but now perhaps no longer always high enough—the new screening system grants much-needed security. This effective fail-safe system will, in turn, indubitably impact on the quality of the case law too. A wholesome side-effect of this development may be that foreign jurisdictions decide to emulate the practice—offering further proof of the Union's 'soft power' in external relations. Of course, every polity gets the judiciary it deserves; yet, when the vast experiences gained with designing judicial selection methods in this part of the world are finally put to good use, the situation in the EU one day ought to become as good as it can ever get. The novel instruments dissected here should, at the very least, bring us one step closer to that goal.

---

[122] cf Engel (n 39) 451.

[123] In 2013, the Czech Republic did for a while refuse to withdraw Mr Peter Mlsna, nominated to take up office in the General Court. It however eventually proceded to retract this candidate, who received a negative opinion from the 255 Panel, in favour of the sitting judge Irena Pelikánová. See Dumbrovský, Petkova, and Van der Sluis (n 22) 476.

[124] cf Alter (n 11) 127, pointing *inter alia* to party affiliation and political connections. Cohen (n 2) 35–6 deftly unveils the nepotism that surrounded some of the first appointments.

[125] Meanwhile, the number of Advocates General at the Court of Justice is already set to rise to 11 by the end of 2015; see Council Decision 2013/336/EU of 25 June 2013 increasing the number of Advocates-General of the Court of Justice of the European Union [2013] L179/92.

[126] In the same sense, Sauvé (n 4) 118.

2

Judicial Performance, Membership, and Design at the Court of Justice

Damian Chalmers

1. Introduction

The performance of the Court of Justice (Court) is coming under ever closer scrutiny. It is deciding more politically salient cases, is subject to increasing national judicial dissent,[1] and its banner achievement, the primacy of EU law, is met with increasing public opposition.[2] The relationship between who does the work of the Court and the quality of that work is, of course, central to all this. To raise questions about performance review or more careful reflection about how judges are selected is often to encounter muttered remarks and frowns of disgust, however, for to do so would be to violate that great taboo: it would infringe judicial independence. Important as the latter is, there is a certain chutzpah in this criticism. Neither current appointment procedures, resting as they do on governmental appointment, nor the possibility for reappointment after a short-ish six-year term safeguard that independence.[3] Furthermore, it is difficult to deny that judges arrive with a certain disposition, skill-set, and life experience which will inform their approach to their job. A better question is, therefore, how these issues are addressed in thinking about whom to appoint to the Court and how this process of reflection should be structured. Agnosticism to these issues simply belies the significance of the judicial office.

---

[1] Pl. ÚS 5/12 *Slovak Pensions*, Judgment of 31 January 2012 (Czech Constitutional Court); 1 BvR 1215/07 *Counterterrorism Database*, Judgment of 24 April 2013, paras 88–91 (German Constitutional Court); *R v The Secretary of State for Transport ex parte HS2 Action Alliance Limited*, Judgment of 22 January 2014, see also Lords Neuberger and Mance, paras 188 and 189 (United Kingdom Supreme Court). On cases within the Netherlands see S Garben, 'Sky-High Controversy and High-Flying Claims? The *Sturgeon* Case Law in Light of Judicial Activism, Euroscepticism and Eurolegalism' (2013) 50 *CMLRev* 15.

[2] A poll by Open Europe in February 2014 found, therefore, that 55 per cent of Britons and 36 per cent of Germans believed that their parliament should be able to veto any new EU law: online at <http://www.openeurope.org.uk/Page/Research/en/LIVE>, last accessed 1 August 2014.

[3] Article 19(2) TEU. On the idea of a nine-year non-renewable term see the Rothley Report of the European Parliament, Session Document A3-0228/93.

This chapter will initially consider the tensions between the twin demands of judicial independence and judicial performance. It shall suggest that the only way of reconciling these demands in a manageable way is to locate them in the particular tasks that are expected of the judiciary at a certain time. Insofar as it relates to judicial appointments, a task-based approach looks at what procedures and skills/experience/disposition would be best suited to realize these tasks. In the subsequent sections it will be argued, through an analysis of the history of the professional backgrounds of the Court, that a failure to do this simply results in the Court setting its own tasks for itself—leading to claims of judicial activism and possible institutional dislocation—and that these tasks invariably reflect the prevailing professional disposition of the Court at the time. The work of the Court is, thus, marked by four eras. In the first, the transitional period, its central task was to establish a template for an EU law. The second, the period prior to Maastricht, was concerned with establishing a legal order with constitutional trappings but was functionally very confined. In the third, the period between Maastricht and Lisbon, a more managerial approach was taken, where there was a concern to organize and generalize, albeit in quite a moderate manner, the legal principles established. The fourth period, since Lisbon, has witnessed a return to a concern with an approach centred on entrenching and extending EU rights and furthering institutional integration. In each of these eras, it will be argued that the prior professional backgrounds of the judges made the approach in question seem natural.

The conclusion of this chapter will argue that the Court now sits at a crossroads, as both the professional composition of the Court changes and the wider political and institutional environment which allowed it to carve out these agendas becomes less supportive. Two visions of the Court's future agendas emerge. One characterizes the Court as a constitutional court. Its judges would come from that background. However, its role would be more confined in terms of its docket than now: deciding fewer cases in less detail, setting out architectonic principles, and engaging more seriously in review of the EU legislature than hitherto. The other sees it as a more managerial court. Its professional background would be more varied and its docket greater. It would be engaging more with dispute settlement and the contribution of law to the realization of Union policies, but less with constitutional principle. Either position is defensible. Less desirable is an intermediate position where the Court has a background which induces it, on the one hand, to set out a constitutional imaginary not justified by the context of the disputes and in turn distorted by that context and, on the other, grants it insufficient expertise to deal with the detail of many disputes. Without thought as to the membership of the Court, its docket, or its internal organization, there is a danger it will drift to that position.

2. Judicial Performance and the False Dilemma of Judicial Independence and Judicial Accountability

The appointment to judicial office matters because of the significance of what that office does. The question of appointment cannot, therefore, be separated from that of judicial performance. Placing judicial appointment within the context of judicial performance raises questions, however, first about the values and parameters by which we are to judge such performance, and second about how appointment is to contribute to these.

If we turn, first, to the values and parameters for judicial performance, for some constitutional settlements, judicial independence is the trumping value. It is the only constitutionally recognized value demanded of the judiciary, therefore, in many European states.[4] At the other end of the spectrum, judicial power is presented as something exercised on behalf of constituents or on behalf of a constituent power. At its most powerful, this judicial accountability can lead, as with many states in the United States, to merit plans whereby the electorate can vote against a judicial appointment at the next subsequent general election.[5] However, within the European Union,[6] both the Spanish Constitution[7] and EU law[8] emphasize the accountability of a judge, and therefore the possibility of state liability for her performance.[9] In reality, most judiciaries operate between these poles, and this is certainly the case with the Court of Justice. There are, on the one hand, guarantees concerning its independence. Judges must be appointed from persons whose independence is beyond doubt.[10] They must not hold political or administrative office, and cannot engage in any occupation, even unpaid, unless granted exemption by the Council.[11] However, the responsibilities with regard to how they exercise their duties are less onerous, requiring that they take an oath to carry them out impartially and respect the secrecy of the deliberations of the court.[12] Countervailing performance duties exist, however. Appointees must possess the qualifications required for appointment to the highest judicial office or be 'jurisconsults of recognised competence'.[13] The oath carries with it a parallel commitment to work conscientiously.[14]

This agnosticism offers little guidance as to the balance between independence and accountability. Independence is clearly to be a central value of the Court of Justice, but it is not to be its only valued characteristic. Insofar as other values will have to be weighed against that of independence, they will necessarily qualify it. Furthermore, this balance need not be a static one. As the nature of the Court's workload changes, it might be that the balance between independence

---

[4] Art 97 German Basic Law; Art 104 Italian Constitution; Art 178 Polish Constitution; Art 87(1) Austrian Constitutional Law.

[5] This is sometimes called the Missouri plan as it was first adopted. It is adopted by 34 states in the United States. On some of the challenges see S Paynter and R Kearney, 'Who Watches the Watchmen? Evaluating Judicial Performance in the American States' (2010) 41 *Administration and Society* 923, 924–6.

[6] Notwithstanding the change in titles and designations since the Treaty of Rome in 1957, the European Union (EU) and EU law are used generally for ease of reference.

[7] Sections 117(3) and 121 Spanish Constitution.

[8] Case C-224/01 *Köbler v Republic of Austria* [2003] ECR I-10239.

[9] The 'Rothley Report', European Parliament Session Document A3-0228/93, suggested parliamentary hearings prior to appointment.

[10] Articles 19(2) TEU and 255 TFEU.   [11] Statute of the Court of Justice, Art 4.
[12] Statute of the Court of Justice, Art 2.   [13] Article 253 TFEU.
[14] Statute of the Court of Justice, Art 2.

and accountability should be modulated. Blockages in the Council, it has been argued, might lead to the neglect of certain interests which can only be protected by the Court. Conversely, if the legislature is working well, there is a less strong case for such intervention.[15]

The second difficulty is a regulatory one, namely the criteria and mechanisms to secure and correct any balance. Criteria for 'judicial performance evaluation' have proven to be a hoary subject in the United States, with no real agreement as to either the criteria or level of detail to be deployed.[16] There is also doubt about the efficacy of the mechanism of appointment and reappointment as a way of safeguarding performance. The evidence as to whether elections rather than appointments lead to a more ideological or less conscientious judiciary is mixed.[17] In like vein, the presence of judicial councils, panels comprising judges and others, to look at budgets, appointments, and performance of courts is associated with both weak and strong judicial performance.[18] This is because a much wider array of features condition performance than appointment procedures. These include relations within any court and the patterns of socialization generated by these; the tasks of the institution and how the main audiences of the court are seen to esteem its work.[19] Any schema regulating all these determinants would simply be too constraining and too rigid to protect judicial independence sufficiently. However, to be indifferent to all this is to be happy with the possibility of an independent donkey for a judge.

This dilemma may be a false one, however, as it rests on an abstract notion of the judge as both fully independent and capable in any equal measure concerning any task. However, any task will involve particular legal norms, a particular procedure involving a particular dispute involving particular litigants, a particular surrounding legal and socio-economic context, and particular interventions from national governments. All these will frame how independence and performance is assessed by the judge and her audience, the arguments she entertains, the reasons she deploys, and the legal resources she invokes.[20] Even at the most formal level, different types of case lead to different forms of reasoning, different levels of intervention from national governments, different styles of litigation, and different sizes

---

[15] This argument has been made most recently through the justification of teleological reasoning used by the Court: namely, that it is to realize the objectives of the Treaty but must respect the judgment of the Union legislature when it has adopted legislation (although apparently not when it has not). K Lenaerts and J Gutiérrez-Fons, 'To Say What the Law of the EU Is: Methods of Interpretation and the European Court of Justice' (EUI Working Paper AEL 2013/9, 2013) 27–9.

[16] J Elek and D Rottman, 'Improving Judicial-Performance Evaluation: Countering Bias and Exploring New Methods' (2013) 49 *Court Review* 140.

[17] For a review of the literature see G Tarr, *Without Fear or Favor: Judicial Independence and Judicial Accountability in the States* (Stanford University Press 2012) 149–50.

[18] N Garoupa and T Ginsburg, 'The Comparative Law and Economics of Judicial Councils' (2009) 27 *Berkeley Journal of International Law* 52.

[19] L Baum, *Judges and Their Audiences: A Perspective on Judicial Behavior* (Princeton University Press 2006) chapter 6.

[20] On how this question of task being performance shapes the reasoning used and who is heard and participates see D Chalmers, 'The Reconstitution of Europe's Public Spheres' (2003) 9 *ELJ* 127.

of chamber hearing the case.[21] Furthermore, the judicial task will combine the different elements set out above—predisposition, skill, judicial setting, audience—in a manner that is distinctive to that case and makes it somewhat artificial to treat them too discretely from one another.

Rooting questions of judicial independence and accountability in the tasks performed by the Court of Justice allows these questions to be approached in a more grounded and manageable manner. The starting point for this would be to consider the types of task in which the Court is most commonly engaged, and then consider the organization and procedures which could allow it to discharge these best. Such an approach respects the independence of the Court insofar as it considers which structures and procedures enable judicial performance, rather than setting these up as parameters to measure its performance. It is also in line with how other EU institutions are organized. The internal organization and institutional relations of the European Central Bank were, therefore, geared to enable it to secure price stability through authorization of the issue of money and the corollary setting of short-term interest rates.[22] These structures have adapted as it has acquired new powers, most notably the prudential regulation of euro-area banks.[23]

It is beyond the scope of this paper to consider what all this may involve. In regard to the question of appointments, however, it would seem that the predisposition, skills, expertise of these appointments should be geared to meeting the tasks envisaged for the institution. These influence how judges envision EU law and the role of the Court of Justice in any case. To fail to have regard to the background of appointments does not merely fail to break the link between the appointment process and how EU law is interpreted and applied, but introduces an element of ad hocery, and allows judges to define the task for the Court rather than others simply by virtue of these tasks being left undefined by the latter.

To substantiate this argument, this paper will divide the history of the Court into four periods: the transitional period up until 1970; the subsequent period up until the ratification of the Maastricht Treaty; the period beyond that until the ratification of the Lisbon Treaty; and the period since the Lisbon Treaty. Each of these periods has distinctive qualities. The transitional period is a period of beginning marked, however, by relatively little EU law entering into force. The period prior to the Treaty on European Union (TEU) is a period of political, legal, and institutional consolidation, so that by 1993 the European Union has an established legal

---

[21] In different styles of reasoning see S Sankari, *European Court of Justice Legal Reasoning in Context* (Europa Law Publishing 2013); on patterns of litigation see D Kelemen, *Eurolegalism: The Transformation of Law and Regulation in the European Union* (Harvard University Press 2011) and on patterns of government intervention see C Carrubba et al, 'Judicial Behavior under Political Constraints: Evidence from the European Court of Justice' 102 (2008) *APSR* 435.

[22] Art 127(1) TFEU.

[23] Regulation 1024/2013/EU conferring specific tasks on the European Central Bank concerning policies relating to the prudential supervision of credit institutions, OJ 2013, L 287/63. Further see D Chalmers et al, *European Union Law* (3rd edn, Cambridge University Press 2014) 733–6.

system, a public sphere, and a high level of institutional consolidation. The period from Maastricht until Lisbon is a period marked by increased political contestation and institutional reform, as well as embarkation on the euro project. The final period since the ratification of the Lisbon Treaty is marked by the fall-out from the sovereign debt crisis but also by a new procedure, that in which judicial panels give their opinions on the quality of candidates. It is possible to associate the Court with the performance of a dominant task in each period. This task was established by the Court with no explicit mandate, and it was easier for it to do this as a consequence of the professional origins of its members during each period: something that has occurred largely by happenstance and relies on a supportive or passive institutional and political environment to happen.

For each period, the prior professional background of each Court of Justice judge and advocate general shall be examined, and shall be given a mark out of 3. This can be broken up in the case of different professional backgrounds. To measure influence, this score is then multiplied by the number of years spent on the Court during that period.[24] A weakness of this measurement is that it assumes professional background weighs on judges equally. It also assumes that each judge has equal influence within the Court. It is unlikely that either assumption is actually true. Furthermore, a higher relative weighting is given to time spent as membership of the senior judiciary, partly to compensate for this being something that can only happen later in a career (unlike in other careers) and partly because it is often the role that the Court is claiming for itself. Prior experience of such a role might weigh more heavily than other careers in such an instance.

All these assumptions are problematic and possibly not true. However, the argument made here is not a strong one that the prior professional background of individual judges causes them to behave in a particular way; it is a weak one that a collective professional backdrop which reflects a balance between certain careers allows a collective disposition which makes it easier for the Court to adopt a particular view of EU law and particular tasks for itself. These assumptions are not sufficiently problematic to falsify this.

3. The Transitional Period and the Establishment of a Template for the EU Legal Order

The transitional period is marked by a number of characteristics. It is associated, first, with *Van Gend en Loos* and *Costa*.[25] This case law differentiated the TEU from international treaties, marking it out as establishing an autonomous legal order which limited the sovereignty of member states, and, consequently,

---

[24] Rounding up usually takes place except in the last two periods, where fractions are kept simply to illustrate emerging trends.

[25] Case 26/62 *Van Gend en Loos* [1963] ECR 1; Case 6/64 *Costa* [1964] ECR 585.

took precedence over national law and generated individual rights which could be invoked in national courts. A new template for both integration through law and law beyond the nation state was, therefore, established, which created new legal subjectivities, configurations of power, and systems of accountability. However, no more than a template was provided, as the second characteristic of this period was that few EU legal provisions had full juridical effects during it. It is not a period marked, therefore, by many significant doctrinal advances in relation to EU substantive law, with perhaps the only lingering advance of note being the extension of Article 101 TFEU, the provision outlawing anti-competitive agreements and concerted practices, to cover not merely restraints between producers, distributors or retailers (horizontal restraints) but also those between actors at different levels of the production and distribution process (vertical restraints).[26] This led to little reaction from domestic judiciaries about its proclaimed distinctive qualities. There was indifference in France[27] and a disposition to treat it like other international treaties in Belgium and the Netherlands.[28] Only the German judiciary engaged with this case law, and then in a highly sceptical manner.[29] This autonomous legal order, in other words, did not exist as a regulatory reality but rather as a legal gambit, left on the table to await eventual reaction. This did not mean that this period was an inactive period. Legal historians have shown that it was marked by the activism of the Commission Legal Service and the establishment of pan-Union associations such as the *Fédération Internationale pour le Droit Européen* (FIDE) and equivalent national associations pressing for the expansion and consolidation of EU law.[30] In particular, these argued for the desirability of an autonomous Union legal order, its presence, and its implications. If much of this was contested, particularly in Germany,[31] this network of academics, practitioners, and Commission officials developed both important ties and reservoirs of arguments and ideas that were to be central to the subsequent development of EU law.[32]

---

[26] Joined Cases 56-58/64 *Consten & Grundig* [1966] ECR 299.

[27] A Bernier, 'Constructing and Legitimating: Transnational Jurist Networks and the Making of a Constitutional Practice of European Law, 1950–70' (2012) 21 *Contemporary European History* 399, 410–13.

[28] On the practice of the Dutch courts up until 1970, albeit that references to the Constitution faded, thereafter see M Claes and B de Witte, 'Report on the Netherlands' 171, 184–5 and H Bribosia, 'Report on Belgium' 3, 11–14 in A-M Slaughter et al (eds), *The European Courts & National Courts: Doctrine and Jurisprudence* (Hart 1998).

[29] 2 BvL 29/63 *Tax on Malt Barley*, Judgment of 5 July 1967. 1 BvR 248/63 and 216/67 *European Community Regulations*, Judgment of 18 October 1967.

[30] K Alter, *The European Court's Political Power* (Oxford University Press 2009) chapter 4.

[31] B Davies, *Resisting the European Court of Justice: West Germany's Confrontation with European Law, 1949–1979* (Cambridge University Press 2012) 64–77; 156–9.

[32] M Rasmussen, 'The Origins of a Legal Revolution: The Early History of the European Court of Justice' (2008) 14 *Journal of European Integration History* 77; A. Vauchez, 'Introduction: Euro-Layering, Transnational Social Fields and European Polity Building' in A Vauchez and B de Witte (eds), *Lawyering Europe: European Law as a Transnational Social Field* (Hart 2014) 6–9.

Table 2.1 Members of the Court of Justice 1958–69

Judge	Politician	Academic	Practitioner	Civil servant	EU institution	Lower Court Judge	Senior Court Judge	Years of service
Serrarens	3							1
Pilotti						2	1	1
Van Kleffens				2		1		1
Riese		15						5
Delvaux	18		9					9
Rueff		4		8				4
Hammes		9		9		9		9
Lagrange				18				6
Roemer			24			12		12
Rossi							18	6
Donner		36						12
Catalano		3		3	3			3
Trabucci		27						9
Lecourt	24							8
Strauss				18				6
Monaco		5				10		5
Gand		10		5				5
Mertens de Wilmars	6							2
Pescatore		2		4				2
Total	51	111	33	53	3	34	19	

Against this context, the Court was, during this time, at its smallest. Table 2.1 indicates that it comprised just 19 members during the 12 years, with three only there for the first year, and there only being three advocates general during the time (Lagrange, Roemer, Gand). It was, thus, a highly personalized court in the sense that both individual personalities and individual turnover could make a significant difference to the dynamics of the Court.[33] The breakdown of backgrounds below suggests a court whose members professional backgrounds are centred on that of the university professor and the national civil servant. There is limited prior judicial expertise, particularly at a senior level, and very little practitioner expertise. It is a body, therefore, whose background is not geared to dispute settlement or the tactics of litigation in a strong way. Instead, its members' orientation was geared more to establishing legal visions, setting out a panorama for the issues to be addressed

[33] M Rasmussen, 'Revolutionizing European Law: A History of the *Van Gend en Loos* Judgment' (2014) 12 *ICON* 136.

by EU law and architecture for how it was to deal with them. Such a background was likely to have a sensitivity which was open to academic arguments about creating and systematizing a public law of the European Union.

However, as Antonin Cohen has noted, the Court was a much more politically embedded institution than these figures suggest. In addition to the four members of the Court with extensive political experience, there were four with close family ties to senior national politicians (Donner, Trabucci, von Kleffens, and Roemer).[34] Furthermore, a number of those with a civil service background had been heavily involved with either negotiating the Treaties (Lagrange, Catalano) or litigating these before the European Coal and Steel Community Court (Mertens de Wilmars, Pescatore, Lagrange, Catalano). It was thus, as Cohen has noted, an institution which was far more exposed to political ties than would subsequently be the case. Many of the judges already had both a prior investment in the Treaties and sensitivity to the types of argument which circulated in national ministries and to which these would be tolerant.

This allowed the Court to sit at a crossroads between politics, policy, and the law and negotiate a pathway for the case law through it, but it also gave individual judges the capacity and expertise to recognize opportunities when they presented themselves and to push forward EU law in significant ways.[35] The provision of a template fitted in with this. The claim that EU law limited national sovereignty fitted an environment in which many national constitutions had included provisions to limit sovereignty or grant domestic effects to treaties.[36] It was a cheeky claim insofar as the national constitutional measures were acts of self-limitation whereas the claim in *Van Gend en Loos* was one of external imposition. Yet, with their contacts, Court of Justice judges could be confident in their actions. The language of the judgments at a superficial level mirrored that of the national constitutional contexts and, in the main, provided a template for future action whose implications could be worked out at a later date in an environment yet to be defined.

4. Constitutional in Form and Functional in Substance: The Institution of an Autonomous Legal Order from 1970 Until Maastricht

The second period, between the end of the transitional period and the entry into force of the TEU, is twice as long—just over 24 years—as the first period. The

---

[34] A Cohen, '"Ten Majestic Figures in Long Amaranth Robes": The Formation of the Court of Justice of the European Communities' in Vauchez and de Witte (n 32) 35–6.

[35] Ibid, 36–41 on how Lagrange worked on and advanced a constitutionalizing agenda both prior to and during his time at the Court.

[36] Article 28, 1946 French Constitution; Article 49bis Luxembourg Constitution as amended by a law of 25 October 1956; Article 11 Italian Constitution 1947; Article 24(2) German Basic Law 1949; Article 66 Netherlands Constitution 1953 and 1956.

period prior to the ratification of the Single European Act is often portrayed as one of Euro sclerosis, with that between the Single European Act and the Danish referendum as one of a welter of EU legislation and support for European integration in the wake of the collapse of the Berlin Wall.[37] As with all general narratives, there is some truth in this, but the history of the period was a little less dichotomous than that.

The 1970s and early 1980s were marked by significant increases in intra-EU trade, the emergence of a significant if industrially dominant public sphere in Brussels,[38] and the appearance of repeat players before the Court of Justice, who increasingly saw litigation through it as an avenue for securing their preferences rather than action through other institutional arenas, be this over trade liberalization or securing rights in the workplace.[39] Alongside this, this era marked a period in the history of the common agricultural policy in which support was being both cut back and retargeted, at a cost to a number of farmers. The Court of Justice was the only venue in which these reforms could be challenged.[40] This period of years was, therefore, one of a significant increase in case law across all heads of jurisdiction, but notably with regard to preliminary references,[41] and a period in which the Court began to acquire its own clear litigant constituencies. It is also the period in which the Euro academy took off. An array of academics, legal secretaries to the Court of Justice, and Commission officials published significant amounts of academic articles in specialized EU law journals, which argued predominantly for advancing and systematizing the development of EU law. The legal activism of the transitional period, with its concern with establishment networks and putting ideas out for academic debate, was replaced with a period marked by the embedding of an epistemic community in which a certain worldview was taken on EU law and its mission. This worldview was much more dominated by public officials and less by academics than is the case for other fields of law.[42] It did not argue for integration for integration's sake. Instead, the development of EU law was seen as necessary to secure the effectiveness of Union

---

[37] Most famously see J Weiler, 'The Transformation of Europe' (1991) 100 *Yale Law Journal* 2403.

[38] On this see N Fligstein and A Stone Sweet, 'Institutionalizing the Treaty of Rome' 29, 47–9 in A Stone Sweet et al (eds), *The Institutionalization of Europe* (Oxford University Press 2001).

[39] Alter (n 31) chapters 6, 8, and 9.

[40] Although the most significant reforms were not to come until 1992 (the Macsharry reforms), a series of ad hoc reforms, co-responsibility levies, quotas, and restrictions on planting were introduced in individual sectors: F Snyder, *Law of the Common Agricultural Policy* (Sweet & Maxwell 1985). On milk in particular see M Cardwell and M Cardwell, *Milk Quotas: European Community and United Kingdom Law* (Oxford University Press 1996) chapters 1 and 4.

[41] Between 1958 and 1975, 499 references were therefore made to the Court of Justice, while 1,191 were made between 1990 and 1995, a much smaller period. T Brunell, C Harlow, and A Stone Sweet, *Litigating the Treaty of Rome: The Court of Justice and Articles 226, 230, and 234* (Newgov, EUI 2008) 27.

[42] Academics accounted for about 57 per cent of the articles in the three dominant EU law journals, whereas they accounted for about 85 per cent of articles in other fields. This increased academic writing by public officials allowed not only for greater intellectual exchange between these and academics but also increased mobility, whereby these could often exchange the academic department for the EU post or vice versa: H Schepel and R Wesseling, 'The Legal Community: Judges, Lawyers, Officials and Clerks in the Writing of Europe' (1997) 3 *ELJ* 165, 172–3.

policies; to grant it the processes and mechanisms found in equivalent national laws; and to advance particular post-national liberal values.

In complementary fashion, the period is possibly that most associated with the caricature of the Court of Justice as an activist court tucked away in Luxembourg, engaged in all kinds of integrationist projects. For it is a period of landmark judgments. Economic freedoms were expanded to cover not merely discriminatory measures but also trade-restrictive ones; the effects of EU law in domestic courts were worked out through the development of direct effect and the emergence of the doctrines of indirect effect, incidental effect, and state liability; competition law was expanded and developed, as were the powers of the European Parliament, the system of Union-exclusive competencies, and the Union's powers in the field of external relations. The Court pushed the rights of working women further than any national laws did at the time and cemented the place of fundamental rights within EU law. This culminated in the early 1990s with the debate on whether the Court had developed the Treaties in such a way that it had inherent jurisdiction and there were limitations on member states' powers to amend the Treaties.[43]

How does the composition of the Court fit in with this? There is continuity in one significant sense, and also one significant discontinuity.

With regard to continuity, there are more judges, as a consequence of the accession of six states. Including incumbents in post on 1 January 1970, there were 59 judges and advocates general of the Court during this time, compared to 19 during the earlier period. However, once the length of the period is taken into account, the highly personal nature of the Court is retained, in terms of both the interpersonal nature of the institution and the influence of individual judges. Central to this, notwithstanding the expansion in the size of the Court, was the institution of the chamber system, which allowed cases to be heard in chambers of three or five judges.[44]

If the institution remains highly interpersonal, with individual judges having a significant say in the trajectory of the case law, there is however a significant change in the backgrounds of the judges. Table 2.2 shows that that academics continue to represent a powerful tradition within the Court. However, the centre of gravity has moved with regard to other backgrounds. Whereas the Court of the transitional period was marked by a large number of former civil servants and judges with political ties and very little prior judicial experience, this composition is reversed for the period up to Maastricht. The amount of judicial experience now becomes significant, with 14 judges having such prior experience for this court. By contrast, the political ties are diluted. To be sure, these were not inconsiderable, but they were concentrated in a number of figures who then went on to spend a number of years in the Court (Pescatore, Due, Mertens de Wilmars, Lenz, Schockweiler, Bosco). Furthermore, the orientations had changed. The majority of these judges had a strong disposition

---

[43] A Arnull, 'Does the Court of Justice have Inherent Jurisdiction?' (1990) 27 *CMLRev* 683; J da Cruz Vilaça and N. Piçarra, 'Y a-t-il des limites matérielles à la révision des traités instituant les Communautés européennes?' (1993) 34 *Cahiers de Droit Européen* 3.

[44] This was introduced in 1974. Rules of Procedure, OJ 1974, L350/1, Article 95. On the autonomy of the Chambers see D Kelemen, 'The Political Foundations of Judicial Independence' in D Kelemen and S Schmidt (eds), *The Power of the Court of Justice* (Routledge 2014).

Table 2.2 Membership of the Court 1970–93

Judge/AG	Politician	Academic	Practitioner	Civil servant	EU institution	Lower Court Judge	Senior Court Judge	Years of service
Roemer		3		3	3			3
Donner		27						9
Trabucci	18							6
Strauss				3				1
Monaco		6				12		6
Gand		2		1				1
Mertens de Wilmars	42							14
Pescatore		15		30				15
Ó Caoimh							30	10
Capotorti		18						6
Bosco	24	12						12
Touffait							18	6
Koopmans							33	11
Due				48				16
Everling				16	8			8
Chloros		3						1
Slynn			22			11		11
Rozès							9	3
Verloren van Themaat		10			5			5
Grévisse							18	6
Bahlmann				6		12		6
Mancini							33	11
Galmot				18				6
Kakouris							30	10
Lenz	27							9
Darmon		9				18		9
Joliet	27							9
O'Higgins							18	6
Schockweiler				24				8
Mischo				10	5			5
Moitinho de Almeida		7		14				7
Da Cruz Vilaca	6							2
Rodriguez Iglesias		21						7

(Continued)

Table 2.2 *Continued*

Judge/AG	Politician	Academic	Practitioner	Civil servant	EU institution	Lower Court Judge	Senior Court Judge	Years of service
Diez de Velasco							15	5
Zuleeg		15						5
Van Gerven		15						5
Jacobs		10	5					5
Tesauro			5	10				5
Kapteyn							9	3
Gulmann		2	2	2				2
Murray			4	2				2
Edward		1	2					1
Total	117	203	40	187	21	53	213	

towards academia. Examples include Ole Due, who went on to a professorship at the University of Copenhagen after his time at the Court. Pescatore is, of course, well known as one of the most eminent writers on the Court.[45] Everling had written the most central work on freedom of establishment.[46] Mertens de Wilmars had a post at the Catholic University of Leuven from 1971 onwards. Early in his career, Bosco had enjoyed stints as an academic at the Universities of Florence and Naples.

This judicialization and academicization of the Court might have led to an institution which, concerned about the independence of the judiciary, is more inclined to view the institution as something geared more to curbing government power than to working with government to realize collective goods. Generationally, its members would be less invested in ownership over the original Treaties, as few had been engaged in their negotiations. It might also be the case that both academics and judges would be more concerned to secure the autonomy and coherence of the EU legal order, making sure that legal principles governed its operations, its norms had legal authority, and it was the central medium through which integration was realized. However, for all this, the Court was marked by the conservative disposition of judicial professions. These were individuals whose professional habitus was geared to securing the development of their domestic constitutional settlements and maintaining the esteem of the judiciary. Neither was protected by a judicial activism which undermined domestic constitutions and pushed interpretation of EU law to the limit through teleological interpretations or wide-ranging application of the implied powers doctrine. There is no evidence, furthermore, that the Court saw itself as an activist court.

---

[45] Indeed, his most seminal work was published during his early time at the Court. P Pescatore, *The Law of Integration* (Springer 1974).
[46] U Everling, *The Right of Establishment in the Common Market* (CCH 1964).

The answer to this puzzle, it will be argued, lies in the content of the docket before the Court during that time. The docket can be crudely dived into three.

There were, first, actions against EU institutions. Insofar as the Court developed doctrines such as fundamental rights or general principles of law, these were, of course, deployed largely to curb EU measures in the fields of external trade or agriculture which would have been quasi-legislation if adopted in a national context. Judgments curbed either supranational activity or measures which were not politically salient. By contrast, considerable legal leeway was granted to EU legislation where it involved the exercise of discretion and politically salient issues, with only the most abusive legislation struck down.[47] The general narrative was thus one of deference to legislative interests. If granting the European Parliament increased *locus standi* and allowing it to insist on certain legal bases being used departed from this narrative, it emerged at the end of this period[48] and in a political climate across Europe where there was a concern to give all parliaments greater supervisory powers over the executive.[49]

The second dominant tranche of case law concerned infringement proceedings against member states. This covered the whole swathe of EU law. However, a feature of this procedure is that the overwhelming proportion of proceedings are settled between the Commission and national government concerned in opaque circumstances, where both parties enjoy maximum discretion over the form of the settlement. Court judgments only occurred, therefore, where there was very little doubt as to the illegality of the practice.[50] While there were exceptions,[51] they rarely developed EU law in controversial ways. Moreover, the period was associated with the Court granting considerable procedural safeguards to states throughout the procedure.[52]

The final swathe of case law concerned preliminary references from national courts. Most of the salient or controversial judgments emerged through this procedure. It could not be controlled by national governments or EU institutions, and national disputes provided a context which incentivized parties to push the envelope of EU law to grant them entitlements or immunities not provided by domestic law. However, a feature of the procedure was that, in material terms, it was extremely confined. Aware of its dangers (from their perspective), EU legislators drafted very few EU provisions in such a manner that they granted rights which could be invoked before national courts. The data set provided by Brunell, Harlow, and Stone Sweet indicated that between 1976 and 1990, five areas (agriculture, free movement

---

[47] Eg Case 80/77 *Ramel v Receveur des Douanes* [1978] ECR 927.

[48] Case C-70/88 *Parliament v Council* [1990] ECR I-2041; Case C-300/89 *Commission v Council* [1991] ECR I-2867.

[49] B Rittberger, *Building Europe's Parliament: Democratic Representation Beyond the Nation-State* (Oxford University Press 2005) chapter 5.

[50] On this see Chalmers et al (n 23) 357–70.

[51] A large number of infringement proceedings were brought setting out the parameters of the prohibition on discrimination against competing imports (eg Case 168/78 *Commission v France* [1908] ECR 347, Case 356/85 *Commission v Belgium* [1987] ECR 3299). There was also significant case law in the field of services: Case 205/84 *Commission v Germany* [1986] ECR 3755. These cases were the exception, however.

[52] On the letter of formal notice see Case 211/81 *Commission v Denmark* [1982] ECR 4547. On the procedural safeguards offered by the reasoned opinion see Case 278/85 *Commission v Denmark* [1987] ECR 4065.

of goods, social security, taxation, and competition) accounted for 64.2 per cent (1,459 out of 2,271 references) of all preliminary references to the Court.[53] Of these areas, two—free movement of goods and competition—were dominated by a discrete number of Treaty provisions, Articles 34–36 TFEU and 101–102 TFEU respectively, and two—social security and taxation—revolved around single pieces of legislation: Regulation 1408/71/EEC in the case of social security and Directive 77/377/EEC in the case of taxation. Other fields accounted for very few references. Approximation of laws accounted for 81 references during this 15-year period, social policy for 70, and environmental law for 22. This pattern does not appear to be unrepresentative. More generalized litigation before national courts illustrates a similar narrow ambit. A study of all reported cases in the first 25 years of British membership of the Union found the Treaty was invoked more than all the Regulations or Directives which had been invoked during that period, and that five Directives accounted for over 73 per cent of all the Directives invoked during that period.[54]

In terms of judicial engagement, the Treaties during this time therefore represented a functional organization with constitutional trappings. Albeit acquiring a constitutionalist tone, the dominant pattern of work of the Court of Justice regarding significant rulings concerned two things: curbing abusive administrative behaviour by EU institutions and developing a robust case law with a clear autonomous legal logic of its own in a number of very discrete policy sectors where the Court saw it was required to take a lead within the integration process. The adoption of such robust case law was quite consistent with judicial deference in a Court dominated by ex-judges and academics with judicial restraint. If it established the disciplines necessary to allow EU law to move from the assertion of a few principles to a detailed operational, autonomous legal system, it did not transgress into sufficient policy sectors to destabilize either Union political processes or domestic ones on a wide-ranging basis.

5. Managing and Generalizing the Legal Order: From Maastricht to Lisbon

The 16-year period between the ratification of the Treaty of Maastricht and the ratification of the Treaty of Lisbon was marked by much stronger political contestation. This took a number of forms: increased Treaty revision and negative referenda; sharper political cleavages within public opinion about the European integration process; and increased pluralization of the Brussels public sphere. Alongside this, the Union witnessed its strongest territorial expansion, going from 12 to 27 member states. It became a much more politically and socio-economically diverse system than previously. This period was also one of great legislative activity, averaging 50 Directives per

---

[53] T Brunell et al (n 41) 27.
[54] D Chalmers, 'The Positioning of EU Judicial Politics within the United Kingdom' (2000) 23 *WEP* 169, 178.

annum.[55] If the single market was initially marked as requiring 279 measures for the 1992 programme, its reach had extended and its bite intensified so that by April 2009 it amounted to 1,606 Directives and 897 Regulations.[56] In addition, extensive legislative programmes were developed in, most notably, financial services and the area of freedom, security, and justice during this period. However, this period also marked a time in which other tools were increasingly deployed to secure integration. In some instances this was because certain policies, such as EMU, relied less on the adoption of swathes of legislation than more established policies. In other fields, most notably employment and those which adopted the Open Method of Coordination, legislation was deliberately eschewed. In more traditional fields of integration, there was, finally, greater resort to a wider array of regulatory processes and instruments, be these agencies, standardization, grant of property rights, or co-regulation.

In short, the Union grew into a political system marked by greater political diversity, contestation, and a wider array of regulatory techniques. Against this background, the Court engaged in a limited generalization of the legal order established by it. The principles set out with regard to free movement of goods were applied across the other economic freedoms.[57] Judgments on free movement of goods moved from being the most common of those on the economic freedoms to the least common. The principle of non-discrimination was extended to protect a wide range of headings, of which the most frequently invoked before the Court was age discrimination. The emerging case law in the fields of environmental and labour law developed considerably, as did the case law on taxation. New areas of case law emerged, most notably those on EU citizenship, free movement on capital, and the area of freedom, security, and justice.

These generalizing qualities undoubtedly extended the reach and salience of the Court of Justice. However, for all of that, the scope of EU judicial involvement as measured by the preliminary reference procedure remained limited, albeit less limited than it was. A study by Chalmers and Chaves found that of the 49 fields of EU law identified by the Court of Justice, only 13 generated an average of five rulings or more per annum. Moreover, 80 per cent of the rulings given between 2007 and 2009 occurred in just seven fields: economic freedoms; harmonization of laws; taxation; the area of freedom, security, and justice; environment; agriculture; and social policy. Furthermore, within some of these, notably agriculture, approximation of laws, and environment, only a tiny proportion of the legislation was litigated.[58] Litigation of EU law before national courts and development of EU law through preliminary rulings

---

[55] The average annual output of Regulations was much higher, but as acts were not categorized into legislative and non-legislative acts prior to the Treaty of Lisbon, Directives, as measures rarely used for non-salient issues, are a better indicator prior to then. On this see D Toshkov, 'Public Opinion and Policy Output in the European Union: A Lost Relationship' (2011) 12 *EUP* 169; D Chalmers and M Chaves, 'EU Law-Making and the State of Democratic Agency' in O Cramme and S Hobolt (eds), *Democratic Politics in a European Union under Stress* (Oxford University Press 2014) 163–4.

[56] European Commission, *Internal Market Scoreboard No 19, July 2009* (Office for Official Publications 2009) 9.

[57] If the 1980s and 1990s were marked by articles arguing for a common approach, the sense of a settlement in this direction was reflected in later pieces which took it for granted: J Snell, 'The Notion of Market Access: A Concept or A Slogan?' (2010) 47 *CMLRev* 437.

[58] D Chalmers and M Chaves, 'The Reference Points of EU Judicial Politics' (2012) 19 *JEPP* 25, 32.

was thus confined to a relatively small fraction of EU law. However, the dynamics of its development were more varied. Chalmers and Chaves identified four types of litigant who tended to be clustered around different sectors of EU law. Transnational enterprises litigated to enforce transnational rules of the game in areas such as harmonization of laws or to contest domestic or transnational taxes. Administrations provoked or entered into litigation in fields such as taxation and environment in order to consolidate or extend the fiscal and regulatory capacities granted to them by EU legislation. Small domestic enterprises challenged domestic fiscal and regulatory burdens through invoking EU tax law or the economic freedoms. Finally, there was litigation by civil society in fields such as anti-discrimination law, EU citizenship, and the area of freedom, security, and justice aimed at extending civil liberties and liberal values. While not hugely plural, the range of litigants, and their corollary interests and expectations, could not be squeezed within a single judicial narrative, with different types of argument dominating different parts of the Court's docket.

How was this to be managed by the Court of Justice? Table 2.3 sets out the background of all the judges and advocates general who served on the Court from 1993 until the entry into force of the Treaty of Lisbon. There are two features of note about this period in relation to its predecessors.

The first is the high number of members of the Court, 81 during this period, compared to preceding periods. There are no signs of increased turnover, and this is almost exclusively a consequence of the enlargement of the Union from 12 members in 1993 to 27 by the end of this period. However, it does change the nature of the institution. The Court almost never sat as a full court, with the overwhelming proportion of cases—90.7 per cent in 2009—heard by chambers of three or five judges.[59] Relations within the Court are thus more attenuated. With eight chambers in 2009, this increased the power of the president of the Court, who could allocate cases to particular chambers, and the presidents of individual chambers also became increasingly salient as each chamber acquired a certain autonomy.

The second was the change in the composition. On its face, the same three dominant backgrounds—academia, the civil service, and the senior judiciary—seem to dominate both periods. However, there has been a significant shift. Most notably, former civil servants acquired a much more prominent role in the Court during this period. In the period prior to Maastricht, they accounted for 18.7 per cent of the total as previously set out, while senior judges accounted for 21.3 per cent and academics 20.3 per cent. In the period prior to Lisbon, the relative figures were 28.4 per cent, 25.8 per cent, and 23.6 per cent. Furthermore, if the figure for judges is broken down, one finds it is concentrated around a number of figures who spend long periods on the Court (La Pergola, Jann, Colmer, Kapteyn). Judicial involvement during this period was also temporarily concentrated in that it increased after the 2004 enlargements, with a number of these states sending former constitutional court judges.

---

[59] *Court of Justice of the European Union Annual Report 2009* (Office for Official Publications 2010) 88.

Table 2.3 Members of the Court 1993–2009

Judge/AG	Politician	Academic	Practitioner	Civil servant	EU institution	Lower Court Judge	Senior Court Judge	Years of service
Due				3				1
Grévisse							3	1
Mancini							18	6
Kakouris							12	4
Lenz	12							4
Darmon		1				2		1
Joliet		6						2
Schockweiler				9				3
Mischo				12	6			6
Moitinho de Almeida		7		14				7
Rodriguez Iglesias		30						10
Diez de Velasco							3	1
Zuleeg		3						1
Van Gerven		3						1
Jacobs		26	13					13
Tesauro			5	10				5
Kapteyn							21	7
Gulmann		13	13	13				13
Murray			12	6				6
Edward		11	2					11
La Pergola							36	12
Cosmas							18	6
Hirsch							18	6
Elmer				6		3		3
Puissochet				36				12
Leger		12		12		12		12
Ragnemalm		10				5		5
Sevón				14			7[1]	7
Fennelly			15					5
Wathelet	16	8						8
Jann							42	14
Colomer							42	14
Schintgen		12		24				12
Ioannou		2		4				2

(*Continued*)

Table 2.3 *Continued*

Judge/AG	Politician	Academic	Practitioner	Civil servant	EU institution	Lower Court Judge	Senior Court Judge	Years of service
Alber	18							6
Saggio			2		2		2	2
Skouris	20	10						10
O'Kelly Macken			15					15
Colneric		12				6		6
von Bahr				12		6		6
Tizzano		9		18				9
Da Cunha Rodrigues				27				9
Timmermans		9			18			9
Geelhoed				12	6			6
Stix-Hackl				18				6
Rosas		14		7				7
Lapuerta				18				6
Lenaerts		12			6			6
Kokott		18						6
Poiares Maduro		18						6
Schiemann			10				5	5
Makarczyk		5		10				52
Kūris							15	5
Juhász	5			10				5
Arestis							15	5
Barthet				15				5
Ilešič		10	5					5
Malenovský							15	5
Klučka							15	5
Lõhmus							15	5
Levits	5						10	5
Ó'Caiomh			10				5	5
Larsen				6		3		3
Sharpston		3	6					3
Mengozzi		9						3
Lindh				6		3		3
Bonichot				6	3			3
Von Danwitz		9						3
Bot				9				3

(Continued)

Table 2.3 *Continued*

Judge/AG	Politician	Academic	Practitioner	Civil servant	EU institution	Lower Court Judge	Senior Court Judge	Years of service
Mazák							9	3
Trstenjak		6	3					3
Arabadjiev							6	2
Toader		4				2		2
Kasel			3					1
Safjan							0.5	0.2
Svaby							0.5	0.2
Berger							0.5	0.2
Jaaskinen							0.5	0.2
Villalon							0.5	0.2
Total	**82**	**292**	**114**	**352**	**41**	**37**	**319.5**	

[1] Sevón spent time as a judge at the EFTA Court, which has been classified here.
[2] The next ten members represent those member states who acceded to the Union in 2004.

This stronger governmental background suggests a more managerial Court with a conservative disposition which is more receptive to administrative concerns. These might be national governmental concerns about excessive integration, judgments which deviate strongly from their preferences, or judgments which have significant dislocating effects. It will also include reluctance to strike EU legislation which has been agreed by at least a qualified majority of governments. This 16-year period is marked, therefore, by fewer of the iconic judgments which marked the period prior to Maastricht. The case law on the effects of EU law in national courts was much more constrained. To be sure, state liability for judicial acts was created and Directives could be invoked against other individuals when considered an expression of the non-discrimination principle.[60] In addition, politically controversial judgments were given on, *inter alia*, the rights of asylum seekers to marry EU citizens,[61] citizens' access to social benefits,[62] the right to a hearing of those suspected of terrorist offences,[63] the organization of a working hours directive,[64] and the set-off of corporate tax.[65] However, it is not possible to point to the radical

[60] Joined Cases C-46 & 48/93 *Brasserie du* and *R v Secretary of State for Transport, ex parte Factortame (No 3)* [1996] ECR I-1029; Case C-144/04 *Mangold* [2005] ECR I-9981.
[61] Case C-127/08 *Metock and Others* [2008] ECR I-6241. On the Danish reaction see M Wind, 'When Parliament Comes First – The Danish Concept of Democracy Meets the European Union' (2009) 27 *Nordisk Tidsskrift For Menneskerettigheter* 272.
[62] Case C-85/96 *Martínez Sala* [1998] ECR I-2691.
[63] Joined Cases C-402/05P & C-415/05P *Kadi and Al Barakaat International Foundation* [2008] ECR I-6351.
[64] Case C-303/98 SIMAP [2000] ECR I-7963; Case C-151/02 *Landeshauptstadt Kiel v Jaeger* [2003] ECR I-8389.
[65] Case C-446/03 *Marks & Spencer* [2005] ECR I-10837.

assertion of principle in perhaps the same way as previously. In many instances, the Court rows back on its doctrines. In the case of invocation of EU law in national courts, restrictive conditions are imposed for the establishment of state liability and the *Mangold* principle is very much confined to the principle of age discrimination rather than being invoked more widely.[66] In like vein, member states are, in principle, allowed to impose demanding residence conditions requiring many years residence before EU citizens can claim social benefits in another state.[67] In other fields, most notably access to publicly funded health care in another member state, the EU legislature follows the example of the Court.[68] Most notably, however, the fields of emergent EU law—be they free movement of capital; prohibition of age discrimination; or the area of freedom, security, and justice—are not developed in a manner that generates such institutional resistance as their predecessors, be they the case law on free movement of goods, the prohibition of sex discrimination, or the rights of Turkish workers and their families under the association agreements. The case law during this period is of a much more institutionally sensitive court. This is borne out with regard to its deference to the EU legislature, with only a single Directive provision being struck down during this period for violating fundamental rights[69] and not a single measure being struck down for violating the subsidiarity principle.

6. Integration and Rights: Legally Onwards from Lisbon?

The period since the Treaty of Lisbon came into force at the end of 2009 is synonymous with the sovereign debt crisis. There has been a deepening of the political contestation surrounding both the European Union's policies and its very existence. Alongside this, there has been a significant tapering off of EU legislation, albeit that there has been a converse significant increase in the workload of EU agencies and standardization bodies. This reduction in EU legislation has, furthermore, been paralleled at the macro level with increased resort to international treaty regimes as direct substitutes for EU law. Finally, stronger cleavages between member states have resulted in greater use of differentiated integration both within and outside the Treaty framework.

If this provides a picture of the European Union with a legal order which is increasingly variegated, and thus marked by fewer unifying characteristics, a paradox of this period has been the involvement of the Court of Justice in ever more prominent cases. In some cases this has been by design, most notably the increased powers granted to it by both the six-pack and the fiscal compact to sanction states for deviant fiscal and macroeconomic policies. However, more often it has simply been by virtue of the range of preliminary references

---

[66] Case C-80/06 *Carp* [2007] ECR I-4501.
[67] Case C-158/07 *Förster* [2008] ECR I-8507.
[68] Directive 2011/24/EU on the application of patients' rights in cross-border healthcare, OJ 2011, L 88/45, Preamble, alinea 10.
[69] Case C-236/09 *Association Belge des Consommateurs Tests-Achats* [2011] ECR I-100.

which now appear in the Court's docket. In addition to the legality of the ESM Treaty,[70] the Court has been asked to adjudicate on issues such as the start of life,[71] the characterization of body shape,[72] parental access rights to children,[73] the parameters of national security,[74] and collective provision for the old.[75] These issues have an iconographic pre-eminence that, no matter how they are dressed up, cases of customs duties on ureaformaldehyde or unpaid utility bills simply do not have.[76]

It is possible to argue, furthermore, that the Court has re-entered another liberal period. In the four years since the Treaty of Lisbon, it developed new lines of reasoning on citizenship in *Zambrano*[77] and on the remit of fundamental rights in *Fransson*.[78] To be sure, it subsequently rowed back on each of these lines of reasoning, but there was, nevertheless, an attempt at activism.[79] The citation of the EU Charter of Fundamental Rights has been extensive in its case law and, for the first time ever, it struck down a whole Directive for violating fundamental rights. This liberalism has been combined with a concern to provide the legal grammar for greater institutional integration, be this through revision of the *Meroni* doctrine to allow EU agencies wider powers[80] or the leeway allowed for EU institutions to acquire powers outside the Treaty framework.[81]

How does this fit with the background of the Court since Lisbon?

The overall picture in Table 2.4 suggests an increased judicialization in the background of the Court. The period served by those with a background in the senior domestic judiciary is considerably larger than any other heading, albeit that the other two traditional headings—academia and domestic civil service—remain significant. The central mover for this does not appear to have been the introduction of tribunals by the Treaty of Lisbon but rather the 2004 and 2007 enlargements. Seven of the initial appointments from these enlargements serving during the time period had this background.[82] There is a further cluster of appointments in October and December 2009 when a further five from that background are appointed; albeit, interestingly, that three of these came from EU15 states (Berger, Jääskinen, Villalón).

---

[70] Case C-370/12 *Pringle*, Judgment of 27 November 2012, n.y.r.

[71] Case C-34/10 *Brüstle* [2011] ECR I-9848.

[72] Case C-354/13 *Kaltoft*, OJ 2013, C 252/37.

[73] Case C-400/10 PPU *McB* [2010] ECR I-8965.

[74] Case C-300/11 *ZZ v Secretary of State for the Home Department*, Judgment of 4 June 2013.

[75] Case C-399/09 *Landtová* [2011] ECR I-5573. An exhaustive study of integration of 'core State powers' in the fields of taxes, defence, and administration found significant integration in all these fields. P Genschel and M Jachenfuchs, 'Conclusion: The European Integration of Core State Powers. Patterns and Causes' in P Genschel and M Jachtenfuchs (eds), *Beyond the Regulatory Polity: The European Integration of Core State Powers* (Oxford University Press 2014).

[76] The facts in Case 26/62 *Van Gend en Loos* [1963] ECR 1; Case 6/64 *Costa* [1964] ECR 585.

[77] Case C-34/09 *Zambrano* [2011] ECR I-1177.

[78] Case C-617/10 *Fransson*, Judgment of 26 February 2013, n.y.r.

[79] In relation to the former see Joined Cases C-356/11 and C-357/11 *O & S*, Judgment of 6 December 2012, n.y.r. and, in relation to the latter, Case C-206/13 *Siragusa*, Judgment of 6 March 2014, n.y.r. The Directive was struck down in Joined Cases C-293/12 and C-594/12 *Digital Rights Ireland*, Judgment of 8 April 2014

[80] Case C-270/12 *United Kingdom v Council & Parliament*, Judgment of 22 January 2014, n.y.r.

[81] Case C-370/12 *Pringle*, Judgment of 27 November 2012, n.y.r.

[82] These are Kūris, Arestis, Malenovský, Lõhmus, Levits, Mazák, and Arabadjiev.

Table 2.4 Membership of Court from 1 December 2009 to end-December 2013

Judge/AG	Politician	Academic	Practitioner	Civil servant	EU institution	Lower Court Judge	Senior Court Judge	Period of service
Skouris	8	4						4
Tizzano		4		8				4
Da Cunha Rodrigues				12				3
Timmermans		1			0.5			0.5
Rosas		8		4				4
Lapuerta		8		4				4
Lenaerts		8			4			4
Kokott		12						4
Schiemann			9					3
Kūris							4	1
Juhász	4			8				4
Arestis							12	4
Barthet				12				4
Ilešič		8	4					4
Malenovský							12	4
Lõhmus							12	4
Levits	4						8	4
Ó'Caiomh			8				4	4
Larsen				8		4		4
Sharpston		4	8					4
Mengozzi		8						4
Lindh				4		2		2
Bonichot				8	4			4
Von Danwitz		12						4
Bot				12				4
Mazák							9	3
Trstenjak		6	3					3
Arabadjiev							12	4
Toader	4					8		4
Kasel				12				4
Safjan							12	4
Šváby							12	4
Berger							12	4
Jääskinen							12	4
Villalón							12	4
Prechal		9						3

(*Continued*)

Table 2.4 *Continued*

Judge/AG	Politician	Academic	Practitioner	Civil servant	EU institution	Lower Court Judge	Senior Court Judge	Period of service
Jarisūnas							9	3
Fernlund				6				2
Da Cruz Vilaca	1		1		1			1
Wathelet	3							1
Vajda			3					1
Wahl		3						1
Rodin		1.5						0.5
Biltgen	1.5							0.2
Jürimäe			0.2		0.2	0.2		0.2
Szpunar			0.3	0.3				0.2
Total	21.5	97.5	36.5	100.3	9.7	14.2	142	

The Court's make-up most closely resembles that, therefore, of the period between the end of the transitional period and the entry into force of the TEU. It will be remembered that this was the period most closely associated with the development of both forceful rights and strongly integrationist agendas. The argument can, indeed, be made (and has been made previously in this chapter!) that the case law has taken a similar path since the Treaty of Lisbon. It is a court dominated by academics and judges concerned with furthering rights and the post-national imagination, but characterized by judicial modesty when it comes to confining the remit of EU institutional action.

The context is, however, very different. Public opinion is more polarized and the Court of Justice is more politically salient. Moreover, the Court's docket involves a greater number of cases which speak far more vividly to both questions of civil liberties, the heartlands of national legal systems, and questions of domestic collective identity. Its activities are subject to much more debate and contention, therefore. It can, of course, be argued that such circumstances demand a strong, independently minded court to combat majoritarian and administrative abuses. Without careful reflection on its limits, such an argument invariably runs the risk of being strongly anti-democratic and, even when this is not the case, brings the ire of powerful populist and administrative voices down on the Court.

Appointments since the entry into force of the Treaty of Lisbon and the institution of judicial panels show, however, a different pattern. The post-Lisbon appointments start with Judge Prechal and involve 11 appointments during the period. Only one, Jarisūnas, involves a senior judicial background. Such a period is not unprecedented. It is possible to find a longer period between 1996 and 2004; however, three features make it a little unusual. First, it parallels a Treaty revision that changes the process of appointment. Second, it comes at a time of reduced trust in EU institutions. Third, and possibly most significantly, we do not see a reallocation of appointments to the traditional sources of judges: academia and the national civil service. Only four appointments during this time have significant prior experience in the senior judiciary, academia, or the national civil service. The sample is too small to do anything more than speculate on this unprecedented development. Albeit that there has been no negative opinion by a judicial panel on a candidate for the Court of Justice, it might be that judicial panels cast a shadow which might deter possible applications.[83] Certain figures (ie senior members of the judiciary) might not wish to offer themselves for assessment by their peers. It might, alternatively, lead to a wider pool being sought from other professional backgrounds, as member states are aware of the duty to account for the appointment and of the possible embarrassment of a negative opinion. There may also be exogenous factures to do with changes in how national governments perceive the function and authority of the Court of Justice which might shape nominations. And a combination of these and possible other factors may be at work.

Be this as it may, the breakdown of the professional background of the Court in 2018 is likely to be very different from that in 2014. A more professionally diverse judiciary might be less keen on developing the constitutionalizing case law of the Court, and may be comfortable with an approach that centres on dispute settlement and judicial reticence. All this remains to be seen. In terms of its professional background, however, the Court is at an unusual crossroads. And the presence of this crossroads is deeply unsatisfactory, whatever one's view on the disposition and activities of the Court. It has happened more by accident and less by design and, if this background matters at all, that cannot be right. Furthermore, it has little regard to the needs of the increasingly diverse docket of the Court. The amount of criminal law on which the Court has to rule has, for example, increased, but only one member, advocate general Bot, has much senior experience in this field. Equally, it is not clear who has expertise to deal with the Court's increasing docket in the field of intellectual property. Little attention is given to the external demands of the institution and the changes in these demands.

7. Conclusion

The tension between judicial independence and judicial accountability arises out of different conceptions of the judiciary. Accounts heralding the former see the judiciary as the main bulwark against public and private power. Its independence must not

---

[83] Further see above ch 1 and below ch 3.

be contaminated or captured by this political or economic power which it stands in opposition to. A vision centred on judicial accountability has a less benign characterization of courts and a less sceptical vision of other sources of concentrated power. It looks at whether courts offer something other government institutions do not: be this dispassion, technical expertise,[84] securing coherent and clear statements of the law,[85] or authoritative restatements of the political morality of the community.[86] There is virtue in both accounts, and it is difficult to take an *a priori* position which always holds one over the other. The balance of the argument will depend on the particular circumstances, and this will usually be shaped by the nature of what the Court is doing.

In this regard, one future possibility is for the Court to be viewed as a quasi-constitutional court for Europe. This would justify a stronger rights-based agenda. It would also require the Court to be less pusillanimous in its judicial review of EU action and clearer in its demarcation of the boundaries between Union and domestic exercise of powers. Constitutional courts confine themselves, however, to elaboration of constitutional principle where grand design is not overly determined by the particular drivers of individual cases. Neither of these is true of the Court at the moment. Furthermore, its membership does not have the authority of a constitutional court (most are too junior). Nor is it clear that it taps into sufficient expertise of domestic constitutional law.

The other possibility is one in which the Court's central role is interpreter of secondary legislation and guardian of the infringement procedure. In this role, it manages the burgeoning law of the European Union pragmatically and sensitively. Architectonic principles are not drawn out of disputes where the weight of argument is finely balanced and complex. A diversity of professional backgrounds and legal expertise is central to such a court as it provides the sensitivity and disposition to respond to the nuances involved. Constitutional sedimentation would be left mainly to the national constitutional courts. The background of the Court might be moving in such a direction but it does not currently reflect that position.

An intermediate position is the worst of all possible worlds. It allows constitutional dogmatism to be imposed on complex areas of the law, making these difficult to change, with all kinds of negative effects. The Court has, for example, through interpreting secondary legislation in the light of the right to life and freedom of expression, given dogmatic interpretations on stem cell research and hate speech which stand out

---

[84] Citations are thus often used as an evaluator: S Choi and M Gulati, 'A Tournament of Judges?' (2004) 92 *California Law Review* 299.

[85] R Wagner and L Pembridge, 'Is the Federal Circuit Succeeding? An Empirical Assessment of Judicial Performance' (2004) 152 *University of Pennsylvania Law Review* 1105.

[86] L Alexander and E Sherwin, *The Rule of Rules: Morality, Rules and the Dilemmas of Law* (Duke University 2001) chapters 1–4; J Penner, 'Legal Reasoning and the Authority of Law' in S Paulson et al (eds) *Rights, Culture, and the Law: Themes from the Legal and Political Philosophy of Joseph Raz* (Oxford University Press 2003).

in their insensitivity to the debates in these fields.[87] Equally, there are questions about the quality of the expertise available to it in relation to some of the fields with which it must now deal. These issues could be addressed through judicial appointments without the sense of any judge feeling the cold shadow of a politician lurking over her shoulder, be it through appointing more former national constitutional court judges or tapping into wider arrays of legal expertise. Either strategy relies, however, on a vision of the central tasks of the Court of Justice. This challenge cannot be addressed by an appointments procedure, but by the 'Masters of the Treaties', whoever they may be, who must decide what they want the Court for.

---

[87] See Case C-34/10 *Brüstle* [2011] ECR I-9848 and Joined Cases C-244/10 & C-245/10 *Mesopotamia Broadcast* [2011] ECR I-8777. For criticisms see G Gaskell, S Stares, and A Pottage, 'How Europe's Ethical Divide Looms Over Biotech Law and Patents' (2012) 30 *Nature Biotechnology* 392, 393; D Chalmers and L Barroso, 'What *Van Gend en Loos* Stands For' (2014) 12 *ICON* 105, 131–3.

3

Selecting the European Union's Judges

The Practice of the Article 255 Panel

Jean-Marc Sauvé

A few years ago, 'methods of selecting judges for European courts' could have been only a topic of largely speculative or future-oriented scholarly studies. Moreover, the issue in itself was of limited interest, or perhaps even stirred no interest at all.[1]

Article 167 of the Treaty of Rome, signed in 1957, foresaw that judges and advocates general shall be 'chosen from persons whose independence is beyond doubt and who possess the qualifications required for appointment to the highest judicial offices in their respective countries or who are jurisconsults of recognised competence'. This phrase is still part of valid law, today contained in Article 253 of the Treaty on the Functioning of the European Union (TFEU). However, up until 2009, it was for each member state alone to assess the independence and the merits of its own candidate.

Within the broader framework of reforms aiming at strengthening the rule of law and judicial independence, the idea of establishing a mechanism that would assist the member states in checking the fulfilment of the criteria set by the TFEU has gradually won broader support. The idea eventually crystallized in the creation of the panel provided for in Article 255 of the TFEU (hereinafter 'Panel'),[2] which became operational on 1 March 2010 and has just completed its first term of office (2010–14).

In order to explain the practice of the Panel, there are three elements that need to be dwelled upon in turn:

1) What were the objectives pursued by establishing the Panel?

2) How does the Panel operate?

3) How can the role of the Panel be evaluated?

---

[1] This chapter was written in collaboration with Olivier Fuchs, member of the administrative tribunal and administrative court of appeal, on secondment with the vice-president of the Council of State.

[2] In the words of the second paragraph of Article 255:

> The panel shall comprise seven persons chosen from among former members of the Court of Justice and the General Court, members of national supreme courts and lawyers of recognised competence, one of whom shall be proposed by the European Parliament. The Council shall adopt a decision establishing the panel's operating rules and a decision appointing its members. It shall act on the initiative of the President of the Court of Justice.

1. Objectives Pursued by Establishing the Panel

Identification of the objectives pursued by establishing the Panel is of crucial importance. Only their full understanding is able to explain the birth of the Panel and to evaluate its activity.

The mechanism that was in place before the entry into force of the Lisbon Treaty was based, in its design as well as in its practice, exclusively on mutual trust. When a judge was nominated, each member state was obliged to trust the state that suggested the candidate. In practice, it was not allowed to voice negative views on a nomination already made. Even if in legal terms the appointments were conditional upon the common accord of the governments of the member states, the appointments in fact depended exclusively on the will of one single government, namely that one which proposed the candidate.

What remains of the previous mechanism is the principle of appointment by common accord of the governments of the member states. However, in addition, a new Panel was established that is called to advise the member states before their collegiate decision is taken. The Panel issues a reasoned opinion, favourable or unfavourable, with respect to the suitability of proposed candidates for the office for which they apply. The opinion is communicated only to the governments of the member states. The Panel has thus been established to strengthen the assessment not only of the candidates' independence, but also their competence and expertise.

In other words, the Treaty of Lisbon inserted into the space between the member states and the judicial system of the European Union an element of independent and impartial evaluation of candidates' ability. What is being sought is to:

1) put the mechanism of judicial appointments at a proper distance from the political heat and power games;
2) make sure that the judges appointed possess the qualities necessary for the holding of their future office.

The aim of the Panel is thus to contribute, commensurably with its powers, to the safeguarding and the increase of an independent, well-qualified, and legitimate judicial power within the European Union. A similar mechanism is indeed original, also viewed comparatively in the context of approaches chosen in other international and regional jurisdictions.[3] The same applies as far as its operation is concerned.

---

[3] See in particular J-M Sauvé, 'Le rôle du comité 255 dans la sélection du juge de l'Union' in A Rosas, E Livits, and Y Bots (eds) *The Court of Justice and the Construction of Europe: Analyses and Perspectives on Sixty Years of Case-Law* (Springer 2013) 99.

2. The Operation of the Panel

The rules and conditions applicable to the composition of the Panel have already been outlined above.[4] One aspect ought nonetheless to be highlighted at this stage: the composition of the first Panel (with term of office 2010–14) was representative of different legal systems as well as different European regions. Moreover, the members of the Panel were drawn from the Union courts and from the national supreme jurisdictions.[5] The Panel could therefore make good use of advanced knowledge of the member states' judicial systems and of the relationships between those systems and the law of the EU, as well as an understanding of tasks, problems, and specific conditions within which European and national courts operate. The diversity and representativeness of the Panel constituted a valuable asset for the exercise of its mandate.

In order to carry out its tasks properly, the Panel has put in place a procedure that allows detailed examination of the candidatures.[6] As a matter of principle, the Panel asks the governments to submit information regarding the national selection procedure that had been employed for selecting the particular candidate, as well as the reasons for the selection. Apart from a curriculum vitae, the candidate's file should also contain a list of the candidate's publications or selected publications, as well as a motivation letter. The Panel also reserves the right to take into consideration any publicly available information brought to its attention. If need be, the information may be subject to a contradictory hearing with the candidate and the member state that has submitted it.

The key component of the Panel's consideration is a private hearing, the duration of which has been set at one hour, and which provides ample space for questions to be asked by the members of the Panel. This practice is essential for the Panel in order to form an opinion, based on evidence beyond the candidate's file, of whether or not the candidate will be able to hold the office she has applied for. In line with the operating rules of the Panel, however, such a hearing takes place only in cases of new candidates, not in cases of judges seeking a renewal of their mandate.

Beyond the way in which candidatures are examined, the Panel, basing itself on the provision of the TFEU, is also called to specify the assessment criteria for the evaluation of candidates.

---

[4] Above ch 2 s 2.1.

[5] The members were: Peter Jann, former judge at the Court of Justice; Lord Mance, judge at the United Kingdom Supreme Court; Torben Melchior, president of the Danish Supreme Court; Péter Paczolay, president of the Hungarian Constitutional Court; Ana Palacio Vallelersundi, professor of law and member of the Spanish Council of State; Jean-Marc Sauvé, vice-president of the French Council of State; and Virpi Tiili, former judge at the General Court. The president of the Panel was Jean-Marc Sauvé.

[6] For a detailed explanation of the examination procedure and assessment criteria for the candidates, see the three activity reports of the Panel: first report of 17 February 2011 (No 6509/11); second report of 22 January 2013 (No 5091/13); and third report of 13 December 2013 (No SN 1118/2014). All three reports are accessible online at <http://curia.europa.eu>.

The examination of two criteria—namely the candidate's legal expertise and pro-fessional experience, with particular regard to the level, length, and diversity of the latter—allows the Panel to assess if the candidate fulfils the conditions required for holding high or even very high judicial office, or if the candidate may be regarded as a jurisconsult of recognized competence, in the sense of Article 253 TFEU. The Panel will equally assess the candidate's ability to perform the duties of a judge, as well as her language skills and her aptitude for working in an international envi-ronment in which several legal traditions are represented. Lastly, the Panel will pay particular attention to the guarantees of independence and impartiality provided by the candidate.

In evaluating whether the candidate meets these criteria, in the course of the hearing, the Panel starts in particular with the candidate's specific experience in order to assess her knowledge and understanding of the key problems and main issues of EU law. The Panel seeks to evaluate the candidate's ability to reason on these subjects as well as on the way in which EU law is applied and the relationship between the EU legal system and the national legal systems. The Panel is open to diverse views, provided they are properly reasoned and are not based on erroneous knowledge. The Panel equally endeavours to check basic knowledge, for instance the scope of the principle of primacy of EU law or the status of the Charter of Fundamental Rights of the EU.

There is one last point relating to the operation of the Panel that needs to be addressed: the absence of publication of the Panel's opinions and, more broadly, the issue of transparency of the Panel's activity. As explained by the Panel in its first activity report, provisions of EU law in the area of protection of personal data as interpreted by the Court of Justice have led the Panel to the conclusion that its opinions cannot be disclosed to the public,[7] be it directly or indirectly. The same applies with respect to the Panel's hearings. The Panel is nonetheless committed to assuring genuine transparency for its activities, which is why it decided to launch and to publish its activity reports.[8] That is also why its mem-bers appear and speak in public, in the European Parliament among others. In these ways, the Panel becomes accountable as to the manner of examination of the candidatures, specific evaluation criteria it employs and their practical application, and detailed statistics of favourable and unfavourable opinions. One should perhaps be careful with calls for greater transparency, as they could result in weakening of the current process. For instance, greater transparency

---

[7] The Panel took into account Regulation (EC) No 1049/2001 of the European Parliament and of the Council of 30 May 2001 regarding public access to European Parliament, Council and Commission documents, OJ [2001] L 145/43, as well as Regulation (EC) No 45/2001 of the European Parliament and of the Council of 18 December 2000 on the protection of individuals with regard to the processing of personal data by the Community institutions and bodies and on the free movement of such data, OJ [2001] L 8/1, as interpreted by the Court of Justice in Case C-28/08 P *Bavarian Lager* [2010] ECR I-6055. On their basis, the Panel concluded that the tenor of the opinions rendered, favourable or not, cannot be disclosed to the public, be it directly or, by the fiat of detailed statistics, indirectly.

[8] See above n 5.

could dissuade applications by candidates who, even though they may not meet certain criteria—in particular, the criterion concerning the length of past legal experience—might be considered on the whole as suitable. Above all, it is necessary to reconcile the principle of transparency with the protection of candidates' private lives, as well as the member states' freedom of choice conferred upon them by the Treaty. Making the opinions or hearings public would be, without good reason, detrimental to candidates who have been judged unsuitable by the Panel. It should be borne in mind that the hearings are not a mere formality and that the opinion issued, even if it seeks to respect the individuals to the fullest, does not hide clear deficits of some candidatures.

Shedding some light on the practice of the Panel is absolutely essential for understanding its genuine operation. It is equally essential for determining and evaluating the impact of its activity.

3. Evaluation of the Role of the Panel

I believe that the first term of office of the Panel justified the choice made by the Treaty of Lisbon. While preserving the powers of the member states, it allowed for the control of manifest error with respect to the choice of the members of the Court of Justice of the EU.

First of all, it should be stressed that the role of the Panel is limited. In particular, its task is not to replace the member states, either with respect to the nomination of the candidates or as far as their appointment is concerned. The former task belongs to each member state acting alone. At present, there are no rules regarding the national selections of candidates. The latter task is the responsibility of the member states acting together. The Panel is furthermore not competent to pass any judgment on a member state's decision not to renew the term of office of a judge. Moreover, the Panel issues mere opinions, which are not binding. As the law stands today, the opinion is concerned with one single candidature for one vacant position; the Panel therefore has no power to rank several candidates. Lastly, as already discussed, the opinion is not published. It will only be communicated to the governments of the member states.

It would nonetheless be a mistake to conclude from the absence of publication of the opinion and from its non-binding, merely consultative nature that the opinions are only of limited influence. The opinions carry, first of all, a certain moral authority, which continues to grow over the years. The gradual emergence and fine-tuning of the Panel's consistent views as to what makes a 'good European judge' contributes to this authority. These views, which are disseminated in particular through the activity reports and, as far as the member states are concerned, can also be inferred from the study of the individual opinions rendered, are among the chief contributions of the Panel.

It should be noted, however, that the absence of opinion's binding force is to a large extent offset by the mechanism of the appointment procedure. With appointment by common accord, ie by a unanimous decision of all member states, being the principle, the disagreement of one single member state suffices for there to be no appointment. Thus, the accord of all member states is in fact needed to overrule an unfavourable opinion of the Panel.

There has never been this kind of unanimity among the member states in the past that would lead to a decision opposing the direction suggested by the Panel. To date, the Panel has issued seven unfavourable opinions. If compared with the 67 opinions rendered by the Panel in total, the percentage of unfavourable opinions might look modest, at slightly over 10 per cent. It should, however, be borne in mind that even if the Panel does not exclude, as a matter of principle, the possibility of issuing an unfavourable opinion with respect to a candidate seeking the renewal of her mandate, this possibility will certainly remain exceptional and has so far never been triggered. The seven unfavourable opinions should therefore be computed against the 32 opinions issued by the Panel with respect to the candidatures for a first term of office, which would then result in about 22 per cent unfavourable opinions issued within this group.[9]

There are two typical cases in which an unfavourable opinion has been issued. In the first type of case, the candidates' length of high-level professional experience was found to be unsatisfactory, perhaps too short, with no possibility of compensating for such length by legal expertise that could be qualified as exceptional. In the second type of case, some candidates' legal expertise appeared inadequate in view of the office for which they applied. The Panel was therefore bound to note that some candidates wholly lacked knowledge of EU law and had insufficient expertise concerning basic notions of EU law and the relationship between legal systems. It was apparent that such candidates would not be in the position to make an effective contribution to the work of EU courts within a reasonable period of time. Similar lack of knowledge in no way undermines the ability of the candidates to hold their office, often a prominent one, at the national level; it just does not recommend them, in the eyes of the Panel, to be appointed to the office for which they applied.

In all these cases, after the unfavourable opinion issued by the Panel, no appointment ensued, which is certainly unprecedented in international courts. One might speculate that any other result would be very difficult: the appointment procedure *de facto* endows the Panel's opinion with force comparable to that of an assent procedure, in particular once the opinion issued is negative.

The system of appointment of EU's judges therefore gives a special weight to the Panel's opinions. The weight of the opinions would carry much less if, by contrast, after the opinion of the Panel was issued, the judges of the Union were appointed or elected by majority in the Council or in the European Parliament. Even if the election of judges by a parliamentary assembly has its advantages in terms of the publicity of debates and votes, it can hardly

---

[9] For more detailed statistics see section I of the Third Activity Report (above n 5).

be substantiated in terms of properly evaluating the relevant criteria and the ability to hold judicial office. Moreover, such a procedure cannot be considered as standard or even prevailing practice for judicial appointments on the national level, within the member states of the EU. The procedure does not necessarily contribute, to put it euphemistically, to prioritizing the consideration of qualifications necessary for the judicial office. In fact, it leaves the door open to purely political mechanisms such as the creation of majorities that may, in some cases, give only little importance to those qualifications. Unfortunately, experience demonstrates that such risk is not just imaginary. Moreover, the domination of political authority in the process of judicial appointments may also be questionable in terms of the requirement of the separation of powers.

***

In conclusion, the Article 255 Panel has accomplished its task in the most rigorous and advanced way possible. It has been aware of the limits of its function as well as of its duties and responsibilities. The judicial selection procedure in which it partakes has confirmed certain candidates, but also rejected others. The procedure therefore cannot be in any way classified as just a formal safeguard, as it contributes effectively to the strengthening of independent, well-qualified, and legitimate judiciary within the European Union. The Panel could perhaps be seen, in full respect of the TFEU and only as far as the appointment of judges is concerned, as a germ of a council of judiciary within the Union. The Panel's activity indeed represents an important step in the appointment procedure. The new procedure allowed the TFEU's innovations in the area of justice to unfold in full and a system of appointments to emerge—a system that ceased to be based exclusively on the sovereign powers of the member states, but that leans on a new method of evaluation and selection of candidates which is more open, objective, impartial, and based on merit.

The steps taken in the past few years with respect to the Court of Justice of the EU and the European Court of Human Rights are essentially aimed at strengthening the authority of the European courts and encouraging acceptance of their decisions by member states, supreme national jurisdictions, and citizens. This is a crucial issue that today is becoming more of a pressing necessity than ever before. The limitations imposed on the member states' prerogatives as far as the selection of judges is concerned are counterbalanced by their enhanced trust vis-à-vis the European courts and by the conviction that justice in Europe is being done with greater competence and efficiency.

Further improvements of the system put in place within the EU could certainly be envisaged or desired. They could follow in particular from further evolution of the role of the Panel, be it in relation to the potential increase of the number of judges at the General Court or, once it becomes relevant, the appointment of an EU judge to the European Court of Human Rights. In both of these cases, a public call for applications could be envisaged and the Panel might in particular be asked to evaluate and rank the candidates according to their merit, a task which would certainly be attainable.

In any case, the activity of the Panel already reaches much further than the apparent modesty of its powers might suggest.

4

The Real Test–How to Contribute to a Better Justice

The Experience of the Civil Service Tribunal

Georges Vandersanden

Looking at the Committee,[1] or rather, to be more exact, at the committees that have been in charge of the selection of judges to the Civil Service Tribunal (CST),[2] what can be added that has not already been said, and said very well, so far? In Chapter 1 of this volume, Henri de Waele described the composition of the three successive committees that have been in charge of the selection of judges to the CST. He also outlined the committees' operation and the way in which they accomplished their task. Furthermore, in Chapter 3, President Sauvé set out the objectives, the operation, the past record, and the prospects of the 255 Panel in charge of evaluating the candidates' suitability to perform the duties of judge at the Court of Justice as well as at the General Court.

In trying to add anything useful to these two excellent chapters, I would like to stress, first, the specific nature of the Committee in charge of the selection of judges to the CST, which is the key to understanding the Committee's operation. Second, I wish to share some of my experience obtained as a member of the second Selection Committee, with a period of office from 2009 until early 2013.

1. A Specific Committee for a Specific Tribunal

The specificity of the CST Committee is two-fold. First, the Committee needs to be distinguished, at least partially, from the 255 Panel. Second, the specificity of the Committee overlaps essentially with the specificity of the CST.

First, in contrast to the 255 Panel (occasionally also called the 'Sauvé Panel', after its distinguished president), which has only been operational since 2010, the

---

[1] This contribution solely expresses the author's personal opinions. It does not bind in any way other members of the Selection Committee of which the author was a member.

[2] Established pursuant to Art 3(3) of the Annex to the Council Decision 2004/752/EC, Euratom of 2 November 2004 establishing the European Union Civil Service Tribunal [2004] OJ L333/7, later

Committee in charge of the selection of judges to the CST became operational in 2005 under the chairmanship of former judge L Sevón. The Committee has therefore played a pioneering role and has introduced a new kind of selection procedure. In particular, the Committee also defined the selection criteria, as has been previously outlined by Henri de Waele.[3] Thus, since the very beginning of its activity, the CST has been composed of judges appointed as a result of this new selection procedure involving the selection committees.

Furthermore, whereas the term of office of the members of the 255 Panel expired for the first time in 2014, there have already been three successive CST Committees. It ought to be stressed that all the members of the respective CST Committee were replaced each time their term of office came to an end without any consideration given to continuity, despite the fact that the relevant legal provision explicitly allows for the possibility of renewal. This is, in my view, regrettable and not entirely understandable.

Another fundamental difference from the 255 Panel is that vacancies for the position of judge at the CST are advertised by publishing a vacancy notice in the *Official Journal of the European Union* as well as in the member states' major newspapers. By contrast, as far as appointments to the Court of Justice and the General Court are concerned, candidatures are submitted by the member states whose judges are to be replaced, following the convention of one judge per each member state.

It follows that whereas the 255 Panel is essentially an evaluation committee of the applications which are, in a way, 'submitted' by the member states, the CST Committees are both: selection committees, since they will short-list the candidates after the call for applications, as well as evaluation committees, since they will afterwards assess the ability, the aptitude, and the competence of the short-listed candidates. This explains the particularly high number of submitted applications once a judicial office at the CST falls vacant.

In the end, the CST Committees function to some extent as a selection panel in qualification-based competitions. First, all the applications received are reviewed. Each member of the Committee is assigned a more or less equal number of applications by the president of the Committee. In ensuing discussions, the candidates with weak or inadequate profiles are eliminated. Eventually, a list of short-listed applicants is drawn up, each of whom will be invited for an interview lasting about 30 minutes. Some of the questions asked in the interviews are identical, in order to enable comparison among the candidates; other questions are more specific and based on the candidate's individual profile.

---

re-enacted as Annex I to Protocol no 3 to the Lisbon Treaty on the European Civil Service Tribunal, OJ [2010] C 83/226.

[3] Above ch 1 s 4.1. Those criteria are indeed common sense and are well suited for the choice that has to be made, given the judicial function that the selected candidates will perform. They reflect the practice of judging and the experience learned from it. The criteria have been taken over without any alterations by the 255 Panel, which thereby recognized and approved their correctness for the purpose of selecting judges for the Court of Justice and the General Court.

Second, the CST Committees must take into account the specialization of the CST: jurisdiction in matters opposing the Union and its officials or agents. This jurisdiction-based specificity of the CST substantially distinguishes the CST committees from the 255 Panel.

Consequently, knowledge of the law of the European civil service will be of primordial importance in the selection process, even if, in the evaluation form used for scoring the individual candidates, this particular criterion is not being awarded the greatest number of points. This knowledge will be even more important in a court composed only of seven judges, where one cannot allow for the luxury of waiting for the newly appointed judges to build up their knowledge in order to become 'operational'. Although certainly not desirable, this may be less problematic in larger courts, such as the Court of Justice or the General Court.

The knowledge criterion, in other words advanced proficiency or even mastery of the field of European civil service law, was nonetheless not the primary focus in the course of the first nominations made by the first Committee (Committee I). This is understandable. The task of the day was to set up a new jurisdiction equipped with a relatively broad competence and, while allowing the necessary time for the new jurisdiction to establish itself, also allowing its members to acquaint themselves—with open spirit, leading perhaps to new directions in the future case law—with the European civil service law as such. Thus, out of the first seven judges selected, only four had some practical experience in the field of international or European civil service law: S Gervasoni, H Tagaras, S Van Raepenbusch, and also, to some extent, the later first elected president of the CST, P Mahoney. The three other judges selected had recognized legal skills in administrative law and, most importantly, in social law. This led, notably, to development of the possibility of friendly settlement of disputes within the CST.

It is to be underlined that all the proposed nominees were of different nationalities. In this, Committee I showed foresight and diplomacy, even if the question of the candidates' nationality does not form the basis for its decision-making. It is for the Council, when making the appointments, to ensure a balanced composition of the CST on as broad a geographical basis as possible from among nationals of the member states and with respect to the national legal systems represented. In any case, Committee I demonstrated good judgement by acting as it did, since the Council approved its choice and appointed the seven persons proposed. Later on, this turned out to be an excellent choice, as the CST proved to be a high-quality jurisdiction that gave new and enriching impulse to the European civil service case law.

As far as Committee II is concerned, all the candidates whom it eventually nominated had good knowledge of European civil service law. In fact, all the nominees were former legal secretaries to judges or advocates general at the Court of Justice. Those persons, definitely brilliant and competent as regards their knowledge of the field, were therefore all able to assume their duties as judges directly. This was also the case with respect to Committee III, which has (so far) proposed to appoint a former Danish legal secretary to the Court of Justice: a nomination that was approved by the Council.

2. Questions and Reflections from the Practice

Having explained the specificity of the CST Committee, in this section I wish to share some thoughts based on my personal experience as member of the second CST Committee.

2.1. Should the Civil Service Tribunal become the privileged 'end-of-career station' for meritorious legal secretaries?

In view of the already discussed high number of former legal secretaries appointed to the CST, the question of whether or not the CST may become an 'end-of-career station' for deserving legal secretaries poses itself with renewed importance. Should that indeed be the case, it could mean that any other candidates, regardless of their qualities and references, would be as good as automatically barred from the possibility of becoming a judge at the CST.

This would be, in my view, regrettable for a number of reasons. First, the CST, in its initial composition, has done remarkable work, even if it was not initially composed only of European civil service law specialists. Second, European civil service law has itself evolved considerably in a direction that requires advanced knowledge of the law of contract. The reason for this is the increased number of contractual agents, who are no longer civil servants and who have been given jobs in the different agencies, offices, and other decentralized bodies of the Union. For this reason, persons with knowledge of labour law, or even the law of contract, are also needed. Third, in European civil service law, general principles of law and fundamental rights derived both from the European Convention for Protection of Fundamental Rights and Freedoms and from the Charter of Fundamental Rights of the European Union play an equally essential role. The knowledge and the previous practice in this field could also be taken into consideration when examining individual applications.

In a nutshell, it seems to me that there might be the need for 'fresh air' in the future in order to avoid the CST becoming a place where only former legal secretaries will be 'crowned'. Another valuable reserve pool of candidates for the CST might come from the ranks of professors or attorneys. This would require, however, that representatives of the latter professions submit applications, which is presently not really the case.

It should also be noted that legal secretaries have acquired experience within the institutions. Without questioning their independence in any way, legal secretaries have been serving the institutions (often within the respective legal service or in other services where they assumed high responsibilities) that are the respondents in civil service-type litigation. It seems to me that this may represent risk of judicial 'conservatism' in favour of the institutions. This would be difficult to reconcile with the early years of the CST, which showed new directions in the case law, such as for example with respect to the duty to state reasons for decisions, non-contractual liability, or questions of dismissal and non-renewal of contracts. In all these fields, the CST sought to limit the broad discretion enjoyed by the institutions. One can also note that in this CST case law, there might be slightly diverging decisions on similar legal issues due to the different composition of chambers.

What ought to be furthermore mentioned is that precisely because of its specificity, the CST may run the risk of becoming an ivory tower of experts. In its current composition, six out of seven judges are former legal secretaries. As will be further discussed at the end of this chapter, experts are not necessarily good judges.

2.2. Re-emergence of nationality-based considerations

The major goal pursued by establishing selection committees is to remove the appointment process from the control of the member states and focus on the quality, ability, and competence of the candidates. Unfortunately, one of the experiences in the course of the work of Committee II went rather in the opposite direction.

In its second session, Committee II was asked to suggest at least six candidates to fill the vacancies opened by three judges leaving: the president, P Mahoney, and judges H Tagaras and S Gervasoni. Mr Gervasoni did not request renewal of his term, but Mr Mahoney and Mr Tagaras did. They were evidently entitled to seek their reappointment. This created, however, some difficulties for the Selection Committee, since there was no reason to question their competence for the job. Thus, the question arose: what should Committee II do? Should the retiring judges seeking reappointment be automatically put on the list of the most able and meritorious candidates, or should they be invited to an interview? Taking the principle of equal treatment into account, it was decided to invite them for an interview, but only in order to get to know their motivation for seeking renewal of their mandate. The Council requires that only one list of candidates is submitted to it. Thus, the names of P Mahoney and H Tagaras were put at the top of the list, preceded by the number 0 and, below on the same list, the names of the six best candidates (two times three) were ranked in order of merit from 1 to 6.

Complete freedom of choice was therefore left to the Council, while at the same time suggesting that the two judges whose first mandate had come to an end deserved, at least as much as the other selected candidates, to be taken into consideration for a second appointment. Reappointment would obviously allow them to continue work already started that required confirmation and consolidation in the long run.

Faced with such a list, the Committee of Permanent Representatives (COREPER) met several times and even asked Judge G Hirsch, who chaired Committee II, to clarify the delivered opinion. In the end, the Council decided not to renew the mandate of the two outgoing judges. It rather applied a rotation rule based on nationality. The Council chose the first three candidates appearing on the list under numbers 1 to 3 and in consequence, the CST once more consisted of seven judges of seven different nationalities, the three latest appointees being Irish (K Bradley), Dutch (R Barents), and Italian (E Perillo). Those three nationalities were not yet 'represented' within the CST. In short, one could describe this appointment policy as 'nationality-based sprinkling' of mandates.

Personally, one does not have to approve or disapprove of the choices made. All of the appointed judges possess acknowledged competence in the specific matters pertaining to the CST jurisdiction. Moreover, it is not for the Committee to express views on this issue. I can, however, understand that the former judges seeking reappointment who were set aside in this way may have felt a certain degree of frustration, if not injustice.

It should be also noted that at the occasion of the first CST renewal in 2008, the Council accepted to reappoint three judges who at the time of their initial appointment were drawn by lot and whose mandate expired after three years already. The Council noted, however, that this was a particular situation, specifically provided for by legislation, and brought about by the need to differentiate the length of mandate of the first court.

It therefore appears that member states chose to apply the principle of rotation based on nationality and, more generally, the already mentioned 'sprinkling' principle that allows all nationalities to access the office of judge. They interpreted strictly, and in my point of view incorrectly,[4] their power to appoint judges 'on an as broad geographical basis as possible'[5]. This, to a certain extent, appears as a 'reinstatement' of the principle of nationality (one judge per state), which cannot in fact be guaranteed, as the number of judges is inferior to the number of member states.

This could lead, if proper care is not taken, to undermining the work and the competence conferred on the selection committees. There is the risk of a return to political nominations, to favouritism, to appointments based on considerations other than merit: in other words, to precisely the practices that were supposed to be weeded out. What will happen when the Committee proposes candidates

---

[4] The 'broad geographical basis' criterion is not a 'corrective' criterion, *a fortiori* not an 'exclusive' one, among the selection criteria as applied by the selection committees and leading to the establishment of a list of 'winners'. It is rather an 'adjustment' and thus just an ancillary criterion, the aim of which is to avoid the creation of an imbalanced composition of the CST due to 'over-representation' of a given nationality. This criterion does not provide any legal basis for selecting a given candidate because of her nationality only. Nothing in the CST founding texts stipulates that its judges ought to be of different nationalities. Quite the contrary: it was precisely to avoid such inflexibility that the selection committees were set up. As far as the fact that it would be desirable to have different national legal systems 'represented' is concerned, ie to have persons of different nationalities, the criterion of nationality in itself appears to be wholly inappropriate for achieving this goal. There are two main reasons for this. First, people often study in several countries precisely to familiarize themselves with different legal knowledge and approaches, seeking to widen their horizon as much as possible. This breaks the link between nationality and legal training. Second, as follows both from the basic texts as well as their interpretation in the case law, European civil service law is one unified field of law with its own, independent content. For these reasons, the alleged necessity to ensure a balanced composition 'with respect to the national legal systems represented' (see notably Art 3(1) of Annex I to Protocol no 3 to the Lisbon Treaty on the European Civil Service Tribunal, OJ [2010] C 83/226) makes no (or no more) sense.

[5] Art 3(1) of Annex I, above (n 1).

whose nationalities are already present within the CST, or candidates of the same nationality? Will the Council go so far as to ask the Committee to submit different names, or even to start its entire work over again? Should this be the case, it would mean, to a certain extent, the end of selection committees, which would have to give way to the distribution of mandates assigned on basis of nationality. This would represent, in short, a deplorable step back.

All this demonstrates the weak position of the CST Selection Committees. It distinguishes them from the 255 Panel, where the nationality question does not matter, since it is undisputedly embedded already in the nomination procedure itself. The natural question to be posed in such situation is to inquire whether the powers of the CST Committees could be reinforced, and how this could be done while not encroaching on the decisional—and therefore political—powers of the member states' choice in appointing judges.

One could imagine that nominations made by the Committees could be given greater weight. Their nominations could be either approved by the Council as they stand or discarded as a whole, provided that the Council is unanimous and has good reasons for doing so. This, obviously, would in turn require that the nominated candidates are ranked in order of merit—as opposed to alphabetical order—so that the Council cannot arbitrarily select specific candidates from the list.

One could equally amend the respective legal provisions and prohibit there being more than two judges of the same nationality within the CST. This would guide the Committee in establishing the list of nominations before submitting it to the Council. Lastly, the Council could also choose to give preference to a given candidate in the case of a tie between two candidates of different nationalities, if the nationality of one of the candidates had not yet been represented within the CST.

3. Some Final Considerations

I would like to conclude with three final thoughts. First, the CST Selection Committees no doubt represent a progressive step towards greater 'professionalism' of judges, focusing on their ability, skills, and competence in relation to the specific jurisdiction conferred on the CST. Although only recently set up, the selection system has rapidly found its own 'cruising speed'. It functions well and deserves to be followed further. It has allowed for efficient work of the CST since its establishment.

For the future, one will have to make sure that the—unfortunately natural—tendency of the member states to push through choices based on exclusively national considerations is limited to ancillary incidents. The main consideration ought to be given to the rankings of candidates established by selection committees and submitted to the Council.

It should also be noted that the work of CST Committees is confidential. There is neither transparency, nor publicity. Equally, neither the work nor its results are reflected in any sort of a public report. The results are accessible only by the Council for the purpose of informing the exercise of its power of judicial appointments. Some people might regret this state of affairs. What appears most important, however, is protection of the rights of the individual candidates throughout the entire procedure of examination of the applications. The candidates can, if they wish to, ask for reasons for an eventual refusal to be stated, and also request further explanation to be given on the matter.

Second, I was struck by the large number of applications for the position of judge at the CST. I have been practising in the field of European civil service law for more than 35 years, first before the Court of Justice, then before the Court of First Instance, and finally before the CST. I was not aware, however, that there are so many of us that are interested in this type of litigation to such an extent as to wish to become judges.

I therefore assume that as a large portion of those candidates had no notable expertise in this field of law, they must have had other motivations for applying. What were they? This question is difficult to answer, since those candidates whose files were not convincing enough were not even interviewed. I think, however, that three observations can be made in this regard. First, there were a great number of applicants coming from the new member states. This shows how attractive the European institutions, notably European judicial institutions, are for these new European citizens. Second, there were very few applications by women. This is reflected in the present composition of the CST, where only one female judge sits. Third, there were also a great number of applications submitted by older candidates, who were close to retirement and have had a career that I would qualify as accomplished within their respective judicial system or within their legal career.

This last point, I believe, can be generalized and extended to all the three levels of jurisdiction within the European judicial architecture: the Court of Justice, the General Court, and the CST. There are several facts that may induce a candidate to apply for the position of judge, even to the CST: a jurisdiction that might be called a 'ground-level' one, without implying any derogatory meaning by using this notion—quite to the contrary. Those incentives are the following: the power inherent in the judicial function; the respect and the social standing that come with the office; and, at the end of the day, also an international-level salary that has no equivalent at the national level, even at the highest echelon of national judiciaries. There are also further non-negligible benefits linked to the office. These incentives might naturally be given different weight in the personal motivation of each individual candidate.

But, even if all these incentives are taken together, they cannot guarantee the identification of a good judge who will deliver sound justice. This observation leads to the third and final point of my final considerations, which may be the most important one: who is a good judge? Answering this question is hard, if not impossible. It is as difficult as trying to define what sound justice might be. All we can attempt is to state that a good judge masters the craft of judging. A good judge wishes to devote herself to this task and to dedicate all her time and zeal to it.

Alas, no selection criterion in the world can ensure this. Equally, no selection committee, as scrupulous as it might be, can be sure that it has identified a 'good judge' who will deliver 'sound judgments'. The craft of judging will be visible only on the job itself, when exercising the judicial office. This art will certainly rest on solid expertise. But that is not all that matters; I would venture to claim that it is even not essential. What counts is the love for the job, for the craft. It is about listening to the parties; about understanding the case; about penetrating beyond what the professional language is hiding, grasping the suffering, anxiety, hunger for justice; about the time spent trying to understand all of these…

Judging is a craft with no place for improvisation. It cannot be learned. One has to want it and to be ready to sacrifice a lot in order to arrive there. It requires humility, dedication, almost devotion.

Such characteristics cannot be ascertained, not even approximately, through a questionnaire or in the course of a short impersonal interview lasting only a few minutes. One does not know, one cannot know, and one will never know what people think, what they really want. This is the real test, the true question. What one does in fact is place a bet, nothing more. This demonstrates the key importance of knowing, above all, the true motivation of candidates. There is no doubt that too little time is spent on this question within the practice of the Committees.

Choosing a good expert for the job is already a step forward. She has in her hands the necessary tools, which she knows how to use. The question nonetheless remains how she will be using them. Nobody knows that, with the exception of perhaps herself—and even that may not be guaranteed, since judging is a job that, most frequently, the person appointed has not done before, and is without any doubt one of the most difficult jobs. It is for the appointee to discover it, and to discover her own personality while doing so. It is only after this first step in the judicial office that we, the first evaluators, will know whether we were right or mistaken. But this first step remains fundamentally unpredictable. As former judge Sevón, who chaired Committee I, rightly noted, 'no filtering procedures will ever succeed in either precisely evaluating personality of candidates or their capacity to decide a case in an efficient way'.[6]

---

[6] Leif Sevón, 'La procédure de sélection des membres du TFPUE', in Le TFPUE 2005-2010: Actes du colloque organisé à l'occasion du 5ème anniversaire du TFP, Luxembourg, 1er octobre 2010, special issue, (2011) 20 *Revue universelle des droits de l'homme* 1–3, 8.

5

(S)electing Judges for Strasbourg

A (Dis)appointing Process?

Koen Lemmens

1. Introduction

The concept of the rule of law,[1] understood as a government of laws, not of men,[2] may explain why legal scholars and lawyers *tout court* tend to focus their work and research on the 'impersonal' aspects of the law: the rules and the institutions. Arguably, this is an evident choice, although in doing so we may not be paying sufficient attention to the role of individuals in the legal system. This is particularly true in the case of the European Convention on Human Rights (ECHR). The meaning of this Convention has radically changed over time due to an expanding case law. Now, this case law is the result of the perseverance of courageous, sometimes perhaps stubborn, applicants willing to bring a case to the European Court of Human Rights (hereinafter 'ECtHR' or just 'Court') who invest many years of their lives, obsessively from time to time, in their struggle against national law. Without Paula Marckx,[3] Christine Goodwin,[4] and Youssef Salduz,[5] to name but three, European human rights would look completely different. Likewise, the European judges play a quintessential role in the evolution of the case law.[6] Yet it is striking that although the ECtHR has been heavily criticized in recent times, particularly for its very activist attitude in the human rights protection,[7] this critique

---

[1] The author wants to stress that although he bears the same surname as his colleague at Leuven University, the Belgian Judge in the European Court of Human Rights, Paul Lemmens, they are no relatives. The standpoints expressed here are strictly personal and Judge Lemmens has nothing to do with this contribution. Criticism voiced in this article should of course not be considered as a hidden critique on Judge Lemmens' election either.

[2] The quote is notoriously attributed to John Adams and is expressed in Article XXX of the Constitution of Massachusetts (1780).

[3] *Marckx v Belgium* App no 6833/74 (ECHR, 13 June 1979).

[4] *Christine Goodwin v UK* App no 28957/95 (ECHR (GC), 11 July 2002).

[5] *Salduz v Turkey* App no 36391/02 (ECHR (GC), 27 November 2008).

[6] See eg Laurence Helfer and Erik Voeten, 'International Courts as Agents of Legal Change: Evidence from LGBT Rights in Europe': <ssrn.com/abstract=1850526>, last accessed 15 February 2014.

[7] I refer, among others, to Lord Hoffmann's *Judicial Studies Board Annual Lecture*: <www.judiciary.gov.uk/media/speeches/2009/speech-lord-hoffman-19032009>, last accessed 15 February 2014; see

was directed at the Court as such; the position or even the impact of the individual judges on the case law is not so much studied, let alone called into question. Only few scholars have made in-depth analyses of the positions and profiles of the judges and tried to link this to the development of the case law. Professor Eric Voeten is most probably the most well-known researcher in this domain. Not surprisingly, he comes from a social sciences background.[8]

In this contribution, I will not focus on the behaviour, attitude, and positions of the individual judges to understand (the evolution of) the Strasbourg case law. Instead, I will limit myself, as a lawyer, to analysis of the procedure of selection of the judges. Other authors in this volume provide critical comments and suggest possible improvements.[9] My perspective here is of course two-fold, as I will focus both on the way in which the Council of Europe approaches the question and how national states deal with it. In section 2, I will sketch the legal framework pertaining to the eligibility of judges. Next, in section 3, I will describe how the Council of Europe conceives the election process.

Finally, in section 4, I will focus on the national dimension. The focus will be on France, Belgium, and the UK, all three states which recently had to organize the selection procedure. A comprehensive comparative study would exceed the scope of this contribution; far from offering a complete panorama of all the problems that may arise in the various states, this contribution will offer a snapshot of some of the most delicate issues that can occur during the election process. It may serve as a basis for a more comprehensive analysis of the national selection procedures. The selection of the three states is inspired not only by pragmatic reasons (knowledge of language and familiarity with the legal systems) but also by genuine comparative motives. Although the three states are all West European 'founding' states of the Council of Europe, they constitute an interesting set of data. France and the UK represent the two major legal systems (civil law and common law) in the Council of Europe.[10] French and English are the only two official languages of the Council of Europe and the Court. The UK has been qualified as a 'poor implementor'[11] and, in recent times, the Court

---

also Marc Bossuyt, 'Should the Strasbourg Court Exercise More Self-restraint? On the Extension of the Jurisdiction of the European Court of Human Rights to Social Security Regulations' (2007) *Human Rights Law Journal* 321–32; Marc Bossuyt, 'Judges on Thin Ice: The European Court of Human Rights and the Treatment of Asylum Seekers' (2010) *Inter-American and European Human Rights Journal* 3–48. For a recent overview: Spyridon Flogaitis, Tom Zwart, and Julie Fraser (eds), *The European Court of Human Rights and Its Discontents* (Cheltenham: Edward Elgar Publishing, 2013).

[8] Erik Voeten, 'Does a Professional Judiciary Induce More Compliance?: Evidence from the European Court of Human Rights': <ssrn.com/abstract=2029786>, last accessed 15 February 2014; 'The Politics of International Judicial Appointments: Evidence from the European Court of Human Rights' (2007) *International Organization* 669, 685–6 and 701; 'The Politics of International Judicial Appointments' (2008–9) 9 *Chicago Journal of International Law* 387–405.

[9] See in particular this volume, ch 6, and further chs 8–10.

[10] Yet, although it is frequently believed that the traditional way of legal reasoning in common law (centred on case law) would favour judicial activism, contrary to the typically French way of arguing (with its focus on the law, because *les juges ne sont que les bouches de la loi*), Voeten has shown that the judges' legal background does not impact on the degree of their activism. See Voeten, 'The Politics of International Judicial Appointments' (n 8).

[11] Voeten, 'Does a Professional Judiciary Induce More Compliance?' (n 8). Yet others argue that the UK is very good at implementing the ECtHR's judgements: Alice Donald, Jane Gordon, and Philip

has been heavily criticized in the UK. Some of the British judges have been among the most outspoken defenders of judicial restraint.[12] The UK is therefore representative of a more ECHR-sceptic state. In this respect, the contrast with Belgium is outspoken: traditionally, the position of the European Convention and the Court is almost uncontested in Belgium.[13] When Professor Voeten established his ranking of the most activist judges, he concluded that two of the three most activist judges were Belgian (judges De Meyer and Tulkens).[14] Belgium can be quite rightly said to be an ECHR-friendly state. France seems to have a position between the two previously described states. Although France recognized the individual complaint procedure (1981) quite late,[15] as of 1975 it accepted (arrêt *Respino*)[16] the direct effect of the Convention. Pursuant to the model of Professor Voeten, the French judges in the Court did not appear to be either extremely activist or extremely restrained.[17] So there are good arguments to suggest that France has a moderate position towards the ECHR and the functioning of the Court.

2. Selecting a Judge for Strasbourg: The Convention's Legal Framework and the Problematic Practice

2.1. The Convention

Before entering into the heart of the matter it is necessary to describe the position of a judge in the ECtHR as it results from the Convention itself, though at the outset, we can already observe that the Convention only pays little attention to the legal status of the judges and the selection process. All in all, only four articles deal with the position and selection of the judges, the most important being Articles 21 and 22 of the Convention. Article 21 reads:

1. The judges shall be of high moral character and must either possess the qualifications required for appointment to high judicial office or be jurisconsults of recognised competence.
2. The judges shall sit on the Court in their individual capacity.
3. During their term of office the judges shall not engage in any activity which is incompatible with their independence, impartiality or with the demands of a full-time

---

Leach, *The UK and the European Court of Human Rights* (Equality and Human Rights Commission 2012) 144: <http://www.equalityhumanrights.com> (last accessed 23 June 2014).

[12] Voeten, 'The Politics of International Judicial Appointments' (n 8).

[13] Guan Schaiko, Paul Lemmens, and Koen Lemmens, 'Belgium' in J Gerards and J Fleuren (eds), *Implementation of the European Convention on Human Rights and of the Judgments of the ECtHR in National Case Law. A Comparative Analysis* (Intersentia 2014).

[14] Voeten, 'Does a Professional Judiciary Induce More Compliance?' (n 8) 685–6.

[15] Gerard Cohen-Jonathan, 'La reconnaissance par la France du droit de recours individuel devant la Commission européenne des Droits de l'Homme' (1981) *Annuaire français du droit international* 269, 271.

[16] Cass (France), judgment Respino, 3 June 1975, n° 75–90.687.

[17] Voeten, 'Does a Professional Judiciary Induce More Compliance?' (n 8) 685–6.

office; all questions arising from the application of this paragraph shall be decided by the Court.

Thus, the criteria for office are here enlisted. Arguably, this list is fairly concise—which entails of course some problems, which we will have occasion to discuss later. Here, it is important to highlight the second paragraph, which stresses that the judges sit in their individual capacity. It follows that judges represent neither the high contracting party nor the Council of Europe. If this is indeed the underlying idea, it is obvious that neither of the two actors concerned should have the exclusive power of appointing the judges. Under such circumstances, it is rather evident that the procedure concerning the appointment of judges reflects the equilibrium between the state party and the Council of Europe. Article 22 of the Convention therefore states: 'The judges shall be elected by the Parliamentary Assembly with respect to each High Contracting Party by a majority of votes cast from a list of three candidates nominated by the High Contracting Party.'

The picture is now complete: judges will act in their individual capacity, but they are appointed pursuant to a procedure in which both the national states and the Council of Europe—through its Parliamentary Assembly—are involved. Yet, although it may be complete, the picture still remains excessively vague. The Convention does not contain precise rules that give us a clear idea on who may sit as a judge, apart from the conditions that they must be of high moral character (could it be otherwise?) and that they must possess the qualifications required for the appointment of a high judge, or at least be jurisconsults of recognized competence. It is hard not to agree with these criteria, as the line of reasoning is almost completely circular. Indeed, what the Convention says is that in order to be able to be elected as a high judge, you should have the capacities to serve as a high judge. This is obviously a reference to national law: candidates should have the capacities to occupy high functions within the national legal system. The question, rather, is: what are those capacities?

Following the text of the Convention, two criteria have to be taken into account.[18] One concerns the personal qualifications of the candidates and is explicitly mentioned in the Convention. The other is more implicit, and follows in a way from the first. Even if the Convention does not mention it explicitly, elected candidates indeed need to have a good command of one of the two official languages of the Court, either French or English. The linguistic capacities of the candidates are in a way part of their personal qualifications. In its advisory opinion, the Court itself stressed that the candidates' linguistic skills are part of their qualifications.[19] It must be noted here that there is indeed a serious problem, not so much with the knowledge of English, but definitely with that of French.[20]

---

[18] Jean-François Flauss, 'Les élections de juges à la Cour européenne des droits de l'homme (2005-2008)' 2008 *Revue trimestrielle des droits de l'homme* 713, 720–22.

[19] European Court of Human Rights, *Advisory opinion on Certain Legal Questions Concerning the Lists of Candidates Submitted with a View to the Election of Judges to the European Court of Human Rights*, 12 February 2008, para 47.

[20] Flauss (n 18) 740–1.

Be that as it may, at this point it seems obvious to draw the conclusion that the Parliamentary Assembly has rather wide discretionary power when it comes to electing one of the three candidates. Even more troublesome is the fact that the Convention gives no indication at all of how the member states should proceed in view of the establishment of the list of three candidates.

2.2. The practice

A succinct, vague, or incomplete legal framework does not necessarily have to cause problems, as long as it is completed by an established and qualitative practice. In reality, we have to admit that over the years, no such practice has come to light. Unfortunately, indeed, over 15 years[21] of elections of judges has shown that in practice, many question-begging incidents have happened. Other scholars have followed the election procedures in detail, especially the late Jean-François Flauss, who has proven to be an insightful and critical observer;[22] regrettably, his research showed that, whereas in the period 2001–4 incidents were still marginal, in recent times elections have become more troublesome. It would lead us way too far off track to go into the salient details of many elections. Yet a random selection of some—even recent—elections gives full credit to the thesis that the procedures were suboptimal. Some authors went even further in their criticism and stated that unfit persons have been proposed for election.[23]

It is indeed shocking to read that on many occasions governments have tried to misuse the election process for their own purposes. This deplorable practice has been quite frequently denounced. Basically, two problems can be distinguished.[24] First, we see that in the past, when sitting judges could still be re-elected for a new term—now impossible, since Article 23 of the Convention states that there is no possibility of renewal of the mandate—states used this renewal to discipline the judges. Docile judges would then be proposed for re-election, but judges who did not necessarily please states would not be re-elected, or would not even be presented as candidates for re-election at all. Since this is a phenomenon of the past, I will not develop this issue.[25] Still, we must realize that there exists a related danger. As judges are elected for one term only, they have to find new professional occupations (save when they have reached pensionable age). For some judges this

---

[21] If we take the creation of the permanent Court as the starting point.

[22] Jean-François Flauss, 'Radioscopie de l'élection de la nouvelle Cour européenne des droits de l'homme' (1998) *Revue trimestrielle des droits de l'homme* 435–64; 'Le renouvellement triennal de la Cour européenne des droits de l'homme' (2001) *Revue trimestrielle des droits de l'homme* 693–713; 'Brèves observations sur le second renouvellement triennal de la Cour européenne des droits de l'homme' (2005) *Revue trimestrielle des droits de l'homme* 5–32; 'Les élections de juges à la Cour européenne des droits de l'homme (2005-2008)' 2008 *Revue trimestrielle des droits de l'homme* 713–41.

[23] Norbert Paul Engel, 'More Transparency and Governmental Loyalty for Maintaining Professional Quality in the Election of Judges to the European Court of Human Rights' (2012) 32 *Human Rights Law Journal* 448. See also below ch 6.

[24] Jean-François Flauss, 'Brèves observations sur le second renouvellement triennal de la Cour européenne des droits de l'homme' (2005) *Revue trimestrielle des droits de l'homme* 5, 9.

[25] See at length Flauss (n 24) 9–12.

may not be too complicated (eg if they return to university teaching), but others may have greater problems. Those who go back to national administrations or who would be interested in appointment to the national judiciary may depend for their further career on the 'goodwill' of the national states. This may, of course, have a chilling effect on relatively young judges, who may be tempted to avoid overly strong criticism of their state in order to avoid endangering their post-Court career.[26]

Second—and this is still, today, a topical problem—some states try to get 'their preferred candidate' elected, even if this implies that they have to influence the election process in a pernicious way, or even bypass it. Other authors have committed themselves to denouncing these irregularities.[27]

3. The Council of Europe's Side of the Selection Process

It goes without saying that both the relative vagueness of the legal framework and the sometimes embarrassing election procedures of some judges called for a more serious approach, which would allow for fine-tuning the existing procedure in order to select those candidates who are fit and proper for the office of judge in the ECtHR. The reform of the selection process has two clear goals: it aims at preserving the impartiality of the Court and at assuring the quality of the judges. Nothing less than the credibility of the Court is indeed at stake.[28]

The malaise caused by some (recent) elections of judges was not only known to the in-crowd of Strasbourg observers, but was also discussed more widely.[29] For instance, at the High Level Conference on the Future of the European Court of Human Rights (Interlaken Declaration, 19 February 2010), the need to maintain the independence of the judges and preserve the impartiality and quality of the Court was stressed.[30] More precisely, the Conference called upon the states and the Council of Europe to:

ensure, if necessary by improving the transparency and quality of the selection procedure at both national and European levels, full satisfaction of the Convention's criteria for office as a judge of the Court, including knowledge of public international law and of the national legal systems as well as proficiency in at least one official language. In addition, the Court's composition should comprise the necessary practical legal experience.[31]

---

[26] Eric Voeten, 'The Politics of International Judicial Appointments' (n 8); Interrights, *Judicial Independence: Law and Practice of Appointments to the European Court of Human Rights* 24 <www.interights.org/jud-ind-en/index.html>, last accessed 15 February 2014.

[27] I refer to the works of Flauss (n 22) and Engel (n 23).

[28] See first paragraph, Guidelines of the Committee of Ministers on the selection of candidates for the post of judge at the European Court of Human Rights, CM(2012) 40, 29 March 2012; Andrew Drzemczewski, 'Election of Judges to the Strasbourg Court: An Overview' (2010) *European Human Rights Law Review* 377, 377.

[29] In 2003, Interrights produced a critical report, 'Judicial Independence' (n 26).

[30] Accessible online at <www.coe.int>, last accessed 8 October 2013.

[31] Point 8a, Action Plan, Interlaken Declaration.

A year later, at the Izmir Summit (26–7 April 2011), the High Level Conference continued to recognize the need for a critical assessment of the existing procedures and a possible improvement. The Conference invited

the Committee of Ministers to continue its reflection on the criteria for office as judge of the Court and on the selection procedures at national and international level, in order to encourage applications by good potential candidates and to ensure a sustainable recruitment of competent judges with relevant experience and the impartiality and quality of the Court.[32]

This insistence of the High Level Conference should not, however, make us forget that for more than a decade, both the PACE and the Committee of Ministers had already taken steps to ameliorate the election process.[33]

An important catalyst here was the entry into force of Protocol no 11 on 1 November 1998. Since that date, the European Court has been a permanent Court, composed of full-time judges. There are as many judges as high contracting parties to the Convention: 47 at present. From that moment onwards, selection of the judges became, of course, of utmost importance, even if little attention was paid to this issue and even if the general rules on the election process had not been changed.[34] That is, however, not to say that no critical reflection on the topic had taken place. In fact, both the PACE and the Committee of Ministers have taken steps to improve the (s)election process, and they continue to do so.

3.1. The Parliamentary Assembly

As early as 1996, the Parliamentary Assembly of the Council of Europe made a first attempt to try to bring some objectivity into the election process. In Resolution 1082 (1996) and Recommendation 1295 (1996), it called upon the candidates and the member states to use a standard model of curriculum vitae.[35] Moreover, it also advocated personal interviews with the candidates by an ad hoc Sub-Committee of the Committee on Legal Affairs and Human Rights. As former judge Hedigan clearly states, some governments would manipulate the presentation of the CVs: instead of transmitting three 'comparable' CVs, they would send two rather short CVs, whereas the preferred candidate's merits would be presented in a lengthier one.[36]

---

[32] Online at <www.echr.coe.int>, last accessed 15 February 2014, p 2.
[33] For a comprehensive overview: Committee on Legal Affairs and Human Rights, *Procedure for electing judges to the European Court of Human Rights*, AS/Jur/inf(2014)03, 7 January 2014. See also Andrew Drzemczewski, 'L'élection du juge de l'Union européenne à la Cour européenne des droits de l'homme' (2013) *Revue trimestrielle des droits de l'homme* 551, 553–8; John Hedigan, 'The Election of Judges to the European Court of Human Rights' in Marcelo Kohen (ed), *Promoting Justice, Human Rights and Conflict Resolution Through International Law. Liber amicorum Lucius Caflisch* (Leyden 2007) 235–49.
[34] Interrights (n 26) 6.
[35] PACE, Recommendation 1295 (1996), 22 April 1996 and PACE, Resolution 1082 (1996), 22 April 1996.
[36] Hedigan (n 33) 238.

The result was still not satisfactory. While the PACE's attention was initially quite understandably focused on the second phase of the election process—ie the period after transmission of the lists with the three candidates—it had to acknowledge, shortly after the 1998 elections, that there were still problems with the selection of candidates at the national level. The PACE observed in particular the existence of four problems: it discovered that

- national selection procedures would strongly vary from one state to another;
- some states would not have any rules governing the selection process;
- some states did not include women in their lists;
- some states would present candidates who did not match the requirements for office.[37]

Recommendation 1429 (1999) tried to tackle these problems by suggesting some, albeit very modest, improvements to the national selection process. Essentially, the governments were invited to advertise in the specialized press in order to attract eminent jurists. Furthermore, it was stressed that candidates should have experience in the field of human rights as practitioners or as activists and that they should be able to work in either French or English. Moreover, governments were advised to select candidates of both sexes and rank them in alphabetical order. Obviously, the idea was that by ranking the candidates in such a way, states could not—not even in a very subtle and implicit way—express their preferences.

Despite these praiseworthy intentions, the election process of 2001 did not turn out to be an improvement on the 1998 elections. As Flauss has shown, most states did not respect all the recommendations.[38]

In 2004, the PACE recalled that the ECtHR would only benefit from citizens' confidence if the selection process inspired this confidence. The need for a transparent and fair national selection procedure was once more underscored. Particular attention was paid to gender balance. The PACE not only called for lists with candidates from both sexes, but also invited the Committee of Ministers to propose an amendment to Article 22 of the Convention. The idea was that the Convention would explicitly mention that the states had to send in a list containing three candidates, representing both sexes.[39] However, Resolution 1627 (2008) in a way softens this obligation, since it offers the states the possibility to submit, in exceptional circumstances, a list containing only candidates of the over-represented sex. The PACE decided, indeed,

to consider single-sex lists of candidates of the sex that is over-represented in the Court in exceptional circumstances where a Contracting Party has taken all the necessary and appropriate steps to ensure that the list contains a candidate of the under-represented sex, but has not been able to find a candidate of that sex who satisfies the requirements of Article 21 § 1 of

[37] PACE, Recommendation 1429 (1999), 23 September 1999.
[38] Jean-François Flauss, 'Le renouvellement triennal de la Cour européenne des droits de l'homme' (2001) *Revue trimestrielle des droits de l'homme* 693–713.
[39] PACE, Recommendation 1649 (2004), 30 January 2004.

the European Convention on Human Rights. Such exceptional circumstances must be duly so considered by a two-thirds majority of the members casting a vote and a majority of the members entitled to vote of both the Sub-Committee and the Committee on Legal Affairs and Human Rights. This position shall be ratified by the Assembly in the framework of the Progress Report of the Bureau of the Assembly.[40]

This should not come as a surprise, since it almost literally copies the conclusion of the Court's advisory opinion on the question of whether lists can be rejected because they do not contain candidates of both sexes. Pursuant to the Court, exceptional circumstances—this is 'where a Contracting Party has taken all the necessary and appropriate steps with a view to ensuring that the list contains a candidate of the under-represented sex, but without success, and especially where it has followed the Assembly's recommendations advocating an open and transparent procedure involving a call for candidatures'—can justify the approval of a list with only candidates of one sex. The Assembly 'may not reject the list in question on the sole ground that no such candidate (i.e. a candidate from the under-represented sex) features on it'.[41]

An important Resolution was adopted in 2009. Resolution 1646 gives a clear overview of the problems encountered and the solutions proposed. First, the PACE recalls that the nomination of candidates to the election process is an important issue, which implies that the procedure must be democratic, transparent, and non-discriminatory. The PACE then warns the states by indication that non-respect of the procedure could be sanctioned. In the absence of a real choice between the candidates, the lists may indeed be rejected by the PACE. The same goes for situations in which national selection procedures did not comply with the requirements concerning fairness, transparency, and consistency.

3.2. The Committee of Ministers

Although the PACE has been taking the lead in stressing the need of an improved (s)election process,[42] the Committee of Ministers has in recent times taken some important steps too. Two elements have to be mentioned here.

In the first place, the Committee of Ministers has established an Advisory Panel of Experts in the slipstream of the Interlaken Conference through Resolution 2010 (26).[43] This panel consists of seven experts whose mission is to examine whether the candidates to be proposed for election by the high parties meet the

---

[40] PACE, Resolution 1627 (2008), 30 September 2008. In 2011, this rule was slightly modified by PACE, Resolution 1841 (2011), 7 October 2011. The exceptional circumstances 'must be duly so considered by a two-thirds majority of the votes cast by members of the Sub-Committee on the Election of Judges to the European Court of Human Rights'.

[41] European Court of Human Rights, *Advisory Opinion on Certain Legal Questions Concerning the Lists of Candidates Submitted with a View to the Election of Judges to the European Court of Human Rights*, 12 February 2008, para 54.

[42] Norbert Paul Engel, 'More Transparency and Governmental Loyalty for Maintaining Professional Quality in the Election of Judges to the European Court of Human Rights' (2012) 32 *Human Rights Law Journal* 448, 451.

[43] Committee of Ministers, Resolution (2010) 26, 10 November 2010.

requirements for office. The idea is that the states, before transmitting the list of candidates to the PACE, forward it first to the Advisory Panel.

According to Article 5 of the Resolution, whenever the Panel finds all candidates suitable, it shall inform the high contracting state of its findings. However, should it find that one or more candidates do not fulfil the requirements for office, its president shall contact the high contracting party to inform it and to obtain further information. If, after having obtained the state's views and possibly some more information, the Panel still finds that one or more candidates are not suitable, it will inform the state and give the reasons for its opinion. This will be communicated in a confidential way.

Equally, should the Advisory Panel consider that the lists of three candidates are in line with Article 22 of the Convention, it will communicate to the PACE its opinion on whether the candidates meet the criteria mentioned in Article 21§1 of the Convention. Again, this communication is confidential.[44]

Second, the Committee of Ministers adopted guidelines on the selection of candidates for the post of judge at the ECtHR.[45] These guidelines aim at mainstreaming the national selection procedures and offer a perfect synthesis of the Resolutions and Recommendations of the PACE, the Declarations of the High Summits, and the observations made by experienced observers.

At this point, I will only deal with the specific recommendations concerning the *modus operandi* of the national procedure. The Committee of Ministers divides this national selection procedure into three different stages: the phase of 'eliciting applications', the phase of establishing the lists, and, ultimately, the phase of finalization of the lists.

Pertaining to the first step in the national selection process, the Committee of Ministers insists primarily on the need for a stable and established procedure. It is clear that states should avoid improvisation, changes in the rules, or their creation *en cours de route*. Furthermore, the Committee of Ministers underscores the importance of casting the net wide: calls for applications should be made largely available. States should take measures to ensure a sufficient number of suitable candidates so as to allow the national selection panels to make a real choice. If third parties are allowed to propose candidates, they should be treated on a par with other candidates. This possibility should not prevent other candidates from applying. It goes without saying that interested candidates should be given sufficient time to submit their applications. In this way, there should be a sufficient number of serious candidates applying, as if it were a matter of mere public procurement.

The second cluster of recommendations concerns the national selection body and its functioning. Not surprisingly, the members of the panel need to have sufficient technical knowledge to perform their task and should themselves inspire confidence. The members of the national panel should have different backgrounds. This suggestion relates of course to the discussion on the composition of the Court itself. Traditionally, some judges are academics, while others come

---

[44] I discuss the (first) findings of this Advisory Panel below in s 3.3.
[45] Committee of Ministers, (2012) 40, 28 March 2012.

from legal practice. Some of them were judges within their national system; others were attorneys; some come from the national administration or diplomacy; and some may even have experience as human rights defenders in non-governmental organizations (NGOs). Obviously, it is felt—and to some extent established—that differences in professional backgrounds may explain why some judges are more activist than others.[46] A national selection panel that is insufficiently mixed may be (unintentionally) inclined to select people with a similar background to the panel members'. In this way, governments could indeed influence the selection process through the selection of the members of the panel. The Committee of Ministers wants to avoid this as much as possible. It is self-evident that the persons sitting on the national selection panels should be able to exercise their functions in all independence, without any pressure. It is highlighted as well that all the members of the national panel should participate on an equal basis in deliberations.

The national selection panel then has to review the applications. In principle, all candidates should be interviewed personally. Ideally, this interview will not be a free discussion, since it should be based on a standardized model. The Committee of Ministers apparently favours the semi-structured model of interviews. Should there be too many candidates, the Committee of Ministers suggests drawing up a short-list based on the written applications.

In any event, whether an interview has been conducted or not, an assessment of the linguistic capacities of the applicants has to be organized. The guidelines do not specify how this assessment should be conceived. They only specify that it should preferably take place during the interview. This seems to imply that the panel members themselves are in charge of the language assessments, but are they sufficiently schooled to do so? It occurs to me that the important question of linguistic knowledge could be dealt with in a more sustainable way. Why not accept that candidates prove their knowledge either by language certificates or equivalent experience, or through a professional language test to be passed on the day of the interview?

The final series of guidelines relates to finalization of the list of possible candidates. Here, the Committee of Ministers suggests basically three things. First, if the national instances that take the final decision on the list decide not to follow the recommendations of the selection panel, they are allowed to do so if they justify this 'by reference to the criteria for the establishment of the list'. Second, rules on confidentiality permitting, applicants should have the possibility to obtain information regarding the examination of their application. Ultimately, the final list should be made public by the national authorities.

3.3. The Advisory Panel

The committee of experts on the Reform of the Court—which is an intergovernmental committee acting under the authority of the Steering Committee for Human

---

[46] Voeten (n 11) 696.

Rights that functions itself under the auspices of the Committee of Ministers[47]—had two meetings with the chairman of the Advisory Panel, Mr Luzius Wildhaber, a former judge of the Court.[48] These meetings took place in April 2012 and January 2013. It follows that the findings of the chairman related essentially to elections of judges that took place in 2011 and 2012.

After only two years, the president of the Advisory Panel clearly had mixed feelings about its functioning, more precisely with regard to co-operation with all the stakeholders. Yet in 2012 he still had a quite positive overall message, since he stated that the Advisory Panel had benefited from 'a most satisfactory level of co-operation' from the states and the Parliamentary Assembly. The most significant problem seemed to be that some states submitted their list at the same time both to the Advisory Panel and the Parliamentary Assembly:[49] needless to say, this attitude reduces the role of the Panel to almost nothing.

In 2013, when president Wildhaber looked back at the Advisory Panel's experience on the occasion of the elections of 2012, he appeared less enthusiastic. In very strong terms, he declared: 'My fellow colleagues and I have the impression that, as things stand at the moment, the Panel's opinion is too often either being disregarded or not considered important enough or necessary by some stakeholders in the election procedure.'[50]

The question, then, is why Mr Wildhaber voiced such a harsh critique. The answer is clearly that the elections of 2012 gave rise to several incidents.[51] The 'feelings of frustration' seem to be related to three types of incidents. First, the president of the Advisory Panel noted that although a list had been approved by the Panel, it had nevertheless been rejected by the Sub-Committee on the election of judges to the European Court of Human Rights of the Committee on Legal Affairs and Human Rights. Next, some states did not wait for the Advisory Panel's answer before introducing their list to the Parliamentary Assembly. As a result, the Parliamentary Assembly elected judges without having regard to the Panel's assessment. This is indeed a strange situation, since the Advisory Panel was created to advise and therefore to help the high contracting parties—if they simply bypass the Advisory Panel, one can indeed question the Panel's *raison d'être*. However, the third problem is perhaps the most embarrassing one. Wildhaber mentions the case of a list on which figured, according to the Panel, one candidate who was included was unfit for the job. However, the state did not withdraw him from the list and the candidate did not set a step aside. Following an intensive strategy of lobbying, the candidate was elected by the Parliamentary Assembly. Although Wildhaber does not mention the

---

[47] <http://www.coe.int/t/dghl/standardsetting/cddh/reformechr/DH-GDR_en.asp>, last accessed 15 February 2014.
[48] Steering Committee for Human Rights, *Ministers' Deputies Exchange of Views with Mr. Luzius Wildhaber, Chairman of the Advisory Panel of Experts on Candidates for Election as Judge to the European Court of Human Rights*, DH-GDR (2013)005, 5 February 2013.
[49] Steering Committee for Human Rights (n 48) 4.
[50] Steering Committee for Human Rights (n 48) 2 (exchange of views of 30 January 2013).
[51] Ibid.

name of the candidate or of the state, there is little doubt that he was referring to the election of the Czech judge.[52]

In this respect, it should be noted that Wildhaber's complaints did not pass unnoticed. Experts working on reform of the Court within the framework of the Steering Committee for Human Rights have been discussing the functioning of the Advisory Panel pursuant to this critique. However, it is clear that the experts do not entirely subscribe to the critique. They agree that states should not transmit lists simultaneously to both the Panel and the Parliamentary Assembly; hence, they suggest that the list be submitted to the Advisory Panel at least three months before the deadline of the Parliamentary Assembly. However, the experts are more hesitant about the problem of following up the Panel's findings. The experts stress that the Panel's assessment is in any event non-binding advice. The Parliamentary Assembly may still decide autonomously whether it follows this advice or not.

The experts express the wish that the Sub-Committee of the Parliamentary Assembly would give 'due consideration' to the findings of the Advisory Panel. Yet, there is clearly no intention of making the advice binding. As a compromise, the experts suggest, among other things, that the Panel inform the government confidentially but comprehensively about why it has found that one or more candidates is/are not fit for the job. Subsequently, the state would have the opportunity to discreetly inform the candidate, and he or she would then have the opportunity to withdraw.[53] The outcome of this reflection on the functioning of the Advisory Panel remains to be seen, but it is clear that if nothing changes, the future of the Panel is very uncertain. Why would experts take up responsibilities in a panel if their work is dismissed, bypassed and not even properly considered?

3.4. An intermediate summary

At this point, it is possible to draw an intermediate conclusion. Undeniably, since the entry into force of the 11th Protocol and the creation of the 'new', ie permanent Court, there have been serious efforts by the Council of Europe's organs to make the selection process more transparent. However, as we have seen, the Council of Europe's organs only intervene in a second phase. The first phase is much more crucial, since it pertains to the establishment of a national list of three candidates. It goes without saying that the role, or at least the influence, of national governments is noticeable. Similarly, the role of the Council of Europe is rather limited at this stage. Apart from suggesting guidelines to the states on how to conduct the national selection procedures in a transparent way, the Council of Europe

---

[52] Norbert Paul Engel did not hesitate to qualify the behaviour of the Czech government as 'disloyal'—above (n 42) 450. For a detailed discussion of the Czech case see also below, ch 6 s 4.

[53] Steering Committee for Human Rights, *Draft CDDH report on the Review of the Functioning of the Advisory Panel of Experts on Candidates for Election as Judge to the European Court of Human Rights*, GT-GDR-E (2013), 19 September 2013, 14 and Steering Committee for Human Rights, *CDDH Report on the Review of the Functioning of the Advisory Panel of Experts on Candidates for Election as Judge to the European Court of Human Rights*, CDDH(2013)R79 Addendum I 29 November 2013, 14.

has to accept that states enjoy a wide discretion when it comes to establishing a list of three candidates.

It would be very naïve to hope that one day the election of judges can be 'depoliticized'.[54] There is evidence that (some) governments try to use appointments to the Court to install judges who share their views on judicial activism/judicial restraint. As Voeten has shown, this can rather easily be done by having a look at the professional career of the candidates: a past as a diplomat or a bureaucrat will lead more often than not to a restrained judge.[55] It is hard to see, especially in our times where the Court is regularly accused of being too activist, why governments would totally give up control over the selection process. Moreover, we could seriously wonder whether reducing the role of governments, the so-called *dégouvernementalisation*[56] of the national procedure, would be sufficient to avoid the influence of politics in the election process. In fact, it should not be forgotten that in the end, the Parliamentary Assembly of the Council of Europe elects the judges. So, however objective, transparent, fair, and neutral the national selection procedures may be, in the end politicians will decide. And as long as the Convention hallows the idea of democratically elected judges, we have to accept the flip side of this coin: lobbying, political games, international wheeling and dealing.

In this respect, I would like to stress that the Parliamentary Assembly consists of 318 members (and 318 substitutes, pursuant to Article 25 of the Statute of the Council of Europe). However, when we take a look at the votes cast, it is striking to see that only relatively few parliamentarians participate in the vote. For instance, with respect to the elections of 2012, approximately 50 per cent of the parliamentarians took part in the elections of the Belgian, Dutch, Czech, Polish, and UK judges.[57] The elections of the judges with respect to Russia, Moldova, Croatia, and Bosnia-Herzegovina benefited from a slightly higher degree of participation (62 per cent), and parliamentarians were remarkably active in electing the Swedish judge (78 per cent). Of course, numbers do not explain everything: it may well be that other points on the agenda of the Parliamentary Assembly explain why more parliamentarians are present at the moment of the vote. However, this fairly weak degree of participation sets the threshold for effective lobbying fairly low: governments do not need to convince too many parliamentarians to support their preferred candidates. Next, organizing a number of elections on the same day or within the same session increases of course the possibility of 'package deals'. Therefore, Flauss was surely right in observing that what could be hoped for was not so much the complete depoliticizing of the election process as the end of partisan influence on the election.[58]

---

[54] Flauss (n 22).　　　[55] Voeten (n 11) 696.

[56] Flauss (n 22) 436; Hans-Christian Krüger, 'Procédure de sélection des juges de la nouvelle Cour européenne des droits de l'homme' (1996) *Revue universelle des droits de l'homme* 113, 115–16.

[57] On 24 April 2012, 163 members voted in the election of the Belgian judge. With respect to Sweden, 250 members participated on 26 June 2012. On 27 June 2012, 162 members voted in the case of the Czech Republic, the Netherlands, Poland, and the UK. For the elections of the judges with respect to Russia, Moldova, Croatia, and Bosnia-Herzegovina, on 2 October 2012, 199 members voted.

[58] Flauss (n 22) 436.

4. The National Side of the Process

In this part of my contribution I want to focus on the national side of the election procedure, but I have to stress that it is extremely difficult, if not impossible, to give a full account of the national election procedures. However, on the basis of the summary of the national procedures, which the governments add to their list of three candidates, it is possible to get in any case an idea of what happened—at least, we may detect some interesting incidents.

4.1. Belgium

The election of the Belgian judge was not very controversial *in se*, although several smaller 'incidents' coloured the election process. First of all, it has to be stressed that the call for applicants was published in the *Moniteur belge* of 30 October 2009.[59] The call had been published in the specialized press, and passed to the supreme courts, the bar associations, and the universities as well.[60] We can regret, however, that the Belgian government did not mention which specific law journals were involved.[61] It is noteworthy too that candidates were given only one month to file their application.

It may seem strange that while the election only took place in April 2012, the selection process had already started in October 2009. The reason for this is the entry into force of Protocol no 14, pursuant to which the mandate of the then sitting Belgian judge, Françoise Tulkens, was extended from the autumn of 2010 to the autumn of 2012. The Belgian government had already included this possibility of the extension of Judge Tulkens' mandate in the original call.

It follows from the chronology of the facts that the Belgian authorities had finished their national selection procedure when they were informed by the Council of Europe that, further to the entry into force on 1 June 2010 of Protocol no. 14, the election process would be stopped. As a result, the national selection had been accomplished, but the procedure on the level of the Council of Europe was annulled. Only in 2011 was the procedure reinitiated, pursuant to the letter of the Parliamentary Assembly informing the Belgian authorities that, since Judge Tulkens' mandate was about to end in the fall of 2012, the national selection of candidates had to be organized.

On 7 July 2011, the Belgian Minister of Justice handed in the list of three candidates that had been established in view of the election initially planned for April 2010. This 'resubmission' of the list without reopening a new 'internal' procedure was, according to the accompanying letter, justified by the fact that all three candidates had

---

[59] *Mon belge*, 30 October 2009, 70784.

[60] PACE, Election of a judge to the European Court of Human Rights, Doc 12789, 14 November 2011, 4.

[61] Contrary, for example, to the Dutch government, which did explicitly mention the specialized journals in which the call was published. PACE, Election of a judge to the European Court of Human Rights, Doc 12936, 22 May 2012, 63.

confirmed their availability for the function of judge, even after the entry into force of Protocol no 14. Yet the main reason for this resubmission of the list is perhaps a consideration of mere internal, constitutional law. In fact, on 13 June 2010 there were federal elections in Belgium. The new government was only sworn in in December 2011—thus terminating what was by far the longest period of government formation in the history of the country. Throughout that time, the exiting government was serving as a 'care-taker' government in demission. In such a period of so-called 'current affairs', the powers of government are limited. The idea is indeed that parliament cannot use the arm of forcing the government (already) in demission to resign. Since parliamentary control does not work in this hypothesis, governments' powers should be restricted. Traditionally, it is said that governments in demission have three competences: 1) they are in charge of normal daily activities without major political significance; 2) they are allowed to deal with urgent matters that cannot be postponed and left to the new government with full powers; and 3) they can continue procedures that were initiated before the government was in demission.[62] I suppose that by reintroducing the list that had already been established, the Belgian government wanted to avoid extra complications pertaining to the question of whether a government in demission had the power to start the internal selection procedure all over again.

How then had this list been established? It follows from the government's explanation that a national selection panel had been created, comprising six members: a member of the judicial service, two parliamentarians, a member of the High Council for Justice, and two members of the office of the government agent before the Court.[63] This panel received in all 13 applications, of which one came from a female candidate, and invited the candidates for interview.[64] According to an interview with professor of human rights Eva Brems published in the Flemish newspaper *De Morgen*,[65] she was the female candidate. The national panel selected five candidates which, upon deliberation, appeared to be the best candidates to hold the position of judge. It transmitted this list to the government, who chose three candidates from these five. Candidates were ranked in alphabetical order and they had used the model CV.

There was, however, a problem with the list, since it contained only male candidates. The government almost apologized for this omission, but insisted on the exceptional circumstances of the present case. It referred to the large call for candidates, the interview, and the high qualifications of the candidates, but explained that although the female candidate met the requirements of Article 21, paragraph 1 of the Convention, she did not have equivalent competence to the three other candidates. Finally, the government argued that since 40 per cent of the judges

---

[62] André Alen and Koen Muylle, *Handboek van het Belgisch staatsrecht* (Kluwer 2011) 153.

[63] Some authors criticize the presence of members of the Governments Office before the Court. See Nicolas Hervieu, 'Point sur l'élection des juges à la Cour européenne des droits de l'homme' in Lettre « Actualités Droits-Libertés » du CREDOF, 1 May 2012, 3.

[64] Declaration of the Minister of Justice, Chambre des représentants, *Compte rendu intégral de la commission de la Justice*, CRIV 53 COM 439, 27 March 2012, 29.

[65] *De Morgen*, 29 January 2011, 8–9.

serving in the Court (at the time of submitting the list) were women, there was no 'manifest gender imbalance'.

The attitude of the Belgian government has been criticized by some scholars in the human rights blogosphere.[66] Nevertheless, the list had been sent to the Parliamentary Assembly and approved, after a change of the rules.[67] No specific reference to the findings of the advisory panel of experts can be found.

What happened then is hard to reconstitute for outsiders. But what we know is that as of 6 December 2011, some months after the submission of the list, there was a new government in Belgium with full competence and a new Minister of Justice. In a parliamentary debate on 27 March 2012, a few weeks before the election of the Belgian judge, the Minister in charge stated that she had convinced the government to withdraw the list. Yet, she added, this had been refused by the Sub-Committee of the Parliamentary Assembly. The reasons for this refusal had not been communicated. The Minister gave this explanation in an answer to a question coming from Eva Brems, who had been newly elected to the federal parliament. Both the member of parliament and the Minister regretted that no female candidate had been placed on the list, although one woman had been found, in compliance with Article 21, first paragraph of the Convention.

It should not have come as a surprise that the withdrawal of the list was refused. In a second advisory opinion on certain legal questions concerning the lists of candidates, given in 2010, the Court had indeed found that states could withdraw lists of candidates as long as this happened before the deadline for submission set by the Parliamentary Assembly.[68] The Court justified this by referring to legal certainty and the transparency and efficacy of the election procedure.[69] I believe a more straight-forward explanation is possible. What sense would it make to stress that the election of judges has to be 'depoliticized' if, at the same time, governments are allowed to withdraw their lists at any moment in time? Should this be accepted, it would be perfectly possible that, in the case of a change of government between the moment of submission of the list and the final vote, the new government withdraws the list introduced by the previous one for merely party political reasons. By setting a time limit, the Court has reduced the risk of such disloyal behaviour.

The question now is how the attitude of the Belgian government in demission should be assessed. Of course, since I have no information about the discussions within the government, it is hard to prove anything and much of my interpretation remains purely guesswork. Yet the critique that Belgium did not care about gender

---

[66] A Remiche, 'Election of the New Belgian Judge to the ECtHR: An All-male Short list Demonstrates Questionable Commitment to Gender Equality', <http://ohrh.law.ox.ac.uk/?p=143>, posted 12 August 2012, last accessed 3 February 2014; A Buyse, 'Committee of Ministers Adopts Guidelines on Selecting European Court Judges', <http://echrblog.blogspot.be/search?q=male+list>, posted 29 March 2012, last accessed 3 February 2012.

[67] See above (n 39).

[68] European Court of Human Rights, *Advisory Opinion on Certain Legal Questions Concerning the Lists of Candidates Submitted with a View to the Election of Judges to the European Court of Human Rights*, 22 January 2010, para 49.

[69] Ibid, para 47.

equality[70] which on first glance may have appeared plausible is probably less so at second glance. The candidate to be elected was to replace Françoise Tulkens, who served 14 years as a judge in Strasbourg with respect to Belgium. Such a long mandate for a female judge is not typical for a 'misogynist' state. Therefore, other considerations may have played an important role. Judge Tulkens, who appeared to be an activist judge according to Voeten's classification, had an academic background but she did not have any prior experience as a judge. We know that in recent times, the Court has been heavily criticized for its activism. It is, therefore, not unlikely that the Belgian government was looking for a judge who would possibly be less activist. Although Voeten has shown that judges with a previous career as professional judges are not less activist than judges coming from other backgrounds,[71] it cannot be excluded that precisely this consideration explained the choice of the Belgian government. All three candidates were, like Professor Brems, highly esteemed academics, although not all of their research interests may have been all focused in great part on human rights. Yet what differentiated them from Professor Brems is that they had all served as high judges in either the Constitutional Court or the Council of State. This is most probably what the government referred to when it declared that the female candidate did not have equivalent competences.

From an internal Belgian perspective, the profiles of the two candidates with most votes are extremely interesting. Both of them are native Dutch speakers (the third candidate was a Francophone). As a consociational democracy, the institutional design and politics of Belgium are based on permanent negotiations and agreements between different linguistic, philosophical, and ideological groups in society. From that angle, it is surely remarkable to see a Francophone[72] female academic replaced by a Dutch-speaking male judge and academic. So many equilibriums are interwoven, and gender is, from a Belgian perspective, but one of the many pertinent criteria to take into consideration.[73]

In any event, the different stages of the Belgian part of the election procedure reveal the extent to which governments still have an important role. Although Belgium followed the various recommendations in order to enhance the fairness and transparency of the election procedure, it is clear that in the Belgian case, the

---

[70] This is not the place to launch the debate, but one could wonder why it is so important to stress gender equality compared to other grounds of possible discrimination. Why are there no non-white judges? Are we sure that philosophical, religious, political convictions are duly represented? What about sexual orientation issues? What about the representation of disabled persons, and so on, and so forth? Should representatives of all groups suffering from under-representation be included in the national lists, they will most probably have to contain more than three persons...

[71] Recalling that former diplomats, for instance, are more restrained: Voeten (n 11), 696. In his new research, Voeten discovered that there is a link, however, between the professional background of the judges and compliance with their judgments. Judgments delivered by professional judges would be better complied with. Voeten, 'Does a Professional Judiciary Induce More Compliance?' (n 8).

[72] Although Judge Tulkens wholeheartedly describes herself as a *Brusseles*—ie an inhabitant of Brussels.

[73] Compare this for instance to the Belgian Constitution. Pursuant to Article 99, the Federal Government is composed of an equal number of Francophone and Dutch-speaking ministers (the Prime Minister excluded). Yet Article 11bis states the government is made of both men and women, so one woman is sufficient to meet this requirement.

key point is the selection made by the federal government. The national selection panel suggested five names, but the government selected three of them. This is a governmental decision, and we can only guess the reasons behind the government's final decision to select three candidates.

4.2. France

The election procedure regarding the French judge started with a publication of the call on the websites of the Ministries of Foreign Affairs and Justice in September 2010.[74] It was also published in several legal journals.[75]

The candidates who appeared most suitable for the job—according to the press there were some 20 applications in total[76]—were interviewed by the French National Group of the Permanent Court of Arbitration. This group was in charge of examining the applications and had to transmit a list of six candidates to the French government. The group consisted of distinguished French jurists. Its president, Gilbert Guillaume, was a judge at the International Court of Justice, the other members being Prosper Weil, professor emeritus of public law; Jean-Pierre Puissochet, former judge at the Court of Justice of the European Union; and Marc Perrin de Brichambaut, former director of legal affairs at the Ministry of Foreign Affairs and secretary general of the Organization for Security and Co-operation in Europe.[77]

Instead of transmitting six names to the French government, they only handed down a list of five candidates. Then, like in the Belgian case, the final decision was to be taken by the government, who disposed of a certain *marge de manoeuvre* when it came to selecting the three candidates.

At that point, something strange happened. It is reported that the national selection body would have stressed that two of the suggested candidates were particularly fit: Ms Edwige Belliard (council of state, co-agent of the French government before the ECtHR) and Mr André Potocki (Court of Cassation). By contrast, Mr Michel Hunault, the third candidate selected by the government, was not included in the list of five names.[78] Mr Hunault, who is a lawyer and professor at Science Po—but apparently without a very good knowledge of English—was also a member of parliament. It is said that a good friend of then-president Sarkozy was interested in the seat occupied by Mr Hunault. Transferring Mr Hunault to Strasbourg would be a gentle way of vacating the seat.[79] The government proposed Mr. Hunault, together with two of the most suited candidates, to the Parliamentary Assembly, though it

---

[74] <www.diplomatie.gouv.fr/fr/IMG/pdf/FichePoste_diffusion.pdf>, last accessed 3 February 2014.

[75] PACE, Election of a judge to the European Court of Human Rights, Doc 12616, 18 May 2011, 4.

[76] Franck Johannès, 'Petite manoeuvre de l'Elysée pour placer un ami', <http://libertes.blog.lemonde.fr/2011/03/14/petite-manoeuvre-de-lelysee-pour-placer-un-ami>, posted 14 March 2011, last accessed 30 January 2014.

[77] PACE, Election of a judge to the European Court of Human Rights, Doc 12527, 25 February 2011, 4.

[78] Ibid.   [79] Engel (n 42) 451.

was so fair to admit that Mr. Hunault was a complementary candidate, who had not been short-listed by the national selection panel.[80]

On 7 March 2011, the Sub-Committee of the Parliamentary Assembly dealt with the lists of candidates.[81] According to press reports, the list was rejected since one of the candidates did not meet the requirements for office.[82] The Advisory Panel would have come to the same conclusion.[83] Apparently, the French government did not want to replace the rejected list, so the candidate himself decided to withdraw.[84] As a result, the procedure was interrupted.[85] France then replaced him and introduced a new list. It contained the two candidates preferred by the national selection panel, completed by a third candidate, Mr Valat (Court of Appeal of Versailles).[86]

However, it is noteworthy to compare the accompanying letters of both lists. What strikes one immediately is that the French government, on transmission of the second list, mentioned the withdrawal of Mr. Hunault, but did not mention that this candidate was never proposed by the national selection panel. A quick reading of the document, without knowledge of the context, would therefore create the impression that Mr Hunault was one of the five candidates proposed by the panel and that, after his withdrawal, the government just had to enlist another candidate. In presenting the case like this, the whole *politikeering* behind the scene of course completely vanished. Finally, André Potocki was elected by the Parliamentary Assembly on 21 June 2011.[87]

Apart from all kinds of politically inspired comments one could voice regarding the election of the French judge, there is of course one more general comment to be expressed. The French government followed the above-mentioned second advisory opinion of the Court with regard to the lists of candidates. In this second opinion the Court indeed held that if the withdrawal of a candidate occurred before the time had come to hand in a list, states could either complete the list or submit a new one. However, if the withdrawal took place after that date—as happened in the French case—the state was only allowed to complete the list.[88] I wonder whether this is an elegant solution to the problem. In the past, serious efforts have been made to convince states not to rank candidates in such a way that the Parliamentary Assembly would be able to deduce a preference for one candidate over the two others. However, in a situation where *in extremis* a candidate is

---

[80] PACE (n 77) 4.

[81] PACE, Committee on Legal Affairs and Human rights, AS/Jur No 2011/02, 15 March 2011, 3.

[82] Johannès (n 76); Nicolas Hervieu, « Cour européenne des droits de l'homme: Conférence de haut niveau sur l'avenir de la Cour européenne des droits de l'homme et Déclaration d'Izmir » in Lettre « Actualités Droits-Libertés » du CREDOF, 1er mai 2011.

[83] Engel (n 39) 451.   [84] Ibid.

[85] PACE, Secretariat, Carnet de bord, 11 April 2011, online at <http://www.assembly.coe.int/committee/bur/2011/BUR005F.pdf>, last accessed 3 February 2014.

[86] PACE, Election of judges to the European Court of Human Rights, Doc 12616, 18 May 2011, 4.

[87] The results can be found in the following document: <http://www.assembly.coe.int/Sessions/2011/ElectionResultsECHRFranceJune2011final.pdf>, last accessed 3 February 2014.

[88] European Court of Human Rights (n 68), paras 55–6.

added to the list, it is clear to everyone that (s)he was either not among the best candidates in the eyes of the national selection panel, or the government, or both. In the case of France, Mr Valat obtained eight votes.[89]

4.3. United Kingdom

Let us then, finally, have a look at the UK election process for the latest appointment of a judge with respect to the UK.[90] When we try to reconstitute the election process, what is most striking is that the information provided by the UK authorities is very detailed, compared to the information given by the French and the Belgian governments. So we know, for instance, that, as in the two other cases, the election procedure began with a wide appeal that started with the publication of the call on 3 November 2011. The UK government explains that this call[91] was published on a 'wide range' of specialized websites, including one focused on female legal professionals, and in the *Times*. Furthermore, the call was published in regional newspapers in Scotland and Northern Ireland. Needless to say, this wide call can be seen as indicating a very smart and anticipative attitude: should no women eventually be classified on the list, the UK government would indeed be able, without any further problem, to refer to the exceptional circumstances clause justifying the introduction of a single-sex list. Wide calls are arguments that may convince the Sub-Committee of the Parliamentary Assembly to accept such a list.[92]

Next, a panel of specialists was entrusted with examination of the candidates. In the letter to the Parliamentary Assembly, it was stressed that there was a clear 'regional' mix, meaning that there were people from England and Wales, Scotland and Northern Ireland. However, although the letter does not mention the names of the panel members, only limiting itself to their function, it is not too difficult to figure out who was sitting in this panel. In a declassified letter from then Lord Chancellor and secretary of state for justice, Kenneth Clarke, it is explained that the panel was made up of five members. Chaired by Lord Mance, Justice of the Supreme Court, it also included Lord Reed, senator of the College of Justice; Professor Rooney, commissioner of the Northern Ireland Judicial Appointments Commission; Ian MacLeod, legal adviser to the Foreign and Commonwealth Office; and Rosemary Davies, legal adviser to the Ministry of Justice.[93]

The panel received 20 applications, of which it found 18 admissible. Ultimately, it selected the best six candidates for an interview. Interestingly enough—and we

---

[89] Madame Belliard obtained 42 votes and the elected judge 110.

[90] The following paragraphs summarize the accompanying letter, PACE, Election of judges to the European Court of Human Rights, Doc 12936, 22 May 2012, 125–6.

[91] The text of which can be found in the paper by Vaughne Miller, 'The European Court of Human Rights: The Election of Judges', 4 May 2011, 9. Online at: <www.parliament.uk/briefing-papers/sn05949.pdf>, last accessed 3 February 2014.

[92] Declaration of Belgian Minister of Justice (n 63) 19.

[93] Letter from K Clarke dated 8 November 2011 on the Election of United Kingdom Judge <http://www.parliament.uk>, last accessed 3 February 2014.

cannot praise this attitude sufficiently—the six candidates were asked to complete a French language test. Then, the interviews were conducted. We understand they consisted of three parts: a presentation, an analysis of a legal problem pertaining to the Convention, and finally some questions. The national selection panel then proposed three candidates to the British government, which accepted the list.[94] The advisory panel confirmed that all candidates were fit for the function. Finally, on 26 June 2012, Paul Mahoney was elected.

Compared to the French and Belgian procedures, it is remarkable how transparent the UK election procedure was. Although the same general framework has been applied in all the three cases (open call—national selection panel), the UK communicated in the most transparent and detailed way regarding how candidates were selected. Moreover, while in the French and Belgian cases governments still insisted on their 'autonomy' by granting themselves the possibility to select three candidates out of a short-list presented by the national selection panel, the UK government fully accepted the suggested list. No political manoeuvres took place at this stage. It is, therefore, unfair to call this procedure 'Byzantine', as even a well-respected English newspaper did.[95]

However, it would be wrong to claim that politics did not play any role in the election of the UK judge. Of course it did. The final election of Mr Mahoney could be seen, given his age, as rather surprising, notwithstanding his previous experience as (deputy) registrar of the Court and president of the European Union Civil Service Tribunal. In fact, for some Court watchers, Ben Emmerson was seen as the favoured candidate for the job.[96] However, according to the press, the British Conservatives campaigned against Mr Emmerson, because he was considered to be too left-wing;[97] moreover, Mr Emmerson had the 'problem' of having defended several terrorism suspects in his practice. The third candidate, Ms Agnello, was a practising lawyer specialized in insolvency and pensions law.

At this point, I do not believe it is very useful to engage in analysis of the possible lobbying activities that took place, if ever there was lobbying. It seems more important to stress that the UK respected the rules of the system.[98] Internally, it gave maximal powers to the national selecting body, thereby preferring merits over political considerations. Next, when the list had been approved and therefore the merits of the three candidates had been ascertained, arguments other than

[94] See also the letter of Kenneth Clarke to the Chair of the Joint Committee on Human Rights (29 February 2012), online at <http://www.parliament.uk>, last accessed 3 February 2014.

[95] Owen Bowcott, 'Paul Mahoney Appointed UK's New Judge in Strasbourg', *The Guardian*, 27 June 2012, online at <http://www.theguardian.com>, last accessed 3 February 2014.

[96] Joshua Rozenberg, 'Matrix Barrister is Clear Front-runner to be Next UK Judge in Strasbourg', *The Guardian*, 8 March 2012, online at <http://www.theguardian.com>, last accessed 3 February 2014; Jonathan Petre, 'QC who Defended Hate Preacher Abu Qatada is Favourite to be Britain's New Judge in Human Rights Court', *Daily Mail*, 23 June 2012, online at < http://www.dailymail.co.uk>, last accessed 3 February 2014; Hervieu (n 63).

[97] Joshua Rozenberg, 'Paul Mahoney: Politics Trumps Merit', *The Guardian*, 27 June 2012, online at <http://www.theguardian.com>, last accessed 3 February 2014.

[98] One can question, however, whether the age of the elected candidate respects at least the 'philosophy' of the recommendations made in the Explanatory Report to Protocol no 14. It was suggested that judges who cannot at least serve half of the term should not be elected.

strictly technocratic ones could be taken in consideration. The politicians in the Parliamentary Assembly are not limited to expressing their preferences on merely technocratic grounds, but they are allowed, should they wish so, to do what politicians often do: they follow the logic of politics, not necessarily that of technocracy. There is nothing wrong with this, all the more since the Convention disposes that the Parliamentary Assembly elects the judges.

5. Conclusion

When analysing the procedure of selecting judges for the ECtHR, it immediately becomes clear that two sets of values conflict. On the one hand, there is the problem of the relative autonomy of the stakeholders. As it stands, the election process involves both the Parliamentary Assembly and the high contracting parties. While the Parliamentary Assembly may try to 'objectivize' or 'depoliticize' the national procedures, it should respect the autonomy of the states. The ECtHR has stressed this in particularly clear terms.[99]

The second conflict of values is that between technocratic legitimacy and democratic legitimacy. The practice of the national selection panels has led to a selection process that is rather based on meritocracy. Unfit candidates should in principle be filtered out at this stage. The role of the Advisory Panel of experts and the sub-committee of the Parliamentary Assembly is, in this respect, to double-check. The French example shows that this can work. Undeniably, at the level of the Parliamentary Assembly, politics play a dominant role; however, since the improved quality check has already filtered out unfit candidates, political games should not have an impact on the quality of the judges to be elected.

Coming back to the small comparison of recent elections (France, Belgium, UK), we have to acknowledge four interesting phenomena. First, the number of candidates in Belgium was remarkable. In the Belgian case 13 candidates applied, whereas 20 candidates applied in France and the UK, albeit both have a considerably higher population (the ratio being almost 6.6).

Second, when it comes to the profiles of the candidates, it is striking that the Belgian candidates all came from the highest Courts. In France, this was only true for two of the three candidates. In the UK, only Mr Mahoney had judicial experience (on the European level). Given that the third candidate was a specialist in insolvency and pensions, we can conclude that the number of applicants with strong profiles for the office of judge in the ECtHR is lowest in the UK. High judges and important human rights scholars apparently did not apply for the job.

At this point, we can only guess why this is so. But a good explanation might be that the knowledge of foreign languages (English and French) is not an insurmountable problem in Belgium, whereas English may still be a problem

---

[99] European Court of Human Rights, *Advisory Opinion on Certain Legal Questions Concerning the Lists of Candidates Submitted with a View to the Election of Judges to the European Court of Human Rights no 2*, 22 January 2010, para 39.

for French candidates, as is French for UK candidates. Furthermore, there may be a link between the transparency of the selection process and reputational costs. The more the selection process is transparent (and objective), the more highly placed candidates may refrain from applying, in order to avoid reputational damage.

Third, as to the election process, it is good to see that all three states formally followed the underlying idea of the election process. The most transparent procedure was followed by the UK authorities, but France and Belgium certainly respected the requirements as well. Yet the degree of political influence on the selection procedure differs greatly. The most outspoken intervention took place in France. What happened was *in se* remarkable: the government overtly explained that it had added a candidate who had not been found fit and proper by the national selection body. It was therefore easy for the Council of Europe's institutions to detect the anomaly.

Finally, the underlying motives of national (ie governmental) conditioning of the election process seem to be different as well. In the Belgian case it could be argued, although it remains speculation, that the Belgian government—at least at the moment of the establishment of the first list—did not have an outspoken preference for one of the candidates, but rather preferred to have a career judge in Strasbourg, presumably because the government believed that career judges would err more on the side of restraint. At least, this can be assumed on the basis of the profile of the three candidates. On the contrary, the French case shows that the French government did not refrain from instrumentalization of the election process for purely internal reasons. The Brits left the real political choices to the Parliamentary Assembly, where political influence can play a role.

It is hard to assess this behaviour. There are of course good reasons to deplore the governmental pressure, the lobbying and such like. But once again, we may not forget that this is the direct result of the (s)election process established by the Convention, with its unique mix of meritocracy and democracy. Therefore, there are reasons to be hopeful. The national selection procedure is becoming growingly meritocratic (transparent, open, fair). Of course, governments sometimes try to bypass the recommendations and guidelines. Political parties can start lobbying in the Parliamentary Assembly as well, and this is, given the existing rules, perfectly acceptable. But, as Nicolas Hervieux suggests, one could also, in perhaps an overly optimistic interpretation of the facts, hold that all this shows that states care about who is elected in Strasbourg.[100] This, undeniably, is an illustration of respect for the Court. These days, that is not an unimportant message. Let it be encouraging for the Court.

There is an ultimate consideration. Both the members of the Parliamentary Assembly and the governments should realize that 'incidents' in the election

---

[100] Nicolas Hervieu, « Désignation de cinq nouveaux juges à la Cour européenne des droits de l'homme (et ses péripéties électorales) » in Lettre « Actualités Droits-Libertés » du CREDOF, 28 June 2012.

process may have repercussions, not only for the image of the Court, but also for the image of the individual judges who, as candidates, are involved in a procedure that they do not control. In the cases I analysed, there is no doubt that the elected judges are irreproachable personalities. It would be a pity for elections of such candidates to be marred by the slightest suspicion of nepotism, irregularities, and such like. The Court and the judges do not deserve that.

6

Selecting Strasbourg Judges

A Critique

David Kosař

1. Introduction

Since the major overhaul of the Strasbourg system of protection of human rights in 1998, thousands of articles have engaged with the case law of the European Court of Human Rights (hereinafter also the 'ECtHR' or just the 'Court') and explained its working.* In contrast, very little scholarly attention has been paid to the actual selection of Strasbourg judges.[1] This is surprising, since everybody knows that it matters who decides cases and, therefore, it matters who picks those people who will eventually decide cases. Moreover, several Strasbourg judges have been subject

* I am grateful to far too many colleagues to mention here (moreover, many of them were willing to discuss these issues only on the basis of confidentiality) for comments and discussions on earlier drafts of this chapter. Usual caveats apply. This chapter reflects the state of the art as of 31 December 2013.

[1] Most exceptions are relatively recent; see Jutta Limbach et al., *Judicial Independence: Law and Practice of Appointments to the European Court of Human Rights* (INTERIGHTS, 2003); JF Flauss, 'Les élections de juges à la Cour européenne des Droits de l'Homme (2005--2008)' (2008) 19 *Revue trimestrielle des droits de l'homme* 713; Andrew Drzemczewski, 'Election of judges to the Strasbourg Court: an overview' ([2010]) *E.H.R.L.R.* 377; Loukis G. Loucaides, 'Reflections of a Former European Court of Human Rights Judge on his Experiences as a Judge' [(2010)] *Roma Rights Journal* 61; Norbert P. Engel, 'More Transparency and Governmental Loyalty for Maintaining Professional Quality in the Election of Judges to the European Court of Human Rights' (2012) 32 *HRLJ* 448; Andrew Drzemczewski, 'L'élection du juge de l'Union européenne à la Cour européenne' (2013) 24 *Revue trimestrielle des droits de l'homme* 551; Başak Çali, Anne Koch, and Nicola Bruch, 'The Social Legitimacy of Human Rights Courts: A Grounded Interpretivist Theory of the Elite Accounts of the Legitimacy of the European Court of Human Rights' (2013) 35 *Hum. Rts. Q.* 955; Tom Zwart, 'More human rights than Court: Why the legitimacy of the EurCourtHR is in need of repair and how it can be done' in Spyridon Flogaitis, Tom Zwart, and Julie Fraser (eds), *The European Court of Human Rights and its Discontents* (Edward Elgar Publishing 2013) 71; and Yuval Shany, *Assessing the Effectiveness of International Courts* (Oxford University Press 2014). On the selection of international court judges in general, see in particular Ruth Mackenzie et al., *Selecting International Judges: Principle, Process, and Politics* (Oxford University Press 2010); Jiří Malenovský, 'L'indépendance des juges internationaux' in *Recueil des cours de l'Académie de droit* international *de la Haye* (Martinus Nijhoff 2011) 1; Daniel Terris, Cesare PR Romano, Leigh Swigart, *The International Judge: An Introduction to the Men and Women Who Decide the World's Cases* (Brandeis University Press 2007) chapter 2.

to criticism in the press, and rumours about how the lists of candidates are made at the national level and how the voting coalitions in the Parliamentary Assembly of the Council of Europe (hereinafter also the PACE) are built have spread across Europe for quite some time.

To be sure, the selection of the Strasbourg judges is a sensitive issue. In addition, it is a political process at both the national and PACE levels. This leads many stakeholders, especially in the PACE, to the view that the solution to the existing problems concerning the selection of Strasbourg judges is also political, by which they mean more PACE recommendations and intensive diplomatic negotiations. Conversely, these stakeholders argue that 'washing their dirty laundry' in public might be detrimental to the legitimacy of the ECtHR, which is particularly fragile these days. This chapter accepts the advantages of political solutions, but believes the problems that bedevil the selection of Strasbourg judges have reached such a pitch that political means alone cannot tackle them effectively and that brushing this issue under the carpet would probably engender resentment and suspicion, which would be much more detrimental in the long term. In other words, the aim of this chapter is to identify problematic issues in selecting Strasbourg judges so that they can be addressed, which in turn should make the ECtHR stronger.

The process of selection of Strasbourg judges is described by Koen Lemmens in Chapter 5 of this volume. This chapter highlights the problematic aspects of this process. It builds heavily on Lemmens' contribution as well as on a seminal article by Norbert Paul Engel, who openly addressed current problems regarding particular elections and particular judges.[2] However, this chapter also looks at the bigger picture. It discusses the recent report on the legitimacy of the ECtHR and, based on its findings, it argues that the inadequate qualifications, experience, and stature of some of the Strasbourg judges are a serious threat to the institutional legitimacy of the ECtHR. This combination of concrete examples and structural issues should provide a reasonably accurate picture of the current state of selection of Strasbourg judges.

Given their breadth, this chapter cannot deal with all problems plaguing the selection process. Nor does it address all selection criteria.[3] Several issues are deliberately omitted, including ad hoc judges,[4] impartiality, social security payable

---

[2] Engel (n 2). See also Flauss (n 2).

[3] For a concise summary of the selection criteria for selecting Strasbourg judges see Guidelines of the Committee of Ministers on the selection of candidates for the post of judge at the European Court of Human Rights, CM(2012)40 final, 29 March 2012 (hereinafter 'Guidelines of the Committee of Ministers'); Steering Committee for Human Rights, *Report of Ad Hoc Working Group on National Practices for the Selection of Candidates for the Post of Judge at the European Court of Human Rights*, CDDH-SC(2011)R1, Appendix III, 14 September 2011; Committee on Legal Affairs and Human Rights, *Procedure for electing judges to the European Court of Human Rights'*, AS/Jur/inf(2014)03, 7 January 2014; Andrew Drzemczewski, 'L'élection du juge de l'Union européenne à la Cour européenne des droits de l'homme', (2013) *Revue trimestrielle des droits de l'homme*, 551.

[4] The issue of ad hoc judges is very specific and, in my opinion, not capable of challenging the institutional legitimacy of the ECtHR.

to Strasbourg judges,[5] and diversity issues. Moreover, substantive criteria for Strasbourg office are prioritized over procedural issues, as the latter usually receive more attention and were sufficiently addressed in the previous chapter. Finally, the PACE part of the selection process is given greater emphasis than the national part.[6]

The structure of this chapter is as follows. Section 2 explains the breadth and depth of the problems concerning the selection of judges of the ECtHR. It highlights the importance of electing stellar judges to the Strasbourg bench for maintaining the legitimacy of the ECtHR. Section 3 briefly summarizes the good practices and recent improvements in the selection process. Section 4 focuses on problems regarding the use of certain substantive criteria. More specifically, it addresses the role of gender, the issue of the minimum and maximum ages of Strasbourg judges, their language skills, their knowledge of national law, and expertise in public international law. Section 5 then discusses recent examples of elections that raised eybrows across Europe and shows the politics behind them. Section 6 revisits the key question of how to attract top candidates to Strasbourg. Section 7 concludes.

2. Breadth and Depth of the Problem

Before this chapter zeroes in on the substantive issues in the selection of Strasbourg judges, it is necessary to understand the breadth and depth of the problem. It seems that many stakeholders, especially within Strasbourg circles, downplay the problem.[7] They either dismiss criticism of the selection process, qualification, and competence of judges as unsubstantiated or blame the signatory parties to the Convention.

For instance, Mr De Vries, the Chairperson of the Sub-Committee on the Election of Judges to the European Court of Human Rights, claims that 'if...the very best candidate is not always elected, it is too easy to blame the Assembly', as '[s]urely here, the principal responsibility rests in the hands of State Parties to ensure that all three candidates submitted are of the highest calibre'.[8] In other words, he suggests that the proverbial ball is in the signatory states' court.

Jean-Paul Costa, the former president of the ECtHR, also considers the logic of criticism concerning the Court's membership 'flawed',[9] because the older signatory states to the Convention had implicitly accepted the ratification of the Convention by 'new democracies' and because 'it is the sovereign states themselves who are responsible for putting forward candidates for the [Strasbourg] Court and it is the

---

[5] Even though this might have been a 'deal breaker' for some qualified candidates in the past; see s 6 below in this chapter.

[6] The national procedures concerning nomination of candidates for Strasbourg office vary from one State to another and over time. It is thus an impossible task for one researcher to understand all the nuances of this process in all 47 member states of the Council of Europe.

[7] See also Zwart (n 2) 76–77.   [8] Id. (both citations).

[9] Jean-Paul Costa, 'On the Legitimacy of the European Court of Human Rights' Judgments' (2011) 7 *EuConst*, 173, 176.

Parliamentary Assembly, made up of delegations from national parliaments, that elects them'.[10] He thus echoes De Vries' argument and likewise blames the states. Moreover, Costa implicitly suggests that 'problematic' candidates come only from Central and Eastern Europe, which is not true.[11]

Another line of defence of the Strasbourg Court is that 'a single judge does not have the power to hold that there has been a violation of the Convention'.[12] It is true that only a three-member panel, a chamber, or the Grand Chamber can do so. However, since the entry into force of Protocol no 14, single judges have filtered cases, and thus they may decide on the outcome of the application. Moreover, legitimacy is not only about outcomes.[13] Even if problematic judges cannot decide a case by themselves or change the outcome of the panel decision, the very fact that they are on the bench is a legitimacy problem. This is so because people in the Council of Europe Member States, or at least domestic elites, constantly compare the credentials of Strasbourg judges with those of judges of domestic apex courts.[14]

András Sajó, a current judge of the ECtHR, provides a more nuanced position and criticizes confusion of the problem of the ECtHR's independence within the Council of Europe with the problem of the ECtHR's 'staffing'.[15] He argues that 'there is little evidence that the quality of judges lies at the heart of the Court's current difficulties' and that '[t]here is no evidence in the scholarly literature of national bias in the Court's judgments... on the contrary, scholarly studies indicate the personal integrity of the judges'.[16] I agree with Sajó that the internal independence[17] of the ECtHR and its judges within the Council of Europe has

[10] Ibid, 176.
[11] As will be shown below in s 5, 'old' Council of Europe member states have also failed to nominate judges of the highest calibre and submitted lists containing candidates below the apex courts and sometimes even below the appellate courts. See also Engel (n 2) or the examples discussed in Chapter 5 of this volume, section 4.
[12] See eg Costa (n 10) 176.
[13] On the distinction between outcome legitimacy and process legitimacy concerns see eg Shany (n 2) 264–7.
[14] See Çali, Koch, and Bruch (n 2), discussed in further detail below.
[15] András Sajó, 'An All-European Conversation: Promoting a Common Understanding of European Human Rights', in Spyridon Flogaitis, Tom Zwart, and Julie Fraser (eds), *The European Court of Human Rights and its Discontents* (Edward Elgar Publishing 2013) 188.
[16] Sajó (n 16) 189. For the actual numbers see eg Martin Kuijer, 'Voting Behaviour and National Bias in the European Court of Human Rights and the International Court of Justice' (1997) 10 *LJIL* 49; Erik Voeten, 'The Impartiality of International Judges: Evidence from the European Court of Human Rights' (2008) 102 *American Political Science Review* 417; or most recently, Erik Voeten, 'Politics, Judicial Behaviour, and Institutional Design' in Jonas Christoffersen and Mikael Rask Madsen (eds), *The European Court of Human Rights between Law and Politics* (Oxford University Press 2011) 61 and ff. Note that Voeten has argued in the above-mentioned articles that there *is* some national bias among Strasbourg judges, but given the large size of panels at the ECtHR, it has a minuscule impact on the outcome of the ECtHR's judgments.
[17] Internal independence means independence within the Council of Europe at large and within the ECtHR itself (that is vis-à-vis the court president and his 'Bureau', the section presidents, and the Registry). In contrast, external independence means independence from actors outside the Council of Europe. For a standard distinction between the internal and external independence of judges see Peter Russell and David O'Brien (eds), *Judicial Independence in the Age of Democracy: Critical Perspectives from around the World* (University Press of Virginia 2001) 11–13. On the related interplay between internal and external judicial accountability see David Kosař, 'The Least Accountable Branch (Review Essay)' (2013) 11 *Int'l J of Const Law* 234, 244–5.

been neglected[18] and that the issue of the independence of Strasbourg judges should not be reduced to the problem of proper 'staffing'. However, the competence[19] of Strasbourg judges actually lies at the heart of the Court's current difficulties and, in fact, presents the major legitimacy challenge for the ECtHR.[20]

For instance, the retired ECtHR judge Loukis Loucaides put it bluntly: 'Lawyers who had no training or even a background acquaintance with human rights and/ or did not have essential or adequate knowledge of one, and on some occasions of both, official working languages of the Court, namely English and French, became members of the Court with self-evident negative consequences.'[21] He concluded that 'the procedure of selecting and appointing judges was quite defective'.[22] Other authors concur:[23] Leif Sevón, former president of the Supreme Court of Finland and former member of the Court of Justice of the European Union, stated that '[a]lthough a number of bodies in the Council of Europe would appear to scrutinize the nominations, there is in practice little meaningful review',[24] and the late Jean-François Flauss identified the key problems plaguing the selection of Strasbourg judges as early as 2008.[25] Norbert Engel assumed Flauss's mantle and updated the list of current problems in his seminal article in 2012.[26] More recently, Andreas Follesdal and Yuval Shany echoed this criticism of the qualifications and experience of Strasbourg judges.[27]

If anything, it is the recent work of Başak Çali, Ana Koch, and Nicola Bruch on the ECtHR's legitimacy[28] that should ring a bell in relevant circles, because it empirically confirms this dissatisfaction regarding the competence of Strasbourg judges. Their study on the Court's legitimacy (hereinafter the '2011 Legitimacy Report') is the most rigorous research on this topic to date.[29] It was based on in-depth interviews with 107 domestic politicians, judges, and human rights lawyers carried out in Turkey, Bulgaria, the United Kingdom, the Republic of Ireland, and Germany between 2008 and 2010. Their central argument is that the social

---

[18] See also Loucaides (n 2). In fact, most PACE documents emphasize only external independence (the latest example being Committee on Legal Affairs and Human Rights, *Need to Reinforce the Independence of the European Court of Human Rights*, AS/Jur (2013) 34, 12 November 2013) and leave internal independence untouched.

[19] The notion of 'competence' is understood broadly here so as to encompass not only Strasbourg judges' knowledge of human rights law, but also their qualification, experience, stature, and language skills.

[20] See Çali, Koch, and Bruch (n 2); Zwart (n 2).   [21] Loucaides (n 2).   [22] Ibid.

[23] For early criticism see Limbach (n 2). See also Mackenzie (n 2) 156–7.

[24] Leif Sevón, 'The Procedure for Selection of Members of the Civil Service Tribunal: A Pioneer Experience', accessible online at <http://curia.europa.eu>, 3.

[25] Flauss (n 2).

[26] See Engel (n 2); Norbert Paul Engel, 'Mehr Tansparenz für die Wahrung professionneller Qualität bei den Richter-Wahlen zum EGMR' (2012) *EuGRZ* 486.

[27] Andreas Follesdal, Johan K Schaffer, and Geir Ulfstein (eds), *The Legitimacy of International Human Rights Regimes* (Cambridge University Press 2013) 287; see also Andreas Follesdal, 'The Legitimacy of International Human Rights Review: The Case of the European Court of Human Rights' (2009) 40 *Journal of Social Philosophy* 595, 605; Shany (n 2) 267.

[28] See Başak Çali, Anne Koch, and Nicola Bruch, 'The Legitimacy of the European Court of Human Rights: The View from the Ground' (2011); Çali, Koch, and Bruch (n 2).

[29] Çali, Koch, and Bruch (n 29).

Table 6.1 Ranking: Performance Dimension, cited from the 2011 Legitimacy Report, p. 13[1]

Normative		Managerial	
Standard	%	*Standard*	%
Transformative quality	44	Length of proceedings	43
Intervention	44	Judges: qualification, experience	26
Balance between law and politics	40	Knowledge of domestic fact/law	20
Living instrument	21	Enforcement	18
Effective HR protection	19	Case law coherence	16
		Judicial independence	16
		Admissibility procedure	12
		Reasoning of a judgment	6
		Judges: selection transparency	6
		Hearing procedure	4

[1] All emphases added; footnotes in the original table are omitted since they concerned only the normative part of the performance dimension.

legitimacy of the ECtHR is built on constant comparison between the purposes and performance of domestic institutions and the purposes and performance of the ECtHR.[30] They include the quality of judges among the criteria of the performance dimension of the ECtHR's legitimacy, and their conclusions are worrying. They argue that 'concerns about the quality of the [Strasbourg] judges…are not only routine criticism but signal legitimacy erosion and inform deeper trends that undermine respect for the institution'.[31]

The 2011 Legitimacy Report, which Çali et al build their theory on, offers additional insights regarding the perception of the quality of Strasbourg judges. First of all, judges' experience and qualification is the second most widely emphasized legitimacy standard in the 'managerial' part of the performance dimension, lagging only behind the well-known problem of the length of proceedings before the ECtHR (see Table 6.1). Interestingly, interviewees found judges' experience and qualifications more important than their independence, and significantly more important than the transparency of their selection. Of all the interviewees, 26 per cent included the experience and qualifications of Strasbourg judges in their accounts, while only 16 per cent mentioned judicial independence and a mere 6 per cent cited transparency of selection of Strasbourg judges (see Table 6.1). This is the reverse order from that which recent PACE documents, which focus primarily on transparent selection and judicial independence, would suggest.

Second, interviews reinforced the view that the quality of judges needed rethinking and improvement.[32] A closer look at the 2011 Legitimacy Report reveals that

---

[30] Çali, Koch, and Bruch (n 2).   [31] Ibid, 981.
[32] Çali, Koch, and Bruch (n 2) 967–8.

assessment of the qualifications and experience of Strasbourg judges was far from positive: on the contrary, of 26 assessments, 16 were negative. This amounts to 62 per cent of interviewees who mentioned judges' qualifications and experience as a legitimacy concern, and 15 per cent of all interviewees.[33] This in itself should be taken seriously. However, things get worse.

Third, perception of the qualifications and experience of the ECtHR's judges is particularly low in the eyes of domestic judges. Judges interviewed were not only more concerned with the qualifications and experience of the Strasbourg Court's judges than other professional groups (40 per cent as opposed to an average of 26 per cent),[34] but also came to a more critical assessment (eight negative, three positive).[35] In other words, the majority of domestic judges who mentioned the quality of Strasbourg judges as a legitimacy factor viewed it negatively. Although this sample of domestic judges is not representative and any overgeneralization should be avoided,[36] this erosion of support among the key allies of the Strasbourg Court should be taken very seriously.

Fourth, given the choice of countries covered by Çali et al, one would expect the UK respondents to be the most critical of Strasbourg judges. However, the actual results were different. The UK interviewees were split regarding the assessment of the qualifications and experience of the Strasbourg Court's judges. Out of eight assessments, four were positive and four negative.[37] Only the Bulgarian respondents, where the quality of the Strasbourg judges is not a significant concern due to the low trust in domestic decision-making, were more positive.[38] In contrast, all the comments of Turkish interviewees on the legitimacy concerns connected with the independence, experience, and selection of judges were negative.[39] Similarly, the quality of the Strasbourg judges was a concern that figured in German interviews.[40] All assessments of the experience and qualifications of Strasbourg judges by German respondents were negative.[41] Irish interviewees also questioned the quality of the Strasbourg judges, as four out of six assessments of judicial qualification and experience were negative.[42]

The key message of this cross-country comparison is that the qualifications and experience of Strasbourg judges have not just been questioned in the United Kingdom: interviewees from all countries covered by Çali's study, apart from Bulgaria, were very critical, and dissatisfaction with the quality of Strasbourg judges is thus more widespread than expected.

---

[33] Çali, Koch, and Bruch (n 29) 17.

[34] Ibid, 19. See also Çali, Koch, and Bruch (n 2) 972.

[35] Çali, Koch, and Bruch (n 29) 19. See also table 'Emphasis on Performance Standards, By Profession' in ibid at 23.

[36] Domestic judges might feel particularly threatened or alienated by activities and competencies of the Strasbourg Court. See also Çali, Koch, and Bruch (n 29) 20.

[37] Çali, Koch, and Bruch (n 29). However, the negative assessments were very harsh; see Çali, Koch, and Bruch (n 2) 970.

[38] Çali, Koch, and Bruch (n 2) 979.   [39] Çali, Koch, and Bruch (n 29) 25.

[40] Çali, Koch, and Bruch (n 2) 971.   [41] Çali, Koch, and Bruch (n 29) 29.

[42] Ibid, 28. See also Çali, Koch, and Bruch (n 2) 971.

In sum, there is a growing consensus that how judges are selected has an impact on the ECtHR's legitimacy.[43] Çali's findings show how widespread and deep the negative perception of the quality of Strasbourg judges is.[44] The criticism raised by other authors confirms the depth and breadth of the problems concerning the selection of Strasbourg judges.[45] The current situation might have become worse than Çali's findings suggest. It is important to take into account the fact that interviews were conducted between 2008 and 2010, before several recent controversies broke concerning the selection of Strasbourg judges,[46] and before the problems concerning the selection of judges became a salient issue in academic literature. The increased turnover of Strasbourg judges after the entry into force of Protocol no 14, which introduced the non-renewable term, further exacerbated these problems. There were times when judges sat in Strasbourg for almost two decades. Now each state has to find three stellar candidates every nine years.[47] All of these arguments call for greater attention to be paid to selecting judges for the ECtHR.

3. The Good

Even though this chapter focuses on problematic aspects of the selection of judges of the ECtHR, it is important to emphasize that, in general, huge progress has been made in improving the process in the last two decades.[48] The Convention itself was amended several times to make this happen. Most importantly, Protocol no 14 introduced a non-renewable term for Strasbourg judges,[49] which eliminated judges' incentives to please their governments in order to secure their renomination.[50] The back-and-forth changes in the upper age limit require a more nuanced assessment,[51] but the new rule introduced by Protocol no 15 may indeed broaden the pool of competent candidates.

---

[43] See Brighton Declaration, para 21; Committee on Legal Affairs and Human Rights, *Nomination of Candidates and Election of Judges in the European Court of Human Rights*, 1 December 2008, Doc 11767, Part B (Explanatory memorandum), para 3; Follesdal (n 28) 601; Mackenzie (n 2) 25 and 177; Shany (n 2) 136–58; Kanstantsin Dzehtsiarou and DK Coffey, 'Legitimacy and Independence of International Tribunals: An Analysis of the European Court of Human Rights' (2014) 37 *Hastings Int'l & Comp L Rev* 271.

[44] Of course, this study must be interpreted with caution. There is no longitudinal study on the legitimacy of the ECtHR and thus we do not know whether the Strasbourg Court was perceived as more legitimate 10 or 20 years ago. Maybe the Court remained the same, but the expectations have changed.

[45] See notes 2 and 24–8 above. [46] See s 4 below, and Engel (n 2).

[47] As will be shown below in s 6 of this chapter, this may prove difficult, especially in small states.

[48] For a succinct summary of these developments see above ch 5, s 2 and 3; see also Committee on Legal Affairs and Human Rights, *Procedure for Electing Judges to the European Court of Human Rights*, As/Jur/Inf (2011) 02 rev 3, 28 June 2011, paras 5–11.

[49] See Art 23(1) ECHR.

[50] But, as will be shown below, it created a new problem, as Strasbourg judges had to seek new jobs after the end of their term, which increased the likelihood that they might try to please their governments. This problem is further exacerbated by the election of young judges to the ECtHR.

[51] The issue of the age requirements is discussed thoroughly below in s 4.3.

PACE and the Committee of Ministers have been particularly active in improving the national part of the selection process. Guided by the principles of transparency, equality, and non-discrimination, they nudged states towards open and fair competition at the national level.[52] They created standardized curricula vitae for candidates seeking election to the ECtHR and required governments to submit their lists of three candidates in alphabetical order,[53] both of which reforms stopped governments clearly prioritizing one candidate[54] and ensured that PACE could make an informed choice.

Positive developments took place also in the Council of Europe's part of the selection process. PACE's Sub-Committee on the Election of Judges to the European Court of Human Rights became a permanent Sub-Committee in 2007,[55] which increased its status within PACE and signalled the growing importance of getting the selection process right. Three years later, the Committee of Ministers introduced an Advisory Panel of Experts on Candidates for Election as Judge to the European Court of Human Rights,[56] which was supposed to add a long-awaited expert element to the selection process.[57]

Finally, all stakeholders devoted resources and time to fine-tuning non-binding substantive criteria. Both PACE and the Committee of Ministers have: steadily raised the standards regarding language skills; fought gender inequality; discussed and eventually approved the pension scheme for Strasbourg judges, the lack of which might have deterred some applicants in the past; tackled the issue of reintegration of Strasbourg judges after the end of their term; and developed additional criteria such as the knowledge of domestic law and public international law.

This is a long list of accomplishments. So what is wrong with the selection of Strasbourg judges? The simple answer is that the current system does not work properly. As will be shown in Sections 5 and 6, it is not able to 'deliver the goods', that is to 'produce' stellar judges, on a consistent basis.[58] The immediate follow-up question is: how is that possible? A response to that question is far more complex—sometimes the criteria themselves are sub-optimal,[59] sometimes

---

[52] See PACE, Recommendation 1649 (2004), 30 January 2004; Committee on Legal Affairs and Human Rights, *Nomination of Candidates and Election of Judges in the European Court of Human Rights*, 1 December 2008, Doc 11767, Part A, para 1 and Part B (Explanatory memorandum), paras 14–22; Committee on Legal Affairs and Human Rights, *National Procedures for the Selection of Candidates for the European Court of Human Rights*, 7 October 2010, Doc 12391 (2010); and Guidelines of the Committee of Ministers (n 4), parts III–V.

[53] See PACE, Resolution 1646 (2009), para 4.3. See also PACE, Recommendation 1429 (1999), 23 September 1999; PACE, Recommendation 1649 (2004), 30 January 2004; Appendix to Resolution 1432 (2005); and Committee on Legal Affairs and Human Rights (n 53), Part B, paras 27–8.

[54] For specific examples of expressions of governmental preference see this volume, ch 5 s 4.

[55] See footnote to Rule 48.6 in the Rules of Procedure of the Assembly, Strasbourg 2008, p 72, and document AS/Jur/Cdh (2008) 05.

[56] See Committee of Ministers, Resolution (2010) 26, 10 November 2010. For a history of the proposal to create such panel see Committee on Legal Affairs and Human Rights (n 53).

[57] On how the Advisory Panel met the expectations see ch 5 s 3.3.

[58] See eg above ch 5; Limbach (n 2), Flauss (n 2), Engel (n 2), Loucaides (n 2), Malenovský (n 2), or Sevón (n 25) 3.

[59] This is the case of a current *maximum* age limit of Strasbourg judges that fails to take into account corresponding age limits of domestic judges—see further below, s 4.3 of this chapter.

the problem lies in the under-enforcement of the existing criteria,[60] sometimes the necessary criterion does not exist at all,[61] and sometimes too many criteria are combined that might dissuade top candidates. To get a more nuanced picture, the next section will address five key substantive criteria for Strasbourg office, point out the current deficiencies, and suggest what can be done to remedy them.

4. The Bad

This Section examines in depth five non-binding[62] substantive criteria for the office of a judge of the ECtHR: gender, language skills, age, knowledge of domestic law, and expertise in general international law. These five criteria are mentioned in almost every PACE document and in the Committee of Ministers' Guidelines, and thus form the core of the non-binding requirements for candidates for Strasbourg judicial office.[63] The order of these criteria does not indicate their relative importance, but rather the attention paid to them. For that reason, this section starts with the gender issue, which resulted in two advisory opinions of the ECtHR, followed by language skills and age requirements, both of which have been discussed widely in numerous PACE documents, and concludes with knowledge of domestic law and expertise in general international law, which have been less salient issues so far.

4.1. Gender

Gender has been the most widely discussed substantive non-binding criterion for selecting Strasbourg judges. PACE adopted several resolutions touching upon the gender issue,[64] the ECtHR's first advisory opinion dealt with the gender balance of the lists of candidates nominated by the states,[65] and scholars have paid significant attention to this issue.[66] One might thus think that this issue is settled. However,

---

[60] Under-enforcement plagues the evaluation of judges' language skills.

[61] A typical example of this type of problem is the lack of a *minimum* age limit; see below in s 4.3.

[62] Some commentators consider one or more of these criteria as 'implicit' requirements set by the Convention, and thus treat them as binding. However, I believe that it is more accurate to treat them as non-binding criteria.

[63] Of course, other criteria are also plausible. For instance, the Advisory Panel seems to prefer the criteria of the so-called 'Article 255 Panel' envisaged by the Treaty on the Functioning of the European Union; see Steering Committee for Human Rights, *CDDH report on the review of the functioning of the Advisory Panel of experts on candidates for election as judge to the European Court of Human Rights*, CDDH(2013)R 79 Addendum II, 29 November 2013, para 19.

[64] See in particular PACE, Resolution 1366 (2004); PACE, Resolution 1426 (2005); and PACE, Resolution 1627 (2008).

[65] See ECtHR, *Advisory Opinion on Certain Legal Questions Concerning the Lists of Candidates Submitted with a View to the Election of Judges to the European Court of Human Rights*, 12 February 2008.

[66] Virtually every law review article touching upon the selection of Strasbourg judges addresses the gender issue. On the role of gender in the selection of international judges in general see Mackenzie (n 2), 47–9.

despite some progress,[67] there is still room for improvement. A typical example is the Belgian 'male only' list submitted in April 2012.[68]

In order to understand the current problems with gender balance on the Strasbourg bench, it is important briefly to address the development of the position of PACE. In fact, the source of the problems that bedevil the national nominations is the fact that PACE went from one extreme to another on the gender issue, and then did not strictly follow the rules it itself set. This created a sense among the states that they did not have to take the gender criterion seriously.

How did the rules change from one extreme to another? Until the 1990s, there was little emphasis on the gender balance of the Strasbourg Court and no criteria for gender-balanced nomination lists existed. However, after the turn of the century PACE started to attach greater importance to the gender balance of the ECtHR and developed criteria in order to ensure that lists contained candidates of the sex that was under-represented in the ECtHR.[69] In 2004, PACE adopted Resolution 1366 (2004) and Recommendation 1649 (2004), which stressed the need for gender balance in the Strasbourg Court. A year later, it amended Resolution 1366 (2004) by Resolution 1426 (2005), under which single-sex lists of candidates could be considered by PACE only if people of that sex were under-represented in the Court.[70] Resolution 1426 (2005) defined the threshold for under-representation as under 40 per cent of judges. Given the composition of the ECtHR at that time, this rule meant that no 'male only' lists were acceptable under any circumstances.

The new strict standard (hereinafter 'the general rule on gender') immediately caused problems. Several states, especially smaller ones which had a limited number of women candidates with credentials equivalent to those of male candidates,[71] argued that they were not able to produce a gender-balanced list without compromising the other selection criteria. As a result of these developments, in 2007 the Committee on Legal Affairs and Human Rights prepared a draft resolution[72] amending paragraph 3.ii of Resolution 1366 (2004), as amended by Resolution 1426 (2005), which would enable the existing general rule on gender to be waived

---

[67] In 2008, the number of women rose to 17 out of 47 judges. On further development see also Engel (n 2) 452–3.

[68] For further details of the selection of a Belgian judge of the ECtHR in 2012 see above, ch 5 s 4.1.

[69] See Committee on Legal Affairs and Human Rights (n 53), Part B, para 26. The reasons behind the lack of women with equivalent credentials are beyond the scope of this chapter. However, it is a well-known fact that in many European states women are still severely under-represented at apex courts as well as in academia. For an excellent overview of the politics behind establishing a new rule of gender balance for the ECtHR, see Stéphanie Hennette-Vauchez, 'More Women—But which Women? The Rule and Politics of Gender Balance at the European Court of Human Rights' (forthcoming in *European Journal of International Law* in 2015).

[70] Article 3.ii of PACE, Resolution 1366 (2004), as modified by PACE, Resolution 1426 (2005).

[71] This, of course, does not mean that the PACE members changed their views within one year. In fact, the people inside the PACE who pushed the gender equality agenda were mobilized for much longer and the topic was already a serious topic of concern by the late 1990s. For further details, see Hennette-Vauchez (n 70).

[72] Committee on Legal Affairs and Human Rights, *Candidates for the European Court of Human Rights*, 19 March 2007, Doc 11208.

in exceptional circumstances. However, this draft resolution was rejected by PACE and the matter eventually ended up before the ECtHR itself. In the key dicta of the 2008 Advisory Opinion, the ECtHR held that

in not allowing any exceptions to the rule that under-represented sex must be represented, the current practice of the Parliamentary Assembly is not compatible with the Convention: where a Contracting Party has taken all the necessary and appropriate steps with a view to ensuring that the list contains a candidate of the under-represented sex, but without success, and especially where it has followed the Assembly's recommendations advocating an open and transparent procedure involving a call for candidatures…, the Assembly may not reject the list in question on the sole ground that no such candidate features on it… exceptions to the principle that lists must contain a candidate of the under-represented sex should be defined as soon as possible.[73]

Following two controversial debates, PACE eventually adopted Resolution 1627 (2008), which allows for exceptions to the general rule on gender, but only when a state demonstrates that it has tried and failed to find a qualified candidate from the under-represented sex. The exception to the general rule on gender reads as follows:

The Assembly decides to consider single-sex lists of candidates of the sex that is over-represented in the Court in exceptional circumstances where a Contracting Party has taken all the necessary and appropriate steps to ensure that the list contains a candidate of the under-represented sex, but has not been able to find a candidate of that sex who satisfies the requirements of Article 21 § 1 of the European Convention on Human Rights.[74]

The report of the Committee on Legal Affairs and Human Rights makes it clear that such exception should be allowed only in 'truly exceptional circumstances'.[75] The states must have taken 'all the necessary and appropriate steps to ensure that the list contains a candidate of the under-represented sex',[76] but 'without success because of the requirement to satisfy the other criteria',[77] and the burden of proof lies exclusively with the state concerned.[78] These stringent criteria for the exception to the general rule on gender were reiterated in the Guidelines of the Committee of Ministers.[79]

The new moderate rule on gender—that is, the general rule with strictly interpreted exceptions—seems to strike a good balance between the need to ensure gender equality on the Strasbourg bench and other criteria for the office. In fact, the risk of compromising the other selection criteria for the sake of submitting a gender-balanced list could easily backfire against the very policy of positive

---

[73] ECtHR, the 2008 Advisory Opinion (n 66), § 54.

[74] PACE, Resolution 1627 (2008), para 4. The second part of this paragraph that stipulates the quorum for accepting such lists is omitted.

[75] Committee on Legal Affairs and Human Rights, *Candidates for the European Court of Human Rights*, 4 July 2008, Doc 11682, para 23.

[76] Ibid, para 24 (emphasis in the original).   [77] Ibid, para 23 (emphasis added).

[78] Ibid, para 24.   [79] Guidelines of the Committee of Ministers (n 4), para II.8.

discrimination of women candidates and eventually undermine the stature and legitimacy of the ECtHR.[80]

Unfortunately, PACE relaxed the criteria for exceptions to the general rule on gender too far. The 2012 Belgian 'male only' list is a prime example. Belgium is not a small country such as Malta. Nor it is a post-communist country with a limited number of qualified women candidates due to a language barrier, social stereotypes, and average legal education. On the contrary, Belgium hosts some of the finest law schools in Europe, most of which have several stellar female professors in their faculties; it is bilingual; and Belgian female judges have been active in various international professional associations of judges. It is thus very implausible that the Belgian government took all the necessary and appropriate steps to ensure that its list contained a candidate of the under-represented sex, and there is no sign that it was asked by PACE to prove it.[81] To be sure, the chapter by Koen Lemmens shows that gender is just one legitimate criterion in Belgium and the Belgian government had to weigh it against other concerns, but this cannot in itself serve as an excuse for submitting a list featuring no women:[82] other governments are in a similar situation and since 2004 all of them, with the exception of the Maltese (in 2004 and 2006), Slovak (in 2004), and Moldovan governments (in 2012) managed to produce a list featuring at least one woman.

This by no means suggests that the candidate who was eventually elected the ECtHR judge on behalf of Belgium was a bad or illegitimate choice. The problem does not lie with the successful candidate, who was a stellar nominee, but exclusively with the PACE. By departing from its own standards on gender in the Belgian case, PACE sent an implicit message to other states that they might submit male-only lists without detailed justification and might still get them through. Even more importantly, one of the cornerstones of the rule of law is the principle that the very body, be it a king, the parliament, or the executive, that issues the rule is itself bound by it.[83] Given the fact that the *raison d'être* of the Council of Europe

---

[80] The other option to ensure a gender-balanced list in countries with a limited number of stellar female candidates—to place women of foreign nationality on the list—was ruled out by the ECtHR as incompatible with the ECHR; see ECtHR, the 2008 Advisory Opinion (n 66), § 52.

[81] The explanation of the 'male only' list provided in this volume, ch 5, s 4.1 is persuasive, but I still respectfully disagree. If we accept that the state may submit a 'male only' list to replace a sitting female judge or that gender is just one criterion among many in compiling the list, then we are not talking about 'truly exceptional circumstances'. See also the Slovak all-male list rejected by PACE in 2004, Malta's all-male lists rejected by PACE in 2004 and 2006, and the Moldovan all-male list presented to PACE in 2012. For further details, see Hennette-Vauchez (n 70).

[82] For instance, at first sight it seems laudable and neutral that the Belgian government preferred candidates with judicial experience at a top national court. But when one takes into account the fact that women are severely under-represented at apex courts in most 'old' EU Member States, this criterion indirectly prioritizes male candidates (note that in 2012 only one out of 12 judges on the Belgian Constitutional Court was female). The Strasbourg selection process thus reveals a deeper problem in striving for a gender balance on the bench. See also n 70.

[83] For a standard account of this principle see FA Hayek, *The Road to Serfdom* (London 1944) 54: '[the rule of law] means that government in all its actions is bound by rules fixed and announced beforehand—rules which make it possible to foresee with fair certainty how the authority will use its coercive powers in given circumstances and to plan one's individual affairs on the basis of this knowledge.'

is to promote the rule of law, PACE should be particularly vigilant in adhering to this principle.

4.2. Language skills

Language skills have always been considered one of the most important non-binding substantive criteria for Strasbourg judges. Several PACE documents even suggest that language skills rank at the very top of the hierarchy among the criteria for Strasbourg office.[84] This is not surprising, since sufficient language skills are vital in an international court for judges to participate effectively in discussions and reading documents.[85] There seems to be a consensus that a lack of sufficient language skills on the part of a Strasbourg judge hampers effective communication with her colleagues as well as with the Registry, prevents her from working as a judge rapporteur and reviewing the validity of translated versions of judgments in the second official language, impairs the functioning of the ECtHR as a whole, and undermines the ECtHR's credibility.[86] In addition, judges' inadequate language skills empower the Registry,[87] as such judges cannot meaningfully fight back if they disagree with the Registry's lawyers who draft most decisions.

But despite the strong emphasis on this criterion, knowledge of the two official languages of the Council of Europe (English and French) among nominees is still a huge problem. For instance, Ruth Mackenzie et al suggested that 'the language skills of the [Strasbourg] judges have become a particularly problematic and controversial issue'[88] and argued that the PACE introduced more stringent language standards '[i]n response to concerns that some recently appointed judges have not had adequate command of both French and English (and in some cases neither)'.[89] Loukis Loucaides,[90] a former Strasbourg judge, and Norbert Engel[91] confirmed these allegations.

---

[84] See eg Committee on Legal Affairs and Human Rights, *Candidates for the European Court of Human Rights* (n 76), para 26: 'There is a clear hierarchy among the various criteria for office'; Committee on Legal Affairs and Human Rights (n 53), Part B, para 24: '... language abilities must be considered among the most important criteria for office' (see also para 41 in ibid).

[85] Brandeis Institute for International Judges, *International Justice: Past, Present and Future* (Brandeis University, 2009), available at <https://www.brandeis.edu/ethics/pdfs/internationaljustice/biij/BIIJ2009.pdf>, 25.

[86] See ibid and Steering Committee for Human Rights, *Report of Ad Hoc Working Group on National Practices for the Selection of Candidates for the Post of Judge at the European Court of Human Rights*, CDDH-SC(2011)R1, 14 September 2011, para 6.

[87] See Paul L McKaskle, 'The European Court of Human Rights: What It Is, How It Works, and Its Future' (2005) 40 *USF L Rev* 1, 28 (raising the problem of registrars' power due to the language deficiencies of judges). The significant powers of the Registry, not envisaged by the ECHR, have recently been subject to strong criticism: see Loucaides (n 2) or McKaskle's article mentioned above in this note, at 26–31. Recent PACE documents have also started addressing the issue (albeit only regarding lawyers seconded to the Registry); see eg Committee on Legal Affairs and Human Rights (n 19), para 33. On the role of the registries and legal secretariats in international courts in general see Stéphanie Cartier and Cristina Hoss, 'The Role of Registries and Legal Secretariats in International Judicial Institutions' in Cesare Romano, Karen Alter, and Yuval Shany (eds), *Oxford Handbook of International Adjudication* (Oxford University Press 2013) 711–36.

[88] Mackenzie (n 2) 170.   [89] Ibid.   [90] See n 22 above.

[91] See Engel (n 2) 452.

In response to these concerns, the PACE has paid significant attention to this problem. In order to understand these developments, where they have succeeded, and where they are still failing, it is important to remember that the requirement of language skills in fact consists of two key issues that are interrelated but separate: (1) language proficiency; and (2) bilingualism (knowledge of both official languages of the Council of Europe).[92] While this chapter acknowledges that both of these aspects are important, it contends that there is a hierarchy among them[93] and that proficiency in judges' 'first language'[94] is more vital for the ECtHR's functioning and legitimacy than bilingualism.[95] For that reason, the issue of language proficiency will be addressed first.

In general, standards regarding proficiency in judges' first language have risen steadily, but perhaps too slowly. As of 2004, it was still enough for candidates to have a 'sufficient knowledge' of at least one of the two official languages.[96] In other words, candidates who had a sufficient knowledge of the first official language and no knowledge of the second were still eligible. This was a rather low standard, as

the requirement that a judge have 'sufficient' knowledge of one language could mean, in practice, that his or her level of proficiency may be below the standard that is necessary in order to be aware of linguistic subtleties and nuances necessary for an understanding of a complex case and which are clearly inherent in legal drafting and arguments.[97]

It was only in 2009 that PACE required candidates to possess an 'active knowledge' of the first language.[98] Finally, the Committee of Ministers increased the first language standard in the 2012 Guidelines that stipulate that '[c]andidates must, as an absolute minimum, be *proficient* in one official language of the Council of Europe'.[99]

The current proficiency standard thus seems to be fine and on a par with standards applicable to other international courts.[100] However, this standard must also

---

[92] There are of course other factors as well. For instance, several PACE documents suggest that knowledge of other languages is also an asset: 'knowledge of other European languages frequently used in the correspondence with the Court by applicants from different countries (such as Russian or German) should also be taken into account in assessing a candidate's language abilities' (Committee on Legal Affairs and Human Rights, n 53, Part B, para 24).

[93] Of course, in the ideal scenario, all nominees (or at least elected judges) should be proficient in both English and French. However, this is not always possible in the real world. Some states, especially small countries, can hardly produce a list with three nominees who are fluent in both.

[94] By 'first language' I mean the one of the two official languages which a given candidate is more proficient in.

[95] Some interviewees with whom I discussed a draft of this chapter went further and suggested that knowledge of the 'second language' is even less important than generally thought, because deliberations are always interpreted into the other official language and each judge of the ECtHR who acts as a judge rapporteur can tell lawyers in the Registry to draft a decision in his 'first language'. I tend to disagree, as textual nuances matter in legal reasoning, and thus all Strasbourg judges should have at least passive knowledge of the 'second language'.

[96] PACE, Recommendation 1649 (2004), 30 January 2004.

[97] Committee on Legal Affairs and Human Rights (n 53), Part B, para 11.

[98] PACE, Resolution 1646 (2009), para 4.4.

[99] Guidelines of the Committee of Ministers (n 4), para II.3 (emphasis added).

[100] See eg Art 36(3)(c) of the Rome Statute of the ICC, which enunciates perhaps an even more stringent standard: 'Every candidate for election to the Court shall have an *excellent* knowledge of and be *fluent* in at least one of the working languages of the Court' (emphasis added).

be enforced. The one way to ensure that the proficiency standard is met is to require thorough language testing (of non-native speakers) in the national nomination contests. This seems to be the current path taken by PACE and the Committee of Ministers to tackle this issue.[101] But this proved to be insufficient. The testing of language skills at the national level has often been less thorough than necessary and, moreover, 'proficiency' in foreign languages in certain countries means a somewhat lower standard than would be expected in Strasbourg circles.

The solution to this problem is three-fold. First, the required level of proficiency should be clarified by reference to the Council of Europe's Common European Framework of Reference for Languages.[102] Second, the Common European Framework of Reference for Languages should also be used in the model curriculum vitae,[103] like the European Language Passport. Third, proficiency in the *first* language should be tested at the Strasbourg level as well. Currently, only the Sub-Committee on the Election of Judges to the European Court of Human Rights can interview candidates. However, this interview has failed to sift out candidates with insufficient knowledge of the first language. Therefore, it would be beneficial both to the states and to the PACE if the advisory panel of experts were allowed to interview the candidates and test their ability to communicate complex legal issues effectively and understand linguistic nuances in official languages[104] of the Council of Europe.[105]

Regarding the second issue, bilingualism, standards have also increased over time. As of 2004, candidates had to possess only a sufficient knowledge of one of the two official languages and hence, *a contrario*, no requirement regarding the second official language was set.[106] This is surprising since the ECtHR's documents have not been produced in both languages.[107] More specifically, according to the Registry of the ECtHR, 'typically around two-thirds of documents before Chambers were in English only and one-third in French only'.[108] Protocol no 14 made knowledge of the second official language even more important. After

---

[101] See Guidelines of the Committee of Ministers (n 4), para IV.3; Committee on Legal Affairs and Human Rights (n 53), Part B, para 24.

[102] See Steering Committee for Human Rights, *Report of Ad Hoc Working Group on National Practices for the Selection of Candidates for the Post of Judge at the European Court of Human Rights*, CDDH-SC(2011)R1, Appendix III, 14 September 2011, para 6, note 5.

[103] 'Proficiency' should mean that C2 level is required for the first language. Or at the very least it should be made clear that, as an absolute minimum, each candidate must be able to speak, read, and write at the 'very good' level (according to the current fair/good/very good scale) in one of the official languages.

[104] This means that both English and French native speakers should be on the Advisory Panel of Experts.

[105] The other option is to make the Sub-Committee's assessment of candidates' linguistic competence public.

[106] PACE, Recommendation 1649 (2004), 30 January 2004.

[107] Note that although simultaneous translation between the two official languages is generally provided during the ECtHR's hearings and deliberations, individual sections often work (and produce their working documents) in only one of the two official languages.

[108] See Steering Committee for Human Rights, *Report of Ad Hoc Working Group on National Practices for the Selection of Candidates for the Post of Judge at the European Court of Human Rights*, CDDH-SC(2011)R1, 14 September 2011, para 6.

its ratification, knowledge of both official languages became increasingly impor-tant, because judges sitting alone decide on the admissibility of applications, and three-judge panels deliver judgments with respect to manifestly well-founded cases.[109] This change inevitably increases the exposure of all Strasbourg judges to both working languages. For that reason,[110] PACE raised the standard for the second language and stipulated that all candidates should possess at least a passive knowledge of the second official language.[111]

This standard regarding bilingualism is far from perfect,[112] but a more stringent standard concerning the second official language, especially in small countries that use neither English nor French as their official language, might eliminate many, or even most, top candidates. On the other hand, bilingualism should not be under-estimated. Apart from changes brought about by Protocol no 14 and the fact that the sections are rearranged every three years, which increases the likelihood that a judge may have to switch working languages, bilingualism is also critical for the consistency and coherence of ECtHR case law. If Strasbourg judges do not have sufficient command of the second official language, there is an increased danger that the 'French strands' and 'English strands' of Strasbourg case law will develop separately over time and unless there is a Grand Chamber judgment on a given issue, the case law might diverge.[113]

Thus, it is important to keep an eye on the candidates' knowledge of the second official language and raise the standard when the time is ripe. Until that moment, the same steps as those regarding proficiency can be taken: (1) to stipulate what a 'passive knowledge' means on the Common European Framework of Reference for Languages scale; (2) to use this scale in the model curriculum vitae; and (3) to test the knowledge of the second official languages at the national as well as the Strasbourg level.

4.3. Age

The age of judges at the moment of taking office at the ECtHR was not, for many decades, at the forefront of discussion concerning the selection of Strasbourg judges. However, it is increasingly understood that this overlooked criterion may have serious repercussions for the functioning of the ECtHR as well as for its legitimacy. The compulsory retirement age of 70 years is perceived by many as too low for an international court and, according to critics, has deterred otherwise

---

[109] See Arts 27 and 28 ECHR.

[110] See Committee on Legal Affairs and Human Rights (n 53), Part B, paras 11–12 and 24.

[111] PACE, Resolution 1646 (2009), para 4.4. See also, more recently, Guidelines of the Committee of Ministers (n 4), para II.3.

[112] Note that for all 'Grade A' positions the Council of Europe requires a very good knowledge of one of the official languages (English or French) and *good* knowledge of the other.

[113] This is, to a certain extent, already happening. Judgments drafted in English tend to cite pri-marily case law available in English, whereas judgments drafted in French prefer case law available in French.

well-equipped scholars and judges from applying for Strasbourg office.[114] This rule came under closer scrutiny when judges who could not finish even half of their term due to their age were appointed to the Strasbourg bench, resulting in an increased turnover of the ECtHR's membership. However, it was the recent appointments of '30-something' judges that came in for severe criticism.[115] The appointment of young judges is not only capable of undermining the legitimacy of the ECtHR, but also creates an additional problem of their subsequent reintegration into their member state.

It is thus clear that there are in fact two issues at stake:

(1) the upper age limit;

(2) the lower age limit.[116]

The recent documents of the Council of Europe attempt to tackle both issues simultaneously. However, as each of these issues raises different problems, they will be discussed separately.

Regarding the upper age limit, the Convention itself has switched back and forth within the last 25 years, always without proper explanation. Until 1998, the Convention set no age limit for Strasbourg judges. It was only Protocol No 11 that introduced a mandatory retirement age of 70 years.[117] This sudden shift was neither properly discussed nor justified.[118] Protocol no 11 also reduced the term for Strasbourg judges from nine to six years. Therefore, if a judge wanted to serve a full term in Strasbourg, she had to be 64 years old or younger at the moment of her appointment. Given the relatively short term, one would expect that the PACE would select only those candidates who could serve a full term, but even during the term of applicability of the six-year mandate it elected several judges who were in their late sixties and did not complete their terms due to their age.[119]

---

[114] See Explanatory Report to Protocol no 14, para 53; and Committee on Legal Affairs and Human Rights (n 19), para 12.

[115] See eg Engel (n 2), Loucaides (n 2), Malenovský (n 2) 187, and Sevón (n 25) 3.

[116] For further discussion of the age requirement see eg Limbach (n 2), Flauss (n 2), Engel (n 2), Loucaides (n 2), Malenovský (n 2) 187, and Sevón (n 25) 3 (regarding the ECtHR); also Malenovský (n 2) 184–8 (regarding international courts in general).

[117] See Art 23(3) ECHR, as amended by Protocol no 11: 'The terms of office of judges shall expire when they reach the age of 70.'

[118] See para 63 of the Explanatory Report: 'Since the Court will function on a permanent basis, it was deemed appropriate to introduce an age limit, as exists in most domestic legal systems.' Note that courts and tribunals established by the UN (the International Court of Justice, the International Criminal Court, the International Criminal Tribunal for the former Yugoslavia, and the International Criminal Tribunal for Rwanda) as well as other regional human rights courts do not provide for a mandatory retirement age. For further details regarding maximum age of judges of international courts see Malenovský (n 2) 184–6.

[119] There are several such judges. Antonio Pastor Ridruejo (Spain) was appointed at the age of 66 years and served five years (1998–2003) in Strasbourg. Giorgio Malinverni (Switzerland) was appointed at the age of 66 years and served only four years (2007–11) as a judge of the ECtHR. In addition, Vladimiro Zagrebelsky was 67 years old when he was re-elected in 2007. Finally, Benedetto Conforti (Italy) was appointed at the age of 68 years and served only three years (1998–2001) at the ECtHR, but this was not a problem as his term of office was to expire after three years due to transitional provisions after the entry into force of Protocol no 11—for further details see Drzemczewski (n 2).

However, the election of judges who could not finish six years on the Strasbourg bench did not provoke much controversy at that time.[120] The rules stipulated by Protocol no 11 regarding the terms of office of Strasbourg judges were eventually modified for another reason. As judges were elected for a period of six years with the possibility of re-election, incentives were created for judges to decide cases in a manner that would not jeopardize their re-election prospects.[121]

Protocol no 14, which came into force on 1 June 2010, echoed this criticism and introduced a non-renewable term of nine years. As the compulsory retirement age of 70 years remained untouched, those candidates who intended to serve a full term had to be 61 years old or younger. The Explanatory Report to Protocol no 14 moderated this criterion and suggested that the two criteria—the nine-year term and the age limit of 70 years—read together 'may not be understood as excluding candidates who, on the date of election, would be older than 61'.[122] However, it also stipulated that 'it is generally recommended that High Contracting Parties avoid proposing candidates who, in view of their age, would not be able to hold office for at least half of the nine-year term before reaching the age of 70'.[123] In other words, every judge was supposed to serve at least 4.5 years. Unfortunately, neither the high contracting parties nor the PACE followed this advice, again electing a judge in his late 60s in 2012.[124]

Yet another change in the maximum age limit, which reflects a recommendation of the Brighton Declaration,[125] is envisaged in Protocol no 15.[126] This Protocol, when it enters into force, will replace the age limit of 70 with a new requirement that judge candidates be no older than the age of 65 when the list of three candidates is requested by PACE.[127] The new rule thus allegedly creates a *de facto* age limit of 74.[128]

There are three rationales for the new rule. First, this modification aims at enabling highly qualified judges to serve the full nine-year term of office and thereby

---

[120] But see Flauss (n 2) 739.

[121] See Committee on Legal Affairs and Human Rights (n 19), para 11. Erik Voeten's empirical study actually provides modest support for the claim that career insecurities made Strasbourg judges more likely to favour their national government when it was a party to a dispute; see Erik Voeten, 'The Impartiality of International Judges: Evidence from the European Court of Human Rights' (2008) 102 *American Political Science Review* 417, 421 and 427–8. See also n 17.

[122] Explanatory Report to Protocol no 14, para 53.

[123] Explanatory Report to Protocol no 14, para 53. See also Guidelines of the Committee of Ministers (n 4), para II.5; Brighton Declaration, para 24.

[124] Paul Mahoney (United Kingdom) was almost 66 years old at the date of his election.

[125] Brighton Declaration, paras 24–5. See also the ECtHR's opinion on the Brighton Declaration, para 29.

[126] For a succinct summary of the innovations brought about by this protocol see David Milner, 'Protocols no. 15 and 16 to the European Convention on Human Rights in the Context of the Perennial Process of Reform: A Long and Winding Road' (2014) 17 *Zeitschrift für Europarechtliche Studien* 19.

[127] Art 21(2) ECHR, as amended by Protocol no 15, reads as follows: 'Candidates shall be less than 65 years of age at the date by which the list of three candidates has been requested by the Parliamentary Assembly, further to Article 22.'

[128] See eg Committee on Legal Affairs and Human Rights (n 19), para 12. However, it will be shown below that the *de facto* age limit will actually be higher.

reinforcing the consistency of the membership of the Court.[129] Second, this change provides for the possibility of electing more experienced judges, as well as judges who are closer to retirement in their home countries and therefore less likely to feel the need to prepare the ground for their future employment once they step down as a judge in Strasbourg.[130] Finally, the third rationale, which is well known in Strasbourg circles but has not been discussed in public, stems from the fact that the only chance of attracting the very top candidates from certain old Council of Europe Member States is to 'hire' them after their compulsory retirement in their home countries.[131]

The change regarding the upper age limit brought about by Protocol no 15 is generally considered to be a good solution to the problems caused by the previous rule. But its justification is again dubious and the new rule must be approached with caution. As to the first rationale, the need to reduce the turnover of Strasbourg judges, it could have been achieved even under the previous rule, had PACE accepted only lists containing candidates aged 61 years or younger. Moreover, judges well into their 70s might cause new problems, be they lower productivity, health problems, or, in the worst-case scenario, even deaths on the bench. Here it should be emphasized that the *de facto* age limit is in fact higher than 74. As the critical date on which the age requirement is checked is the date when PACE requests the list of three candidates,[132] and given the length of the process leading to election of a judge, a judge who was 65 years old at the critical date will most probably be 66 when elected, if everything goes well. If the nomination list is rejected, which might happen and has already happened,[133] she will be even older. In other words, the *de facto* maximum age limit is at least 75. One thus wonders why, if judges in their mid-70s are still considered suitable for Strasbourg office, the upper age limit should not be abolished altogether?

The second rationale sought by the new rule, to reduce the need for the reintegration of Strasbourg judges within their home countries and thereby strengthen judicial independence, is also questionable. First of all, if a Strasbourg judge is good she will have no problem finding an appropriate job afterwards, although not necessarily in her home country and not necessarily within the judiciary. In fact, a recent study revealed that former Strasbourg judges often do not return to their home countries:[134] out of a sample of 30 recently retired judges, three were

---

[129] Explanatory Report to Protocol no 15, para 12.

[130] Committee on Legal Affairs and Human Rights (n 19), para 12.

[131] Put more bluntly, for most lawyers in the United Kingdom being a judge of the Court of Appeal or the Supreme Court of the United Kingdom means more than being a judge of the ECtHR. The same logic applies to several other 'west' European countries. A good indicator of this phenomenon is the number of judges of apex courts on the nomination lists submitted to PACE.

[132] In this aspect the final wording of Protocol no 15 differs from the wording of the Brighton Declaration, which proposed 'that judges must be no older than 65 years of age at the date on which their term of office commences' [see Brighton Declaration, para 25(f)]. For justification of this departure see Committee on Legal Affairs and Human Rights (n 19), para 13.

[133] Note also that the list can be rejected more than once.

[134] But it must be noted that many of the following positions, especially at supranational or international institutions, are dependent upon nomination by a home state.

appointed to positions at international organizations such as the United Nations or European Union institutions, six were appointed or elected to other international courts or tribunals, ten were appointed or elected to be judges on national courts or to serve as ombudspersons, at least four worked for some time as academics, eight served in their national administrations as, for example, advisors, and some of them even became MPs and ministers.[135] Moreover, virtually any law school in Europe, and even beyond, would like to have a former Strasbourg judge as a member of its faculty.

Of course, it would be desirable if a national judge who finished her Strasbourg term returned to at least the same position within the domestic judiciary she originally came from.[136] However, this is not always possible, because the number of seats at apex courts is often fixed and there is no immediate vacancy.[137] The situation regarding constitutional justices is even more complex, as most European constitutions set a non-renewable term for constitutional justices and hence there is no chance to return to the same post at all. But these are the terms of Strasbourg judicial office and everybody knows them in advance. In addition, there is no evidence of national bias in the ECtHR's judgments and virtually all scholarly studies indicate the personal integrity of Strasbourg judges.[138] The recent study on the legitimacy of the ECtHR confirms this state of affairs by showing that judicial independence is not perceived as a major legitimacy issue by the relevant stakeholders.[139] Finally, the new rule cannot prevent the reintegration of Strasbourg judges entirely, since at several European constitutional courts there is neither a maximum age nor a compulsory retirement age for their justices.[140] In other words, some Strasbourg judges will always try to seek reintegration within the domestic judiciary. In sum, reintegration's threat to judicial independence is doubtful at best, especially when we compare Strasbourg judges with their Luxembourg colleagues.[141]

The third rationale, to attract top national judges after their compulsory retirement in their home countries, thus seems the most promising explanation of why the new rule came into being. For instance, justices of the German Constitutional Court face compulsory retirement at the age of 68, and thus the increase in the upper age limit brought about by Protocol no 15 might indeed increase their interest in Strasbourg office. The same logic applies to judges in other states that stipulate the retirement age for judges as 65 years or below.[142] Moreover, even those

---

[135] See Nina Vajić, 'Some Remarks Linked to the Independence of International Judges and the Observance of Ethical Rules in the European Court of Human Rights' in *Grundrechte und Solidarität:Durchsetzung und Verfahren Festschrift für Renate Jaeger* (N. P. Engel Verlag 2010) 179, 185 (cited also in Committee on Legal Affairs and Human Rights, n 19, para 21).

[136] See also Committee on Legal Affairs and Human Rights (n 19), paras 22–3.

[137] Forcing governments to keep the seat of a Strasbourg judge vacant for nine years is quite a stretch.

[138] See n 17 above.   [139] See Çali, Koch, and Bruch (n 29), discussed in section 1.

[140] This applies, for instance, to the Italian Constitutional Court.

[141] Judges of the Tribunal and the Court of Justice of the European Union not only face the same hurdles regarding reintegration, but also have to seek reappointment every six years.

[142] According to the 2012 CEPEJ Report the retirement age of judges or ordinary courts varies between 63 years (Cyprus) and 72 years (Ireland); see CEPEJ, *European Judicial Systems, Edition 2012 (Data 2010): Efficiency and Quality of Justice*, available at <http://www.coe.int/t/dghl/cooperation/cepej/evaluation/2012/Rapport_en.pdf>, p 274.

judges who face compulsory retirement at the age of 70 may give the Strasbourg application a thought, as it would prolong their active judicial careers for several more years. However, if this was the intention of the drafters of Protocol no 15, they should have studied the maximum age of domestic judges more systematically to choose the 'right' maximum age.

In contrast to the upper age limit, the Convention never explicitly set a minimum age requirement. The only formal limit set by the Convention can be found in Article 21(1) ECHR, which states: 'The judges shall be of high moral character and must either possess the qualifications required for appointment to high judicial office or be jurisconsults of recognised competence.' It was suggested that the criterion of eligibility for 'high judicial office' in this article may, in itself, amount to an implicit lower age requirement,[143] but in practice states as well as the PACE interpreted this criterion in a very flexible way and the PACE elected several judges in their thirties.[144]

Despite growing criticism of this phenomenon,[145] little attention was paid to it in Strasbourg circles.[146] However, this ignorance soon backfired against the ECtHR. When in 2009 the PACE elected a 36-year-old Ukrainian lawyer, who was working at the ECtHR's Registry at the moment of her election, many commentators felt that this was too much and started criticizing this practice openly.[147] This is somewhat unfair vis-à-vis the Ukrainian judge,[148] because seven other judges elected since the establishment of the permanent Court in 1998 had been under 40 at the moment of their election.[149] Moreover, the election of a Ukrainian judge in 2009 was rather special, because there had been no Ukrainian judge since 2007[150] and the selection process was severely protracted due to the battle over the lists of candidates.[151]

---

[143] See eg Committee on Legal Affairs and Human Rights (n 53), Part B, paras 5 and 32; or Malenovský (n 2) 186.

[144] These judges came from Albania (Kristaq Traja, 33 years old, 1998–2008), Lithuania (Danutė Jociene, 34 years old, 2004—13), Latvia (Ineta Zimele, 35 years old, 2005–), Georgia (Nona Tsotsoria, 34 years old, 2007–), Albania (Ledi Bianku, 36 years old, 2008–), San Marino (Kristina Pardalos, 36 years old, 2009–), Ukraine (Ganna Yudkivska, 36 years old, 2010–), and Estonia (Julia Laffranque, 36 years old, 2011–).

[145] See the references to this problem in Limbach (n 2) and Flauss (n 2).

[146] For exceptions see eg Committee on Legal Affairs and Human Rights (n 53), Part B, para 32.

[147] See eg Engel (n 2), Loucaides (n 2), Malenovský (n 2) 187, Sevón (n 25) 3.

[148] The low age of the Ukrainian judge seemed to operate as a mere proxy. What was more controversial was the length and nature of professional experience she had acquired before she was elected a judge of the ECtHR; see also s 4.4 below in this chapter.

[149] See n 145 above.

[150] As a result, ad hoc judges had to be appointed for applications concerning Ukraine (which was among the top four countries against which the ECtHR issued judgments at that time) between 2007 and 2009.

[151] Ukraine withdrew the entire list of three candidates after one of the initial three had indicated she was no longer interested for personal reasons, and submitted an entirely new list. PACE disagreed with this solution and asked Ukraine to add only a new third candidate. This dispute eventually came before the ECtHR, which sided with PACE; see ECtHR, *Advisory Opinion on Certain Legal Questions Concerning the Lists of Candidates Submitted with a View to the Election of Judges to the European Court of Human Rights (No 2)*, 22 January 2010.

Thus, it is the considerable number of '30-something' judges on the Strasbourg bench that is staggering, and the election of a Ukrainian judge was just the proverbial straw that broke the camel's back. These '30-something judges'[152] may currently present the biggest problem for the legitimacy of the ECtHR. Recent appointments of such young judges have been criticized by scholars as well as national judges, and they significantly reduce the legitimacy of the ECtHR in comparison to domestic courts.

Most national legal systems stipulate a lower age limit for judges of top ordinary courts as well as for justices of the Constitutional Court. For instance, justices of the Czech, German, Slovak, Slovenian, and Turkish Constitutional Courts must be at least 40 years old. Other national systems require a minimum number of years of professional experience: for instance, the Czech Republic requires ten years of such experience for appointment to the apex courts, and Montenegro requires 15 years.[153] Even those countries that do not lay down any formal requirement concerning the minimum age, such as the United Kingdom, set a *de facto* minimum age limit, as judges under 40 years are never appointed to the High Court or above. Interestingly, the Article 255 Panel also made clear that it is no longer possible, as a general rule, to appoint someone in her mid-thirties to the Court of Justice of the European Union (CJEU) or even to the Tribunal.[154] This view is shared by the Advisory Panel.[155]

These states, as well as the European Union, do not lay down minimum age and/or minimum professional experience criteria just for the sake of having them. They have reasons for introducing them. They want their apex court judges to possess sufficient experience and wisdom to deal with complex legal issues and their judgments to carry sufficient weight vis-à-vis other constitutional organs, such as the parliament, the head of state, the Prime Minister, the ministries, senior civil servants, and so on. Judges at top courts simply must have sufficient gravitas. If this is perceived as crucial for domestic judges, it is at least equally important for Strasbourg judges. In other words, if the ECtHR wants its judgments to carry sufficient weight among key stakeholders in the signatory states, Strasbourg judges must have proper stature, experience, and credentials,[156] which should translate into a minimum age requirement.

A recent PACE document reacted to this criticism and suggested that 'States Parties (and the Assembly) ought perhaps to be more vigilant in the nomination of candidates and election of judges who may still be in their 30s or early 40s when more experienced candidates can be elected.'[157] The Advisory Panel echoes this call

---

[152] The specific historical situation in some countries (eg Baltic states in the 1990s) might have justified the exceptional election of younger judges in the past. However, times have changed and these specific historical circumstances no longer exist.

[153] Sometimes, both a minimum age and a number of years in practice are required.

[154] Further see above ch 3 s 2.

[155] See Excerpt from GT-GDR-E(2013)004, published as Appendix to Steering Committee for Human Rights (n 64).

[156] See also Resolution 1764 (2010), para 2 (which emphasizes the necessary 'qualifications, experience and stature' of Strasbourg judges).

[157] Committee on Legal Affairs and Human Rights (n 19), para 25.

and suggests that 'the European Court of Human Rights, by its nature, status and pan-European role assumes that its members already have, on election, all the fully developed judicial qualities that come from long experience', as a result of which '[i]t would appear unlikely to find such qualities in a candidate of a relatively young age'.[158]

This effort to raise the lower age limit of Strasbourg judges is laudable, but one should be careful not to 'throw out the baby with the bathwater'. First, if the PACE increases the lower limit, either *de iure* or *de facto*, too much, it will just perpetuate the problems experienced in the 1990s and the early 2000s. As Malenovský has suggested, in several Central and Eastern European countries judges of the old guard are disqualified, either because they do not speak English and French or due to their co-operation with the previous regime, and thus these states tend to nominate younger judges.[159] The statistical data confirm this claim: out of eight judges under 40 elected between 1998 and 2013, five came from post-Soviet countries (three from the Baltic states, one from Ukraine, and one from Georgia), two from Albania, and one from San Marino.[160]

In addition, if the PACE prefers candidates in their late 50s or 60s, it may be forced to compromise on other selection criteria, since lawyers who graduated from the reformed law schools in the mid-1990s are still in their 40s, and there will again be a very small pool of good candidates. Also, age diversity on the Strasbourg Court is healthy, as it invites a richer and more robust debate. Moreover, younger judges have some comparative advantages too, as they may have better knowledge of new technologies or EU law.[161] Finally, the fact that judges return from the ECtHR to their 'home base' also has several positive effects, since 'former [Strasbourg] judges are likely to enrich the legal profession's knowledge of Strasbourg case law with their uniquely acquired European experience'.[162]

Therefore, it would suffice if a reasonable lower age limit were added to the Convention[163] or, at least, were *de facto* required by the PACE, as suggested by the Advisory Panel.[164] A good starting point is to look at the minimum age limit for constitutional court justices, because constitutional courts are the closest equivalents to the ECtHR at the domestic level. The most common minimum age for constitutional justices is 40 years, which is suitable for Strasbourg judges too. The minimum age of 40 years would improve the stature of the ECtHR, but at the same time would keep the pool of candidates large enough. Contrary to

---

[158] Excerpt from GT-GDR-E(2013)004, published as Appendix to Steering Committee for Human Rights (n 64) (both citations).

[159] Malenovský (n 2) 187. See also ch 12 s 4.   [160] See n 145 above.

[161] This applies in particular to judges from new EU member states, where EU law was not taught until the late 1990s.

[162] Committee on Legal Affairs and Human Rights (n 53), Part B, para 38.

[163] Art 21(2) of ECHR, as amended by Protocol no 15, could read as follows: 'Candidates shall be *more than 40 years* and less than 65 years of age at the date by which the list of three candidates has been requested by the Parliamentary Assembly, further to Article 22.'

[164] See Excerpt from GT-GDR-E(2013)004, published as Appendix to Steering Committee for Human Rights (n 64).

what some commentators claim,[165] it would not unduly limit the choice from post-communist states in Central and Eastern Europe, as they already have enough lawyers trained in the democratic regime and well versed in foreign languages who are in their mid-40s. This also means that I disagree with the Committee on Legal Affairs and Human Rights, which suggests that judges in their early 40s present a problem.[166] There are quite a few constitutional justices on the Continent who were appointed in their 40s, and some of them assumed the highest offices.[167] The current president of the Federal Constitutional Court of Germany, Andreas Voßkuhle, is a prime example. He was elected a justice and vice-president of the Federal Constitutional Court of Germany when he was 44 years old and became president of the Federal Constitutional Court of Germany at the age of 46.

I prefer the minimum age requirement to the minimum professional experience requirement, because the new rule must be easy to police and because critics care primarily about judges' young age.[168] Viewed from this angle, age is objective and universally accepted. In contrast, a minimum professional experience limit requires diving into national laws and discovering what counts as 'practice' in each Council of Europe member state, because the criteria are not uniform. Moreover, even the requirement of 15 years of practice, as suggested by a former Strasbourg judge, Elisabeth Palm,[169] may not be enough. In some countries legal education takes only four years and if someone finishes law school at the age of 22 years, after 15 years of practice she will still be only 37 years old. Finally, length of practice itself is not a good indicator of judicial capacity, as one must also take into account the nature of the practice.[170]

In sum, getting judges' minimum and maximum age limits right presents a big challenge for the Advisory Panel, PACE, and signatory states. However, the key stakeholders must rise to this challenge. Setting the maximum age limit too low may dissuade good candidates, but if it is too high it may jeopardize the functioning and legitimacy of the ECtHR. Any rule on minimum age contains the same trade-off, but the need to entrench a proper minimum age requirement is even more critical, as '30-something judges' have had deleterious effects on the Court's legitimacy.

---

[165] See, most recently, Committee on Legal Affairs and Human Rights, *Reinforcement of the independence of the European Court of Human Rights*, 5 June 2014, Doc 13524, Part C (Explanatory memorandum), para 32.

[166] See n 158 above.

[167] For other advantages of the age diversity on the ECtHR, see n 162 above.

[168] PACE documents and the majority of commentators seem to prefer the latter. See Committee on Legal Affairs and Human Rights (n 53), Part B, para 5; Drzemczewski (n 2) 381–2; Malenovský (n 2) 188. I also accept a *de facto* minimum professional experience requirement, but under the knowledge of domestic law criterion; see s 4.4 below in this chapter.

[169] See Committee on Legal Affairs and Human Rights (n 53), Part B, para 5. See also Drzemczewski (n 2) 381–2; Malenovský (n 2) 188 (both quoting Palm's suggestion with approval).

[170] See Steering Committee for Human Rights, Ministers' Deputies exchange of views with Mr Luzius Wildhaber, Chairman of the Advisory Panel of Experts on Candidates for Election as Judge to the European Court of Human Rights, DH-GDR (2013)005, 5 February 2013, 2 (exchange of views of 4 April 2012), para 9; and Excerpt from GT-GDR-E(2013)004, published as Appendix to Steering Committee for Human Rights (n 64).

4.4. Knowledge of national law

Like the age requirements, knowledge of domestic law has not attracted much attention as a criterion for Strasbourg office. However, its importance should not be underestimated. The study on the ECtHR's legitimacy conducted by Başak Çali et al[171] showed that stakeholders ranked this criterion very highly.[172] They considered knowledge of domestic law and fact the third most important legitimacy standard in the 'managerial' part of the performance dimension, lagging behind only the length of proceedings before the ECtHR and the qualification and experience of Strasbourg judges (see Table 6.1 in section 1).

The importance of knowledge of domestic law was stressed also by the ECtHR. In its first advisory opinion the Grand Chamber rejected the argument that in order to fulfil the criterion concerning the sex of candidates, states can be forced to nominate non-nationals. It provided the following explanation:

> this would be liable to produce a situation where the elected candidate did not have the same knowledge of the legal system, language or indeed cultural and other traditions of the country concerned as a candidate from that country. Indeed, the main reason why one of the judges hearing a case must be the "national judge", a rule that dates back to the beginnings of the Convention and is today enshrined in Article 27 § 2, is precisely to ensure that the judges hearing the case are fully acquainted with the relevant domestic law of the respondent State and the context in which it is set.[173]

This requirement was further reiterated by the Committee of Ministers, which stressed that '[c]andidates need to have knowledge of the national legal system(s)'[174] and suggested that 'a high level of knowledge…[of the national legal system] should be taken as an implicit requirement for candidates for judge at the Court and relative levels of knowledge could be taken into account when choosing between applicants of otherwise equal merits'.[175]

Sufficient exposure to the national legal system is a critical requirement for Strasbourg judges also for another reason. The ECtHR judge is often the only senior lawyer from her country in Strasbourg who can explain to her colleagues how the respective law applicable in a given case works at the national level, including all the nuances, such as whether and how it was modified by case law, how it fits into the legal system as a whole, what the specifics of a given legal culture are, what the view of doctrine is about this law, what the vexing human rights issues are in a given country and what are not, and so forth.[176] This problem is exacerbated by the fact that many lawyers at

---

[171] See s 2 above.

[172] See also Lucius Caflisch, 'Independence and Impartiality of Judges: The European Court of Human Rights' (2003) 2 *The Law and Practice of International Courts and Tribunals* 169, 173; Malenovský (n 2) 110.

[173] ECtHR, the 2008 Advisory Opinion (n 66) § 52. See also Brighton Declaration, para 22 *in fine.*

[174] Guidelines of the Committee of Ministers (n 4), para II.4.

[175] Explanatory Memorandum to the Guidelines of the Committee of Ministers on the selection of candidates for the post of judge at the European Court of Human Rights, CM(2012)40 addendum final, 29 March 2012, para 27.

[176] See, *mutatis mutandis*, ECtHR, the 2008 Advisory Opinion (n 66), § 52.

the Court's Registry are junior lawyers[177] who joined the ECtHR soon after graduation and/or have little experience of practising law in their home countries. But even if there are senior lawyers from a given country in Strasbourg, they do not take part in deliberation and cannot communicate the nuances of national law as effectively as judges themselves.[178]

In other words, a Strasbourg judge must be fully acquainted with the relevant domestic law. This means that 'globetrotters' who spent their entire careers outside the country of their nationality, including in the Council of Europe organs, and have never practised, lectured, or served as judges, or did so only for a marginal period of time, in the national jurisdiction from which they come are not good candidates for the position of judge in the ECtHR.

If the PACE decides otherwise, it invites easy criticism. The recent elections of Ukrainian and British judges are typical examples.[179] Ganna Yudkivska became a Strasbourg judge in 2009, even though she was called to the Ukrainian Bar only in 2003 and started to work as a lawyer at the Court's Registry after a mere two years. This is in fact a far more controversial aspect of her election than her relatively young age.[180] The election of Paul Mahoney in 2012 is even more problematic in this respect. After a short period of legal practice in London in the 1970s, Mahoney worked for three decades in various posts at the ECtHR and then served as Judge and President of the European Union Civil Service Tribunal in Luxembourg between 2005 and 2011. In other words, he did not practise in the United Kingdom for four decades in a row. Even though one should certainly approach the *Daily Mail* with caution, it is not surprising that it calls Mahoney a 'Eurocrat' and 'celebrated' his election with the headline 'Meet our new Euro human rights judge...who's not even a real judge: Top Strasbourg job for man who's never sat in a British court'.[181]

The headline is, typically for the *Daily Mail*, misleading. I do not want to convey the message that Strasbourg judges should recruit only from among national judges. However, Strasbourg judges should recruit from among lawyers who have substantial experience with the national legal order, culture, and traditions, irrespective of whether or not this experience is of a judicial nature. Even though I strongly disagree with the content and style of the *Daily Mail* reporting about the ECtHR, this article also shows how easy it is to delegitimize the choice of the PACE by claiming that the elected judge is 'not one of us',[182] which implicitly

---

[177] Note that this does not apply to all sections.
[178] Moreover, some senior lawyers at the Registry did not practise law in their home countries at all.
[179] These two elections are also problematic for another reason. They create the sense that ECtHR's 'insiders' have an extra advantage in the PACE stage of the election process. However, this issue is beyond the scope of this chapter.
[180] On the latter, see s 4.3 above in this chapter.
[181] James Slack, 'Meet our New Euro Human Rights Judge...Who's Not Even a Real Judge: Top Strasbourg Job for Man Who's Never Sat in a British Court', *Daily Mail* (27 June 2012), online at <http://www.dailymail.co.uk>, last accessed 15 April 2014.
[182] This may happen also at the national level. The recent appointment of Justice Marc Nadon to fill the Quebec seat at the Supreme Court of Canada is a prime example. When Prime Minister Stephen Harper announced that he intends to fill the Quebec spot with a *federal* judge it was perceived

suggests that he might not share 'our values'. In other words, sufficient professional experience of a Strasbourg judge in *her* country of nationality is important not only for 'functional' reasons (expertise in national law and ability to explain the national law and legal culture to other Strasbourg judges), but also for 'legitimacy' reasons (the people and the legal community of the judge's home country[183] must treat 'their' judge as 'one of them'). Otherwise, there is a danger that a Strasbourg judge can be easily labelled as a part of a 'transnational power elite'.[184]

On the other hand, the requirement of knowledge of national law should not be applied too strictly. For instance, if someone is *at the moment of* the election holding a position outside the state of her nationality, she should not be excluded, provided that she was sufficiently exposed to national law prior to her appointment abroad. By 'exposure' to national law I mean clerkship, attorney's practice, lecturing, serving as a national judge, or being a member of another legal profession. 'Sufficient' exposure is more difficult to define, but I believe that any candidate, at the moment of her election, should have been exposed to the national legal system for at least ten years throughout her career, although not necessarily in the period immediately before her election. This period should be enough to ensure that a Strasbourg judge has the necessary gravitas not only on the transnational plane, but also within the domestic legal and political milieux.[185]

4.5. Expertise in general international law

Under this heading I would like to raise one issue, which is often overlooked. Despite some efforts to prevent it,[186] expertise in general international law, in contrast to human rights specialization, on the Strasbourg Court has been declining for a while. If we leave aside a huge group of judges elected in 1998 immediately after the entry into force of Protocol no 11, the only expert in general international law elected to the ECtHR between 1999 and 2011 was Ineta Ziemele.[187] The situation improved after 2011 because several generalists, such as Helen Keller (2011–), Linos-Alexander Sicilianos (2011–), Erik Møse (2011–), and Iulia Motoc (2013–), joined the ECtHR, but if it had not been for these recent additions to the Strasbourg bench, the expertise in general international law among its judges could have withered away completely.

by the province's legal community as 'a blow in [their] faces, a disavowal of the Quebec bench': for further details see Sean Fine, 'The Secret Short List that Provoked the Rift between Chief Justice and PMO', *The Globe and Mail* 23 May 2014. Note that Justice Nadon was eventually found ineligible to fill the Quebec Supreme Court spot by the Supreme Court of Canada in *Reference re Supreme Court Act, ss 5 and 6*, 2014 SCC 21.

[183] I leave aside here that some small states occasionally nominate a judge of other nationality.
[184] See this volume, ch 12 s 2.   [185] See this volume, ch 12 s 4.
[186] See in particular Guidelines of the Committee of Ministers (n 4), para II.4, and Explanatory Memorandum to the Guidelines of the Committee of Ministers (n 176), para 27, discussed below.
[187] Of course, the definition of a 'generalist international law expert' is somewhat subjective. Some commentators might also include Davíd Thór Björgvinsson (2004–13), Mark Villiger (2008–), Işıl Karakaş (2008–), and Ledi Bianku (2008–), all of whom taught international law, but I believe that their primary specializations were human rights, general legal theory, and/or EU law.

There may be several reasons behind this decline, including the changing perception of the role of the ECtHR and its constitutionalization. But, irrespective of one's position in the 'ECtHR-as-a-constitutional-court' debate,[188] the ECtHR is still an *international* human rights court and must tackle many vexing issues of general international law, such as international responsibility of states,[189] implementation of the United Nations Security Council resolutions,[190] prosecution of war crimes,[191] the law of armed conflict,[192] and the law of the sea.[193] In addition, it needs to maintain expertise beyond the narrow confines of human rights law to maintain a dialogue with and be taken seriously by other international courts, such as the International Court of Justice (ICJ), the International Criminal Court (ICC), or the International Tribunal for the Law of the Sea.

The recent tendency to prefer human rights specialists and scholars is not *per se* bad, but it should not go too far. There should be a plurality of backgrounds among judges so that both human rights and general international law expertise is guaranteed. This does not mean that the pendulum should swing back to the 1980s, when the majority of Strasbourg judges had a background in international law. However, a 'critical mass' of judges who are well versed in general international law must be ensured at all times. The ECtHR has always been and will always be an international court and thus it should be staffed accordingly.

Therefore, it is laudable that the 2012 Guidelines of the Committee of Ministers on the selection of candidates for the post of judge at the European Court of Human Rights explicitly stress that '[c]andidates need to have knowledge of the national legal system(s) and of public international law'[194] with the following justification: '[a]s the [Strasbourg] judges sit on an *international* court playing a subsidiary role in supervising national implementation of the Convention, it is

---

[188] For supporters of the constitutionalization of the ECtHR see Luzius Wildhaber, 'A Constitutional Future for the European Court of Human Rights?' (2002) 23 *HRLJ* 161, 161; Alec Stone-Sweet, 'Sur la constitutionnalisation de la Convention Européenne des Droits de l'Homme: Cinquante ans après son installation, la Cour Européene des Droits de l'Homme conçue comme une cour constitutionelle' (2009) 80 *Revue trimestrielle des droits de l'homme* 923; Steven Greer, 'What's Wrong with the European Convention on Human Rights?' (2008) 30 *HumRtsQ.* 701. For a more sceptical view, see Nico Krisch, 'The Open Architecture of European Human Rights Law' (2008) 71 *MLR* 183, 184; David Kosař, 'Policing Separation of Powers: A New Role for the European Court of Human Rights?' (2012) 8 *EuConst* 33, 60–2.

[189] See, most recently, ECtHR, *Al-Skeini and Others v the United Kingdom* [GC], 7 July 2011, no 55721/07; ECtHR, *Al-Jedda v the United Kingdom* [GC], 7 July 2011, no 27021/08; ECtHR, *Ivanţoc and Others v Moldova and Russia*, 15 November 2011, no 23687/05.

[190] See eg ECtHR, *Bosphorus Airways v Ireland* [GC], 30 June 2005, no 45036/98; or ECtHR, *Behrami and Behrami v France* (dec) [GC], 2 May 2007, no 71412/08.

[191] See eg ECtHR, *Kononov v Latvia* [GC], 17 May 2010, no 36376/04; ECtHR, *Maktouf and Damjanović v Bosnia and Herzegovina* [GC], 18 July 2013, nos 2312/08 and 34179/08; ECtHR, *Marguš v Croatia* [GC], 27 May 2014, no 45036/98.

[192] See eg *Varnava and Others v Turkey* [GC], 18 September 2009, nos 16064/90 and other (concerning the Turkey–Cypriot issue); *Sarusyan v Azerbaijan* (dec) [GC], 14 December 2011, no 40167/06 (concerning the Armenian–Azerbaijani conflict over Nagorno-Karabakh); or the cases in the previous three footnotes.

[193] See eg ECtHR, *Medvedyev and Others v France* [GC], 23 March 2010, no 3394/03; or ECtHR, *Hirsi Jamaa and Others v Italy* [GC], 23 February 2012, no 27765/09.

[194] Guidelines of the Committee of Ministers (n 4), para II.4.

important for them to have knowledge of *both public international law* and the national legal system(s).'[195] As a result, 'a high level of knowledge... [of public international law] should be taken as an implicit requirement for candidates for judge at the Court and relative levels of knowledge could be taken into account when choosing between applicants of otherwise equal merits'.[196]

Finally, one caveat must be added here. If the European Union indeed accedes to the Convention, which seems very likely now, there may be pressure to increase the number of judges with sufficient expertise in EU law in future. However, there is a danger in the overrepresentation of EU law experts on the Strasbourg bench, because it might lead to reading EU law into the Convention at the expense of states that are *not* members of the EU.[197]

5. The Ugly

The previous part addressed systemic problems. This part provides several examples of the controversial techniques[198] employed in recent elections of Strasbourg judges. These examples are not so much about general criteria, but rather about ways of rigging or bypassing these criteria. Some of them might have resulted from sloppiness, but most were driven by politics. This part builds heavily on Norbert Engel's account, but adds a few more examples of the use of questionable tricks. Finally, it provides a more detailed account of the 2012 election of the Czech judge that provoked the greatest shockwaves behind the scenes.

Problematic cases which were eventually contained concern Spain, Bulgaria, France, and Slovakia.[199] The Spanish case reminds us that there must be someone who checks the accuracy of information on nominees' CVs. According to Engel, the Spanish government submitted the curriculum vitae of a candidate who had wrongly claimed to have held high office.[200] This deception was revealed at the national level by a leading newspaper and the PACE eventually rejected the nominee. The Bulgarian case serves as an example of blatant nepotism, as a minister of justice put his wife's name on the list of nominees. This time, it was noticed only at the Strasbourg stage, by a non-Bulgarian member of the PACE. As a result, the PACE eventually rejected the nominee.

[195] Explanatory Memorandum to the Guidelines of the Committee of Ministers (n 176), para 27 (both emphases added).

[196] Ibid. (both emphases added).

[197] This is already, to some extent, happening. See eg ECtHR, *Schalk and Kopf v Austria*, 24 June 2010, no 30141/04, §§ 60–1.

[198] It is important to stress that I do not consider the exercise of political influence or politicking problematic as long as political manoeuvres do not aim at pushing through an ineligible candidate and do not deceive the members of PACE. Like Koen Lemmens, I believe that a complete 'depoliticization' of the election process is neither healthy nor possible; see above ch 5 s 3.4.

[199] The first three examples are covered by Engel (see Engel n 2, 450–1); the last has not, to my mind, been discussed by scholars. I do not include the Moldovan case discussed by Engel as it concerns the re-election of Strasbourg judges, which is no longer relevant.

[200] Engel (n 2) 450.

The French case is more complex and involves sophisticated politicking on the national level. In a nutshell, the French government pushed forward its protégé, a law professor and MP who was not short-listed by the national selection panel, in order that he would vacate the seat held by him in the French parliament.[201] This is not as such condemnable.[202] Moreover, the French government transparently acknowledged that it put on the list a complementary candidate who had not been short-listed by an expert panel. The problem was that the French government favoured a candidate who had so little knowledge of the second official language (English)[203] that he was rejected by both the Advisory Panel and the Sub-Committee on the Election of Judges to the European Court of Human Rights.[204]

The election of the Slovak judge in 2004 reveals an even more intricate plan. It is a perfect example of the risk described by the late Flauss that the states might not put together a list with equivalent candidates and, instead, intentionally submit a list in which one candidate stands out and the other two are supposed to play the role of mere 'figurants'.[205] That is exactly what happened in Slovakia. Prior to the 2004 vote in the PACE, everything was cleared at the national level to pave the way for the election of the former Justice of the Slovak Constitutional Court to the ECtHR. There was a 'careful' selection of two weak opponents at the national level, with no experience at the top courts, so that a justice of the Slovak Constitutional Court clearly stood out among them.[206] Nevertheless, the rumour about the rigged selection process at the national level reached the PACE, which eventually elected someone else.

In the previous cases, 'fire alarms' worked. The PACE eventually either rejected the list containing a problematic nominee or elected another candidate. In contrast, the election of a Czech judge in 2012 was fatal. To sum up, the PACE chose a candidate whose knowledge of both English and French was questionable at the time of the elections, whose writings on the law of the Convention were considered marginal even in the Czech Republic,[207] whose expertise in general international

---

[201] Franck Johannès, 'Petite manœuvre de l'Elysée pour placer un ami', *Le Monde*, 14 March 2011: <http://libertes.blog.lemonde.fr/2011/03/14/petite-manoeuvre-de-lelysee-pour-placer-un-ami/> accessed 15 April 2014.

[202] See n 199 above.

[203] Note that 'for judges whose native tongue is one of the official languages, the level of proficiency required for the other may well be pitched higher than for judges for whom both official languages are foreign' (Committee on Legal Affairs and Human Rights, n 53, Part B, para 24 *in fine*).

[204] Engel (n 2) 451. Further see ch 5 s 4.2.

[205] Flauss (n 2); see also Malenovský (n 2) 120; John Hedigan, 'The Election of Judges to the European Court of Human Rights' in Marcelo Kohen (ed), *Promoting Justice, Human Rights and Conflict Resolution Through International Law. Liber amicorum Lucius Caflisch* (Leyden 2007) 238.

[206] Unfortunately, similar problems plagued the national selection of three Slovak nominees in 2013 and 2014 (note that the first as well as the second Slovak list was rejected by PACE). However, I refrain from commenting on this process since, at the point this chapter was submitted, it is not yet finished.

[207] If one looks at the case law of all three Czech apex courts, which is available online, as of 31 March 2014 Pejchal's publications are cited once by the Constitutional Court in a decision dismissed at the admissibility stage, twice by the Supreme Court, and not at all by the Supreme Administrative Court. Moreover, all three citations refer to the co-authored commentary on the Czech Act on the Advocacy.

law was minimal, who had been twice rejected as a candidate for the position of justice of the Czech Constitutional Court, and who had very close ties to the former president of the Czech Republic.[208]

So why did the election of the Czech judge in 2012 go wrong? There is no easy, straight-forward answer to this question. The following paragraphs will show that, for one thing, the (s)election process of the Czech judge was far more complex than generally acknowledged.[209]

First of all, it must be stressed that the selection process started at the national level as early as 2009, because Protocol no 14 had not yet been ratified by Russia, and the term of Karel Jungwiert, a Czech judge of the ECtHR since 1993, was supposed to expire in October 2010. In fact, the government of the Czech Republic adopted Rules on the Selection of Candidates for the Position of a Judge of the European Court of Human Rights (hereinafter only 'Czech selection rules') as early as August 2009.[210]

The Czech selection rules defined the criteria in abstract terms, taking the view that individual invitation calls would specify them. They looked perfect on paper. Article 1 clearly defined the timeframe—the invitation to submit names must be made at least 14 months prior to the expiry of the term of the sitting Strasbourg judge on behalf of the Czech Republic and candidates must have at least two months to lodge their applications. Article 2 defined substantive criteria, both compulsory and 'bonus' ones,[211] which closely followed the PACE's recommendations. Article 3 required the Minister of Justice to ensure 'the broadest possible publicity' for the invitation by uploading it on his website as well as distributing the invitation to courts, prosecutors' offices, professional organizations, and law schools. Article 4 defined the composition of the selection panel: the Minister of Justice (chairman), the Czech agent before the ECtHR, one member nominated by the Minister of Foreign Affairs, two members nominated by the Minister of Justice from jurisconsults of recognized competence, the Chief Justice of the Constitutional Court; the Chief Justice of the Supreme Court; the Chief Justice of the Supreme Administrative Court; and the Ombudsman. Article 5 then set detailed criteria on how the selection panel should proceed. It stipulated, among other things, compulsory interviews with candidates and careful consideration of gender issues.

The first invitation was issued on 1 September 2009. At that time, 13 candidates applied, including the Chief Justice of the Supreme Court, another judge of the Supreme Court (who was elected a judge of the ICC in 2011), and the Czech

---

[208] I would doubt whether all members of PACE had this information on the day of the Czech judge's election.

[209] Note that I co-authored a casebook on Czech constitutional law and two policy papers on the state of the Czech judiciary with one of the unsuccessful Czech candidates in 2012, Zdeněk Kühn (full disclosure). However, I personally believe that even under the somewhat more relaxed PACE criteria applicable in 2012, this entire list should have been rejected.

[210] Decision of the Government of the Czech Republic No 1063 adopted on 26 August 2009.

[211] The 'bonus' criteria included perfect knowledge of both official languages, age sufficient to allow a candidate to serve a full term on the ECtHR, and no necessity to appoint ad hoc judges for complaints against the Czech Republic; see Art 2(2) of the Czech Selection Rules.

agent before the ECtHR (currently the chairman of the Steering Committee for Human Rights). The national selection panel eventually short-listed the following three candidates: Iva Brožová (Chief Justice of the Supreme Court), Robert Fremr (at that time a judge of the Supreme Court, now a judge of the ICC), and Mahulena Hofmannová (at that time a law professor at the University of Giessen).

However, Russia ratified Protocol no 14 in February 2010, as a result of which the mandate of the then sitting Czech judge, Karel Jungwiert, was extended from the autumn of 2010 to the autumn of 2012.[212] This timing of the entry into force of Protocol no 14 did not work well for the Czech selection process. The two-year postponement made a huge difference. What changed during those two years? The Chief Justice of the Czech Supreme Court was no longer interested due to her age. Robert Fremr, another short-listed candidate in 2009, chose a different career path, ran for the position of judge of the ICC in 2011, and was eventually successful. He was elected to the ICC on 13 December 2011.

Therefore, when the second invitation was issued on 8 August 2011, only one short-listed candidate from the 2009 call, Mahulena Hofmannová, applied. The other factor that came into play in 2011 was the fact that between 2012 and 2015 a complete reshuffle of the Czech Constitutional Court was due,[213] and many potential candidates preferred a post at the Constitutional Court to the Strasbourg one. All in all, the above-mentioned personal circumstances and institutional factors led to a very low number of applications in 2011. Out of six applicants, there was no justice of the Constitutional Court, no judge of the Supreme Court, only one judge of the Supreme Administrative Court, and two law professors (Mahulena Hofmannová and Pavel Šturma).[214] Things got worse as two applicants withdrew before the interview stage, including Professor Šturma, who was elected to the UN International Law Commission in November 2011.

The selection panel short-listed Mahulena Hofmannová, at that time a law professor at the University of Luxembourg, and Zdeněk Kühn, a judge of the Supreme Administrative Court. Actually, it was not 'short-listing' in the true sense, because the panel found the other two candidates ineligible. As a result, the third position remained vacant. Interestingly, Aleš Pejchal did not answer the August invitation. Later, he explained in an interview with the Czech law journal *Právní rádce* that his view was that 'answering the open call is for recent law school graduates' and that he preferred the 'prior practice, when respectable institutions...nominated their candidates'.[215]

A separate invitation for the third vacant position on the list was eventually issued on 15 December 2011. This time two candidates applied: Aleš Pejchal, a member of the Czech Bar and a personal advisor to the president of the Czech

---

[212] For a similar scenario, with somewhat different consequences, see above ch 5 s 4.1.

[213] Due to the flawed design of the Czech Constitution, which does not stipulate a staggered system of appointing justices of the Czech Constitutional Court, virtually the entire Constitutional Court is staffed *de novo* every ten years.

[214] The other three candidates included one judge of the regional court, one advocate in his early 40s, and one advocate in his mid-30s.

[215] *Vyšlo to moc hezky*, Právní rádce, 23 August 2012, p 42.

Republic; and Jana Reschová, assistant professor at the Faculty of Law at the Charles University. Out of the two candidates who replied to the December call, the selection panel eventually short-listed Aleš Pejchal. Subsequently, the Czech government submitted the complete list to the Advisory Panel and the PACE.

What happened next at the Strasbourg level is difficult to piece together as the relevant documents are confidential. According to Engel, the Advisory Panel concluded that 'in view of [Mr. Pejchal's...] professional career to date and the list of his publications on the area of law relating to the Convention, [he...] did not have the necessary qualification for the office of judges in Strasbourg',[216] while Czech sources suggest that the panel simply was not satisfied that Mr Pejchal qualified as a jurisconsult of recognized competence.[217] Luzius Wildhaber, the chair of the Advisory Panel, indirectly confirms the latter version, even though he does not mention Mr Pejchal explicitly.[218] Engel also claims that PACE's Sub-Committee on the Election of Judges to the European Court of Human Rights, after interviewing all three Czech nominees, had likewise voted not to recommend Mr Pejchal to the plenary for election.[219] I can neither support nor refute this assertion conclusively, but Engel's claim is not consistent with the subsequent practice of the Sub-Committee once it declassified its advice.[220]

In the meantime, the Czech government intensified its lobbying in the PACE. According to Engel, the Czech Ministry of Justice sent a letter to PACE members in which he underlined his support for the election of Mr Pejchal, even though the latter was considered unsuitable.[221] Engel's account is to some extent misleading. The Czech Minister of Justice did not support Mr Pejchal as a person, but rather lobbied in order to prevent the rejection of the entire Czech list[222] and to save the reputation of the Czech Republic. Here it is important to recall that all other participants in the national selection process were found *ineligible*. The Czech government was simply desperate, because it had no candidate on the reserve list and, given the extremely low number of responses to the previous two invitations to

---

[216] Engel (n 2) 450.

[217] Note that Mr Pejchal had never served as a judge before he was put forward as a candidate for the ECtHR and thus he had not had sufficient judicial experience either.

[218] Steering Committee for Human Rights, Ministers' Deputies' exchange of views with Mr Luzius Wildhaber, Chairman of the Advisory Panel of Experts on Candidates for Election as Judge to the European Court of Human Rights, DH-GDR (2013)005, 5 February 2013, 2 (exchange of views of 30 January 2013).

[219] Engel (n 2) 450.

[220] The practice of the Sub-Committee, once it declassified its advice, is to recommend the most qualified candidate(s) and not to discuss eligibility of the candidates on the list; see eg Conclusions of the Sub-Committee on the lists of candidates submitted by Iceland, Lithuania and the Slovak Republic, Contracting States to the European Convention on Human Rights Progress report, Doc 13233 Addendum II, 17 June 2013. The Czech sources likewise suggest that the Sub-Committee merely chose and recommended the most qualified candidate and did not discuss Mr Pejchal's eligibility.

[221] Ibid, 450.

[222] According to Czech insiders, the Advisory Panel had some doubts not only about Mr Pejchal, for the reasons previously mentioned, but also about Mr Kühn because of his youth and relatively short judicial experience and about Mrs. Hofmannová because of her limited exposure to Czech law (as she had spent most of her career before her candidacy abroad).

apply, the prospects of another round were dim. It was Mr Pejchal, his wife,[223] and his supporters,[224] not the Czech government, who successfully lobbied the Czech delegation in PACE, which in turn lobbied for Mr Pejchal in other delegations.

Due to these efforts, the Czech list eventually was not rejected. On the very day of the first round of elections, one more attempt to reconsider Mr Pejchal's eligibility was made: Lord Tomlinson wanted to comment on his qualifications in an open assembly, but he was silenced on the ground of confidentiality.[225] As a result, the election of the Czech judge could proceed. The first round of elections ended inconclusively. In the second round, Mr Pejchal was eventually elected by a qualified majority,[226] despite the negative assessment by the Advisory Panel and not being recommended by the PACE's Sub-Committee.

In order to get the full picture, it is important to add Mr Pejchal's own account of the election process at the Strasbourg level, published in a Czech law journal shortly after his election:

> We must acknowledge that *selection* ended on the Czech level, on the European level it was *election*... It was on each candidate to persuade the Parliamentary Assembly that he or she is the most suitable candidate... It was not about comparing knowledge [of the nominees]. The important thing was to impress MPs and persuade them, either directly on the Sub-Committee... or by one's CV or by greater support of NGOs.[227]

He thus indirectly confirms his active lobbying in PACE. It sounds like crude politics. However, that is how it works in other cases too,[228] and it is not *per se* reprehensible.[229]

What Pejchal does not mention, though, is that he had an unfair advantage in terms of access to the PACE's members in comparison to the other two candidates. It is a public secret in the Czech Republic that Pejchal's wife, who was at that time working for the lower chamber of the Czech parliament, was in dubious circumstances 'assigned' to the Council of Europe before the election of a new judge on behalf of the Czech Republic.[230] What exactly Pejchal's wife did in Strasbourg is difficult to tell, but appearances matter. All insiders in Strasbourg circles and in the Czech Republic, as well as the other two candidates, interpreted her 'assignment'

---

[223] On the 'assignment' of Mr Pejchal's wife to PACE see below.

[224] According to Czech sources, the Czech Bar Association and the Archbishop of Prague, among other actors, wrote letters of support for Mr Pejchal to PACE.

[225] Lord Tomlinson wanted to quote from the Sub-Committee's recommendation, which is confidential. See 2012 Ordinary Session (Third part), Report, Twenty-first Sitting, Tuesday 26 June 2012 at 10 am, Document AS (2012) CR 21, available at <http://assembly.coe.int>.

[226] The final election result of 27 June 2012 was as follows: Pejchal 90, Kühn 40, Hofmannová 24 votes.

[227] *Vyšlo to moc hezky*, Právní rádce, 23 August 2012, p 42 (emphasis added).

[228] Actually, most accepted as well as rejected candidates whom I interviewed attest to it. See also Erik Voeten, 'The Politics of International Judicial Appointments: Evidence from the European Court of Human Rights' (2007) 61 *Int'l Org* 669; or, more broadly, Erik Voeten, 'The Politics of International Judicial Appointments' (2009) 9 *Chicago J of Int'l L* 387.

[229] See n 199 above.

[230] The circumstances were dubious, because the Czech Republic has a permanent representative to the Council of Europe and the Czech Parliament had never made such 'assignment' before or after this case.

as a way of lobbying in PACE for her husband. It is also obvious that the other two candidates could hardly match that.

The 2012 election raised many eyebrows in the Czech Republic. In fact, PACE managed something that no one else has achieved so far—to unite Czech lawyers irrespective of their political affiliation and judicial philosophy. NGOs, advocates, and judges in unison shook their heads at PACE's choice. Not only the ECtHR's, but also the PACE's and the Council of Europe's credibility suffered. Czech elites' already low trust in European institutions was further reduced. As mentioned above, Pejchal had twice been rejected as a nominee for the Czech Constitutional Court.[231] Many people in the Czech Republic thus wonder how someone like him could have been elected to the ECtHR. Czech commentators also pointed to double standards: on the one hand, the PACE requires maximum transparency in the national selection process, but then it keeps most of its own documents confidential. Similarly, the PACE requires national governments to justify any departure from the trio of candidates short-listed by the national selection panel, but finds it normal to ignore the advice of the Advisory Panel as well as of its own Sub-Committee. From a pragmatic point of view, it may prove difficult to attract top candidates from the Czech Republic in the next election round. They will think twice before they apply, because the process at the Strasbourg level is unpredictable and the PACE is not following even its own criteria.

Finally, it is useful to make a short detour and look at the selection of a Czech judge to the EU's Tribunal which took place a year later. The Czech government of the day wanted to place its protégé at the EU's Tribunal in 2012. This time it completely ignored the advice of the national selection panel, which recommended renewing the term of the then sitting judge at the Tribunal, Irena Pelikánová, and instead nominated one of its ministers, Petr Mlsna, who was 34 years old,[232] had never held judicial office, and had spent his entire career as a civil servant at the Office of the Czech Government. The Article 255 Panel rejected Mlsna and, after several months, Irena Pelikánová was reappointed. This example thus shows that the 255 Panel worked properly,[233] whereas the PACE failed.

The Czech case teaches us several lessons. First, it reminds us that virtually nothing is known publicly about the internal mechanics of the election process within PACE.[234] To my knowledge, no comprehensive study has been conducted on the selection of Strasbourg judges that is comparable to analysis of the selection of judges of the ICJ and the ICC by Ruth Mackenzie, Kate Malleson, Penny Martin, and Philippe Sands. We do not know the lobbying strategies of governments and other actors, how voting coalitions are built, whether package deals are struck, or how often members of the PACE are told to vote for a particular candidate. While

[231] See also Engel (n 2) 450, note 4.

[232] Mr Mlsna famously compared himself to Koen Lenaerts, who became a judge of the Court of First Instance of the European Communities (the predecessor of the Tribunal) at the age of 35.

[233] However, it is important to acknowledge that the Czech government that initially nominated Mlsna was replaced in the meantime.

[234] For brief remarks on this subject see Engel (n 2) 453. However, this lack of information on the election mechanics is not specific to the ECtHR; see Mackenzie (n 2) 100.

it is clear that lobbying and political deals cannot be eliminated, it is necessary to adopt basic rules on lobbying in the PACE, including the disclosure of candidates' family ties. Second, the confidentiality of the Advisory Panel's assessment and Sub-Committee's position is problematic as it benefits ineligible and weak candidates. No matter how well PACE defines the criteria for Strasbourg office, if it does not effectively police their fulfilment, it is of little use. Moreover, the functioning of the 255 Panel shows that public rejection of a Tribunal/CJEU candidate does not discourage good candidates from applying. On the contrary, it stops ineligible or weak candidates from being put forward.

6. How to Attract Top Candidates?

The previous sections have addressed improvements in the selection of Strasbourg judges (the good), explained the problems concerning selected substantive criteria (the bad), and pointed to the worst examples of rigging the selection process (the ugly). Not unlike the PACE's documents, several improvements have been suggested and a few amendments recommended. However, one should not forget the ultimate aim of these efforts. As Mackenzie and others concluded regarding the selection of judges for international courts in general,

[a]ny proposal for reform in relation to judicial appointments should start with the caveat that the role of the procedures and practices in determining the nature and quality of the courts should not be overstated. An entity is only as good as the individuals that are nominated and elected. We can have the best procedure and criteria, but that doesn't guarantee you a great court.[235]

In other words, all efforts to improve the selection procedure of Strasbourg judges should aim at electing judges of the highest calibre,[236] and everything thus boils down to a simple question: how can one attract top candidates?

Put more bluntly, if Çali and her colleagues are right,[237] then people in the United Kingdom compare Strasbourg judges with judges of the Supreme Court of the United Kingdom, Germans compare them with justices of the *Bundesverfassungsgericht*, Frenchmen with judges of the *Conseil d'État*, Poles with judges of the *Trybunał Konstytucyjny* and so forth. If they think that judges of their top domestic courts perform better, then the social legitimacy of the Strasbourg Court is in danger. The key question thus can be rephrased as: how can one lure judges of *these* courts, and candidates from other legal professions with the same gravitas, to Strasbourg?

Finding an answer to this question requires a holistic, proactive, and knowledge-based approach. First, the Council of Europe shall address the

---

[235] Mackenzie (n 2) 177.
[236] See Committee on Legal Affairs and Human Rights (n 53), Part A, para 1; Resolution 1764 (2010), para 1; and Brighton Declaration, para 22.
[237] See s 2 above in this chapter.

recruitment of Strasbourg judges in a holistic way. Hitherto, most documents drafted by the PACE or Committee of Ministers have been good at detail, but one could not see the wood for the trees. Even some amendments to the Convention have suffered from the same malaise. The back-and-forth changes in the upper age limit for judges serve as a prime example.[238] New rules on the upper age limit in Protocols no 11, 14, and 15 were just quick fixes done in a piecemeal fashion, with no vision regarding the big picture. There simply has not been any serious debate about how the new rule affects the selection of Strasbourg judges as a whole.

Instead of discussing how to attract top candidates, states and PACE blame each other for being responsible for electing less-than-stellar judges. To be sure, PACE is right that 'it is the principal responsibility of *states* to submit... lists of top quality candidates'.[239] In other words, '[i]f good candidates are not put forward, or do not come forward, the election procedure cannot lead to good results'.[240] However, PACE must also understand that its actual choices have an impact on who may apply in the future. If it eventually does not elect the very best candidate from the list or, even worse, elects the worst candidate, top candidates may not apply in future at all. At the same time, less-than-stellar candidates will get the message that they indeed have a chance. In other words, top candidates will not apply as the PACE is unpredictable and unprincipled, whereas less-than-stellar candidates will apply precisely because the PACE is unpredictable and unprincipled.

However inconvenient it is, the PACE should also acknowledge that there is 'high demand and low supply' of well-qualified candidates for the position of an international judge.[241] In particular, smaller EU member states have to find stellar nominees for the Luxembourg Courts, namely for the CJEU, the Tribunal, and the position of advocate general; may want to nominate candidates for international courts such as the ICC or the ICJ; and, of course, want to keep some of their best legal minds for their apex courts.[242] Other competent candidates are not willing to apply to the ECtHR for personal or family reasons, and yet another group of candidates consists of those recently appointed to another position who do not want to be perceived as ungrateful or as 'ruthless promotionists'.[243] As a result, some states are not always able to submit a list of three top candidates as they are simply not available at that moment.[244] In addition, the PACE must recognize

---

[238] Further above s 4.3 of this chapter.

[239] Introductory statement made by Mr De Vries at the Standing Committee's meeting held in Paris on 8 March 2013, published in Committee on Legal Affairs and Human Rights, *Information Note: Standing Committee's Exchange of Views with the Sub-Committee's Chairperson*, As/Jur/Cdh (2013) 05, 29 April 2013, p 3 (emphasis in the original).

[240] Michael Wood, 'The Selection of Candidates for International Judicial Office: Recent Practice' in Tafsir M Ndiaye and Rüdiger Wolfrum (eds), *Law of the Sea, Environmental Law and Settlement of Disputes* (Koninklijke 2007) 357, 357–8.

[241] See also Mackenzie (n 2) 61.

[242] See eg the situation in the Czech Republic in 2011 described above in s 5.

[243] For instance, it is considered *chucpe* if someone who was appointed to the domestic apex court just two years before the vacancy for the ECtHR arose applies for Strasbourg office. There is always an unwritten rule that such a judge must serve several years or a substantial part of her term before seeking another position.

[244] The Advisory Panel seems to be aware of this problem; see Excerpt from GT-GDR-E(2013)004, published as Steering Committee for Human Rights (n 64) ('in countries with a small population it

that governments will, from time to time, decide not to follow the advice of their advisory bodies and will place their own protégés on the list.[245]

In such situations, the role of the PACE is to choose the best out of the three, or at least not to elect a candidate who clearly does not meet one of the key requirements such as language skills and knowledge of domestic law, or whose experience or age would raise an eyebrow. Unfortunately, the PACE has recently elected several judges who were unfit for Strasbourg office, while disregarding its own criteria. If the PACE itself is not able to identify such problematic candidates, then another filtering body must do that job. The PACE's Sub-Committee on the Election of Judges to the European Court of Human Rights has been the subject of severe criticism[246] and, judging by recent embarrassing examples, has failed to fulfil this 'sifting' role. It is thus surprising that the Advisory Panel, which is the expert body, is not allowed to interview the candidates and check their language skills and other eligibility criteria.[247]

One caveat must be added here. For an outsider who does not live in Strasbourg and does not have access to confidential information, it is difficult to identify what went wrong between the PACE and the Advisory Panel. In my opinion, the Advisory Panel should not act as a 'ranking agency',[248] but must be able to stop ineligible candidates from going any further. Otherwise it does not make sense to have it. However, the PACE and the Committee of Ministers think differently.[249]

Second, the Council of Europe must also be more active in attracting top candidates.[250] It is now generally accepted that any improvements at the nomination and selection stages 'should be coupled with efforts to expand the selection pool through proactive efforts to seek out highly qualified candidates who might not be as visible as those in traditional networks'.[251] The Steering Committee for Human Rights (CDDH) did a good job on this issue and proposed the following measures:

- maximum transparency in the selection procedure;
- awareness-raising on the work and life of a judge in Strasbourg, including with a view to correcting misconceptions about the conditions of employment;
- transmitting information to legal networks about the imminent call for applicants;

---

might prove to be difficult to find three candidates of an equally long professional experience'). See also Malenovský (n 2) 187.

[245] See this volume, ch 5 s 4.2 and Engels (n 2) for specific examples.

[246] Limbach (n 2) 20–3; Sevón (n 25) 3; Lord Hoffmann, *The Universality of Human Rights*. Judicial Studies Board Annual Lecture, available online at <https://www.judiciary.gov.uk>, last accessed 19 March 2009, para 38. See also Mackenzie (n 2) 156–7.

[247] See above, ch 5 s 3.3.

[248] This role seems to be played by the Sub-Committee on the Election of Judges to the European Court of Human Rights.

[249] See the contributions of Mr Cilevičs and Mr de Vries, published in Committee on Legal Affairs and Human Rights (n 240), pp 2 and 4; Steering Committee for Human Rights (n 64), paras 31–2.

[250] See Izmir Declaration, p 2.   [251] Mackenzie (n 2) 179.

- particular measures aimed at increasing applications by people from backgrounds that are historically less likely to produce applicants;
- asking relevant independent persons/organizations to encourage potentially suitable people to apply;
- the use of new media, including government websites;
- taking measures to ensure the availability of suitable professional opportunities for former judges upon leaving office.[252]

Third, the Council of Europe should also know what top judges and top candidates from other legal professions care about, or, more precisely, what is a deal-breaker for them. Is it the salary? Is it the suspension of the pension scheme in their home countries? Is it the need to reintegrate after the end of their Strasbourg term? Is it their inability to choose their own law clerks themselves? Is it the difficulty for their partners to find jobs in Strasbourg? Or is it something else? Do they consider the nine-year term too short to justify moving to another country or, rather, too long? Unless the Council of Europe knows the answers to these questions, it can hardly solve the problem of attracting top candidates effectively and systematically.

Hitherto, this chapter has proceeded on the assumption that the current system of selection of Strasbourg judges can still be improved to produce stellar judges whose independence, qualification, and stature would be beyond doubt. However, it is perhaps time to start thinking outside the box and question the very foundations of the current system of electing Strasbourg judges, because the view that the current procedure is 'undoubtedly a major success story'[253] is no longer shared by many.

The current system rests on three basic principles:

(1) that *each* State nominates its own candidates;

(2) that each State submits a list of *three* candidates;

(3) that the *PACE* elects Strasbourg judges.

The first and the third principles will hardly be abandoned without a complete overhaul of the selection process, but changing the second one should be considered. It was mentioned above that some smaller states in particular sometimes have problems putting together a list of three stellar candidates.[254] The key question is thus whether reducing the number of candidates to two or just one would mitigate this problem.[255]

---

[252] Steering Committee for Human Rights, *Report of Ad Hoc Working Group on National Practices for the Selection of Candidates for the Post of Judge at the European Court of Human Rights*, CDDH-SC(2011)R1, 14 September 2011, p 18.

[253] Introductory statement made by Mr. De Vries at the Standing Committee's meeting held in Paris on 8 March 2013, published in Committee on Legal Affairs and Human Rights, *Information Note: Standing Committee's Exchange of Views with the Sub-Committee's Chairperson*, As/Jur/Cdh (2013) 05, 29 April 2013, p 3.

[254] See nn 242–245 above.

[255] I am grateful to Daniel Kelemen for raising this issue at the Bruges conference.

Whether having two instead of three candidates on the list would have any positive impact is unclear, but switching to one would certainly make the selection process easier. The responsibilities of the relevant players would be clearer and states could no longer blame PACE for not choosing the first best candidate. Similarly, governments would have no incentive to prioritize 'their' candidate.[256] There is one more advantage. All candidates for Strasbourg office are risk averse and no one wants to be labelled as an 'unsuccessful candidate for the position of a judge of the European Court of Human Rights'. Especially for top candidates, such 'rejection' has reputational costs. Hence, switching to one candidate would put pressure on the nominating government to submit the best possible candidates and increase the chances that the top candidates would be willing to join the contest.[257]

This solution thus seems to be a 'win–win' one. However, there is always a trade-off. In this case, the reduction of the number of candidates to one would change the PACE's role. It would no longer have a real choice. Instead, it would become a veto gate. But that is the way it works in Luxembourg, and it works much better than the Strasbourg rule. To my knowledge, no one has questioned the qualifications, experience, or stature of Luxembourg judges.[258] Moreover, the PACE itself has already indicated that it invites the prioritization of candidates by national governments in order to make its choice 'easier'.[259]

7. Conclusion

Mr De Vries, a member of the PACE and its Sub-Committee on the Election of Judges to the European Court of Human Rights, said in his speech on 8 March 2013 that '[the] procedure [of selecting Strasbourg judges] is undoubtedly a major success story, despite occasional mishaps or unpleasant surprises, which to us, parliamentarians, well versed in the daily realities of power-politics and behind-the-scenes arrangements, comes as no surprise'.[260] This chapter respectfully disagrees. It argues that there are flaws in the procedure and, more importantly, there is no room for further 'mishaps' or 'unpleasant surprises'.

The very legitimacy of the Strasbourg Court is at stake. Recent empirical studies and the burgeoning literature on the selection of judges of the ECtHR show that Strasbourg judges' qualifications and experience rank among the most important legitimacy criteria for key stakeholders, and that a significant number of these

---

[256] Note that the requirement to present the three nominated judges in alphabetical order, as stipulated by PACE, Resolution 1646 (2009), para 4.3, is often not followed in practice—see eg Malenovský (n 2) 121. For further discussions of the pros and cons of the prioritization of candidates by governments see Committee on Legal Affairs and Human Rights (n 53), Part B, paras 27–8.

[257] One reviewer suggested that non-nomination on the national level has similar reputational costs for a rejected candidate. I disagree: the reputational costs are far lower on the national level as the names of candidates are known to only a few insiders.

[258] Further see this volume, Chapters 1–3.

[259] See Committee on Legal Affairs and Human Rights (n 53), Part B, para 23 *in fine*.

[260] Introductory statement made by Mr. De Vries at the Standing Committee's meeting held in Paris on 8 March 2013, published in Committee on Legal Affairs and Human Rights (n 240), p 3.

stakeholders assess this criterion negatively. Given the recent 'mishaps', especially in the 2012 elections, this picture has become even dimmer and the reservoir of trust in the ECtHR has shrunk further. It is important to keep in mind that the election of one sub-optimal judge to the ECtHR has more far-reaching consequences for the Court's legitimacy than one controversial judgment. Most controversial rulings are forgotten after a few years or can at least be moderated by subsequent judgments, but a problematic judge will take part in thousands of decisions. Such a judge thus not only undermines the legitimacy of the ECtHR at the moment of her election, but also becomes the Court's 'legitimacy baggage' for nine years.[261]

It is thus unfortunate that the problems regarding the selection of judges have only recently started to be openly discussed. While it is understandable that procedural reforms of the Convention, such as reducing the time for lodging an application to the ECtHR or efforts to reduce the backlog, receive more attention than institutional issues, such as upper age limits or language skills of Strasbourg judges, it is short-sighted to underestimate the latter. The ECtHR is not an 'it', but a 'they'. It is thus critical to move beyond second-tier principles such as non-politicization, diversity, and the transparency of national procedures[262] and pay more attention to the higher-level principles of professional competence and integrity.[263] This means that we must start addressing key questions such as which substantive criteria are the most important, which standards cannot be compromised under any circumstances, how to attract the top candidates to Strasbourg, and how to eliminate those whose presence will not advance Strasbourg's reputation. The recent controversies regarding selection of Strasbourg judges may in fact lead to increased institutional robustness of the ECtHR vis-à-vis its critics and make it stronger.[264] There is still time to do so. But if the current problems are not taken seriously now, we may soon learn that it is too late to save the Court.

---

[261] Moreover, there is neither initial nor in-service training for Strasbourg judges; see Egbert Myjer, 'Are Judges of the European Court of Human Rights so Qualified that They Are in No Need of Initial and In-Service Training? A "Straatsburgse Myj/mering" (Myjer's Musings from Strasbourg) for Leo Zwaak' in Yves Haeck et al (eds), *The Realisation of Human Rights: When Theory Meets Practice: Studies in Honour of Leo Zwaak* (Intersentia 2014).

[262] In fact, several commentators on the draft of this chapter provocatively suggested that the road to hell (the best candidates do not apply) is often paved with good intentions (that is with a transparent national selection process).

[263] For the distinction between these two tiers of principles involved in selecting international judges see Mackenzie (n 2) 137.

[264] The current criticism of selection of Strasbourg judges is thus not by definition a sign of defeat; see this volume, ch 12 s 1.

7

On the Democratic Legitimacy of Europe's Judges

A Principled and Comparative Reconstruction of the Selection Procedures

Armin von Bogdandy and Christoph Krenn

1. Introduction

For a long time the appointment of judges to international courts has been an issue for diplomats:[1] brewed in ministerial corridors, decided behind closed doors, directed by the wisdom of national governments.[2] At a time when international adjudication was rare and 'blessed with benign neglect',[3] when international judicial decisions had little effect on our daily lives, on democratic institutions or social conflicts, executive wisdom and diplomatic skills could indeed be seen as the best way to choose those suited to populate such remote institutions.

Today the situation is different. International and supranational courts effectively impact on the world we live in. Among them the European Court of Human Rights (ECtHR) and the Court of Justice of the European Union (CJEU) stand out. Being political achievements of a post-war Europe, they have

---

[1] We are grateful to Markus Fyrnys, Matthias Goldmann, Jannika Jahn, Isabelle Ley, Karin Oellers-Frahm, Stefan Ruppert, Daniel Sarmiento, and Stephan Schill for valuable advice and critique.

[2] For a vivid description see Ruth MacKenzie and Phillipe Sands, 'Judicial Selection for International Courts: Towards Common Principles and Practices' in Kate Malleson and Peter H Russell (eds), *Appointing Judges in an Age of Judicial Power: Critical Perspectives from Around the World* (University of Toronto Press 2006) 213 and Paul Mahoney, 'The International Judiciary—Independence and Accountability' (2008) 7 *Law and Practice of International Courts and Tribunals* 313, 324; see also Michael Wood, 'The Selection of Candidates for International Judicial Office: Recent Practice', in Tafsi Malick Ndiaye and Rüdiger Wolfrum (eds), *Law of the Sea, Environmental Law and Settlement of Disputes. Liber Amicorum Judge Thomas A. Mensah* (Nijhoff 2007) 357, 358.

[3] See, famously, Eric Stein, 'Lawyers, Judges and the Making of a Transnational Constitution' (1981) 75 *AJIL* 1, 1.

developed in an unforeseeable manner into powerful institutions.[4] Their judges empower citizens,[5] restrain trade unions,[6] define employment conditions,[7] or determine child custody.[8] In more conceptual terms these courts contribute to social interaction as multifunctional institutions and have thereby left the traditional understanding, which conceives of international courts only as dispute settlement bodies, far behind.[9] Sure enough, the ECtHR and the CJEU resolve disputes—but they also *stabilize* normative expectations in reasserting the validity and enforcement of the law they apply. Moreover, they develop the law and thus *create* normative expectations,[10] often called, even by the courts themselves, case law. Law-making through precedents is their business, too.[11] Important social questions are framed and regulated by their decisions. Finally, they control and legitimate the authority exercised by others. Also in this respect, they resemble national constitutional or supreme courts.[12] In performing those manifold functions the ECtHR's and the CJEU's authority is little determined by the law,[13] so that judges shape the legal order according to their ideas and convictions. Although the courts have no direct coercive mechanisms at their hands, their authority is often hard to withstand.[14] In other words, the ECtHR and the CJEU are multifunctional institutions that exercise public authority.[15] This

---

[4] Steven Greer, *The European Convention on Human Rights: Achievements, Problems and Prospects* (Cambridge University Press 2006) 9; Karen Alter, *The European Court's Political Power* (Oxford University Press 2009).

[5] *Hirst v UK (No. 2)* App no 74025/01 (ECHR, 6 October 2005) (enhancing the political rights of prisoners).

[6] Case C-438/05 *Viking Line* [2007] ECR I-10779.

[7] Case C-426/11, *Mark Alemo-Herron* [2013] OJ C260/10 (severely restricting the effects of collective labour agreements in the case of transfer of an undertaking).

[8] *Zaunegger v Germany* App no 22028/04 (ECHR, 3 December 2009).

[9] Armin von Bogdandy and Ingo Venzke, 'On the Functions of International Courts: An Appraisal in Light of their Burgeoning Public Authority' (2013) 26 *Leiden Journal of International Law* 49.

[10] Marc Jacob, *Precedents and Case-Based Reasoning in the European Court of Justice: Unfinished Business* (Cambridge University Press 2014); Markus Fyrnys, 'Expanding Competences by Judicial Lawmaking. The Pilot Judgment Procedure of the European Court of Human Rights' in Armin von Bogdandy and Ingo Venzke (eds), *International Judicial Lawmaking* (Springer 2012) 329.

[11] In more detail Marc Jacob, 'Precedents: Lawmaking Through International Adjudication' (2011) 12 *German Law Journal* 1005. This law-making happens although a decision is legally binding only upon the contending parties in the litigated matter and has no further binding effect.

[12] Samantha Besson, 'European Human Rights, Supranational Judicial Review and Democracy. Thinking Outside the Judicial Box' in Patricia Popelier, Catherine Van de Heyning, and Piet Van Nuffel (eds), *Human Rights Protection in the European Legal Order: The Interaction Between the European and the National Courts* (Intersentia 2011) 97.

[13] For this point, exemplified in the example of the judicial development of EU internal market law, see Stephen Weatherill, 'The Court's Case Law on the Internal Market: "A Cirumloquacious Statement of the Result, Rather than a Reason for Arriving at It"?' in Maurice Adams et al (eds), *Judging Europe's Judges. The Legitimacy of the Case Law of the European Court of Justice* (Hart 2013) 87.

[14] Armin von Bogdandy and Ingo Venzke, 'In Whose Name? An Investigation of International Courts' Public Authority and Its Democratic Justification' (2012) 23 *EJIL* 7; in full detail Armin von Bogdandy and Ingo Venzke, *In wessen Namen? Internationale Gerichte in Zeiten globalen Regierens* (Suhrkamp 2014), 150–155.

[15] On this important point, von Bogdandy and Venzke, *In wessen Namen?* (n 14) 16–30, 136–155.

raises the question of their legitimacy, not least their democratic legitimacy,[16] and prompts us to consider judicial selection to the Strasbourg and Luxembourg courts in a new light.

Nevertheless, many will wonder whether the selection of judges can be meaningfully construed as a democratic endeavour. Many perceive judicial appointments as rather technical and legally framed decisions, applying given criteria and aiming to select—out of a number of candidates—the best legal expert to fill a vacancy at a court.[17] Such technical decisions primarily demand judgement, expertise, and assessment of past merits. Accordingly, they are often seen as ill-suited to be treated in the democratic process and rather to be left to specialized institutions like expert panels. To improve selection procedures, the argument goes, one should aim to 'depoliticize' rather than 'democratize' the process, putting it in the hands of independent experts and taking it off the diplomatic parquet. This position is prevalent in the discussion on appointing judges to the ECtHR and the CJEU.[18]

However, if we zoom into the process' actual working, the dominant view loses plausibility. The selection of judges to the ECtHR and the CJEU can hardly be squared with the notion of a decision predetermined by the respective treaties. Both the Convention and the EU Treaties paint only a very vague picture of the personalities of which a court bench should be composed. The Treaty on the Functioning of the European Union (TFEU) requires independence and professional expertise (Art 253 para 1 and Art 254 para 2 TFEU); the Convention speaks of candidates' 'high moral character' and their juridical competence (Art 21 para 1 ECHR). This picture needs to be refined to be operable. Indeed, selection bodies for the ECtHR and the CJEU have done precisely this, giving very specific meaning to the notions of expertise and independence and developing additional criteria.[19] Like norms, they have laid them down in general instruments, namely in resolutions, recommendations, and activity reports. The selection bodies do not only apply the law; they also engage in law-making.[20]

A further doubt comes from comparison. If selecting judges were a mere technical exercise, one could hardly explain why many national constitutions assign the

---

[16] In western modern normative thinking the paramount form of legitimacy for public authority is democratic legitimacy; Pierre Rosanvallon, *La légitimité démocratique. Impartialité, reflexivité, proximité* (Seuil 2008) 9; for the 'post-national constellation' see Jürgen Habermas, 'Konstitutionalisierung des Völkerrechts und die Legitimationsprobleme einer verfaßten Weltgesellschaft' in *Philosophische Texte Band 4. Politische Theorie* (Suhrkamp 2009) 402.

[17] Contrast above ch 3 s 3.

[18] See the discussion on the introduction of the expert panel involved in judicial selection for the EU courts set up by Article 255 TFEU: Final Report of the discussion circle on the Court of Justice in the European Convention CONV 636/03 (25 March 2003) para 6 and Ricardo Passos, 'Le système juridictionnel de l'Union' in Giuliano Amato, Hervé Bribosia, and Bruno de Witte (eds), *Genèse et destine de la Constitution européenne* (Bruylant 2007) 565, 585; for such an argument as regards judicial selection in the ECtHR see for instance Christoph Grabenwarter and Katharina Pabel, *Europäische Menschenrechtskonvention* (5th edn, Beck 2012) 40.

[19] This will be developed in detail below in s 3 of this chapter.

[20] A notion we employ to describe not only legislative acts *stricto sensu* but also other, 'softer' forms of regulation and standard-setting. For a conceptualization of international soft law see Matthias Goldmann, 'We Need to Cut Off the Head of the King: Past, Present, and Future Approaches to International Soft Law' (2012) 25 *Leiden Journal of International Law* 335.

selection of judges for constitutional courts to parliaments[21] or involve members of parliament in judicial selection committees.[22] This reveals that such decisions are of great importance for a political community. Since the ECtHR and the CJEU have a comparable impact, a technocratic take on selecting their judges is hardly convincing from a comparative perspective. The moment of selection of Europe's judges is a moment to take a principled decision as to what kind of personalities should fashion court decisions which may deeply affect individuals, the further path of the law, and the courts' institutional development and success.[23]

To pre-empt misunderstandings: a reconstruction of the selection of judges in light of their democratic legitimacy is not a call for wholesale politicization. We do not advocate direct elections along the lines of the examples of the US or Bolivia.[24] Nor do we understand judges as representatives.[25] What we call for is, first, that representative institutions develop the criteria and procedures for becoming a judge in an open and co-operative fashion; and second, that these criteria are applied in a transparent and deliberative manner in concrete selection cases. This should also forestall concerns that the principle of democracy might negatively affect the independence of courts. To be clear, independence and impartiality are preconditions for the set-up and functioning of courts.

To substantiate our claim, we will first present the democratic principles of the Treaty on European Union (TEU) and the corresponding standards within the Council of Europe (section 2). They provide the basis for a comparative appraisal of the selection of judges to the ECtHR and the CJEU. Section 3 assesses the respective selection procedures. Three theses will guide our contribution: first, in the European Union, when it comes to selecting CJEU judges, reality lags behind the democratic project laid out in Articles 9 to 12 TEU; second, when comparing the judicial selection process in the EU and the Council of Europe the latter fares

---

[21] See Art 94 German Basic Law; Art 147 Constitution of Austria; Art 135 Constitution of Italy; Art 194 Constitution of Poland; Art 159 Constitution of Spain; Art II 2 (2) US Constitution. In detail, Andreas Voßkuhle, *Rechtsschutz gegen den Richter: Zur Integration der Dritten Gewalt in das verfassungsrechtliche Kontrollsystem vor dem Hintergrund des Art. 19 Abs. 4 GG* (Beck 1993) 47–50, 63–4. It is a peculiarity of the appointment of the highest court judges that the number of cases is so few that parliamentary bodies can potentially handle them with all the case-specific factual assessments involved; on the benefits of developing the law, inspired by concrete cases, see Christoph Schönberger, 'Höchstrichterliche Rechtsfindung und Auslegung gerichtlicher Entscheidungen' in *Grundsatzfragen der Rechtsetzung und Rechtsfindung. Veröffentlichungen der Vereinigung der Deutschen Staatsrechtslehrer, vol 71* (De Gruyter 2012) 296, 312–13.

[22] See for instance Art 95 para 2 German Basic Law; Article 197 and 187 Constitution of Poland; Section 178 Constitution of South Africa.

[23] On the ECtHR see only Mikael Rask Madsen, 'The Protracted Institutionalization of the Strasbourg Court: From Legal Diplomacy to Integrationist Jurisprudence' in Jonas Christoffersen and Mikael Rask Madsen (eds), *The European Court of Human Rights between Law and Politics* (Oxford University Press 2013) 43, 48.

[24] For the US Russell Wheeler, 'Judicial Independence in the United States of America' in Anja Seibert-Fohr (ed), *Judicial Independence in Transition* (Springer 2012) 521, 528–39; on the problems of direct elections in federal states see Charles G Geyh, 'Judicial Election Reconsidered: A Plea for Radical Moderation' (2012) 35 *Harvard Journal of Law and Public Policy* 623, 631–8; for direct elections of judges as foreseen in the 2009 Bolivian Constitution see Amanda Driscoll and Michael J Nelson, 'The 2011 Judicial Elections in Bolivia' (2012) 31 *Electoral Studies* 628.

[25] Von Bogdandy and Venzke, *In wessen Namen?* (n 14) 204.

far better; however, third, the Council of Europe institutions' lack of respect for the very law they have developed is deeply problematic from a democratic perspective.

2. Concurring Democratic Principles in the EU and the Council of Europe

This section develops the concurring democratic principles in EU law and the law of the Council of Europe that will, in a second step, be applied to the selection procedures in the following section 3. To be sure, this is not about developing principles that carry claims of illegality, holding certain rules or practices illegal. We are here concerned with guiding principles that legally justify a doctrinal reconstruction and proposals for reform.

In the EU, where the transformative and intrusive effects of public authority beyond the state have been most visible and articulated, the development of democratic principles has progressed furthest. For more than 20 years efforts have gone into carving out legitimating models, strategies, and venues to justify the operation of EU institutions.[26] They resulted in Articles 9 to 12 TEU, the Union's 'democratic principles'. Inserted by the Treaty of Lisbon into primary law, they frame the Union based upon representative, responsive, deliberative, and transparent institutions. These articles have been elaborated in one of the most involved political processes that the European continent has ever seen, and its enactment has gone through very burdensome procedures, mostly constitutional amendment procedures. They have also been the object of detailed judicial review.[27] Accordingly, there is much to be said for the view that the concept of democracy as laid down in these articles enjoys the consent of the vast majority of European citizens. Given their wording and systematic outlook, they apply to all EU institutions, including the CJEU.[28]

The Council of Europe cannot claim to have a similar set of inclusively elaborated democratic principles. Nonetheless, its democratic commitment is prominently laid down in its Statute. The Council's founding document refers to its

---

[26] The debate gained new impetus in the context of the financial and sovereign debt crisis from 2008 onwards: see Ingolf Pernice et al, *A Democratic Solution to the Crisis. Reform Steps towards a Democratically Based Economic and Financial Constitution for Europe* (Nomos 2012); Miguel Poiares Maduro, Bruno De Witte, and Mattias Kumm, 'The Euro Crisis and the Democratic Governance of the Euro: Legal and Political Issues of a Fiscal Crisis', Policy Report 10 May 2012: <http://globalgovernanceprogramme.eui.eu/wp-content/uploads/2012/06/Policy-Report10May20121.pdf>, last accessed 15 November 2014; see in general Beate Kohler-Koch and Berthold Rittberger (eds), *Debating the Democratic Legitimacy of the European Union* (Rowman & Littlefield 2007).

[27] Spanish Constitutional Court, Case Rs. 1/2004, Judgment of 13 December 2004; German Federal Constitutional Court, Judgment of 30 June 2009, BVerfGE 123, 267, 353; Czech Constitutional Court, Case Pl. ÚS 50/04, Judgment of 8 March 2006; Case Pl. ÚS 66/04, Judgment of 3 May 2006, para 53; Case Pl. ÚS 19/08, Judgment of 22 November 2008, para 97.

[28] Art 10 TEU speaks generally of '*the Union*' which shall, according to Article 9 TEU, be democratic '*in all its activities*'. A differentiation as regards the respective institutions only happens in Art 13 TEU (emphasis added).

devotion to democracy.[29] Safeguarding and realizing democratic ideals and principles is among the Council's aims.[30] It is acknowledged that the Council itself is bound to respect the democratic standards it was set up to safeguard;[31] however, given the lack of a catalogue of democratic principles, one may wonder what these precise standards are. As will be shown in a minute, very much like in the EU, the ideas of representation, transparency, and deliberation are of crucial importance. This can be discerned from the Council's institutional law and a number of its secondary legal instruments. It should have become clear by now that our assessment of selection procedures is not a free-standing exercise but strives to take seriously the *legal* commitment of the EU and the Council of Europe to democratic principles.

2.1. Representative democracy

The member states conceive of themselves as representative democracies; therefore, in many domestic contexts, parliaments have a say in the selection of judges to constitutional or other important courts.[32] Because such judicial appointments are deemed important and contingent, it is for representatives of the community to choose who is best suited to sit on these courts.[33] Article 10 TEU also founds the EU on representative democracy. However, it adapts this principle, quite remarkably, for the supranational realm. Its second paragraph installs two lines of democratic legitimation that form the basis for a composite and multilevel democratic structure: European citizens are represented in the European Parliament, which they elect by direct and universal suffrage. The member states' democratically organised peoples in turn are represented in the European Council and the Council composed of national executives. The latter are accountable to member states' parliaments or directly to member state citizens. The key role of national parliaments is further accentuated by Article 12 TEU, which assigns to these assemblies a significant position in shaping and controlling EU politics. Citizens

---

[29] See Recital 2 Preamble of the Statute of the Council of Europe (5 May 1949) 87 UNTS 103, ETS 1.

[30] Art 1 of its Statute (n 29); the effective implementation of its aims are of such importance to the organization that it foresees a mechanism that can, in extreme cases, lead to the exclusion of a member state seriously impairing the Council's aims; see Art 8 CoE Statute; in the EU it took until the 1997 Amsterdam Treaty to emphasize its commitment to common principles in a similar manner, drawing up a comparable mechanism, now enshrined in Art 7 TEU.

[31] See Council of Europe (Committee of Ministers), 'Access to Council of Europe documents' (12 June 2001) CM Res 2001/6: 'Convinced that the application by the Council of Europe of the principles and standards which it lays down for its member states is a fundamental element of the Organisation's credibility and consistency.'

[32] See nn 21–2.

[33] Consequently many national courts decide in the community's name: see § 25 para 4 of the German Federal Constitutional Court Act: 'Die Entscheidungen des Bundesverfassungsgerichts ergehen im Namen des Volkes'; Art 454 of the French Code of Civil Procedure: 'Le jugement est rendu au nom du peuple français'; Art 101 para 1 of the Constitution of the Republic of Italy: 'La giustizia è amministrata in nome del popolo'.

are today not only member state nationals, but also members of a bigger political community.[34] Such a multilevel structure for democratic governance demands we conceive selecting judges to be a *shared responsibility.*

Also, the Council of Europe's main organs, the Committee of Ministers and the Parliamentary Assembly (PACE), are composed of 'representatives', as the Council's Statute informs us.[35] The law hence points to these institutions when we query the institutional locus of politics in this organization. The Committee of Ministers is composed of foreign ministers or high-ranking national diplomats;[36] the PACE unites members of parliament sent by their national parliaments.[37] Like the EU,[38] the Council of Europe has seen a certain pull toward strengthening its parliamentary component. Early on, the PACE programmatically changed its name from 'consultative' to 'parliamentary' assembly, making ample use of those competences granted to it, one particular example being the election of judges. Albeit not directly elected, it represents citizens' interests from a transnational perspective.[39] A lot speaks therefore in favour of also understanding the PACE as an institution entrusted with democratic representation.

Of course, there are important differences from the European Parliament: whereas the PACE follows the path of international parliamentarism, ie the collaboration between national parliamentarians, the EU parliament represents a new polity. This difference, however, does not affect our point: that both institutions serve the function of democratic representation beyond the state.

2.2. Transparency, participation, and deliberation

To be sure, representative democratic processes are difficult to reproduce beyond the state.[40] Most importantly, supra- and international parliamentary assemblies are little embedded in public discourses. This speaks for the significant involvement of national parliaments, as laid down in Article 12 TEU. Beyond this, it has prompted many to investigate the actual processes of decision-making. In the EU, important scholarship focuses on the promise of deliberative settings to enhance the legitimacy of EU governance.[41] The question how a decision is rendered moves

---

[34] Dora Kostakopoulou, 'European Union Citizenship: Writing the Future' (2007) 13 *ELJ* 623; Jürgen Habermas, 'The Crisis of the European Union in the Light of a Constitutionalization of International Law' (2012) 23 *EJIL* 335, 343.

[35] Articles 14 and 25 of the *CoE Statute* (n 29).

[36] See Article 15 of the *CoE Statute* (n 29).

[37] See Article 25a of the *CoE Statute* (n 29).

[38] Berthold Rittberger, 'Institutionalizing Representative Democracy in the European Union. The Case of the European Parliament' (2012) 50 *JCMS* 18 (seeking to explain the institutional choices that led to the EP's empowerment).

[39] Isabelle Ley, *Opposition im Völkerrecht. Ein Beitrag zu den legitimationstheoretischen Grundlagen internationaler Rechtserzeugung und ihrer Anwendung* (Springer 2015) 232–6 (showing that decisions in the assembly can be explained along both, political and national lines).

[40] Jürgen Habermas, *Der gespaltene Westen* (Suhrkamp 2004) 137–42.

[41] See in particular the work done by Christian Joerges and Jürgen Neyer, 'From Intergovernmental Bargaining to Deliberative Political Processes: The Constitutionalisation of Comitology' (1997) 3 *ELJ* 273 and more recently 'Deliberative Supranationalism Revisited', EUI Working Papers LAW

to the foreground. Put pointedly: even more so than their domestic counterparts, public institutions beyond the state have to *earn* democratic legitimacy.

This insight has found its way into the EU Treaties and is reflected in Article 11 TEU.[42] This provision demands that decisions be taken as openly as possible,[43] that venues for participation are opened, and that deliberation be the dominant decision-making paradigm. The integration of diverse views and their open and deliberative processing can inform decisions in many ways.[44] Transparency allows the relevant knowledge for active engagement. The comprehensibility and the possibility of attributing accountability is a democratic essential, in particular in a complex multilevel system. Accordingly, the CJEU unequivocally holds in its recent case law that transparency in EU law has a pronounced democratic meaning and establishes a presumption of democratic openness that needs to be rebutted by institutions which seek confidentiality.[45] Participation, deliberation, and transparency are important elements of democratic governance in the EU.

Similar democratic principles can be found in the Council of Europe, though directed more toward state behaviour than toward the authority of the Council itself.[46] Nevertheless, an acknowledgement of the value of deliberative and participatory governance can, for instance, be discerned in rules of the Committee of Ministers that institutionalize consultations of and discussions with other institutions and experts.[47] As regards transparency, the Council of Europe's 2009 Convention on Access to Official Documents sets the tone by stressing the 'importance in a pluralistic, democratic society of transparency of public authorities'.[48] From a democratic perspective, this must also comprise supranational and international public authorities.[49] Accordingly, the Council does not confine itself to setting up standards for its contracting states; it also commits itself to transparency and openness, establishing that for its own work, 'transparency is the rule and confidentiality the exception'.[50]

No. 2006/20; see also Erik O Eriksen, *The Unfinished Democratization of Europe* (Oxford University Press 2009).

[42] In detail, Joana Mendes, 'Participation and the Role of Law After Lisbon: A Legal View on Article 11 TEU', (2011) 48 *CMLRev* 1849.

[43] See also Art 1 para 2 TEU and Article 15 TFEU.

[44] Concepts of participatory and deliberative democracy have by now entered the mainstream of democratic thought: see Jan Klabbers, Anne Peters, and Geir Ulfstein, *The Constitutionalization of International Law* (Oxford University Press 2009) 268–71; Deirdre M Curtin, *Postnational Democracy: The European Union in Search of a Political Philosophy* (Kluwer 1997) 53–61; Amartya Sen, *The Idea of Justice* (Lane 2009).

[45] Joined cases C-39/05 P and C-52/05 P *Sweden and Turco v Council* [2008] ECR I-4723, paras 45–6 and case C-280/11 P *Council v Access Info Europe* [2013] n.y.r., paras 32–3.

[46] See however, *CM Res 2001/6* (n 30).

[47] Council of Europe (Committee of Ministers), 'Rules of Procedure for the Meetings of the Ministers' Deputies' (4 July 1955, now 4th rev edn 2005), Art 15; see also Council of Europe (Secretariat of the Committee of Ministers) 'Hearings and exchanges of views within the Ministers' Deputies' (11 March 2008) CM/Bur/Del(2008)2 revised.

[48] Council of Europe, 'Convention on Access to Official Documents' (18 June 2009) CETS 205, Preamble 4th recital.

[49] See Anne Peters, 'Towards Transparency as a Global Norm' in Andrea Bianchi and Anne Peters (eds), *Transparency in International Law* (Cambridge University Press 2013) 534, 562–6.

[50] Council of Europe (Committee of Ministers) 'Access to Council of Europe Documents' (12 June 2001) CM Res 2001/6, Preamble 3rd recital; see also Council of Europe (Parliamentary Assembly) 'Transparency of the Work of the Committee of Ministers' (4 November 2005) Doc 10736.

3. Judicial Selection for the ECtHR and the CJEU:
A Democratic Reconstruction

Democratic principles are not operative by themselves, but need concrete procedures and practices. These need to be reconstructed if we want to appraise the democratic quality of the selection of judges for the ECtHR and the CJEU. This will be done on the following pages. In our analysis we will distinguish between the development of criteria for the selection of judges (3.1) and the actual selection process (3.2). We hence discuss first how abstract criteria on what makes a good judge are developed; only then, in a second step, will we discuss how individual candidates are picked. Certainly, in practice the two questions are intertwined. For an analysis guided by a democratic perspective it is, however, useful to distinguish between general and open norm development and norm application in concrete cases.[51]

Before starting the comparative endeavour a possible objection should be addressed, namely the comparability of judicial selection in the CJEU and the ECtHR. Certainly, the two courts and their judges differ in important respects. In Strasbourg judges have to interpret and apply a catalogue of human rights; in Luxembourg this covers just a small percentage of a judge's job description. More importantly, the Luxembourg judge sits on a court that is part of the judiciary of an autonomous and fully developed legal order, where her judgments have, in particular through the preliminary reference procedure, immediate effects in national law. Against this backdrop, what justifies our comparison? It is the fact that both courts exercise public authority in the European legal area and thereby contribute to shaping it. The diverging exigencies and challenges for judges in both systems have to be taken into account when selecting—but this very process can be reconstructed in light of democratic principles and, on this basis, can be compared.

3.1. Laying down the standards

In the EU and the Council of Europe alike, the crude criteria for the selection of judges set out in the Treaties and the Convention respectively are specified—albeit in markedly different ways. In Strasbourg the PACE is the driving force, interacting with national governments, the Committee of Ministers, and the ECtHR. It has set up a number of criteria in what can be denoted as a deliberative and open procedure, creating the kind of democratic noise often lacking in international politics, and has thereby addressed crucial but contested issues (section 3.1.1). While there is lively noise in Strasbourg, an eerie silence persists in Brussels when it comes to debating what constitutes a good judge. Here, the Article 255 Panel has taken the lead, presenting, in activity reports, a number of criteria it deems

---

[51] Generally, Christoph Möllers, *The Three Branches: A Comparative Model of Separation of Powers* (Oxford University Press 2013), 80–109.

important. In these reports, political choices have been couched in terms of expertise (section 3.1.2).

3.1.1. Noise and co-operation in Strasbourg: international parliamentarism in action

The selection of judges is one of the PACE's most visible and prominent competences. From the mid-1990s it has taken an active role in shaping the selection process.[52] It has set a number of political priorities: core themes include the improvement of national selection procedures, the language proficiency of judges at the court, as well as the goal to raise the proportion of female judges at the ECtHR to at least 40 per cent. In an array of law-making documents, namely recommendations, resolutions, and reports, the PACE has painted a clear picture of what kind of person it believes a European judge shall be and on which bench she shall sit.[53] It is of a judge who is not only competent but also communicative; who has an understanding of people and society, courtesy, and humanity and a commitment to public service.[54] She sits on a bench that is gender-balanced and multilingual.[55]

Whether all of these criteria are convincing can be debated. However, what is initially interesting from our perspective is the process through which this profile was devised. A good case in point is the development of a specific subset of criteria, namely those concerned with a gender-balanced bench. To achieve this latter end the PACE demanded that national lists be 'mixed' unless the list contains only candidates of the underrepresented sex or if exceptional circumstances exist.[56] This concern has been subject to intensive parliamentary debate, with the PACE's stance on the matter being subject to open contestation and reconsideration. On the one hand the PACE reacted to the lack of progress it observed in the contracting states;[57] on the other it engaged in an intensive exchange with the Committee of Ministers and national governments.

Early on, the PACE's broader views on the importance of gender balance at the court had, in principle,[58] been accepted and reinforced by the Committee of

---

[52] A number of procedural adjustments aim at increasing the depth and objectivity of the factual basis for the Assembly's decision. This includes standardized *curricula vitae* and personal interviews to be conducted by one of the Assembly's Sub-Committees. They were introduced in PACE Resolution 1082 (1996), then again debated after first experiences and refined in PACE Resolution 1200 (1999). Further see above ch 5 s 3.1.

[53] For a good overview of all the reforms initiated by the PACE see the report prepared by its Committee on Legal Affairs and Human Rights, AS/Jur/Inf (2012) 02 rev4 (7 December 2012).

[54] For a list of personal qualifications the Assembly considers in its interviews see PACE, Report of the Committee on Legal Affairs and Human Rights, Doc 9963 (7 October 2003), para 56.

[55] PACE, Report of the Committee on Legal Affairs and Human Rights, Doc 9963 (7 October 2003), para 10.

[56] PACE Resolution 1366 (2004), subsequently modified by Resolution 1426 (2005), Resolution 1627 (2008), and Resolution 1841 (2011).

[57] PACE Resolution 1627 (2008) and Resolution 1841 (2011).

[58] As to the details, the Committee of Ministers has always insisted on the possibility of exceptions to mixed lists.

Ministers.[59] Nevertheless, in practice, the mixed-lists approach had been subject to challenge. During the Maltese selection process in 2006 the government of Malta did not provide a mixed list, claiming difficulties after having issued public calls for candidature which nevertheless did not lead to qualified female candidates applying. The PACE insisted on a mixed list. Malta claimed that the PACE had no competence to reject its list since Article 21 ECHR, regulating the criteria for becoming a ECtHR judge, was silent on the issue of gender balance.

The ECtHR rendered an advisory opinion to help overcome the disagreement.[60] Its approach is remarkable. The Court took 20 of the total 30 pages of its opinion to develop the procedural history of the dispute. It highlighted the host of discussions in the Assembly and the agreement with the Committee of Ministers on the importance of gender balance. Moreover, it embedded the issue in a broad comparative analysis of international and contracting state highest court practice, documenting a movement toward gender-balanced benches.[61] In light of this record, the Court did not push its own concept of gender-balanced benches but called for possible exceptions where all appropriate steps had been taken to find female candidates, in particular if open calls for candidature had been issued. The PACE reacted to the Court's opinion by revising its procedure and establishing that unusual circumstances that allow deviation from the mixed-lists rule can be established by a two-thirds majority in the PACE's responsible Sub-Committee.[62]

The PACE therefore strengthened the legitimatory basis of its proposals by reaching basic agreement with the Council of Europe's 'second chamber', the Committee of Ministers, by engaging with the legal assessment of the ECtHR, and by showing responsiveness to national stakeholders. This co-operative, multilevel, and deliberative outlook is convincing in light of democratic principles. What is more, the figures suggest that such a democratic strategy is apt to contribute to good results. Today, out of 47 judges, 18 are female—a quota of 38 per cent, which is in sharp contrast to 19 per cent at the CJEU.[63]

The process of defining what constitutes a good judge in the Council of Europe has allowed inclusive articulation of criteria that are politically sensitive and potentially controversial. Another important procedural innovation can be read in this light: the PACE arguably had the necessary political weight to be able to increase—together with the Committee of Ministers—pressure on national governments to lift the quality of their procedures to set up candidate lists: a potentially thorny but important issue, given the shared responsibility of national and transnational actors for selecting Europe's judges.

---

[59] Guidelines of the Committee of Ministers, CM(2012)40 final (29 March 2012), II.8.

[60] ECtHR Grand Chamber, *Advisory Opinion on Certain Legal Questions Concerning the Lists of Candidates Submitted with a View to the Election of Judges to the European Court of Human Rights* (12 February 2008).

[61] *Advisory Opinion* (n 60) paras 34–5 and 49.

[62] PACE, Resolution 1841 (2011), para 6.3.

[63] At the Court of Justice, of 37 judges and advocate generals, only seven are women. At the General Court the situation is only slightly better. Of 28 judges, six are women, which corresponds to 21 per cent female judges (as of 1 August 2014).

As it is, according to Article 22 ECHR, the PACE selects a candidate from a list of three drawn up by the national government. In this context, the PACE has developed the practice to accept the lists drawn up by the national governments and to choose among the candidates proposed if certain procedural criteria are fulfilled: national selection processes have to 'reflect the principles of democratic procedure, transparency and non-discrimination'.[64] The formulation of these conditions can be solidly based on the idea that the national and international components of the selection process cannot be strictly separated, that the outcome's legitimacy results from the supplemental working of national and transnational institutions.[65] Equal treatment, transparency, and democracy are anchored in the national laws of contracting states *and* the Convention,[66] providing a common framework that guides and contains the exercise of public authority.[67] The PACE does not impose substantive criteria for the composition of candidate lists, nor does it spell out national selection procedures *en détail*. Rather, it aims to secure the legitimacy of domestic selection procedures and to thereby activate the potential of a complex legitimatory mechanism.[68]

3.1.2. Silence and solitude in Brussels: experts in charge

The situation is different in the European Union. The central visible actor in the process is the recently established Article 255 Panel.[69] Its primary task is to prepare the final selection decision of the 'representatives of the governments of the Member States'[70] by rendering opinions—not disclosed to the public—on

---

[64] PACE Resolution 1646 (2009), para 2. See already PACE Recommendation 1649 (2004). This can mean, for instance, public and open calls for candidatures and the consultation of national parliaments. This has been supported by the Committee of Ministers; see CM (2012) 40 final (29 March 2012).

[65] This is reflected, most visibly, in PACE Resolution 1646 (2009) para 1: '[The Assembly] underlines the importance of appropriate national selection procedures in order to ensure and reinforce the quality, efficacy and authority of the Court.' See also earlier Recommendation 1429 (1999).

[66] For the principle of democracy see the ECHR's Preamble: 'fundamental freedoms [...] are best maintained [...] by an effective political democracy.' The ECtHR moreover reads Articles 10 (freedom of expression) and 11 (freedom of association) as prerequisites for the functioning of democracy, for example in *Lingens v Austria* App no 9815/82 (ECHR, 8 July 1986) para 42 (as regards Article 10) and in *United Communist Party v Turkey* App no 133/1996/752/951 (ECHR, 30 January 1998) para 25 (as regards Art 11). For the principle of non-discrimination see Art 14 ECHR and the general non-discrimination provision in Art 1 of the 12th Additional Protocol, entered into force in 2005.

[67] Daniel Halberstam, 'Local, Global and Plural Constitutionalism: Europe Meets the World' in Gráinne de Búrca and Joseph Weiler (eds), *The Worlds of European Constitutionalism* (Cambridge University Press 2012) 150, 170–5 (employing voice, rights, and expertise as a basic 'grammar of legitimacy').

[68] The PACE is quite successful. The German Federal Ministry of Justice, for instance, issued public calls for candidacy for the nomination of the German judge to the ECtHR for the first time in 2010; the UK has done this since 1998: on this see Henry G Schermers, 'Election of Judges to the European Court of Human Rights' (1998) 23 *ELRev* 568, 574.

[69] The details of its working are laid down in Art 255 TFEU and Council Decision 2010/124/EU relating to the operating rules of the panel provided for in Art 255 of the Treaty on the Functioning of the European Union [2010] OJ L50/18.

[70] In contrast to appointments to the executive board of the European Central Bank (Art 283 para 2 TFEU) or the Court of Auditors (Art 286 para 2 TFEU), which are carried out by the EU

candidates' qualifications. In three activity reports, it has presented a number of criteria it deems relevant when judging applicants. The 255 Panel is composed of seven experts, mainly national and former EU judges, one of which is proposed by the European Parliament.

To be sure, its establishment constitutes a significant improvement of the selection process. The integration of expertise-based elements is meaningful to thoroughly assess candidates' professional credentials.[71] However, from the perspective of democratic principles the role of experts should be narrowly tailored,[72] in particular as regards further specifying selection criteria and procedures. This does not only derive from Article 10 TEU that privileges democratically representative institutions to discuss issues of principle; it also follows from the 255 Panel's procedure: it neither holds public meetings,[73] nor is it obliged to provide reasons that can publicly be discussed.[74] Moreover, these experts are themselves selected by a judicial expert, accounting for a critical element of co-optation in the procedure: it is for the president of the CJEU to present a proposal for the Panel's composition,[75] which the governments of the member states so far have followed.[76]

In fact, the 255 Panel itself has recognized that its role must be a limited one. It stresses, for instance, that it is not entrusted to deal with the composition of the Court.[77] Questions of social representativeness or gender balance are beyond its mission.[78] This sort of self-restraint is double-edged: on the one hand, it is to be welcomed in light of the Panel's limited democratic legitimacy; on the other hand it is regrettable that important political issues are not brought to the fore, but are nevertheless decided. The 255 Panel cannot help but make important political choices. To give an example: when reviewing professional experience, one of the six criteria which the Panel relies on,[79] it has underlined the particular importance it attaches to candidates' views on the 'nature, role and scope of the office of Judge or Advocate-General'.[80] This suggests that the Committee should assess candidates' professional convictions. Here, highly diverse views on the role of a judge may

---

institutions themselves, ie the European Council and the Council respectively, the selection of CJEU judges rests in the hands of the 'governments of the Member States'; cf Arts 253 and 254 TFEU.

[71] This point will be developed further: see text to n 110 *et seqs*.

[72] See Andreas Voßkuhle and Gernot Sydow, 'Die demokratische Legitimation des Richters' (2002) 57 *Juristenzeitung* 673, 677.

[73] Council Decision 2010/124/EU (n 70) Annex, Art 5.   [74] Ibid. Arts 7 and 8.

[75] Art 255 para 2 TFEU.

[76] The grounds on which the president bases his decision and who are potential *souffleurs* is unclear. It has been suggested that in the context of the first round of Panel appointments, President Skouris was heavily lobbied; see above ch 1 s 2.

[77] Third Activity Report of the Panel Provided for by Article 255 of the Treaty on the Functioning of the European Union, 13 December 2013, 11.

[78] See Lord Mance, 'The Composition of the European Court of Justice'. Talk given to the United Kingdom Association for European Law on 19 October 2011, 14–17.

[79] The other five are legal expertise, the ability to perform the duties of judge, independence and impartiality, language skills, and the ability to work in an international environment.

[80] (First) Activity Report of the Panel provided for by Article 255 of the Treaty on the Functioning of the European Union, 17 February 2011 (Council Doc 6509/11), 10.

exist: a judge may see her task as purely cognitive act[81] or as creative legal work;[82] she may be sceptical of a *gouvernement des juges*[83] or support judge-driven integration;[84] moreover, she may see the Union as a new federal polity or merely an instrument for international co-operation; she may conceive member state governments or EU citizens as the normative vanishing point for the judicial decision.[85] These are possible understandings that inform different yet legitimate conceptions of the 'nature, role and scope of the office of Judge or Advocate-General'. Openly discussing them neither gears toward equating judges to politicians,[86] nor should be seen as impairing the independence of the judiciary.[87] Basic convictions and assumptions necessarily flow into a court's jurisprudence.[88] This is, hence, not to blame the Panel's work. Rather than criticizing the Panel, we observe it to be in a double dilemma: it rightfully refrains from addressing manifestly political questions. However, like anyone pondering what constitutes a good judge, it cannot help but make important value judgements, which it needs to hide under the guise of expertise. Another, similarly important point is the composition of the Court. Although officially beyond the mission of the 255 Panel, it could be suggested that under the Panel's auspices, candidates with a profile comparable to that of many Panel members—namely that of the domestic judge—may be more successful than academics or diplomats in finding their way onto the CJEU's bench.[89]

Certainly, all this would raise less concern were the political process to fully review the Panel's evaluation: giving political orientation where it is deemed necessary and re-evaluating political choices made by the experts. According to Articles 253 and 254 TFEU, this is the task of the governments of the member states.

---

[81] See such an understanding promoted by the German judge at the CJEU, Thomas von Danwitz, 'Funktionsbedingungen der Rechtsprechung des Europäischen Gerichtshofes' (2008) 43 *Europarecht* 769, 769–770.

[82] G Federico Mancini and David T Keeling, 'Democracy and the European Court of Justice' (1994) 57 *Modern Law Review* 175, 186 (arguing that CJEU judges are held to implement the 'preference for Europe' enshrined in the Treaties).

[83] Jean-Pierre Colin, *Le gouvernement des juges dans les communautés européennes* (Pichon et Durand-Auzias 1966).

[84] Giandomenico Majone, *Dilemmas of European Integration. The Ambiguities and Pitfalls of Integration by Stealth* (Oxford University Press 2005) 155–6.

[85] See for the latter, famously, Pierre Pescatore, 'The Doctrine of "Direct Effect": An Infant Disease of Community Law' (1983) 8 *ELRev* 155, 157.

[86] See Christoph Möllers, 'Legalität, Legitimität und Legitimation des Bundesverfassungsgerichts' in Matthias Jestaedt, Oliver Lepsius, Christoph Möllers, and Christoph Schönberger (eds), *Das entgrenzte Gericht* (Suhrkamp 2011) 281, 314–318 (making the case against equating highest courts to small-scale parliaments even if the election of judges is highly politicized).

[87] Here, other issues are pertinent, such as the possibility of renewing the term in office pursuant to Arts 253 para 4 and 254 para 2 TFEU, which is problematic for the independence of CJEU judges. The Council of Europe recently changed the term for ECtHR judges to a non-renewable nine years; see Protocol no 14 entered into force on 1 June 2010.

[88] See Gil Carlos Rodriguez Iglesias, 'The Judge Confronts Himself as Judge' in Robert Badinter and Stephen Breyer (eds), *Judges in Contemporary Democracy. An International Conversation* (New York University Press 2004) 275, 281.

[89] See T Dumbrovský, B Petkova, and M Van der Sluis, 'Judicial Appointments: The Article 255 TFEU Advisory Panel and Selection Procedures in the Member States', (2014) 51 *Common Market Law Review* 460, 482. See also generally above ch 2 s 6.

They literally have the final word. The judicial selection process in the EU is—quite anachronistically[90]—exempted from judicial review.

Unfortunately, it is hard to tell how the member states perceive and exercise their role. They neither issue reasoned statements on judicial selections nor open discussions to the public. The institutional dynamics of EU judicial selections nevertheless speak for a tempered role of the other member states. Before the 255 Panel was established, member states had given the green light to every single candidate proposed by another member state.[91] The Panel's introduction can be seen as a direct answer to this practice of diplomatic courtesy and the perceived lack of critical assessment.[92] Against this backdrop, governments of the member states may well feel obliged to follow the Panel's lead. With a slight hint of satisfaction, the latter revealed in its Third Activity Report that all its opinions, including seven which had been unfavourable, had been followed by the governments of the member states.[93] The context of the Panel's establishment has created high argumentative and reputational hurdles to depart from its judgement. It has led to the process of selecting Europe's judges being framed as a technocratic exercise. This does not correspond to the true nature of appointing CJEU judges. Moreover, it does not allow disappointment with the Panel's selection criteria to be formulated in reasoned political form.[94] Important issues such as the composition of the CJEU that would warrant political discussion[95] have in the EU no forum to be addressed in.

An improvement in light of democratic principles could be the involvement of the European Parliament, which has, since the 1984 *Spinelli* report,[96] longed for a role in appointing European judges.[97] This step corresponds to the legitimatory logic

---

[90] See the appointment of the executive board of the European Central Bank (Art 283 para 2 TFEU) or the Court of Auditors (Art 286 para 2 TFEU), where the European Council or the Council respectively decide whose decisions are reviewable pursuant to Art 263 para 1 TFEU.

[91] Above, ch 1 s 1 and ch 3 s 1. See also Ulrich Karpenstein, 'Article 253 TFEU' in Eberhard Grabitz, Meinhard Hilf, and Martin Nettesheim (eds), *Das Recht der Europäischen Union* (Beck 2013) para 10.

[92] See Ricardo Passos, 'Le système juridictionnel de l'Union' in Giuliano Amato, Hervé Bribosia, and Bruno de Witte (eds), *Genèse et destine de la Constitution européenne* (Bruylant 2007) 565, 585.

[93] Third Activity Report of the Panel Provided for by Article 255 of the Treaty on the Functioning of the European Union, 13 December 2013, 9–10.

[94] See the speech delivered by Advocate General Jääskinen at King's College London in February 2013 entitled *Through Difficulties towards New Difficulties—Wandering in the European Judicial Landscape* (who mentions a rather problematic form of 'political' reaction of member states to the rejection of a candidate: some refrain from nominating a new candidate, which leads to an impasse at the Court): <http://www.kcl.ac.uk/law/research/centres/european/Kings-College-Jaaskinen.pdf>, last accessed 15 November 2014.

[95] See on the importance of having legal experts with different professional backgrounds on the bench above, ch 2; on gender balance below, ch 10 s 3.2.

[96] The therein encompassed Draft Treaty Establishing the European Union [1984] OJ C77/33 foresaw in Art 30 para 2 that '[h]alf the members of the Court shall be appointed by the Parliament and half by the Council of the Union. Where there is an odd number of members, the Parliament shall appoint one more than the Council.'

[97] For an overview see Gregorio Garzón Clariana, 'Le rôle du Parlement européen dans le développement de la Cour de justice' in Ninon Colneric et al (eds), *Une communauté de droit. Festschrift für Gil Carlos Rodríguez Iglesias* (BWV 2003) 21, 25ff.

of Article 10 TEU;[98] it also appears to be the most promising way to increase the discursive quality of the process and raise public awareness—not least for the CJEU's work in general.[99] It would be possible to involve the European Parliament without amending the Treaties. It could act in the form of resolutions[100] and elaborate, even with the help of the 255 Panel,[101] principled criteria for the selection of judges. Such active engagement of the European Parliament would arguably steer discussion and incite the governments of the member states to reflect upon and justify their work and take a more active role in the process.[102]

3.2. Applying the law

Certainly, not every appointment must lead to broad, principled discussions on the traits of a good judge. Some cases may incite engagement in general debates and reconsideration of past decisions, others may not. When it comes to applying those criteria that have been carved out before, the focus rests first and foremost on gathering and thoroughly assessing information on individual candidates. Here, the emphasis on expertise and objective assessments is well placed. Nevertheless, this stage is also important from the viewpoint of democratic principles. Three issues are particularly pertinent: the proposal of candidates by national governments (3.2.1), the involvement of expert panels (3.2.2), and the actual decision (3.2.3).

3.2.1. Proposing candidates

In both regimes the procedure kicks in with the proposal of candidates by a member state. This moment is decisive for the whole process; deficits can hardly be compensated later. National authorities therefore have a huge responsibility.[103] Open

---

[98] The lack of EP involvement is, moreover, striking from a systematic perspective: appointments to other independent institutions like the European Central Bank or the Court of Auditors include at least a consultative role for the EP; see Art 283 para 2 and Art 286 para 2 TFEU.

[99] Renaud Dehousse, *The European Court of Justice. The Politics of Judicial Integration* (Macmillan 1998) 14 (linking the diplomatic, sheltered character of judicial appointments to the CJEU to the lack of controversy surrounding the Court's legal work).

[100] See Rule 120 of the European Parliament's Rules of Procedure.

[101] Arts 5, 7, and 8 of Council Decision 2010/124/EU (n 70) Annex would have to be adapted in conformance.

[102] Arguably a slight shift in such direction can already be discerned. Early after the establishment of the 255 Panel, one finds in appointment decisions the formula: 'The panel set up by Article 255 of the Treaty on the Functioning of the European Union has given a *favourable* opinion on the suitability of [...]'; see for instance Council of the EU, 'Decision of the representatives of the governments of the Member States appointing a Judge to the Court of Justice' (31 May 2010) Doc 9720/10. Surprisingly, in later decisions, the word *favourable* has silently disappeared, referring now only to the 'opinion' of the Panel. Now the formula reads: 'The panel set up under Article 255 TFEU has given an opinion on the suitability of...' see for instance, Council of the EU, 'Decision of the representatives of the governments of the Member States appointing a Judge to the General Court' (16 October 2013) Doc 14468/13. This semantic nuance could be read as a hint that the governments of the member states are not blindly following the Article 255 Panel.

[103] See the Declaration adopted at the High Level Conference on the Future of the European Court of Human Rights (Izmir, Turkey, 26–7 April 2011); PACE Resolution 1646/2009 ('In the

calls for application and transparent, reasoned selection could help find qualified candidates.[104] The involvement of national parliaments could improve transparency and the public visibility of the processes. Here, much needs to improve in both systems.[105] What differs, however, is the lever employed: while the PACE has openly stated that it would reject lists if the national process does not conform with a number of basic principles, such a stance cannot be observed in the EU. It appears from the Panel's activity reports that it conceives the national and supranational elements of the selection process as two separate and detached spheres. In the 255 Panel's conception, a candidate who emerges from a deficient, if not corrupt, national pre-selection can proceed to the CJEU's bench under the sole condition that she conforms with the Panel's substantive criteria.[106] This means the fact that deficient national pre-selection might have excluded a host of excellent candidates is, according to the Panel, none of its business. It even goes so far as to set the national pre-selection of judges outside the scope of EU law,[107] an argument which is utterly unconvincing in light of the composite structure of European governance framed by common principles.[108] The PACE on the other hand underlines the *shared* responsibility of national and transnational institutions by insisting on *shared* principles for the selection. Only if these principles have been respected by all involved can the whole process claim to have been legitimate.

The composite nature of the selection process has moreover implications for the number of candidates proposed. In the EU, where only one candidate is presented, her rejection involves high reputational costs for all actors involved, including the candidate herself. A list of at least three candidates, as practised in Council of Europe selection procedures, appears preferable. This can be easily achieved in the EU: nothing in the text of the relevant provisions, namely Articles 253 and 254 TFEU, regulates how many candidates national governments initially nominate.

3.2.2. Involving experts

A second important element shared by both systems is the involvement of expert panels. Recently, the Council of Europe has come up with its own 'panel of seven',

---

absence of a real choice among the candidates submitted by a State Party to the Convention, the Assembly shall reject lists submitted to it').

[104] The Austrian Constitution provides a promising solution that potentially increases transparency and deliberation: according to Art 23c paras 1 and 2 Federal Constitution, the federal government has to reach agreement with parliament's main committee in nominating a candidate. In practice, however, the main committee does not discuss several applications but merely rubber-stamps the candidate proposed by the government. For the opposition's critique on the occasion of judge Kreuschitz' nomination to the General Court see <http://www.parlament.gv.at/PAKT/PR/JAHR_2013/PK0067> (last checked: 15 November 2014).

[105] See the survey prepared by PACE Committee on Legal Affairs and Human Rights, AS/Jur (2008) 52 (1 December 2008).

[106] Third Activity Report of the Panel provided for by Article 255 of the Treaty on the Functioning of the European Union (13 December 2013) 14.

[107] Ibid. The Article 255 Panel holds that it is 'aware that the selection procedure is the sole responsibility of the Member States and is not framed by the TFEU'.

[108] See only Art 2 TEU.

informally named after its first president, Luzius Wildhaber, to advise governments on the suitability of their candidates before a proposal is made to the PACE.[109] The inclusion of experts into the selection procedure is valuable, also from a democratic perspective. Certainly, it cannot be their task to define broad general criteria nor to make ultimate decisions; rather, they should apply the criteria spelled out in the political process[110] and inform decision-makers' choices. In general, due to their personal and professional experience, they are in a unique position to gather information, structure it, and assess it for instance as regards the legal expertise, independence, and impartiality of candidates. Legal technique and knowledge gained in a professional environment and demonstrated in practice and academia is important for any judge to professionally perform her function, but also for the trust invested in the—compared to national courts—young and fragile institutions of which they are part.[111]

What is critical in regard to the assessment produced by these panels is how it is subsequently processed. It is essential that the grounds revealed by experts are presented to all decision-makers to enrich their deliberations.[112] Moreover, citizens should be able to understand the bases on which judges were selected. To enable transparency, accountability, and public debate, expert opinions as well as the leading grounds of selection decisions should be made public, having due regard to legitimate privacy interests.[113] Publicness is not to put—as a matter of principle—candidates under the spotlight. However, if selection bodies treat candidates fairly and respectfully, someone inclined to seek highest judicial office, who has a passion for the cause, should have the stomach and ability to stand a certain degree of public scrutiny. It may well even be in candidates' own interest.[114] In this regard there remains much to be done in the Council of Europe and the EU.[115] However, the transparency already in place in the Council of Europe has led to a number of occasions on which newspapers or

---

[109] Council of Europe (Committee of Ministers) Resolution CM/Res(2010)26.

[110] In this respect the tendency of the Wildhaber Committee to borrow from the criteria proposed by the EU's 255 Panel instead of seeking orientation from the Parliamentary Assembly is rather alarming.

[111] See Vicki C Jackson, 'Judicial Independence: Structure, Context, Attitude' in Anja Seibert-Fohr (ed), *Judicial Independence in Transition* (Springer 2012) 19, 65.

[112] See the Draft CDDH report on the review of the functioning of the Advisory Panel of experts on candidates for election as judge to the European Court of Human Rights, GT-GDR-E(2013)R2 Addendum II (19 September 2013).

[113] For a convincing proposal see below ch 9.

[114] There is little that is more damaging to a professional career than rumours based on unsuccessful candidates' CVs published in the *EU Official Journal* or on the CE homepage respectively; see for instance the Greek candidate for the General Court who, despite being an experienced EU lawyer, had been rejected (Council Doc 61/25, 9 February 2010), giving rise to wild speculation in the Greek press: see Γιάννης Πρετεντέρης, 'Κοσμοπολιτικός πατριωτισμός', Το Βήμα (Αθήνα, 6 June 2010), <http://www.tovima.gr/opinions/article/?aid=335911>, last accessed 15 November 2014; 'Γιώργος Δαράτος, 'Όταν οι κουτόφραγκοι δεν τρώνε open gov…', Ελευθεροτυπία (Αθήνα, 16 October 2010): <http://www.enet.gr/?i=news.el.article&id=214092>, last accessed 15 November 2014 (both articles present the Article 255 Panel as an effective check against personal and political favouritism that was allegedly behind the ultimately rejected Greek proposal).

[115] See above ch 6; see also the study prepared by Jutta Limbach et al, *Judicial Independence: Law and Practice of Appointments to the European Court of Human Rights* (Interights 2003): <http://www.interights.org/document/142/index.html>, last accessed 15 November 2014.

members of parliament revealed information that brought about the withdrawal of unsuited candidates.[116] Certainly, often a delicate balance has to be struck; nevertheless, it is beyond doubt that more transparency is needed. [117]

3.2.3. Deciding

So far, we have focused on developing criteria for selecting judges and on the procedures for their application. This should not lead, however, to overlooking the actual moment of decision. In a publicly rendered decision, the endpoint of the process crystalizes. It should assure the procedure's legitimate course and is the instance which public scrutiny can most easily attach to and new discussions be sparked. This is facilitated by an open vote, as foreseen in the law of the Council of Europe.

4. Conclusion

Today, democracy is an imposing principle for the selection of Europe's judges. In light of their public authority, the selection of ECtHR and CJEU judges needs to be reconstructed and lived as a democratic process. What this demands can be derived from the concurring democratic principles in the TEU and the law of the Council of Europe, which provide criteria for the selection procedures and show the shared responsibility of national and transnational institutions. The legal framework in the Council of Europe is, against this backdrop, much more convincing than the one elaborated for the selection of EU judges. Much can be said for the point that the Council of Europe conceptually leads the way when it comes to selecting Europe's judges. Accordingly, the EU should take the Council of Europe as an example—but only as regards its law, not its practice. The best procedures and standards are of little value if they are not lived by. In this regard, in Strasbourg, huge problems persist.[118] The Council of Europe institutions and the member states have to respect the laws which they themselves have set up. Otherwise, what we call democracy turns out to be a travesty.

---

[116] For a number of examples see Norbert Paul Engel, 'More Transparency and Governmental Loyalty for Maintaining Professional Quality in the Election of Judges to the European Court of Human Rights' (2012) 32 *HRLJ* 448, 450–1.

[117] In the Council of Europe important steps are taken to develop the Wildhaber Panel in this sense, seeking to establish a fruitful relationship with the Parliamentary Assembly; see the Draft CDDH report (n 112).

[118] See the critical analyses above in ch 6 of this volume as well as in Engel (n 116).

8

Can Judicial Selection Secure Judicial Independence?

Constraining State Governments in Selecting International Judges

Aida Torres Pérez

1. Introduction

Since the end of the Second World War, international courts have flourished across the world.* A wide array of tribunals has been established to adjudicate disputes of various types. Understandably, the increasing influence and power of international courts over a broad range of issues, from the economy to human rights, has raised concerns regarding the legitimacy of these tribunals.[1]

At the domestic level, the legitimacy of the adjudicative power vested in courts is premised to a large degree on the principle of judicial independence. While the independence of domestic courts has undergone thorough analysis in an extensive body of literature, it has only been in the past decade that several scholars have begun to devote increasing attention to the independence of the international judiciary.[2] Given

* Financed by *MICINN DER2011-29207-C02-01*.

[1] Armin von Bogdandy and Ingo Venzke, 'In Whose Name? An Investigation of International Courts' Public Authority and its Democratic Justification' (2012) 23 *European Journal of International Law* 7.

[2] See, among others, Ruth Mackenzie and Philippe Sands, 'International Courts and Tribunals and the Independence of the International Judge' (2003) 44 *Harvard International Law Journal* 27; Eric A Posner and John C Yoo, 'Judicial Independence in International Tribunals' (2005) 93 *California Law Review* 1; Laurence R Helfer and Anne-Marie Slaughter, 'Why States Create International Tribunals: A Response to Professors Posner and Yoo' (2005) 3 *California Law Review* 899; Daniel Terris, Cesare Romano, and Leigh Swigart, *The International Judge: An Introduction to the Men and Women who Decide the World's Cases* (Oxford University Press 2007); Eric Voeten, 'The Impartiality of International Judges: Evidence from the European Court of Human Rights' (2008) 102 *American Political Science Review* 417; Paul Mahoney, 'The International Judiciary—Independence and Accountability' (2008) 7 *Law and Practice of International Courts and Tribunals* 313; Clifford J Carrubba, Matthew Gabel, and Charles Hankla, 'Judicial Behavior under Political Constraints: Evidence from the European Court of Justice' (2008) 102 *American Political Science Review* 435; Roberto Toniatti, 'L'indipendenza dei giudici sovranazionali ed internazionali' (2010) IV *Diritto Pubblico Comparato ed Europeo* 1733;

the diverging institutional and political frameworks of domestic and international courts, the principles developed at the domestic level cannot be automatically transposed to the international one, and the notion of international judicial independence needs to be better conceptualized.[3]

The selection of judges is regarded as crucial from the perspective of judicial independence.[4] At the same time, as several scholars have pointed out, judicial independence might be conditioned by a much broader range of factors, including tenure and reappointment; the composition of the court; dissenting opinions; remuneration and financing; judicial discretion and control over material and human resources;[5] diverse formal and political mechanisms;[6] exit, non-compliance, and legislative override;[7] and interstate and inter-branch competition.[8]

This chapter will examine the process of judicial selection in light of the goal of ensuring judicial independence. The first part will reflect upon the notion of judicial independence of international courts.[9] Before continuing, two initial caveats are warranted: first, the purpose is not to argue that there is a single model of judicial independence that will fit all international courts, just as no single model for judicial independence exists at the domestic level. This notion needs to be responsive to the specificities and challenges of the setting in which international courts operate. The degree of desirable independence might vary according to the diverse goals, functions, audience, and institutional and political context. Second, judicial independence is not to be conceived as an end in itself, but rather as an instrument that enhances legitimacy of courts from an institutional perspective.[10] Legitimacy, in turn, might also depend on other factors, including accountability, transparency, or the quality of legal reasoning.[11]

Eyal Benvenisti and George W Downs, 'Prospects for the Increased Independence of International Tribunals' (2011) 12 *German Law Journal* 1057; James Crawford and Joe McIntyre, 'The Independence and Impartiality of the "International Judiciary"' in Shimon Shetreet and Christopher Forsyth, *The Culture of Judicial Independence* (Martinus Nijhoff Publishers 2012); Dominik Zimmermann, *The Independence of International Courts* (Nomos 2014).

[3] Mackenzie and Sands (n 3) 274–76; Crawford (n 3) 190–1, Mahoney (n 3) 316–18; Tom Ginsburg, 'Political Constraints on International Courts' in Cesare Romano, Karen Alter, and Yuval Shany (eds), *The Oxford Handbook of International Adjudication* (Oxford University Press 2014) 191.

[4] Kate Malleson and Peter H Russell (eds), *Appointing Judges in an Age of Judicial Power* (University of Toronto Press 2006); Ruth Mackenzie, Kate Malleson, Penny Martin, and Philippe Sands, *Selecting International Judges* (Oxford University Press 2010) 144–52; Mahoney (n 3) 324–30; Terris et al (n 3) 154–5; Mackenzie and Sands (n 3) 216.

[5] Robert O Keohane, Andrew Moravcsik, and Anne-Marie Slaughter, 'Legalized Dispute Resolution: Interstate and Transnational' (2000) 54 *International Organization* 457.

[6] Helfer and Slaughter (n 3).

[7] Carruba, Gabel, and Hankla (n 3); Alec Stone Sweet and Thomas L Brunell, 'The European Court of Justice, State Noncompliance, and the Politics of Override' (2012) 106 *American Political Science Review* 204.

[8] Benvenisti and Downs (n 3).   [9] Terris et al (n 3) 149.

[10] James L Gibson, Gregory A Caldeira, and Vanessa A Baird, 'On the Legitimacy of National High Courts' (1998) 92 *American Political Science Review* 343; Marc Bühlmann and Ruth Kunz, 'Confidence in the Judiciary: Comparing the Independence and Legitimacy of Judicial Systems' (2011) 34 *West European Politics* 317.

[11] For the distinction between legitimacy and legitimization see below ch 12 s 2.

The second part will focus on the selection of international judges. The decision-making process that determines the composition of the bench represents an extremely important avenue through which an international court can be influenced. Both the nomination of candidates at the national level and their election or appointment at the international level tend to be processes wholly centralized under the control of state governments. Finally, several strategies to constrain the appointment power of state governments will be examined with respect to the Court of Justice of the European Union (CJEU) and the European Court of Human Rights (ECtHR).

2. The Independence of the International Judiciary

According to the *Burgh House Principles On The Independence Of The International Judiciary*, judicial independence implies that 'the court and the judges shall exercise their functions free from direct or indirect interference or influence by any person or entity'.[12] This concept of independence needs to be unpacked: independence of whom (court and judges), from whom (any person or entity), and from what (direct or indirect interference or influence)? The answers to these questions will enable us to better frame the notion of independence that interests us.

Independence is a concept that refers to relations: whose independence should be ensured and from whom is independence sought? The notion of independence might be referred to judges, to the court in which they sit, or to the judiciary as a whole. At the international level, one usually finds single courts within an international organization. We might focus on international judges individually considered and the sort of influences upon them, or on the court as an institution. Judicial selection would be relevant from the perspective of both.

From whom should judges and courts be independent?[13] To begin with, judges are required to maintain independence from the parties in each case brought to them and from the object of the process. This roughly corresponds to the notion of 'impartiality'. The logic expressed in terms of a triad for conflict resolution demands that judges not be perceived as allies of either of the parties.[14]

Next, judges must possess a degree of independence from other judges in the same judicial system (what is known as 'internal judicial independence'). At the international level, as mentioned earlier, it is rare to find more than one court within the same organization.

Finally, and with this we come to the aspect of independence on which we will focus, judicial independence might be endangered by outside actors (this

---

[12] The *Burgh House Principles On The Independence Of The International Judiciary* were formulated by the Study Group of the International Law Association on the Practice and Procedure of International Courts and Tribunals, in association with the Project on International Courts and Tribunals.
[13] Owen M Fiss, 'The Right Degree of Independence' in Irwin P Stozky (ed), *Transition to Democracy in Latin America: The Role of the Judiciary* (Westview Press 1994) 55–6.
[14] Martin Shapiro, *Courts. A Comparative and Political Analysis* (University of Chicago Press 1981).

quality is referred to as 'external judicial independence').[15] At the international level, states, and in particular state governments, pose the main threat to judicial independence. Yet states are not the only source of concern. Judicial independence might also be jeopardized by the actions of institutions belonging to the international organization under whose auspices the court or tribunal is established.[16] Additionally, there are other private actors that can at times exercise particular leverage at the international level, including but not limited to powerful companies and non-governmental organizations (NGOs) that exert pressure in the process of judicial adjudication.

Whenever one of the parties before an international court happens to be a state, concern for external judicial independence largely coincides with that of impartiality. Still, independence generally refers to matters of an institutional or structural nature ('potential threats that may exist in the abstract'), while impartiality refers to specific cases before the court ('[threats] arising in the particular case as a result of a real or apparent concurrence of interests between the judge and one of the parties or their position').[17]

While judges need to be free from direct or indirect interference or influence when deciding cases, independence cannot be understood in absolute terms. As Fiss once put it, the goal should be to 'optimize, rather than maximize independence'.[18] The notion of independence does not require freedom from all influence, but only from influence that might distort the decision-making process by factoring in considerations extraneous to the adjudication process—factors such as political allegiance and opportunity for personal gain. Indeed, certain constraints on judicial power might very well be justified in order to bolster accountability.[19] Drawing the line between proper and improper influences or constraints is therefore necessary from a normative perspective, albeit difficult.[20] In this chapter, the focus will be on undue influences or interference coming from outside actors.

2.1. From arbitration to adjudication

As the number of international courts and tribunals has increased and their functions have diversified, the ethos has shifted from arbitration to adjudication. In the past, international tribunals were mainly conceived as bodies for the resolution

---

[15] Fiss (n 14) 56 uses the notion 'political insularity' to refer to the independence from other governmental institutions.

[16] *Burgh House Principles on the Independence of the International Judiciary*: '1.2 Where a court is established as an organ or under the auspices of an international organisation, the court and judges shall exercise their judicial functions free from interference from other organs or authorities of that organisation. This freedom shall apply both to the judicial process in pending cases, including the assignment of cases to particular judges, and to the operation of the court and its registry'; Mahoney (n 3) 319.

[17] Crawford and McIntyre (n 3) 201.   [18] Fiss (n 14) 56.

[19] Ginsburg (n 4); Mahoney (n 3) 339–46.

[20] John A Ferejohn and Larry D Kramer, 'Independent Judges, Dependent Judiciary: Institutionalizing Judicial Restraint' (2002) 77 *New York University Law Review* 962, 963.

of disputes between states in the form of *ad hoc* arbitration tribunals or panels for which states directly appointed arbitrators for specific disputes.[21]

Ad hoc arbitration bodies reflect the logic of the triad for conflict resolution based upon consent, in which the parties in discord agree on the norms to be applied and the third party to settle the dispute.[22] The legitimacy of such tribunals under this model is perceived as stemming directly from the disputing parties' consent. Describing developments at the domestic level, Shapiro observed that as societies became more complex, they tended to substitute 'law and office' for consent. As such, both the law and the judge were provided by the state and the parties no longer had a choice of arbiter.[23] As he argues, 'the substitution of law and office for consent entails major destabilizing pressures on the triadic structure'.[24] A court might now be seen as an ally of one of the parties, or as representing a new, third interest, that of the legal regime itself. It is in the context of this shift that judicial independence becomes a primary source of legitimacy.

At the international level, to some extent, a shift from 'consent' to 'law and office' can be observed as a consequence of the creation of permanent courts with compulsory jurisdiction within multilateral regimes, such as the ECtHR, the CJEU, or the International Criminal Court (ICC). Furthermore, and this is paramount for the discussion, individuals have over time gained access to certain international courts—whose jurisdiction, therefore, is no longer limited to disputes between states. The legitimacy of these courts, hence, can no longer be solely grounded upon state consent. Indeed, the predominance of states in the operation of international courts might undermine the perception of independence and thus the legitimacy of these courts in the eyes of less influential states, individuals before the court, and even the public opinion as a whole. Judicial independence thus becomes crucial to a claim of legitimate authority.

Notwithstanding, the shift from 'consent' to 'law and office' has not been completed. The role of consent is still quite relevant at the international level. Indeed, the notion of 'law and office' differs significantly at the international and national levels. With regard to 'office,' the domestic judiciary comprises one of three branches of power established directly by the Constitution and enjoys compulsory jurisdiction. A set of mechanisms have been put in place to secure independence and impartiality. In contrast, international courts are set up by international treaties; their jurisdiction is not always compulsory; and they lack the coercive power to enforce their decisions. State consent is central in the creation of international courts, the recognition of their jurisdiction, and the compliance with their decisions.[25]

In addition, the 'law' applied by international courts is international law, which does not possess the same 'democratic pedigree' as domestic legislation. The democratic origin of state legislation—inasmuch as it is the outcome of an institution

---

[21] Mackenzie et al (n 3) 7; Thomas Buergenthal, 'Proliferation of International Courts and Tribunals: Is It Good or Bad?' (2001) 14 *Leiden Journal of International Law* 267.
[22] Shapiro (n 15) 1–2.   [23] Ibid, 5.   [24] Ibid, 8.
[25] Mahoney (n 3) 317; Crawford and McIntyre (n 3) 191.

representative of the people—is a source of legitimacy for domestic courts.[26] On top of that, at the international level, law and politics are inextricably intertwined.

On the whole, the transition from a model based on consent to that of 'law and office' remains incomplete, and as a result a pervasive tension exists between state consent and judicial independence as the ultimate sources of legitimate authority. In fact, the relative weight of consent itself varies from one international court to the next.

2.2. Towards a check and balance approach

Over time, and in particular since the Second World War, the functions performed by international courts have diversified. If their main function was previously the resolution of conflicts between states, they now contribute to the credibility of international commitments and the maintenance of co-operative regimes. They enhance norm-compliance, monitor the exercise of national and international authority, and engage in law-making.[27] The ECtHR and CJEU offer prominent examples of the diverse functions fulfilled by international and supranational courts nowadays.

The diversification of functions and the extension of jurisdiction over a variety of fields have buttressed the power of international courts and their ability to pass judgment on very sensitive issues that directly involve state sovereignty, such as prisoners' right to vote,[28] amnesty laws,[29] or immigration law.[30] Doctrines such as the primacy of EU law or the conventionality control under the Inter-American Convention of Human Rights were crafted by the CJEU and the Inter-American Court of Human Rights (IACtHR), respectively.

Moreover, the indeterminacy of the law, and in particular international law, requires much interpretation, affording judges a wide margin of discretion. The image of the judge as merely the *bouche de la loi*—the law's mouthpiece—is long gone. Given the power of international courts to check state action and engage in law-making, the fear of a *gouvernement des juges* has reappeared at the international level.

It is, in my view, excessive to describe international justice as 'a tyranny of unaccountable foreign judges applying vague humanistic standards which they, the judges, interpret at their will, often ignoring the clear intentions of the drafters of the international instrument being interpreted'.[31] Yet to the

---

[26] Von Bogdandy and Venzke (n 2).

[27] Lawrence R Helfer and Anne Marie Slaughter, 'Toward a Theory of Effective Supranational Adjudication' (1997) 107 *Yale Law Journal* 273; Yuval Shany, 'No Longer a Weak Department of Power? Reflections on the Emergence of a New International Judiciary' (2009) 20 *The European Journal of International Law* 73; Armin von Bogdandy and Ingo Venzke, 'On the Functions of International Courts: An Appraisal in Light of the Burgeoning Public Authority' (2013) 26 *Leiden Journal of International Law* 49.

[28] *Hirst v UK*, App no 74025/01 (ECtHR, 6 October 2005).

[29] *Gelman v Uruguay* (IACtHR, 24 February 2011).

[30] Case C-34/09 *Gerardo Ruiz Zambrano* [2011] ECR I-1177.

[31] Mahoney (n 3) 319–20 opposing this view.

extent that adjudication is not solely an operation involving syllogisms, and international courts exercise public power and monitor the action of democratic governments, their power needs to be counterbalanced to avoid the risk of abuse.[32]

Political constraints or other mechanisms of accountability for international courts are not precluded by the principle of judicial independence, as long as those mechanisms do not amount to 'undue' influences or pressures.[33] Actually, judicial independence and accountability might be conceived as two sides of the same coin.[34]

At the international level, judicial independence should not be understood in terms of total insularity. The strategy of insulating international courts from other political actors is neither feasible, given the predominant role of states, nor desirable, from the standpoint of legitimacy. While judges must be free to make decisions on the basis of established law, judicial institutions themselves must also be embedded in a broader system of institutional checks and balances.[35]

To what extent might a system of checks and balances be transposed to the international sphere? Clearly, the political and institutional framework in which international courts operate is very different from that at the domestic level, so classic separation of powers does not apply. At the same time, the national and the international are becoming increasingly intertwined and the line separating one from the other increasingly blurred. Moreover, we ought to move beyond a monolithic conception of the state. The state is easily conceptually disaggregated into a set of related yet distinct public institutions which interact with other similar sets at the international level.[36] The principle of checks and balances can be applied to those interactions in order to prevent abuses, but doing so requires conceptualizing the exercise of public power as a continuum in multiple spheres in which national and supranational authorities interact.

Continuing along this perspective, we need to consider which institutions (international and/or national) could provide an appropriate check to the power of international courts, which interests and values those institutions might represent, and what the adequate mechanisms for implementing constraints might be. The answers might very well differ for each type of international court. The various functions and settings in which international courts operate are relevant in the evaluation of the appropriate constraining mechanisms and the potential threats to their independence. Next, we will explore the power of judicial selection in light of the checks and balances principle applied to international courts.

---

[32] Shapiro (n 15) 34.

[33] Ferejohn and Kramer (n 21); Peter H Russell, 'Conclusion' in Malleson and Russell (n 5) 426–7.

[34] Stephen B Burbank, 'Judicial Independence, Judicial Accountability, and Interbranch Relations' (2007) 95 *The Georgetown Law Journal* 909, 911–12; Mahoney (n 3) 320.

[35] Ferejohn and Kramer (n 21).

[36] Anne-Marie Slaughter, *A New World Order* (Princeton University Press 2004).

3. The Dominance of State Governments in Selecting International Judges

It has been claimed that 'the appointment of judges to international courts has long been an unstudied area of sovereign activity'.[37] The predominant role of states in selecting international judges is easily explained from the perspective of state sovereignty. To the extent that international courts are liable to constrain state action, and by virtue of the fact that these courts are created by states, it is easy to see why states might decide to put in place mechanisms to retain control over those institutions.[38]

At the same time, there might be good reasons to attribute the power of judicial selection to the states under a system of checks and balances. Attributing power to select judges to states may constitute an appropriate mechanism to counterbalance the courts' power to exercise public authority and monitor state action. Moreover, assigning judicial appointment to (democratic) states might be one way to address (somewhat indirectly) the lack of democratic accountability at the international level. This rationale would not be entirely different from the decision to vest the president of the United States with the power to appoint federal judges, or to grant political actors (parliament and government) the power to propose constitutional court judges in several European countries. Furthermore, attribution of the power to appoint international courts' judges to state governments may well promote states' acceptance of international courts and their decisions.

Yet, from a disaggregated perspective of the state, the selection of international judges has been centralized in the hands of state governments. As a general trend, the transference of public power to the international and supranational spheres has enhanced executive power vis-à-vis other branches and contributed to the exaggeration of executive power across the globe.[39]

The selection of international judges takes place in two stages: first, nomination of candidates at the national level, and second, election or appointment at the international one. Governments are usually in charge of both nominating the candidates (by proposal of the ministry of justice or foreign affairs) and electing or appointing them at the international level. Even when the election or appointment corresponds to an international, multilateral body, in most cases those are institutions that represent the state governments, such as the Assembly of State Representatives for the ICC; the General Assembly for the IACtHR; the Dispute Settlement Body for the World Trade Organization (WTO) Appellate Body; or the member states in the council for the CJEU. There are some exceptions, such as the Parliamentary

---

[37] Lord Mance, *The Composition of the European Court of Justice*, UK Association for European Law, 19 October 2011.

[38] Helfer and Slaughter (n 3) 44: 'even after states have created a permanent tribunal with compulsory jurisdiction and tenured judges, they face a second level of design decisions in which they must fine-tune their influence over the tribunal and its jurisprudential output using a diverse array of structural, political, and discursive controls.'

[39] Slaughter (n 37).

Assembly of the Council of Europe (PACE) for the ECtHR. State governments, hence, are dominant in both the national and international spheres.

In this context, it is possible to distinguish between full representation and selective representation courts. Selective representation courts are those which have fewer judges than member states, so not all states have a judge in the court—this is the case, for instance, of the International Court of Justice (ICJ), the ICC, and the IACtHR. In these courts, the election process at the international level becomes highly politicized.[40] State governments will seek the support of other member states for election of the candidate in question. Mackenzie and others have shown that, for the ICJ and the ICC, campaigning and vote-trading are central to candidates' success.[41] This is also the case for the IACtHR.[42] The election of judges is not too different from the election of members to other international bodies.

In full representation courts, such as the ECtHR and the CJEU, state governments do not need to engage in campaigning and vote-trading, since each state may appoint a judge. This leaves, however, no incentives for states to vet or second-guess candidates from other member states, or to seek support for their own candidates.[43] The selection process is thus less constrained by the need to gain the support of others, and governments enjoy wider discretion. The politics of selection are mainly relegated to the national level.

In both types of court, to the extent that selection is allocated to political actors, the process cannot be stripped of political considerations. As such, the judicial selection process inevitably involves a significant degree of politics, be it at the national or international stage.[44]

Regardless of the exact amount of politics involved, if judges are appointed on the basis of political considerations rather than competence and merit, the quality of the reasoning and the overall perception of the court's legitimacy in public opinion might be undermined. Moreover, when international courts possess jurisdiction over individuals, appointment by governments creates the risk of perceiving the triad as 'two against one'.

In practice, the motivations behind judicial appointments vary greatly. As Voeten pointed out, 'governments are neither simply picking the best qualified candidate nor are they singularly obsessed with limiting sovereignty costs'.[45] Motives for judicial selection might include a desire to signal a credible commitment to a certain cause, concerns over the implications of court rulings, and rewards for political loyalty, but selection may well also be influenced by norms regarding what

---

[40] Terris et al (n 3) 154.   [41] Mackenzie et al (n 3) 100–28.

[42] Héctor Faúndez Ledesma, 'La independencia e imparcialidad de los miembros de la Comisión y de la Corte: paradojas y desafíos' in Juan Méndez and Francisco Cox (eds), *El futuro del sistema Interamericano de los Derechos Humanos* (IIDH 1998) 187.

[43] Eric Voeten, 'The Politics of International Judicial Appointments' (2009) 9 *Chicago Journal of International Law* 387, 401–2.

[44] Regarding judicial appointment at the domestic level, Russell (n 34) 422 stated: 'our choice is between a process in which the politics is open, acknowledged, and possess some degree of balance or a system in which political power and influence is masked, unacknowledged, and unilateral.'

[45] Voeten (n 44) 389.

an appropriate judge should be and the aspiration to advance norms of liberal internationalism.[46]

Furthermore, once appointed, the capacity of governments to influence judges,[47] and the capacity of those judges to influence court decisions, depends on a much wider set of factors, including term length, the possibility of reappointment, the composition of the court, and the particular decision-making process within multilateral courts.

It might be useful to begin by distinguishing between the independence of the judge and the degree of independence (or politicization) of the selection process. That the selection process is highly politicized or political considerations are involved does not necessarily mean that the judges will be influenced by the government that appointed them or that those governments will be able to influence the court's decisions.

In sum, the greatest problem for judicial independence is not so much that states retain power over judicial selection or that selection is influenced by political considerations. There actually exist reasons, from the perspective of checks and balances, for states to hold selection power as a political constraint on international courts. Yet to the extent that selection power is concentrated in the hands of the executive, the process risks abuse by state governments who may be tempted to nominate loyal judges who will defend the interests of the government. The risk to independence materializes when governments select judges on the basis of motives extraneous to their judicial duties, out of a desire to influence judicial outcomes. Instead of attempting to completely depoliticize the process—whether or not that objective is even feasible—we should consider possible appropriate constraints on the executive to encourage the selection of independent and highly qualified judges.

4. Mechanisms for Constraining State Governments

With regard to the selection of international judges, there might be institutional arrangements that offer incentives for governments to seek and appoint the most suitable candidates without denying the role politics inevitably play. In this section, several mechanisms to constrain executive power in the aim of encouraging the selection of independent judges will be examined.

Such checks on state governments can be implemented in either the national or the international sphere. This analysis will however focus only on mechanisms to constrain governments at the international level; that is, once the candidates have already been selected at the national level. Specifically, the following mechanisms

---

[46] Ibid, 391–2.
[47] Ibid, 403: 'Understanding if and how governments influence judicial behavior requires an understanding both of government motives and of the institutional opportunities to act upon these motives.'

will be examined with respect to the CJEU and the ECtHR from a comparative perspective: parliamentary bodies, expert panels, transparency, and tenure.

4.1. Parliamentary bodies

The participation of parliamentary bodies in the process of judicial selection, both at the national and international levels, might provide a democratic check on state governments. The forms which parliamentary participation might take are diverse, including election of the judicial candidates or other forms of intervention such as prior consent or consultation. In the international sphere, parliamentary bodies are not available to most international courts, and when they are, their shortcomings in terms of representation and operation give cause for caution.

In the EU and the Council of Europe, the intervention of the respective parliamentarian institutions differs greatly. In the Council of Europe, the Parliamentary Assembly (PACE) is vested with the power to elect ECtHR judges by majority vote from a list of three candidates nominated by member states following interviews with the candidates conducted by the Sub-Committee on the Election of Judges to the ECtHR, within the Committee on Legal Affairs and Human Rights.[48] Starting in the 1990s, the PACE adopted several resolutions and recommendations to improve the procedure for selecting Strasbourg judges,[49] which included requiring the names of candidates to be transmitted to the PACE in alphabetical order, providing standardized CVs,[50] requiring the lists to be gender-balanced,[51] and laying out proposals for improving the process of nominating judges at the national level.[52]

Nevertheless, in 2003, the 'Limbach Report'[53] harshly criticized the performance of the Sub-Committee and the overall process for electing judges. The report sustained that the mechanism was 'fundamentally flawed,' stating: 'The Sub-Committee consists of parliamentarians, most of whom lack human rights or international law expertise [...] There have been cases where its ranking of candidates has appeared to be based on or influenced by party politics rather than the merits of the prospective judges.'[54] The report went on to decry the limited information on candidates provided to the PACE and the lobbying of states and,

---

[48] Art 22 ECHR. Further see ch 5 ss 2 and 3.

[49] See Parliamentary Assembly, Sub-Committee on the Election of Judges to the European Court of Human Rights, Procedure for Electing Judges to the European Court of Human Rights, AS/Jur (2010)12 rev3, 11 October 2010; Norbert P. Engel, 'More Transparency and Governmental Loyalty for Maintaining Professional Quality in the Election of Judges to the European Court of Human Rights' (2012) 32 *Human Rights Law Journal* 448, 451–2.

[50] Resolution 1646 (2009), Nomination of Candidates and Election of Judges to the European Court of Human Rights'.

[51] Resolution 1366 (2004), subsequently modified by Resolution 1426 (2005) and Resolution 1627 (2008); Recommendation 1649 (2004).

[52] Recommendation 1429 (1999); Resolution 1646 (2009).

[53] Jutta Limbach (ed), 'Judicial Independence: Law and Practice of Appointments to the European Court of Human Rights' (Interights 2003) 9.

[54] Ibid, 9.

on occasion, of candidates themselves, which 'jeopardizes the future independence (actual and apparent) of judges'.[55] The report questioned the ability of members of the Sub-Committee to assess judges, the manner in which interviews were carried out, the lack of transparency, and the influence of party politics. More recently, the operational performance of the system has also been critically assessed by others.[56]

Moving to the EU, the role of the European Parliament in the selection of Luxembourg judges is nearly insignificant. Again, going back to the 1990s, the European Parliament has demanded greater participation in the process of judicial selection. Proposals included, for instance, granting it the power to nominate half of the judges; or at least conditioning the appointment to parliamentary consent; and also public hearings of the candidates before the Parliament.[57] The Lisbon Treaty eventually granted the European Parliament the power to nominate one of the seven members of the Advisory Panel for judicial selection (Article 255 TFEU). If the aim was attaining some sort of democratic legitimacy, it has not been achieved, but rather appears to be a symbolic concession to the European Parliament.

Attributing power to elect judges to international or supranational parliamentary institutions, or assuring them some sort of participation, such as parliamentary approval or evaluative hearings, could potentially create greater democratic legitimacy, open deliberation, and transparency. Notwithstanding, the intervention of a parliamentary body does not necessarily or automatically advance those values. First, without going into discussion of democratic deficits, the lack of existence of a regional *demos* and a full-fledged democratic system weakens the capacity of international–regional or supranational parliamentary institutions to provide democratic legitimacy. It is therefore unclear whether such parliamentary institutions are better placed than state governments (indirectly democratic) to provide democratic legitimacy in the judicial selection process. Second, even if the election of judges is assigned to an international parliamentary body such as the PACE, the lack of transparency in the process could lead to a failure to deliver the benefits of open deliberation.[58] Third, from the perspective of judicial independence, the intervention of international or supranational parliamentary bodies does not make the process less political,[59] as the selection process might remain highly politicized along political party lines. Furthermore, given the important role played by state governments in the international sphere, their capacity for lobbying should not be overlooked. In the end, even if parliamentary participation could strengthen democratic legitimacy and deliberation, parliaments are liable to be captured by political interests, which would not advance judicial independence much further than its current position.

---

[55] Ibid.   [56] See above ch 6; Engel (n 50).

[57] Sally J Kenney, 'Breaking the Silence: Gender Mainstreaming and the Composition of the European Court of Justice' (2002) 10 *Feminist Legal Studies* 262.

[58] Engel (n 50).

[59] Above ch 7, where Armin Von Bogdandy and Christoph Krenn argue that what is needed is not less politics but rather more democratic politics.

4.2. Advisory expert panels

Advisory expert panels set up to assess the competence and merit of judicial candidates represent a way to introduce a screening mechanism at the international level that might constrain executive power in the judicial selection process. Advisory expert panels for judicial selection are rare at the international level, with some important exceptions. One is the screening committee for selection of the seven members of the WTO Appellate Body. Its role is to assess the candidates nominated by the member states and submit the candidates to be selected by consensus of the WTO Dispute Settlement Body.[60] The Rome Statute setting up the ICC contained a provision for the establishment of the ICC Advisory Committee on Nominations,[61] but it was not established until 2013.[62]

Advisory panels called to scrutinize the suitability of candidates for judicial office have recently been set up by the Lisbon Treaty (Article 255 TFEU) and a Resolution of the Committee of Ministers on the establishment of an Advisory Panel of Experts on candidates for the Election as Judge to the European Court of Human Rights (CM/Res(2010)26).[63] In the case of the CJEU, Articles 243 and 254 TFEU lay down that judges and advocates general of the Court of Justice and judges of the General Court 'shall be appointed by common accord of the governments of the Member States..., after consultation of the panel provided for in Article 255'. This represents a ground-breaking step forward, one that removes judicial selection from the exclusive power of state governments.[64] With regard to the ECtHR, the Resolution of the Committee of Ministers that set up the Panel states that before submitting a list of candidates to the Parliamentary Assembly, each state will forward to the Panel the names and curricula vitae of the intended candidates.[65]

Assessing the independence of candidates has proven difficult for these bodies, as documented in the activity reports published by the 255 Panel.[66] In its Second Activity Report, the Panel argued that, although independence beyond doubt is

---

[60] Mackenzie et al (n 5) 157–8 indicate that the Selection Committee takes an 'overtly political role in consensus building'; see also Richard H Steinberg, 'Judicial Lawmaking at the WTO: Discursive, Constitutional, and Political Constraints' (2004) 98 *American Journal of International Law* 247, 264.

[61] Rome Statute of the International Criminal Court, Art 36(4)(c), which entered into force in 2002.

[62] The Advisory Committee held its first meeting on 19 April 2013. Report of the Advisory Committee on Nominations of Judges on the work of its first meeting, ICC-ASP/12/23.

[63] For further description see above ch 1 (Art 255 Panel) and ch 5 (Advisory Panel).

[64] Tomáš Dumbrovský, Bilyana Petkova, and Marijn Van Der Sluis, 'Judicial Appointments: The Article 255 TFEU Advisory Panel and Selection Procedures in the Member States' (2014) 51 *Common Market Law Review* 455.

[65] Resolution of the Committee of Ministers on the establishment of an Advisory Panel of Experts on candidates for the Election as Judge to the European Court of Human Rights, CM/Res(2010)26, para 5.

[66] Activity report of the panel provided for by Article 255 of the Treaty on the Functioning of the European Union, 6509/11, Brussels 17 February 2011 ('First Activity Report'); Activity report of the panel provided for by Article 255 of the Treaty on the Functioning of the European Union, 5091/13, Brussels, 22 January 2013 ('Second Activity Report'). The Third Activity Report has recently been published: Third Activity Report on the panel provided for Article 255 of the Treaty on the Functioning of the UE, 13 December 2013.

explicitly mentioned as a criterion in the evaluation of candidates (Articles 253 and 254 TFEU):

> …the fulfilment of this requirement, which is indispensable, is undoubtedly difficult to assess solely on the basis of candidates' dossiers as submitted by Member States' governments and hearings conducted by the panel where appropriate. The panel does, however, endeavour to establish whether there are factors of any kind which are likely to lead the panel to express reservations as to the ability of the candidate to perform the duties of Judge independently and impartially. The panel may therefore need to question the candidate or the government which submitted the proposal on one or more aspects of the candidature which might give rise to doubts that the candidate would be able to perform the duties of Judge completely independently and impartially.[67]

In this context, the 255 Panel might take into account the national process of selection as a proxy for judicial independence. In its First Activity Report, the 255 Panel declared that:

> …to support its assessment of the candidate's legal expertise, experience, suitability for the office of Judge, independence and impartiality, the panel may take into account the conditions under which the Member State concerned selected the candidate and, in particular, whether there is a national merit-based selection procedure and, if so, how it is organised (transparency and objectivity of the procedure, involvement of a national selection committee, composition of that committee, and so on).[68]

The PACE has gone even further by requiring that, when submitting the names of candidates to the Assembly, state governments describe the manner by which the candidates were selected. Furthermore, it has declared that 'in the absence of a fair, transparent and consistent national selection procedure, the Assembly may reject such lists'.[69]

While these panels are meant to assess suitability in terms of both independence and competence, in practice their main task becomes evaluation of whether candidates possess the minimal qualifications for judicial office. To the extent that, in practice, poor qualifications and close connections to the current government might go hand in hand, the guarantee of independence could therefore arise as a by-product of assessments of competence and merit. Admittedly, highly competent candidates might also demonstrate loyalty to the government that appointed them, but at least candidates nominated on the basis of loyalty who lack minimum credentials will encounter an obstacle to their appointment.

In practice, the Second Activity Report of the 255 Panel indicated in broad strokes that the reasons for issuing unfavourable opinions involved the short length of high-level professional experience, the 'complete absence of any professional experience relevant to EU law', and the inadequacy of candidates' legal abilities.[70] The stated reasons thus involve competence and merit, but at least one

---

[67] Second Activity Report (n 67) 13 and Third Activity Report (n 67) 19.
[68] First Activity Report (n 67) 6–7.
[69] Parliamentary Assembly Resolution 1646 (2009), para 2.
[70] Second Activity Report (n 67) 13.

of the candidates deemed unsuitable was a close family member of the respective country's president. In the context of the ECtHR, one candidate who received a negative assessment by the Advisory Panel due to a lack of necessary qualifications happened to be a close legal advisor to the President of the Czech Republic and, despite the Panel's opinion, that government managed to push through his election by the PACE.[71]

From the perspective of the effectiveness of these advisory panels, the non-binding nature of their opinions might undermine their effectiveness, as evidenced in the example just mentioned. The report on the review of the functioning of the Advisory Panel published by the Steering Committee for Human Rights indicates that the Panel members 'shared in general a feeling of frustration, exacerbated by the perceived lack of co-operation, or even interest on the part of the other stakeholders in the election procedure'.[72] On some occasions, lists of candidates have been transmitted to the PACE without awaiting for the Advisory Panel's opinion.[73]

In the EU, according to the Third Activity Report, state governments have always followed the opinions of the 255 Panel. Thus, there is some evidence that the Panel's role is not limited to rubber-stamping the candidates put forward by the state governments and that it has had some bite in practice. Although the opinions are not binding, the 255 Panel's intervention is compulsory according to the TFEU.

In the end, assessment by expert panels might have a deterrent effect. The existence of the check represented by assessment of an independent body might discourage governments desirous of influencing the court from advancing low-quality candidates with close ties to the government. Scrutiny at the European level by expert panels may well encourage governments to exclude candidates whose prospects of positive assessment are poor.

4.3. Transparency

The selection of international judges usually takes place in dark corners of political negotiation and deal-making. As Dehousse graphically put it, 'it is in the muffled atmosphere of ministerial cabinets and diplomatic meetings, sheltered from the public gaze, that the members of the Court of Justice are appointed'.[74] A transparent process of judicial selection might bolster independence by publicly revealing the connections between judicial candidates and the governments that proposed them, as well as facilitating scrutiny of suspicious grounds for selection. Greater

---

[71] Engel (n 50) 450; Steering Committee for Human Rights (CDDH), Draft CDDH report on the review of the functioning of the Advisory Panel of experts on candidates for election as judge to the European Court of Human Rights, CDDH(2013)R79 Addendum II, 29 November 2013 ('CDDH report'), para 30.

[72] CDDH report (n 72) para 29.   [73] Ibid, para 33.

[74] Renaud Dehousse, *The European Court of Justice* (Macmillan 1998) 14.

transparency could hence result in both the selection of more independent judges and greater legitimacy in the eyes of public opinion.

At the domestic level, there exist several means capable of enhancing the transparency of judicial selection: public announcements advertising openings in newspapers or the specialized press, or on the internet; consultation with civil society organizations such as NGOs or academia; or public hearings before parliamentary commissions or other advisory bodies.[75] Within the Council of Europe, the PACE has issued a recommendation urging the states to issue public and open calls for candidates[76] and the Committee of Ministers has issued guidelines that require the procedure for eliciting applications to be established in advance, and inclusive of calls for applications that are widely available to the public.[77]

On the European stage, instruments for transparency are quite limited, particularly in the EU. Transparency might be sought with reference to several objects and moments in the process of judicial selection. First, with regard to the judicial candidates in the Council of Europe, the CVs of the three candidates proposed by each state are published on the Council of Europe's website. Thus, the public has knowledge about all candidates' backgrounds. In contrast, in the EU, no information about the judicial candidates' profiles is published before the appointment.

Second, the hearings before the 255 Panel and the PACE Sub-Committee are held in closed sessions. Arguably, private hearings allow for more open and flexible discussion. The proposal for public hearings before the European Parliament was actually rejected by the CJEU, with the argument that those would undermine judicial independence and introduce the risk of prejudging issues that might subsequently be brought before the court.[78] Given the more technical than political character of the 255 Panel and its objective of advising the member states with regard to candidates' suitability, there may well be good reason to hold the interviews in private. In contrast, given the political nature of the PACE Sub-Committee, public hearings would strengthen the democratic legitimacy of the process. At the same time, questions that might reveal judges' ideological positions toward certain issues do not necessarily undermine independence.

Third, the opinions about candidates' suitability rendered by both the Luxembourg and Strasbourg advisory panels are confidential. The 255 Panel's reasoned opinion for each candidate is communicated to member state governments but is not published. The public at large therefore lacks access to information about the outcome of the assessment and the reasons behind it. For its part, the reasoned opinions of the Strasbourg Advisory Panel are confidential and only shared with the respective state government. In addition, the Advisory Panel shall

---

[75] Committee on Legal Affairs and Human Rights, 'Nomination of Candidates and Election of Judges to the European Court of Human Rights. Part B of the Appendix to Assembly Doc 11767: Overview of Member States' Replies to a Questionnaire', AS/Jur (2008) 52, 2 December 2008.

[76] Recommendation 1646 (2009), Nomination of Candidates and Election of Judges to the European Court of Human Rights, para 4.1.

[77] Guidelines of the Committee of Ministers on the Selection of Candidates for the Post of Judge at the ECtHR, 29 March 2012.

[78] Anthony Arnull, *The European Union and its Court of Justice* (Oxford University Press 2006).

make available to the Parliamentary Assembly its views, in writing yet in confidentiality, as to whether the candidates meet the criteria stipulated in Article 21(1) of the European Convention on Human Rights (ECHR).[79] A copy of the Advisory Panel's opinion, including indication of which, if any, candidates were found to lack the necessary qualifications, is shared in confidence with the members of the Sub-Committee.[80]

Several reasons have been put forward to justify the confidentiality of the panels' opinions, which primarily involve the 'chilling effect' that publicity could have on potential candidates, protection of personal data, and reduced effectiveness of the panel.

First, regarding the 'chilling effect', Lord Mance, who is a member of the 255 Panel, claimed that 'it would deter and be unfair to candidates if [the opinions] were to be public'.[81] As for the Strasbourg panel, the Steering Committee for Human Rights has stated that publication might discourage potential candidates who risk serious reputational costs if given a negative assessment.[82] Apparently, however, it is only when the candidates' merits are clearly inadequate for judicial office that the advisory panels will issue a negative opinion. According to the Second Activity Report, the 255 Panel has rejected candidates possessing 'complete absence of any professional experience relevant to EU law' or whose legal abilities were 'inadequate'. To the extent that the Panel will only reject candidates who do not fulfil the minimum requirements to become judges, the deterrent effect would involve low-profile candidates.

Second, with regard to the argument for confidentiality in order to protect personal data, the 255 Panel justified in its First Activity Report the decision not to publish its candidate evaluations in terms of privacy protection. The Report argued that, according to Article 4(1)(b) Regulation (EC) Nº 1049/2001 of the European Parliament and the Council of 20 May 2001 *regarding public access to European Parliament, Council and Commission documents*, there exist grounds for an exception to the right of access to EU documents when their dissemination may affect the protection of private life and integrity. The Panel considered an evaluation of a person's ability to perform the function of judge or advocate general to be personal data pursuant to Article 2(a) Regulation (EC) No 45/2001 of the European Parliament and of the Council of 18 December 2000 *on the protection of individuals with regard to the processing of personal data by the Community institutions and bodies and on the free movement of such data*. The purpose of the evaluations is to help member states make informed decisions for judicial appointments. Publishing the Panel's opinions would, according to the report, amount to using personal data for ends different from those for which the data was collected, violating Article 6 Regulation 45/2001.

Notwithstanding the sensitive information which the evaluations admittedly contain, however, the objective pursued through making them public is in fact

---

[79] Resolution of the Committee of Ministers (n 66) para 5.
[80] CDDH report (n 72) para 26.   [81] Mance (n 38) 9.
[82] CDDH report (n 72) para 54.

no different from the purpose for which the data was collected. The function of the 255 Panel is to assess candidates' suitability for important public positions. Publishing the opinions would reinforce the role of the 255 Panel since, if the opinions were made public, state governments would feel more pressure to withdraw candidates who receive a negative assessment. To strike a better balance between the protection of personal data and the need for greater transparency, the publicity could be limited to the end result, whether positive or negative.[83]

Third, in the Council of Europe, the concerns expressed by the Steering Committee regarding publication of the Advisory Panel's evaluations included the consequences for its effectiveness vis-à-vis state parties. Confidentiality, the argument goes, allows for more room for manoeuvre. Furthermore, publishing the reports could have a 'chilling effect' on the Advisory Panel itself by making it more reticent to issue an unfavourable opinion. One should bear in mind that the Advisory Panel in Strasbourg finds itself in a somewhat different position from the 255 Panel in Luxembourg, since the former was set up by the Committee of Ministers and is not established by the Convention. This Panel's role is to advise individual governments on the suitability of candidates whose election falls to the Parliamentary Assembly.[84] Given the Panel's role and the fact that the PACE is ultimately responsible for the election of the judges, more transparency in the process could be demanded from this parliamentary body. One possible measure could be making public the report issued by the Sub-Committee after holding the interviews, which contains its recommendations and reasoning, instead of exclusively transmitting it to the members of the PACE. This report would ideally include the conclusions reached by the Advisory Panel.[85]

In the end, as stated earlier, expert panels provide a check on state governments that can improve the selection of independent judges, but they carry out their functions in the shadows. The lack of transparency at every stage weakens their role. Moreover, negative evaluations do not necessarily prevent candidates from receiving their appointments, and such occurrence would transpire outside public knowledge. Publishing the panels' opinions and evaluations, or at least their conclusions, would put pressure on state governments not only *ex post*, but also *ex ante*. Publication of the opinions could enhance the deterrent effect of the panel by discouraging state governments from selecting candidates on the basis of political loyalty alone, as that motive might become public knowledge.

In terms of transparency, the activity reports published by the 255 Panel are a welcome development. These reports contain valuable information concerning the number of opinions rendered, their results (without revealing candidate

---

[83] For further details see below ch 9.

[84] Engel (n 50) 449 argued that it would be advisable to communicate the opinion to other state governments that could exert some peer pressure.

[85] Ibid, 449.

identities), the manner by which interviews are conducted, and the criteria taken into account. In the Council of Europe, although the Advisory Panel has suggested that it might publish an annual report to the Committee of Ministers, so far it has not done so. The Steering Committee for Human Rights has at least published one report that includes information about the operation of the Panel and an evalua-tion of its performance, indicating several problems. In addition, the PACE rec-ommendations and resolutions have provided information about what is expected of the judicial candidates advanced by the states parties.

4.4. Tenure and reappointment

Besides the selection process, there are other institutional features that are relevant from the perspective of independence and might work to counterbal-ance the governments' appointment power, notably tenure and reappointment. For instance, in the US Supreme Court, judicial independence is served not through the appointment process, but rather life tenure. The terms of office of international judges, in contrast, tend to be short (ranging from four to nine years) and renewable.[86] For instance, judges at the ICJ serve for a term of nine years and may be re-elected; judges at the IACtHR are elected for six-year terms and are also eligible for re-election (but only once); and International Criminal Tribunal for the former Yugoslavia (ICTY) judges serve for four years and may be re-elected. In the CJEU, terms last six years and the judges may be reappointed without limit. Short terms and the possibility of reappointment might undermine judicial independence.[87] Judges might be inclined to please the state that nominated them (or others that supported their candidature) in order to obtain re-election or secure future job prospects. Voeten argues there is some evidence that career insecurity makes judges more likely to favour their national government when it is a party to a dispute.[88]

The design of newer international courts responds to this concern. For the ICC, nine-year non-renewable terms have been established. For its part, the Council of Europe's Protocol no 14 amended the ECHR in order to extend the length of judges' mandates from six to nine years and ban the possibility of reappointment. The explanatory report emphasizes that this amendment is aimed at strengthening the independence and impartiality of the ECtHR.[89]

---

[86] Terris et al (n 3) 155; Dinah Shelton, 'Legal Norms to Promote the Independence and Accountability of International Tribunals' (2003) 2 *The Law and Practice of International Courts and Tribunals* 27, 37–8.

[87] Terris et al (n 3) 155; Mackenzie and Sands (n 3) 279; Voeten (n 44) 400; Mahoney (n 3).

[88] Eric Voeten, 'The Impartiality of International Judges: Evidence from the European Court of Human Rights' (2008) 102 *American Political Science Review* 417, 417.

[89] Explanatory Report to Protocol no 14 to the Convention for the Protection of Human rights and Fundamental Freedoms, amending the control system of the Convention, para 50: 'The judges' terms of office have been changed and increased to nine years. Judges may not, however, be re-elected. These changes are intended to reinforce their independence and impartiality, as desired notably by the Parliamentary Assembly in its Recommendation 1649 (2004)'.

Scholars generally agree on the risks posed by reappointment from the perspective of independence. At the same time, life tenure does not seem advisable for international courts in order to enhance renewability and, in selective representation courts, geographical representation and diversity. As such, relatively long, non-renewable terms appear to be the most advisable terms to safeguard judicial independence vis-à-vis state governments.[90]

5. Concluding Remarks

The legitimacy of the adjudicative power exercised by international courts is partly premised upon judicial independence. While the principle of judicial independence might not be immediately transposable from the domestic to the international level, it does not follow that judicial independence is not applicable to international courts. At the same time, the role of state consent and the institutional and political setting in which international courts develop their functions need to be taken into account. Over time, the functions of international courts have diversified and their power has increased, resulting in a need for counterweights. The independence of international courts should thus not be understood in terms of insularity, but rather in terms of a broader institutional framework integrated under the principle of checks and balances.

Vesting states with power over judicial selection might be conceived so as to provide an appropriate check on international courts. Concentrating this power in the hands of state governments, however, increases the risk of abuse. State governments might be tempted to appoint loyal judges who will defend state interests and to use the appointment power to exert influence over judges. From the perspective of institutional design, additional mechanisms to constrain state governments must therefore be introduced, be it at the national or the international level. Because of the disparity of the selection processes at the national level, there is increased pressure for such mechanisms at the international level. Several strategies at the international level have been discussed regarding the CJEU and the ECtHR, including the participation of democratic parliamentary bodies, advisory expert panels, transparency measures, and structural arrangements. Despite the inherent difficulty of controlling the independence of judges during the selection process, advisory expert bodies and improved transparency may represent the most suitable means available to improve the chances of selecting independent judges by enhancing the roles of expert scrutiny, peer pressure, and public opinion.

In any event, *ex ante* scrutiny of judicial candidates will always be an imperfect process that cannot completely guarantee the independence of the candidates selected. Practically speaking, the motivations behind governments' judicial appointments are extremely varied and the capacity to influence the court will

---

[90] Terris et al (n 3) 155.

always be a function of a set of institutional and structural arrangements that goes far beyond the selection process for judges. Ultimately, respect for judicial independence is contingent on the legal and political culture, and the culture of judicial independence at the international level remains tenuous. The process of building a robust culture of judicial independence will be long and gradual, and incumbent on political actors and judges themselves.[91]

---

[91] Shimon Shetreet, 'Creating a Culture of Judicial Independence: The Practical Challenge and the Conceptual and Constitutional Infrastructure' in Shimon Shetreet and Christopher Forsyth (eds), *The Culture of Judicial Independence: Conceptual Foundations and Practical Challenges* (Martinus Nijhoff Publishers 2011).

9

How Transparent is Transparent Enough?

Balancing Access to Information Against Privacy in European Judicial Selections

Alberto Alemanno

1. Introduction

The establishment of two dedicated advisory bodies to scrutinize the suitability of judicial candidates to the Court of Justice of the EU (CJEU) and the European Court of Human Rights (ECtHR) represents so far the most significant reform of their respective appointment systems. After having enjoyed wide discretion in selecting their judges, member states in the EU and contracting parties in the Council of Europe have—as a result of this reform—lost their monopoly in assessing the independence and merits of their own candidates.

In 2010, the very same year the panel provided by Article 255 of the Treaty on the Functioning of the European Union (TFEU) (hereinafter 'the 255 Panel') began its work, the Committee of Ministers of the Council of Europe also established a seven-person panel, the Advisory Panel on Candidates for Election as Judge to the European Court of Human Rights ('the Advisory Panel'),[1] and entrusted it with a similar task.[2] Although the two panels enjoy different prerogatives and are called to operate within different selection frameworks, their establishment responds to a common and immediate concern: to guarantee that proposed judicial candidates are of the highest standards.

Given the prominent role of both European courts and the ensuing need for judicial competence and efficiency in *dicere legem*, the process of selecting judges

---

[1] Committee of Ministers, 'Resolution on the Establishment of an Advisory Panel of Experts on Candidates for Election as a Judge to the European Court of Human Rights' (2010)26 (CM/Res). This panel has operated since 8 December 2010 and is composed of seven members '... chosen from among members of the highest national courts, former judges of international courts, including the European Court of Human Right and other lawyers of recognised experience, who shall serve in their personal capacity...'.

[2] The panel is expected 'to advise the High Contracting Parties whether candidates for election as judges of the [ECtHR] meet the criteria stipulated in Article 21 para 1 of the [ECHR]'. See CM/Res (n 1), point 1.

has progressively come under scrutiny.[3] Because the governments of the member states have traditionally dominated the selection of judicial candidates, this process has over the years remained not only fragmented, but also highly politicized.[4] As a result, it has failed to provide sufficient assurance regarding the quality of the proposed candidates for judicial office.[5]

Although reliance on the informal and widespread 'old boys' networks' in the selection process has in some states led to the selection of good candidates,[6] this method has been criticized for jeopardizing the principle of judicial independence: national selection procedures tend to be neither open nor accountable to the public.[7] As an example of the broad discretion traditionally enjoyed by each member state in selecting its judicial candidate, it is noteworthy that, over the years, zero nominees have been formally rejected. In the absence of a centralized quality oversight system over judicial appointments, member states lacked incentives to oppose other countries' candidates.

It is against this backdrop that the two advisory panels have been entrusted with a common mission: scrutinizing the quality of the candidates proposed for judicial posts by the member state concerned through the adoption of reasoned opinions. Although these opinions are merely advisory in nature, they are producing profound transformative changes in the way in which judges are selected in Europe. While the 'quality check' undertaken by these advisory bodies does not automatically translate into unified, objective procedures of selection—these procedures remain under national control—in each legal system, it is significantly shaping the judicial selection process by rendering it more objective and, inevitably, is affecting the outcome of this process. In particular, through the exercise of their fact-finding

[3] For a detailed analysis of this process, see above ch 7 s 1.

[4] See the Final report of the discussion circle on the Court of Justice CONV 636/03 (25 March 2003) para 6.

[5] The literature focusing on the process of appointment judges to both courts is limited. On the EU Courts, see, eg, Sally J Kenney, 'The Members of the Court of Justice of the European Communities' (1998) 5 *Colum J Eur L* 101; Iyiola Solanke, 'Independence and Diversity in the European Court of Justice' (2009) 15 *Colum J Eur L* 91; Karen J Alter, *The European Court's Political Power* (Oxford University Press 2010) 126; Antonin Cohen, 'Ten Majestic Figures in Long Amaranth Robes' in Antoine Vauchez and Bruno De Witte (eds), *Lawyering Europe: European Law as a Transnational Social Field* (Hart Publishing 2013). On the ECtHR, see, eg, Andrew Drzemczewski, 'Election of Judges at the Strasbourg Court: An Overview' (2010) 4 *Eur HR L Rev* 377; Jutta Limbach, *Judicial Independence: Law and Practice of Appointments to the European Court of Human Rights* (Interights, 2003); Erik Voeten, 'The Impartiality of International Judges: Evidence from the European Court of Human Rights' (2008) 102 *American Political Science Review* 417; Norbert P Engel, 'More Transparency and Governmental Loyalty for Maintaining Professional Quality in the Elections of Judges to the European Court of Human Rights' (2013) 32 *HRLJ* 448.

[6] Bo Vesterdorf, 'La nomination des juges de la Cour de Justice de l'Union européenne', (2012) 47 *Cahiers de droit européen* 610.

[7] See, eg, Tomas Dumbrovsky, Bilyana Petkova, and Marijn van der Sluis, 'Judicial Appointments: The Article 255 TFEU Advisory Panel and Selection Procedures in the Member States' (2014) 51 *CMLR* 455; Limbach (n 5). See also the 2004 *Burgh House Principles on the Practice and Procedure of International Courts and Tribunals*, which were issued in 2004 by the Study Group of the International Law Association. They recommend that 'appropriate personal and professional qualifications must be the overriding consideration' and 'procedures...should be transparent and provide appropriate safeguards against nominations, elections and appointments motivated by improper considerations' (paras 2.2 and 2.3).

prerogatives and pedagogical missions vis-à-vis the appointing authorities, the two panels are progressively influencing the national selection process by *de facto* harmonizing—through a set of minimum standards—not only the criteria candidates must satisfy but also the overall transparency of that process. This harmonization occurs both upstream (during the selection process at the national level) and downstream (when the appointing authority completes the process). Thus, for instance, both panels encourage member states to publish open calls for applications to the judicial posts, and pay attention to these national procedures.[8]

Yet, paradoxically, neither of the two panels operates in a context of transparency equal to what they require from the member states when selecting their judicial candidates. In particular, dissemination of the panel opinions is extremely limited, as these are exclusively forwarded to the representatives of the governments of the member states (in the case of the EU) and to the individual government concerned (in the case of the Council of Europe). The role the panels play within the respective selection process emerges therefore as a 'black box': neither their input (candidates' CVs, records of the national procedure, etc) nor their output (panel's opinion) is public. To the contrary, confidentiality appears built into the functioning of both advisory bodies. The principle of confidentiality is mentioned on several occasions in the basic texts of the panels,[9] and any departure from it is currently perceived as unavoidably compromising the panels' operation.[10]

However, given the profound transformative effects that these panels are having on European courts' judicial selection, their current restrictive policy of transparency does seem to raise important and unaddressed questions of democratic legitimacy and accountability. Neither panel is subject to any form of democratic oversight. As a result, it may freely interpret—and even alter—the requirements foreseen for holding judicial office. Moreover, the selection of the panels' own members is equally shielded from external scrutiny.[11] What is more, due to the direct involvement of the EU Courts' respective presidents in the panels' composition,[12] both entities are becoming progressively more expressions of the judiciary than the executive. This may give rise to some embryonic form of unintended judicial self-government.

Against this background, this chapter provides a detailed legal and policy analysis of how the panels currently balance access to information and privacy in

---

[8] Activity Report of the Panel provided for in Article 255 of the Treaty on the Functioning of the European Union, Brussels, 11 February 2011, 6509/11, COUR 3 JUR 57, p 6 and Parliamentary Assembly Resolution 1646 (2009), para 2.

[9] For the EU, see point 5 ('the deliberations of the panel shall take place in camera') and point 8 ('the panel's opinion shall be forwarded to the Representatives of the Governments of the Member States') of Council Decision 2010/124/EU of 25 February 2010 relating to the operating rules of the panel provided for in Art 255 of the Treaty on the Functioning of the European Union [2010] OJ L50/18 (255 Panel Operating Rules). For the Council of Europe, see point 5(3) of the Operating Rules of the Advisory Panel ('If, in the light of the written submissions and any comments obtained, the Panel considers that one or more of the persons put forward by a High Contracting Party are not suitable, it shall so inform the High Contracting Party, giving reasons for its view, which shall be confidential'). See above CM/Res (n 1).

[10] In a similar vein see Sauvé above in ch 3.   [11] See above ch 1 s 2.

[12] See below s 2.2 of this chapter.

their respective selection procedures. While noting the specificities of each panel within its own judicial selection system, it argues that more transparency, far from compromising their function, would in fact maximize their pedagogical mission while at the same time tackling part of the legitimacy concern currently brought to the fore by their operation. The chapter also offers some suggestions on how to improve that balance in judicial selection in order to address the legitimacy and accountability concerns raised by their operation.

The chapter proceeds as follows. First, it provides a comparative analysis of the judicial panels' missions, prerogatives, and operating rules within their respective and differing institutional contexts. Second, it identifies and discusses the actual impact that these two panels are generating within their respective judicial selection systems. Third, it analyses the overall level of transparency surrounding access to the information gathered by the panels, by exploring and critically analysing the arguments generally adduced against further disclosure of their activity. Fourth, it provides a critical look at their actual publicity policy by highlighting unaddressed legitimacy and accountability concerns. Fifth, it formulates some recommendations aimed at striking a more adequate balance between access to the information these panels generate and the candidates' privacy.

2. Comparing the Panels' Roles in Selecting Europe's Judges

This section provides a comparative analysis of the role played by the 255 Panel and the Advisory Panel within their respective judicial selection systems. It highlights the mandate, composition, institutional contexts, operating rules, and prerogatives of both judicial panels.[13]

2.1. Mandate

In order to ensure the continuing effectiveness and legitimacy of the European courts, the panels' mission is to guarantee that proposed judicial candidates are of the highest standards. However, as the institutional contexts in which they are called upon to operate differ from one another, their respective roles and, as a result, impact upon the overall selection process vary considerably in the two legal orders. We will illustrate how these institutional and operational differences determine the overall level of transparency in the operation of the two panels.

2.2. Composition

The composition and appointment procedures for the panels' members are largely similar. Both panels are composed of seven members who are appointed by representatives of the respective organizations' member states: the Committee of

---

[13] For further details on the operation of both selection mechanisms, see above ch 1 and ch 5.

Ministers, following consultations with the president of the ECtHR, on the one hand, and the Council of the EU, on the initiative of the president of the CJEU, on the other.[14] As for their background, in both instances members are drawn from among former members of the respective European courts, members of the highest national courts, and lawyers of recognized competence. In the EU system, however, the term of judicial office is four years, instead of three as at the ECtHR, and the European Parliament proposes one of the seven members. In the Council of Europe system, there is a specific reference aimed at ensuring that the composition of the Panel 'be geographically and gender balanced'.[15]

2.3. Context

The institutional context in which the two panels exercise their mandate differs in part. While the selection process itself occurs at national level in both legal systems, the appointing authority is different. The judges at ECtHR are *elected* by the Parliamentary Assembly, whereas the members of the EU courts are *appointed* by the common accord of the member states.

The mission entrusted to the two panels therefore plays out differently within the respective judicial selection systems and, as a result, they have different impacts within these systems. While the activity of the Advisory Panel takes place in a process involving two principal actors, the states parties to the Convention, who propose, and the Parliamentary Assembly of the Council of Europe (hereinafter PACE), who elects, the 255 Panel only interact with the governments of the member states (via the Council).[16] In particular, in the judicial selection process within the Council of Europe, the Advisory Panel precedes and passes its advice on to the concerned government as well as to another 'quality review' body, the Sub-Committee of the PACE. The latter is also entrusted to assess, autonomously and independently, the candidates' qualities.[17] The 'quality review' exercised by the Advisory Panel intervenes before the candidates' list is transmitted to the PACE and triggers the intervention of its Sub-Committee. This, in turn, is entrusted with preparing a recommendation, after having heard the candidates, addressed to the PACE which identifies the most qualified candidate. Finally, while the Advisory Panel is called to operate within a selection procedure that begins—like in the EU—with a designation made by the concerned government, it is expected to assess the suitability of three candidates instead of one. This institutional feature inherently provides the Advisory Panel as well as the Sub-Committee greater choice.

---

[14] See CM/Res (n 1), point 2; Art 255 TFEU and 255 Panel Operating Rules (n 9), Art 2, and Council Decision 2010/125/EU on appointing the members of the panel provided for in Article 255 TFEU [2010] OJ L50/20.

[15] CM/Res (n 1), point 2.   [16] CM/Res (n 1), point 8.

[17] ECtHR, *Advisory Opinion on Certain Questions Concerning the Lists of Candidates Submitted with a View to the Election of Judges to the ECHR*, 12 February 2008, para 43.

This set of circumstances shows that while the two advisory bodies are both expected to prepare an opinion on the suitability of the candidates, they do so through a very different selection process. In particular, the Council of Europe's selection system requires the Advisory Panel to interact with many different actors and—due to the role of the Sub-Committee of the Parliamentary Assembly regarding the election of judges—also to compete for visibility. In contrast, the 255 Panel, being the only body in charge of assessing the quality of the judicial candidates, does not face a similar competition dynamic; as a result its output emerges, at least on paper, as more salient and authoritative. This appears all the more true when one examines the operating rules, prerogatives, and publicity surrounding their activities.

2.4. Prerogatives and operating rules

The Advisory Panel is not, unlike the 255 Panel, empowered to hear the candidates in person. This is a prerogative that belongs only to the previously mentioned Sub-Committee of the PACE.[18] This seems to weaken the Advisory Panel's ability to fully discharge its mandate by making its scrutiny essentially documentary and remote. It may ask questions but, unlike what occurs in the EU context, these should be addressed to the concerned government and not directly to the candidate. To assess the qualifications of the candidates the Panel may, by virtue of the Supplementary Operating Rule, also use 'other sources of information'. However, unlike the 255 Panel's autonomous fact-finding prerogatives, it is the relevant government that must provide these extra sources. While the default procedure for its examination of the candidates uses written format, a look at the current practice shows that meetings to discuss candidates' qualifications have become the rule and not the exception.[19]

As far as the evaluation criteria are concerned, despite the different language employed, both panels are expected to carry out suitability assessments on the basis of pre-established, formal requirements listed in the respective systems.[20] Interestingly, because they are articulated in greater detail, the Advisory Panel has recently made reference to the evaluation criteria interpreted by the 255 Panel, which have thus become a substantive and reliable source of inspiration for the Advisory Panel's current assessment practice.[21] This is an interesting, yet isolated, instance of cross-fertilization in the operation of the two advisory bodies.

---

[18] The recommendations of the Sub-Committee on the Election of Judges to the ECHR are confidential, but they are made available to all members of the PACE and not only to the relevant government, like those of the Advisory Panel.

[19] Steering Committee for Human Rights (CDDH), *Report on the Review of the Advisory Panel of Experts on Candidates for Election as a Judge to the European Court of Human Rights*, DH-GDR(2013) R79, Addendum II, Strasbourg, 29 November 2013, 9.

[20] Arts 253 and 254 TFEU and Art 21 ECHR.   [21] Above (n 19) 11.

3. How the Advisory Panels are Transforming the Selection of European Judges

Despite the different institutional context in which they are expected to operate, both panels are producing significant—yet largely indirect—effects in the national selection procedures leading to the appointment, in the case of the CJEU, and election, in the case of the ECtHR, of these courts' members. This result is *prima facie* surprising, as neither of them is empowered to issue legally binding opinions that could prevent their members from appointing the candidate they desire. The panels' mission is more modest: to provide an expert opinion, favourable or otherwise, about the proposed candidates' suitability to exercise a judicial function in relation to a set of pre-defined formal criteria.

Notwithstanding their apparently limited role, neither panel hesitates to fully exercise its prerogatives. As a result, both have gained the respect of their organizations' member states over time. Thus, for instance, since the establishment of the 255 Panel, the EU governments have followed all its negative opinions, thus ultimately deciding not to appoint their originally chosen candidates. While the same cannot be said of the Advisory Panel—whose opinions, together with the recommendations of the Sub-Committee, have at times been disregarded[22]—there exist other, subtler effects produced by both panels' oversight activities within their respective judicial selection systems.

First, their opinions, regardless of their actual publicity and dissemination, are known to exist. This mere fact—even if it is not accompanied by their disclosure—breaks the routine of previous selection systems. It disrupts earlier institutional practices characterized by opacity at both national and supranational levels.

Second, the panels' advisory role is not limited to a 'quality check' of actual candidates, but also includes the possibility to provide guidance on how member states ought to select judges. Due to their inherent 'pedagogical' role vis-à-vis national authorities, both panels are thus expected to shape the upstream phase of the selection process. As a result, in both legal orders, the respective panels are changing the ways in which individual governments approach the issue of judicial selection. Thus, in the contexts of both the EU and the Council of Europe, the panels have better defined not only the criteria the candidates must satisfy but also the procedures for identifying those candidates at the national level. As a result, although the criteria established for the selection of courts' members are dictated by both their foundational texts—the Treaty on the Functioning of the EU (TFEU)[23] and the ECHR[24]—both panels have contributed to rendering them clearer and more precise, and at times have even generated new criteria.[25] In addition, through

---

[22] Further see in particular above ch 5 s 3.3 and ch 6 s 5.
[23] Arts 253 and 254 TFEU.   [24] Art 21 ECHR.
[25] Thus, for instance, the 255 Panel has elaborated an assessment criterion that consists of the 'aptitude for working as a part of a team in an international environment in which several legal systems are represented'. See Council of the European Union, 'First activity report of the panel provided for

the exercise of their 'quality review' mission, the panels encourage national authorities to open up their respective selection procedures by asking for information
about how the selection process has been organized.[26] As a result, the panels lead
national authorities to operate in a less opaque manner not only downstream—at
the moment of the appointment or election of the candidates—but also upstream,
during the selection process.

In other words, by operationalizing the criterion of judicial independence, the
panels are promoting a more open, procedure-based, and predictable national
selection procedure. This process should be capable of guaranteeing both the
independence and the qualifications of the candidates for the job, and possibly of
attaining the ultimate goal of ensuring judicial quality of the bench, thus strengthening its authority.

Third, the panels' review of the suitability of candidatures creates an external
scrutiny capable of generating incentives for a meritocratic search as opposed to
a loyalty-reward system. Which country would draw satisfaction from receiving
an unfavourable opinion? While greater disclosure of the relevant opinion would
maximize this mechanism based on 'peer pressure', even the confidential transmission to the concerned state—as is the case in the Council of Europe—appears
capable of producing similar self-policing effects.[27]

While both panels prompt these transformative, yet largely indirect, effects
within their respective selection systems, their individual contributions to that
result differ. In the context of the Council of Europe, the driving force behind
this attempt at guiding national selection procedures has been the PACE, largely
through its dedicated Sub-Committee, which has 'over the years used its direct
practical experience to develop a body of recommendations to States Parties
concerning national procedures for the selection of candidates for judge at the
Court'.[28] Many of these recommendations have been incorporated into the

---

by Art. 255 of the TFEU (1st Activity Report)' COUR (2011) 6509/11, 11; Council of the European
Union, 'Second activity report of the panel provided for by Art. 255 of the TFEU (2nd Activity
Report)' COUR (2013) 5091/13, 12; Council of the European Union, 'Third activity report of the
panel provided for by Art. 255 of the TFEU (3rd Activity Report)' COUR (2014) 1118/14, 17.

[26] This conclusion is however subject to an important caveat. It must be observed that the 255
Panel has—for the time being—only defined the assessment criteria, without yet determining the
standards applicable to the national selection procedures (eg establishment of independent national
expert bodies, publication of calls for expression of interest, etc). It has however clearly expressed its
preference for the establishment of national procedures enabling the merits of the candidates to be
assessed in an independent and objective manner. It stated that while the absence of this procedure
would not be sufficient for 'considering a suitable candidate unsuitable', a national procedure comply-
ing with the above-described features may 'work in the candidate's favour'. See Second Activity Report
(n 25) 10.

[27] See, on this point, Engel (n 5) 448.

[28] Unlike the EU, the appointing authority is not composed of government representatives but is
rather the PACE. The ECtHR held that Art 22 of the Convention does not limit the PACE to assessing candidates only against the criteria set out in Art 21(1) of the Convention; it may elaborate on
Art 21(1) by introducing additional criteria that 'flow' from them and 'explain them in greater detail';
and it may apply other legitimate principles (such as gender balance), provided that in doing so it does
not impede satisfaction of the Art 21(1) criteria. See PACE Sub-Committee on the Election of Judges

Committee of Ministers' guidelines and have at times seen the involvement of the ECtHR itself.[29] They are intended to cover all stages of this procedure, including the establishment of the procedure, the identification of criteria applicable to the inclusion of candidates on a list, the composition and procedures of the selection body responsible for recommending candidates to the final decision-maker, and the role of the final decision-maker.

The two panels thus differ as to their influence over the national selection procedures. While the Advisory Panel merely enforces the (additional) criteria and standards established by the PACE by advising only the relevant government, the 255 Panel acts *de facto* as if it were the PACE itself: it contributes to defining the assessment criteria and refers to the selection procedures in order to inject some transparency at the national level.

In other words, the Advisory Panel's role in judicial selection exhausts itself in the preparation of an assessment of the candidates' suitability in relation to a set of pre-established criteria and procedures (best practices). In so doing, it inevitably offers guidance on how to interpret and apply both the selection criteria and the national procedures. Yet, given the limited diffusion of its opinion (only the individual, concerned member state), the pedagogical effects stemming from its opinion remain—especially if compared with those of the 255 Panel—very limited.

Conversely, in the absence of any policy guidelines aimed at streamlining the national procedures and clarifying the selection criteria, the 255 Panel is in a position to provide both an *in abstracto* and *in concreto* assessment of the candidates' suitability. In other words, the 255 Panel contributes to the same rules that it is entrusted to apply when making its suitability analysis of a proposed candidate. This feature renders the 255 Panel similar to the Sub-Committee of the Parliamentary Assembly.

Given their distinctive institutional contexts as well as the variance in the impact of each panel upon the respective selection systems, the question of the optimal level of transparency that the two panels should guarantee in their respective contributions to the selection process requires some distinctions.

In particular, in the case of the selection system within the Council of Europe, any change in the confidentiality policy of the Advisory Panel may affect—more than would be the case in the EU system—not only the nature of its work and its relations with the Sub-Committee and the PACE, but also the freedom to elect judges entrusted to the PACE by the contracting parties. Therefore, when examining the transparency of the judicial selection system for the ECtHR, the analysis should focus on the overall quality review system of judicial appointments; it therefore cannot be limited to the Advisory Panel but should include the Sub-Committee.

---

to the European Court of Human Rights, 'Procedure for electing judges to the European Court of Human Rights', AS/Jur (2010)12 rev3, 11 October 2010.

[29] ECtHR Grand Chamber, Advisory Opinion on certain legal questions concerning the lists of candidates submitted with a view to the election of judges to the European Court of Human Rights (12 February 2008).

It is therefore time to consider the level of transparency that the panels currently ensure in relation to the exercise of their 'quality review', before illustrating why this is problematic and providing some recommendations on how to strike a better balance between privacy and transparency.

4. The Challenge of Transparency in Judicial Selection

In discharging their 'quality review' task, both panels receive and collect, and may solicit, a significant amount of information about both the candidate and the selection process through which (s)he has been chosen.[30] Of these materials, ranging from the candidate's CV to the record of the national selection procedures, only the panels' opinions are disclosed. Yet the circulation of their opinions is extremely limited, as they are exclusively forwarded to the government concerned in the case of the Council of Europe, and to the representatives of governments of the EU member states in the EU context.

While no specific rules nor clear statements exist vis-à-vis access to the panels' input,[31] a more articulated policy exists in relation to the panels' output: their opinions. As previously mentioned, neither panel is currently subject to transparency duties equivalent to those which they impose on national authorities during the selection procedures. In particular, both panels refuse—in the name of a set of legal and policy-based arguments—disclosure of their opinions to third parties beyond the contracting party concerned (in the case of the ECtHR) or the member states (in the case of the CJEU).

Both panels justify their stance on public access by invoking the protection of privacy of the candidates as well as the related interest of protecting reputation; they also cite a potential 'chilling effect' that the disclosure might have on future candidates by dissuading them from going through the selection process.[32] In so doing they rely on textual arguments drawn from their respective operating rules.[33] In these circumstances, the question arises as to whether the panels' opinions as well as the other information collected in the file should be proactively disclosed to the public, or whether third parties ought to be granted access upon request.

---

[30] See CM/Res (n 1), point 6(2). For an overview of the input received and collected by the 255 Panel, see Second Activity Report (n 25), p 9.

[31] While the 255 Panel presented its policy *vis-à-vis* third-parties access to its documents in its First Activity Report in 2011 (n 25), nothing is said about access to the candidate's file. The other annual reports have not remedied the situation.

[32] For the perspective of the Council of Europe, see eg, CDDH (n 19). For the EU, see above ch 3 s 2.

[33] For the EU, see point 5 ('the deliberations of the panel shall take place **in camera**') and point 8 ('the panel's opinion shall be forwarded to the Representatives of the Governments of the Member States') of the 255 Panel Operating Rules. For the Council of Europe, see point 5(3) of the Operating Rules ('If, in the light of the written submissions and any comments obtained, the Panel considers that one or more of the persons put forward by a High Contracting Party are not suitable, it shall so inform the High Contracting Party, giving reasons for its view, which shall be **confidential**.').

While one may intuitively understand the need for discretion, the current transparency policy of the panels, regardless of its legal correctness, seems to question the legitimacy of the panels themselves. This is true because, despite their mere advisory role, both panels play a significant role not only in the outcome of the selection process but also in the input to that process, by interpreting the selection criteria and applying them to the candidates. How can it be ensured that the panels' assessment is in line with its mission and selection criteria? In other words: who guards the guardians? The ensuing democratic legitimacy concern is heightened when one considers the opaque modalities of selection and composition of the two advisory panels.

Four major arguments are invoked to refuse third party access to the panels' opinions. They can be summed up as follows:

(i)   duty of confidentiality;

(ii) data protection;

(iii) reputation;

(iv) potential chilling effect on future candidatures.

4.1. Duty of confidentiality

Both panels are subject to a duty of confidentiality in their operation. According to point 5(3) of the Operating Rules of the Advisory Panel, 'If, in the light of the written submissions and any comments obtained, the Panel considers that one or more of the persons put forward by a High Contracting Party are not suitable, it shall so inform the High Contracting Party, giving reasons for its view, which shall be **confidential**'. In the case of the 255 Panel, a duty of confidentiality arises from the combination of point 8 ('the panel's opinions must be forwarded to Representatives of the Governments of the Member States') and point 5 of the Operating Rules, which provides that the panel's deliberations take place *in camera*.[34] From the joint reading of these two provisions, it would emerge—in the interpretation provided by the 255 Panel—that *'the [...] opinions were intended exclusively for Member States governments in the context of appointing [...] European Judges'*.[35]

While the confidentiality of the Advisory Panel's output seems textually well anchored, it appears to be less so in relation to the opinions of the 255 Panel. With respect to the 255 Panel's output, one could argue, on the basis of a textual *a contrario* argument, that nothing prohibits disclosure of the opinions. Indeed, the relevant provisions only expressly require confidentiality for public hearings. The current texts do not therefore appear an insurmountable obstacle to greater disclosure. This is demonstrated by the actual policy undertaken by the 255 Panel to publish an annual report providing a considerable amount of information

---

[34] See also First Activity Report (n 25) 5.   [35] Ibid.

regarding the working modalities and the reasoning leading to adoption of the individual opinions. The level of detail of this document seems at times to undermine the 255 Panel's commitment to confidentiality.

4.2. Data protection

Both panels justify their restrictive stance vis-à-vis public access to information by invoking the protection of candidates' privacy. Thus, by referring to its own 'analysis of Regulation 1049/2001 and 45/2001 as interpreted by the Court of Justice in *Bavarian Lager*',[36] the 255 Panel concludes that 'the content of the opinions it gives, whether favourable or not, may not be made public either directly or even, through statistical details, indirectly'.[37]

It is necessary to pause and unpack this legally dense statement by collecting the various bits of legal reasoning offered by the Panel in its first and subsequent activity reports. In the 255 Panel's view, the opinion on a candidate's suitability constitutes a document covered under the Union's general transparency rules. As such it falls under Article 4 of Regulation 1049/2001.[38] Under this provision, the Council is bound to refuse access to a document where disclosure would undermine 'the privacy and integrity of individuals, in particular with regard to the protection of personal data'.

The 255 Panel inferred from this provision, read in conjunction with the judgment of the Court of Justice in the *Bavarian Lager* case, that its opinions on individual candidates are to be qualified as 'personal data' within the meaning of Article 2(a) of Regulation 45/2001, which includes 'any information relating to an identified or identifiable natural person'. As the processing of these personal data was intended solely to help the representatives of the member state governments to take decisions on the judicial appointment, the 255 Panel considers that the communication of these opinions to any other entity than those listed in point 8 of the operating rules, ie the member state governments, could constitute processing of personal data for a purpose other than those for which they have been collected, contrary to Article 6(1) of Regulation 45/2001. Therefore, third party disclosure of the opinion would breach both Regulation 45/2001 (processing of personal data for other purpose than a member state's support) and Regulation 1049/2001, as it would undermine the protection of privacy and the integrity of the individual within the meaning of its Article 4(1)(b). As a result, the Panel holds that its opinions ought not be disseminated to the public.[39]

---

[36] Case C-28/08 P *European Commission v The Bavarian Lager Co. Ltd* [2010] ECR I-6055.

[37] First Activity Report (n 25) 3.

[38] Regulation 1049/2001 regarding public access to European Parliament, Council and Commission documents [2001] OJ L145/43. The legal basis for this regulation is contained in Art 15(3) TFEU second subparagraph. This regulation is currently under revision: Proposal for a Regulation regarding public access to European Parliament, Council and Commission documents, 30 April 2008, COM(2008) 229 final, 2008/0090(COD).

[39] Ibid. See also Lord Mance, 'The Composition of the European Court of Justice', talk given to the United Kingdom Association for European Law, London, October 2011, 19–20.

Thus, according to the 255 Panel, the opinion on the candidate's suitability and the 'documents it draws up or receives in the context of its proceedings' are third party documents within the meaning of Article 4(4) of Regulation 1049/2001. Consequently, it is for the institutions of the Union, provided that they receive a request in this regard, to communicate documents emanating from the 255 Panel which they have received. The institutions are obliged to consult the 255 Panel before any communication in order to determine whether an exception to the right of communication is applicable, unless it is immediately clear that the document should or should not be disclosed.

Such a conclusion assumes, first, the applicability *ratione personae* and *ratione materiae* of both regulations to the 255 Panel output. Second, it fails to determine the status of the other information contained in the candidate's file and collected by the 255 Panel. Assuming that both regulations are indeed applicable to the 255 Panel, they indicate in which circumstances the public may gain access to the 255 Panel's output.

It is undisputed that opinions of the 255 Panel, which include an assessment of the suitability of the candidates for the office of Judge at the Court of Justice or the General Court, contain personal data within the meaning of Article 2(a) of Regulation 45/2001. This does not automatically imply, however, that access to the opinion should be denied. Rather, as interpreted by the Court of Justice of the EU in several cases,[40] institutions should, in dealing with requests for access to documents containing personal data, apply the provisions of Regulation No 45/2001. Under this regulation, publication of personal data may be justified if the disclosure is necessary in a democratic society for a legitimate public interest. Moreover, personal data could be transferred to the applicant under Article 8(b) of Regulation No 45/2001 if he or she establishes the necessity of having the data transferred and if there is no reason to assume that the data subject's legitimate interests might be prejudiced. Because the majority of judicial candidates with respect to whom one may request access to the 255 Panel's opinion have already been appointed to the post, none of his/her legitimate interests appear at stake. As for the negative opinions, according to settled case law, 'the institutions are obliged to balance, before disclosing information relating to a natural person, the European Union's interest in guaranteeing the transparency of its actions and the infringement of the rights recognized by Articles 7 and 8 of the Charter'.[41] In conclusion, it might be suggested that, when balanced with democratic concerns, the judges of the Court of Justice 'cannot demand the anonymity of earlier years, hiding behind literal or metaphorical wigs'.[42]

---

[40] Joined Cases C-92/09 and C-93/09 *Schecke* [2010] ECR I-11063; Case C-28/08 *European Commission v The Bavarian Lager Co. Ltd* [2010] ECR I-6055, paras 75–9; Case T-190/10 *Hackett* [2010] n.y.r.

[41] *Schecke* (n 40), para 85 and *Bavarian Lager* (n 40), paras 75–9.

[42] See Kate Malleson, 'Parliamentary Scrutiny of Supreme Court Nominees: A View from the United Kingdom' (2007) 44 *Osgoode Hall L J* 557, ('Citizens have a right to be properly informed about the people who sit in their top courts and determine controversial issues of great moral and political sensitivity').

4.3. Reputation

The major argument invoked by both panels to oppose public access to their output is the need of protecting the reputation of candidates *pro futuro*.[43] The integrity of the candidates could be put at stake—the argument goes—should their opinions be rendered public, and this remains so even in the case of subsequent appointment of the candidate in question. However, the argument does not seem persuasive when considered in the context of the current selection practice. As will be illustrated below, the current confidentiality policy not only falls short of protecting the candidates' reputation, but—by denying access to the reasons leading to the panels' opinions—also threatens it.

Let's start with an examination of how the current confidentiality policy protects candidates' reputations through an analysis of its broader reputational effects. First, under both systems, while the reasons leading to a negative opinion remain confidential, both the identity of the candidate and the outcome of the panels' opinions are publicly known. This is because, with the designation of the candidate by the relevant member state being public and announced in the media, her/his non-confirmation automatically suggests that something went wrong. In other words, it is easy to deduce from the current selection system whether a given candidate has received a favourable or unfavourable opinion.[44] Therefore, since the current policy only succeeds in protecting the reasons why but not the person who has received an unfavourable opinion, it fails to ensure the respect of the reputation of the candidates. But there is more.

Second, as the first years of operation of both panels have shown, a situation in which the identity of the candidate who failed is widely known but the reasons that led to that conclusion are not lends itself to gossip. By preventing the public from knowing the reasons why a particular candidate has failed to receive a positive assessment by the Panel, the actual confidentiality policy opens a door for speculation, chattering, and manipulation. Virtually no observer belonging to the EU legal epistemic community—which is by nature the most merciless in judging the candidate and prone to speculating about the reasons for her/his failure—is currently unaware of the outcome and presumed reasons that have led to a negative opinion. One may therefore contend that the current policy seems more effective in protecting the panels' operation from public scrutiny than the candidates' reputation.

---

[43] See Lord Mance (n 39) 9 and CDDH report (n 19) para 54.

[44] In the framework of the CoE, the negative opinion by the Advisory Panel may be inferred by the non-inclusion of the designated candidate in the list of candidates submitted to the PACE as provided for in Art 22 of the ECHR. In case of negative opinion on one or more of the candidates, the 'Panel shall in a similar manner consider one or more candidates who would subsequently be presented by the High Contracting Party'. See CM/Res (n 1) point 5. The choice of the Sub-Committee on the Election of Judges to the ECtHR occurs within a roster of three names and generally results in a ranking of those candidates. In principle, the first name is the preferred one, being the most suitable for the job. See, eg, Jutta Limbach, Pedro Villalon, Roger Errera, Lord Lester of Herne Hill QC,

It is submitted that the legitimacy of a judge increases, rather than decreases, if the public is aware of the reasons that judge was appointed or not. The disclosure of the opinion of the panels would therefore increase the perception of personal integrity of the judge and, as a result, of the jurisdiction to which she belongs to. This increases the democratic legitimacy of the courts and does not necessarily harm—rather, it protects—the rejected candidate.[45] It has thus been shown that, in countries in which judicial candidates for the highest court are confirmed by a public hearing (such as the United States), disclosing the reasons why a candidate was confirmed or rejected can increase both the independence and legitimacy of a court in the eyes of the public without harming the reputation of rejected candidates, who were largely rejected based on legitimate factors such as partisanship, political philosophy, or insufficient experience.[46] This is in keeping with the facts that judges are beholden to internal and external pressures and must maintain a strong judicial reputation within the judiciary and outside of it, and that it has been shown repeatedly that both internal and external pressures are vital to the functioning and overall reputation of courts.[47]

Finally, when considering the inevitable repercussions on the candidate's reputation which stem from a negative opinion, we should not forget the limited scope and intensity of the review exercised by both panels upon the choice of the candidates.[48] As stated by Jean-Marc Sauvé in his chapter, in the case of an unfavourable opinion motivated by limited expertise, 'similar lack of knowledge undermines in no way the ability of the candidates to hold their office, often a prominent one, on the national level; it just does not recommend them, in the eyes of the Panel, to be appointed to the office for which they applied'.[49]

4.4. The chilling effect on candidatures

Another related argument that is often invoked to justify the policy of limited disclosure pursued by both panels has to do with the concern that publicity would

---

Tamara Morschakova, Lord Justice Sedley, and Andrzej Zoll, *Judicial Independence: Law and Practice of Appointments to the European Court of Human Rights* (Interights, 2003) 5.

[45] One may contend that this may not be the case when an unfavourable opinion causes repercussions for the exercise of a different governmental job (eg a Minister of Justice designated judge). Yet this collateral effect must—if examined in the light of the objective pursued by the advisory panels—be welcome, as it might discourage inadequate candidacies. More transparency could therefore produce welcome chilling effects on inappropriate candidates.

[46] The reasons a candidate was not appointed to the USSC are openly discussed. See, eg, eJournal, *Issues of Democracy*, Bureau of International Information Programs, US Department of State (April 2005): <photos.state.gov/libraries/amgov/30145/publications-english/EJ-courts-0405.pdf>. See also William G Ross, 'The Ratings Game: Factors that Influence Judicial Reputation' (1996) 79 *MARQ L Rev* 401.

[47] See Nuno Garoupa and Tom Ginsburg, 'Judicial Audiences and Reputation: Perspectives from Comparative Law' (2009) 47 *Columbia Journal of Transnationational Law* 451.

[48] Jean-Marc Sauvé describes the review entrusted and exercised by the 255 Panel limited to the control of 'manifest error'. See above ch 3 s 3.

[49] Ibid.

discourage further candidatures for the judicial jobs. It is believed that more openness might lead to a domino effect whereby potential candidates would be dissuaded from allowing their name to go forward.[50]

However, this argument relies on a set of unproven assumptions; the risk of a chilling effect on candidatures is not empirically established. Moreover, due to the limited confidentiality ensured by the current system, some risk of chilling effect is inherent to any form of 'quality review' whose mission is to exercise external scrutiny on governmental choice. Again, since both the identity of the candidate and the outcome of the 'suitability review' mechanisms are *de facto* known, it is not the disclosure of the opinions that may have a chilling effect, but the mere fact of the review itself. Indeed, the former president of the General Court of the EU contended *in tempore non suspecto* that the procedure as it is already threatens to put off prospective candidates, who may either fear a negative result or believe the whole scheme violates their dignity.[51]

This legal and policy analysis demonstrates that the arguments generally adduced to defend the status quo fail to justify the actual policy of confidentiality pursued by the two judicial advisory panels.[52] It rather suggests that there is a case for striking a better balance between the imperative of transparency and the need to protect privacy. Indeed, a close examination of these arguments seems to question the belief that disclosure of the panels' opinions would automatically jeopardize the functioning of their respective selection systems.

It is against this backdrop that the next and final sections provide a few recommendations on how to better balance the imperative of transparency with the candidates' privacy concerns.

5. Towards More Transparency in Judicial Selection

The current lack of transparency of panels' activities seems questionable not only from a purely legal standpoint but also from at least three other additional perspectives.

First, the limited access to the panels' input and output may compromise the pedagogical function which both panels are called upon to exercise vis-à-vis the member states. As a matter of fact, given the limited diffusion of the panels' opinion, there is a risk that countries might fail to understand how both panels discharge their oversight duties upon each individual candidate. A more transparent policy regarding panels' output would maximize the effectiveness of their respective 'quality reviews' through strategic use of, *inter alia*, 'peer-pressure' and

---

[50] Jean-Marc Sauvé, 'Le rôle du comité 255 dans la sélection du juge de l'Union', in *The Court of Justice and the Construction of Europe: Analyses and Perspectives on Sixty Years of Case-law* (Springer, 2013) 116.

[51] Vesterdorf (n 6) 610.

[52] In the case of the Advisory Panel, however, the legally required confidentiality that was previously discussed represents a stumbling block against a possible reconsideration of the current policy.

'name-and-shame' mechanisms. This appears especially the case for the Advisory Panel's opinions, whose *ex ante* transmission to all Council of Europe contracting parties could provide this entity more teeth and help it gain more respect from all governments.

Second, the current confidentiality policy raises significant legitimacy concerns. This seems especially the case when examined in the light of the panels' broad discretion in interpreting and applying the selection criteria to the candidates, as well as to their increasing voice in the selection process. This legitimacy concern seems all the more worrying in the light of the rather vague rules governing selection of the panels' members.[53] There is indeed a risk that, given the important say that the presidents of both courts have in the appointment procedure, as well as the substantial presence of former members in the resulting panels, the two systems of selection may head towards some form of judicial self-government.[54] While this is unlikely to automatically translate into an empowerment of the judiciary at the expense of the executive,[55] there is clearly a case for enhancing the transparency of the two panels' operation in order to legitimize that process if it should occur.

Third, no democratic oversight is foreseen for the panels when discharging their advisory duty. Indeed, despite their significant authority in shaping the selection process, their working methods and how they actually follow the selection criteria they have contributed to defining remain mostly outside public scrutiny. As a result, no one is entitled to verify whether and how the panels are abiding by the selection criteria and the duty to state reasons for their choice. This seems particularly disturbing should one consider the difficulty of drawing the line between expertise-checking and opinion-checking in any form of suitability assessment. Suppose that a candidate has written extensively in favour of a judicial doctrine that has traditionally been opposed by one of the two courts (eg directive's horizontal effect): this might alter the perception of the candidate's suitability to take up the job. In the absence of public access to the relevant opinions, who would be able to demonstrate that such a bias played a role in the suitability analysis? Likewise, since one of the new criteria developed by the 255 Panel relates to the candidate's views about the 'nature, role and scope of the office of Judge or Advocate-General',[56] its assessment inevitably involves some substantive value judgement. To adequately address these sorts of risks of opinion-checking disguised under the label of expertise-checking, it would probably be more appropriate to organize a public hearing than to merely allow access to the opinions of the panels. This would enable both selection systems to discuss openly—rather

---

[53] According to the Resolution establishing the Advisory Panel, its members '[...] shall be appointed by the Committee of Ministers following consultations with the President of the European Court of Human Rights. Proposals for appointment may be submitted by the High Contracting Parties'. In the case of the 255 Panel, its members must be appointed by the Council and '*it shall act on the initiative of the President of the Court of Justice*' (Art 255 TFEU), who is the one who proposes the names to the Council.

[54] Jean-Marc Sauvé perceives in the 255 Panel a 'germ of a council of judiciary within the Union'. See above ch 3 s 3 as well as the concerns expressed by von Bogdandy and Krenn above in ch 7 s 3.1.2.

[55] Contra see Dumbrovsky, Petkova, and van der Sluis (n 5) 481.

[56] See First Activity Report (n 25) 10.

than behind closed doors—different understandings of the act of judging, as these will inevitably inform adjudication and reflect into the case law of each legal system. This seems particularly relevant when one learns that, from an empirical perspective, candidates whose profile is aligned to those represented within the 255 Panel seem more likely to be appointed than those who have a more academic or practitioner-type background.[57] In other words, a risk of *de facto* co-optation seems very high under the current selection system, at least within the EU.

In order to address some of these concerns, the 255 Panel prepares an annual activity report that, although in an abridged version, is publicly available. Its declared objective is

> not only to give account of the panel's activities, but also to allow the Union's institutions, the governments of the Member States, and, where appropriate, future candidates for the duties of Judge and Advocate-General of the Court of Justice and the General Court to become better acquainted with the procedures established for examining candidatures and with the panel's interpretation of the provisions it is required to apply.[58]

This is the pedagogical role previously evoked. While the Advisory Panel releases no such reports, the PACE regularly publishes documents aimed at providing guidance to its contracting parties about how to select and examine its candidates. Yet, in the absence of third-party access to their *in concreto* suitability assessment, such as opinions and the information collected in the candidate's files, one may, again, wonder: who guards the guardians.

6. Conclusion: Transparency as a Recipe for Effectiveness, Legitimacy, and Accountability of Judicial Selection

The establishment of two European expert bodies exercising quality oversight over judicial selection signals a progressive shift from the rubberstamping of judicial appointments to a more reflexive, at times discursive, selection of candidates for judicial posts both at the ECtHR and the CJEU.[59] While this is a positive development, their operation inevitably affects the balance of powers in the processes of judicial appointment, and brings to the fore fundamental issues of legitimacy and accountability. The foregoing analysis demonstrates that the current policy of limited disclosure pursued by both panels in relation to their input and output renders those concerns even more acute. This seems especially true for the 255 Panel, which is progressively turning into 'a germ of a council of judiciary within the Union'.[60]

---

[57] See above ch 2 s 6.
[58] Second Activity Report (n 25) 6.
[59] This is especially so in the case of the CoE, where the current selection system being based on the dual legitimacy of governmental and parliamentary input has ensured an informed debate about the political and not exclusively technical nature of the judicial selection process.
[60] Above (n 54).

It is submitted that greater publicity of the panels' output could not only maximize the effectiveness of their respective pedagogical missions, but also enhance the democratic legitimacy and accountability of the respective judicial selection processes. This might in turn strengthen the authority of the European courts in the eyes of the general public as a whole.

To maximize the pedagogical mission entrusted to the panels, their opinions, be they favourable or unfavourable, should be circulated *ex ante* (ie before the actual appointment or election) to a larger category of addressees and in a broader set of circumstances. Thus, it is argued that the opinions of the 255 Panel should be distributed among the EU member states also in the case of a candidate's withdrawal.[61] This would act as an important deterrent to unqualified but 'politically supported' candidates ready to force the system by hiding behind the secretive character of the process. There are examples of candidates who have 'tested' the 255 Panel but then withdrew in the aftermath of the hearing, thus preventing the formal adoption of the Panel's opinion.

In the case of the Advisory Panel, its opinions should be circulated among all contracting parties so as to amplify the (albeit non-public) political peer pressure on both the relevant government and its elected representatives in the PACE. This might discourage the relevant government from maintaining a candidate who was found not to be qualified by impeding both the Sub-Committee and the PACE to support such candidate. This change in its confidentiality policy could transform the Advisory Panel from an exclusive advisor to the government concerned to an advisor to the PACE as a whole. However, while this 'upgrade' in the mission entrusted to the Advisory Panel would strengthen its authority, it will not formally impact the autonomy enjoyed by the PACE in electing judges.

But this *ex ante* circulation of the opinions might not be enough to address the legitimacy and democratic accountability concerns raised by the panels' operation. As panels' authority and impact are set to grow over time, their operation is increasingly likely to reflect—given their own composition—the judicial agenda pursued by the advisory bodies over that of the executive and legislative. This seems to call for greater public scrutiny of their role, membership, and operation.

This can only be guaranteed by also publicizing their output *ex post* (ie after the actual appointment or election). This might lead the 255 Panel on the one hand, and the Advisory Panel and Sub-Committee on the other, to initially and proactively release to the public their respective output once a decision has been made.[62] As previously illustrated, given the unavoidable repercussions stemming from the mere existence of an (undisclosed) unfavourable opinion on a candidate's reputation, it appears to be in the interest of all judicial candidates to allow circulation of the motivations leading to that opinion. In other words, the candidates themselves would actually be better served by the public disclosure of a reasoned

---

[61] Interestingly enough, a similar withdrawal scenario is not likely to occur in the selection for a judge to the ECtHR insofar as a candidate is not the addressee of the Advisory Panel's opinion. See on this point CDDH (n 19) 10.

[62] Currently the recommendations of the Sub-Committee are given to the members of the PACE.

opinion than by the current policy of partial confidentiality. The organization of public hearings might attain a similar objective. Finally, since the legitimacy of a judge increases, rather than decreases, if the public is aware of the reasons for that judge's appointment, disclosing the opinion of the panels would increase not only the perception of the judge's personal integrity but also the authority of the courts to which she belongs. Indeed, contrary to conventional wisdom, full disclosure of panels' activities and output might increase the legitimacy of the courts without necessarily harming the rejected candidate's reputation. Rather, by allowing the public to understand and evaluate the process, it might better protect the candidate from inevitable speculation about what went wrong in their individual assessment. Measured against this argument, the current confidentiality policy appears more effective in protecting the panels' operation from public scrutiny than the candidate's reputation, especially when one indeed considers its modest record of success in protecting the latter.

This chapter provided an analysis of why and how the 'quality review' panels should review their current policy of confidentiality. It demonstrated that it is not only legally possible but also in line with societal expectations for the two advisory panels to gradually shift the balance away from privacy concerns towards more openness both during and after the selection process. This would allow the panels to address the significant democratic legitimacy and accountability concerns raised by their operation and help them discharge their final mission: to strengthen the authority of European courts by facilitating acceptance of their rulings in the eyes of the public.

10

Spillovers in Selecting Europe's Judges

Will the Criterion of Gender Equality Make it to Luxembourg?

Bilyana Petkova

1. Introduction

The influence between the national and the supranational judicial tiers, as well as between the two supranational courts in Europe, in establishing new norms for the selection of judges has hardly been theorized.[1] In this chapter, I will argue that new standards of judicial appointments are being formed in a circle of normative change. In other words, I demonstrate that standards that have often been experimented with at the national or the supranational level in Europe have seeped into sister systems. On the one hand, what used to be a highly politicized and exclusively executive-dominated process of appointing judges to the Court of Justice of the European Union (CJEU) and the European Court of Human Rights (ECtHR) is now gradually changing, partly due to the supranational pressure for opening up to scrutiny the appointment process, into a more participatory and merit-based form of judicial selection.[2] On the other hand, the criterion of requiring gender balance on the bench, though not yet firmly entrenched on the national or supranational levels, is slowly making its way onto the reform agenda in both the national and the supranational arenas. While not advocating that there should be one single 'best' model for judicial selection or that spillovers are mechanical and inevitable, the chapter shows that minimum standards of legitimate judicial appointments form through mutual standard-borrowing and are subject to change.

My goal is to explain both horizontal and vertical spillovers in judicial selection in Europe. By 'spillovers' I mean the non-accidental legal and ideational similarities between jurisdictions. Despite their varying degree of causality and/or causation,

---

[1] Many thanks to Judith Resnik and Reva Siegel for the many thought-provoking conversations. The usual disclaimer applies.

[2] I made that claim first in T Dumbrovsky, B Petkova, and M Van Der Sluis, 'Judicial Appointments: The Article 255 Advisory Panel and Selection Procedures in the Member States' (2014) 51 *Common Market Law Review* 455.

spillovers characterize the constant intellectual import and export of institutional design between and across the jurisdictional levels in Europe.[3]

Horizontally, I examine the influence between the Luxembourg and Strasbourg courts in terms of the establishment of advisory panels that vet the national nominations. In this sense, I argue that one can easily discern a causal link in the ECtHR's addition of an extra step to the selection process for judges in Strasbourg: the Strasbourg Court's reformers drew inspiration from the Panel established pursuant to Article 255 on the Treaty of the Functioning of the European Union (the 255 Panel). Both the legal base (or the lack thereof) and the structure of the ECtHR's Advisory Panel are slightly different from those of the 255 Panel. One could say that the ECtHR's Advisory Panel has been adapted to better fit the needs of the Strasbourg system, where the Parliamentary Assembly of the Council of Europe (PACE) plays an important role in the selection of judges, unlike the processes of selection to the Court of Justice (ECJ) and the General Court (GC). Be that as it may, the EU experience has served as a significant intellectual catalyst. I use gender balance on the bench as a further case study for a potential horizontal spillover. Whether gender balance, already promoted to a certain extent in Strasbourg and in a handful of the European states, will gain the same widespread recognition as a legitimating value of judicial selection that expertise has gradually acquired remains to be seen. I will argue that since the two systems—the EU and the European Convention on Human Rights (ECHR)—will soon be interlocked with EU accession to the ECHR, the pressure to consider gender balance among the selection criteria for the bench in Luxembourg is likely to increase. Although the two courts are different in terms of jurisdiction and institutional set-up, their interdependence has always existed and is growing. There are no compelling reasons why ensuring that gender plays a role in the nominations in Strasbourg, but not in Luxembourg, should continue to be accepted as a legitimate part of the process of judicial selection to the latter court.

Vertically, I ask whether the expert advisory panels that now exist at both European levels have in any way influenced the often criticized national procedures used to nominate judges to the European bench. Further, when analysing vertical spillovers, I find interdependences also in the other direction—from the national to the supranational judicial tier. In order to elaborate specific criteria that could put flesh on the bones of the high-level or meta-criteria enshrined in the EU Treaties for selecting judges at the ECJ and the GC, the 255 Panel has looked for guidance in the national criteria for holding office at the highest courts of the member states.

---

[3] Although I have adapted the term 'spillover' to better fit the context of judicial selection, my account is not divorced from that first coined in the classic work of Ernst Haas, *The Uniting of Europe. Political, Social and Economic Forces 1950–1957* (Stevens and Sons 1958). In observing the spillovers of European law from one area to the other, Haas has held that interdependence generates more interdependence. Inasmuch as I believe that interdependence in Europe is present vertically (from the supranational to the national tier) but also horizontally, between the Council of Europe and the EU, as well as between the EU member states, my conceptual understanding of spillovers does not conflict with Haas's. However, I try to avoid the automaticity of neo-functionalism by arguing that certain spillovers are normatively more appealing than others.

The chapter proceeds as follows: I first sketch out the theoretical argument on legitimacy as a dynamic concept and interdependence as inherent to norm formation, then turn to the horizontal spillovers between Luxembourg and Strasbourg, in the specific contexts of ensuring gender balance on the bench and establishing supranational judicial panels. I then review vertical spillovers in terms of the emergence of national judicial commissions that resemble the 255 Panel and the ECtHR's Advisory Panel, and trace the fleshing out of criteria for judicial selection adopted by the supranational panels. I conclude by analysing both the horizontal and the vertical spillovers of judicial selection in Europe that can be categorized by a model of convergence and mutual engagement with norms originating from European jurisdictions. I argue that a third model—that of absolute institutional resistance to standards of judicial selection practised in sister jurisdictions—is both unjustified and unwarranted.

2. The Concept of Legitimacy: As Elusive as an Eel

The concept of legitimacy is a favourite topic of debate among many political philosophers and lawyers.[4] Legitimacy can be viewed as a Weberian or empirical concept or as a normative idea. The empirical part of how we look at legitimacy is dependent on sociological studies: is the ECJ *perceived* by relevant audiences such as academics, national judges, politicians, the media, and the public at large, as more legitimate after the Lisbon reform of the appointment process? Or, is the ECtHR *perceived* as more legitimate[5] after the establishment of an advisory panel that pre-examines the lists of national nominations before sending them to the Sub-Committee of the PACE? From a normative perspective, however, the question one wants to ask is somewhat more ambitious. It looks at legitimacy not as a static concept but as one evolving over time; not as a binary property, but as a matter of degree. In this vein of thought, we might want to ask whether the changing social mores require yet new features to be added to the process of selection of European judges at the ECtHR and the CJEU in order for these courts to be regarded as legitimate.

What the ECJ's Judge Lenaerts writes in a recent piece about the principle of democracy can in fact be paraphrased and extended to our understanding of standards of good governance and institutional legitimacy in a judicial context:

... [Legitimacy] is a dynamic concept, which evolves hand in hand with societal changes. Whilst some components of [democratic legitimacy] are always constant,

---

[4] The reference in the section heading is to Lord Lester's famous criticism of the 'margin of appreciation' for being 'as slippery and elusive as an eel': 'Universality v. Subsidiarity: A Reply?' (1998) 1 *European Human Rights Law Review* 73, 75.

[5] Note that strengthening the legitimacy of the Strasbourg Court is among the main reasons given for the introduction of the ECtHR's Advisory Panel: see 'Draft CDDH report on the review of the functioning of the Advisory Panel of experts on candidates for election as judge to the European Court of Human Rights', Strasbourg, 31 October 2013, p 2.

others have appeared more recently (e.g.... the democratization of alternative means of policy-making and the principle of transparency). This shows that [legitimacy] must be regarded as incorporating elements of both 'continuity and change'. I refer to 'continuity' because some institutional, substantive, and procedural elements cannot be detached from a form of [judicial decision-making] without depriving it of its... character. I refer to 'change' because no form of [decision-making] can ever convincingly argue that its [legitimacy] is flawless and immutable, as new challenges may appear to which [legitimacy] must adapt.[6]

On this account, one can perceive as legitimate certain standards of judicial selection to the highest courts that have accrued over time and have by now become constant for the national as well as the international or transnational levels: arguably, among these are judicial independence, high moral qualities, and professional experience, of which legal education is a core pre-requisite.[7] Other requirements specific to the transnational context (such as the ability to work with diverse legal orders and in a multilingual culture) have been added later in the process. Transparency at the stage of advertising the candidacies, as well as gender equality, are now slowly becoming universal bedrock principles of (judicial) legitimacy and good governance too. Furthermore, as I discuss in detail below, whereas executive-dominated judicial selection for the two European courts used to be the norm, this is certainly not the case any more. Arguably, whereas the first-order criteria of legal merit—independence and professional competence—will stay unaltered, there might be other selection criteria and procedures that will start being taken into consideration in order to enhance the legitimacy of the (European) highest courts.

One such criterion is gender equality. If the fact that court benches were once *de jure* reserved for and then *de facto* overwhelmingly populated by white men was considered legitimate *at some point in the past*, this does not mean that the same is still true *now*. For Judith Resnik:

That the legitimacy of courts depends in any part on women serving as judges is an outgrowth of political and social movements reinterpreting the role of courts in democratic market economies. Adjudication is an ancient form, but only during the course of the

---

[6] K Lenaerts, 'The Principle of Democracy in the Case Law of the CJEU' (2013) 62 *International and Comparative Law Quarterly* 279.

[7] My co-authors and I showed in previous research that these are the formal requirements for both national, ECJ, and GC judges in 14 EU member states: Dumbrovsky, Petkova, and Van Der Sluis (n 1). The same formal requirements apply also to the ECtHR, as discussed in further detail in section 3.1 of this chapter, and are true for most international courts; more generally, see R Mackenzie and P Sands, 'Judicial Selection for International Courts: Towards Common Principles and Practices', in K Malleson and PH Russel (eds), *Appointing Judges in an Age of Judicial Power. Critical Perspectives from Around the World* (University of Toronto Press 2006) 213–40; P Mahoney, 'The International Judiciary—Independence and Accountability' (2008) 7 *Law and Practice of International Courts and Tribunals* 313; R Mackenzie, Kate Malleson, Penny Martin, and Phillippe Sands, *Selecting International Judges, Principle, Process and Politics* (Oxford University Press 2010). To what extent these formal requirements are complied with goes beyond the scope of my point here.

twentieth century did courts come to be obliged to welcome all persons as equals—as litigants, witnesses, jurors, staff, lawyers, and judges.[8]

The normative claim for female judges is thus both a symbolic–egalitarian one (if women are men's equals, why are they not equally represented on the bench?) and a substantive one (if more women are on the bench, will that not impact on the way the law is interpreted?).[9] One prong of the argument is therefore that the diverse, real-life personal experiences of judges will provide balanced perspectives to judicial decisions and substantively affect the law. A second is that even if the personal experience of the judges does not—or, as some would argue, should not—affect the law in a substantive way, the presence of under-represented groups on the bench conveys a sense of inclusiveness and procedural fairness, which encourages more members of such groups to enter the legal profession and to make use of the judicial system. Judges should be impartial when it comes to the outcome of their judgments, but in terms of their judicial deliberations, the diversity of their background enriches the process of constitutional interpretation. Using the above framework, calls for gender equality on the bench can be interpreted as an element of change in the normative aspect of judicial legitimacy.

How to arrive at a gender-balanced bench in turn provokes broader questions on the legitimacy of positive action measures, which are not without their opponents. For instance, at least in Europe,[10] such measures aiming at gender equality are attacked on universalist counts rooted in the idea of one indivisible *body politic* that both representative institutions and, by extension, the courts are there to serve in the public interest. In the words of a Spanish Constitutional Court judge:

In Western democracies, the primary function of political representation is to transform the initial plurality into 'a' political will because it is worthwhile that the heterogeneity of races, religions, cultures, languages, places of birth, etc., do not pose an obstacle to the legal status of the citizen. It is the citizen and only the citizen ... The question we must ask ourselves is whether it is conceivable to divide the political representatives into categories in order to facilitate or ensure that each category is represented without severely affecting the principle of unity and homogeneity of the citizenry. If the answer is 'yes', this will enable the legislature in the future to impose on the electoral body electoral nominations integrated into groups defined by race, language, sexual orientation, religion, certain genetic handicaps, by young people, seniors, etc.[11]

---

[8] J Resnik, 'Representing What? Women, Judges and Equality in the United States', Paper presented at the conference 'The Judge is a Woman', Université Libre de Bruxelles, Brussels, Belgium, 7 November 2013, on file with the author.

[9] J Resnik, ' "Naturally" without Gender: Women, Jurisdiction, and the Federal Courts' (1991) 66 *NYU L Rev* 1682; J Resnik, 'Visible on "Women's Issues" ' (1991) 77 *Iowa L Rev* 41, arguing that beyond questions on non-discrimination decided by the courts, women judges matter in other, more trivial areas of law because lawsuits involving property, contracts, and jurisdiction can have gender implications.

[10] For the range of arguments for and against affirmative action in the US context, see R Siegel, 'From Colorblindness To Antibalkanization: An Emerging Ground of Decision in Race Equality Cases' (2011) *Yale Law Review* 120.

[11] Constitutional Court of Spain, STC Decision No. 12/2008 (2008), Dissenting Opinion of Magistrate Rodríguez-Zapata, at para 2, author's own translation.

The logic of universalism exemplified in the dissenting opinion of the Spanish judge is arguably not confined to concerns for the representative bodies, and it is definitely not unique to Spain. It would rather appear that there has been a horizontal spillover from French constitutional thought and developments that were also discussed in other EU member states.[12] In defence of positive action, however, the French idea of parity has come about to vindicate the legitimacy of gender quotas for political parties and on corporate boards across Europe. Parity was conceived of 'as a formula for making the tradition of French universalism compatible with the political inclusion of women, as one half of humanity'.[13] The introduction of a selection criterion for gender equality across the European courtrooms is therefore related to the ways in which wider debates on positive action unfold. Once parity[14] has made inroads as a legitimate argument for positive action in other domains of the political and social life of European societies, it should be seen as the element of 'change' in the framework of judicial legitimacy espoused earlier.

In turn, judicial independence, once regarded as an unessential attribute to judicial legitimacy, has made a leap into the category of 'continuity' in judicial legitimacy; in other words, into the selection criteria that are now indispensable for the position of a judge. It must be acknowledged that judicial independence did not always rank high on the legitimacy scales of courts. What now seems unthinkable was once the norm: in medieval England, the courts existed only at the whim of the king and in order to carry out the responsibilities and powers of the king. As judges were an integral part of the king's administration, 'the distinction between judicial and administrative duties would have been rather obscure'.[15] As Shetreet writes,

---

[12] The Court and the dissent explicitly made a mention of French history and more recent developments. The dissent distinguished the Spanish context from that of France and Italy, where positive measures for gender equality were enacted after constitutional reforms: ibid. In 1982, the French Constitutional Council struck down party quotas on the ground that 'constitutional principles "preclude any division of persons entitled to vote or stand for election into separate categories"'. Constitutional amendments were eventually introduced in 1999 and 2008 as a result of new feminist arguments which managed to convincingly construe gender parity on electoral lists and corporate boards in universalist hues. See J Suk, 'Quotas and Consequences: A Transnational Re-evaluation' in D Hellman and S Moreau (eds), *Philosophical Foundations of Discrimination Law* (Oxford University Press 2013).

[13] Blanca R Ruiz and Ruth Rubio-Marín, 'The Gender of Representation: On Democracy, Equality, and Parity' (2008) 6 *International Journal of Constitutional Law* 287, 301.

[14] Whether parity can in turn obfuscate the claims of other historically excluded groups is immaterial to the discussion on the process of norm formation in judicial appointments in Europe to which the chapter aspires to contribute. For instance, it is possible that 'Arguments for gender parity blur justice and legitimacy claims, fusing questions of biology, social structure, and democratic theory…by depicting gender as a universal difference—the one difference we all share, a difference supposedly unlike race, ethnicity, and religion': R Siegel, 'Positive Action in the Crucible of Political Conflict', unpublished paper prepared for the conference of the International Society of Public Law, 'Rethinking the Boundaries of Public Law and Public Space', June 26–28, Florence, Italy (2014), on file with the author.

[15] S Sheetreet, *Judges on Trial: A Study of the Appointment and Accountability of the English Judiciary* (N Holland 1976) 2.

This seemingly impossible beginning for the judiciary was not, however, one which gave rise to much concern. At that period, the judges undoubtedly were not independent, being under strict royal control. The king enjoyed the cooperation of the judiciary. This collaboration was *harmonious and widely accepted*, due to the fact that the sovereign did not seek to use judges as instruments in political struggles.[16]

Thus, it was not until the seventeenth century, with the clash between the parliament and the king, that judicial independence made its way up the legitimacy ladder. Since after the establishment of judicial tenures the king could no longer hold the threat of dismissal over a judge's head, and since parliament could not twist a judge's arm to attain its own ends under the threat of withdrawing said judge's remuneration, independence became a reality. About the same time and in the wake of public outcry, judges were also banned from simultaneously serving in high governmental offices. This led to the disposal of the last remnants of the judiciary's medieval dependence on the executive.[17]

It took some time before judicial independence reached the international level—this happened after the Second World War, when it came to be vehemently defended in the case law of the ECtHR and other international bodies, and was declared an international custom by the UN special rapporteur.[18] Further, international professional organizations and non-governmental organizations (NGOs) begun issuing statements and working on international standards related to judicial independence, the Mt Scopus Standards being a case in point.[19] Once taken up at the supranational and international levels, the norm of collective judicial independence was reinforced back at the national level.[20] For instance, the reform of the post of the Lord Chancellor that spurred a number of judicial reforms in the UK, leading to the establishment of an appointments commission, was to a large extent triggered by the need to comply with the ECHR and the ECtHR's case law that signalled the deficiencies of the Lord Chancellor's office from a separation-of-powers standpoint. Sheetreet points in particular to the ECtHR rulings in *Procola* and *McGonnell* as casting doubt on the legality of the institute of the Lord Chancellor. Thus, reinforced on the supranational level, the norm of judicial independence became incompatible with the national institute of the UK's Lord Chancellor. The Lord Chancellor used to preside over appeals in the House of Lords, while simultaneously being a member of the British cabinet.[21] This started

---

[16] S. Sheetreet, 'The Normative Cycle of Shaping Judicial Independence in Domestic and International Law: The Mutual Impact of National and International Jurisprudence and Contemporary Practical and Conceptual Challenges' (2008) 10 *Chicago Journal of International Law* 299, emphasis added.

[17] Ibid.   [18] Ibid, 305–6.

[19] See the Mt Scopus Standard from 2012, elaborated by the International Association of Judicial Independence and World Piece, available at: <http://www.jiwp.org> (last accessed on 22 July 2014).

[20] Above n 15. See also S Sheetreet, 'Creating a Culture of Judicial Independence: The Practical Challenge and the Conceptual and Constitutional Infrastructure', in S Sheetreet and C Forsyth (eds), *The Culture of Judicial Independence. Conceptual Foundations and Practical Challenges* (Martinus Nijhoff 2012).

[21] *Procola v Luxembourg* (1995) 326 Eur Ct HR (series A); *McGonnell v United Kingdom* (2000) 30 *Eur HR Rep* 289, quoted in Sheetreet (n 15) 319.

to be seen as problematic and unsatisfactory for judicial independence, since the Lord Chancellor could review the self-same decisions he or she had made as a member of the executive branch.

Similarly, it is hard to believe today that some of the first judges at the ECJ's predecessor court were not professional lawyers and instead came from professional backgrounds as diverse as high school teacher or economist, and that a legal degree was not required in order to wear the robe in Luxembourg.[22] No matter how awkwardly this may sit with contemporary standards of judicial legitimacy, it was not considered to be illegitimate at the time. Both judicial independence and professional experience have since been accepted as pillars of judicial legitimacy in the selection of judges. Widely enshrined in constitutional provisions or courts' rules of procedure at the national as well as the transnational and international levels, they can now be considered the element of continuity in Lenaerts's above framework. At the same time, among the elements of change in judicial legitimacy can be, certainly gradually, enlisted the value of transparency in publicizing judicial openings and that of gender balance on the bench. I will elaborate in section 3.2 below why the latter, sometimes linked to the former, has been promoted in both national and international fora.

3. Horizontal Spillovers Between the CJEU and the ECtHR

Do lawyers necessarily hate spillovers? Heather Gerken and Ari Holzblatt claim that 'If you want to know what unites the burgeoning work on horizontal federalism [in the domestic context of federations] and illuminates the hidden logic of its doctrine, you need only know one fact: Lawyers hate spillovers.'[23] They describe a horizontal spillover as the laws of one jurisdiction affecting another. Of course, the matter of how one state's regulations affect residents in another state is a different matter from how one supranational organization's reforms are taken up by another. In the first scenario, Gerken and Holzblatt set up a framework that shows why horizontal spillovers may be desirable; with respect to the second, I will argue that, at the very least, such cross-fertilization is a natural consequence of the development of the Luxembourg and Strasbourg judicial machineries.

3.1. The 255 Panel and the Advisory Panel

The ECtHR's judicial reform, which resulted in the establishment of an advisory panel, used as a blueprint both the institutional design of the 255 Panel and the criteria that the Panel later elaborated. As is known on the subject of appointments to the ECtHR,[24] each contracting party submits a short-list of three candidates

---

[22] Above ch 1 s 1.
[23] H Gerken and A Holtzblatt, 'The Political Safeguards of Horizontal Federalism', forthcoming (2014) 112 *Michigan Law Review*.
[24] In detail above ch 5.

who, in accordance with Article 21.1 ECHR, need to be 'of high moral character and must either possess the qualifications required for appointment to high judicial office or be jurisconsults of recognised competence'. After the Sub-Committee of PACE examines the curricula vitae and interviews the candidates, it gives its recommendation to the plenary that is empowered under Article 22.1 ECHR to elect, by majority vote, the new judge. Concerns that the authority of the Strasbourg Court might be undermined due to the not-always-satisfactory quality of judges nominated by contracting states were voiced as far back as 2006, when the so-called Group of Wise Persons envisaged the screening of candidates 'by a committee of prominent personalities possibly chosen from among former members of the Court, current and former members of national supreme or constitutional courts and lawyers with acknowledged competence'.[25]

In the meantime, similar concerns prompted by the EU's eastern enlargement contributed to the setting up of the 255 Panel, which has in turn used as a blueprint an adapted version of the procedure and, above all, the substantive criteria first set in motion for appointments to the EU Civil Service Tribunal.[26] The Group of Wise Persons' proposal was soon renewed in the contribution to the Interlaken Conference made by the secretary general of the Council of Europe.[27] However, it was not until former president of the ECtHR, Jean-Paul Costa, wrote[28] to the permanent representatives (ambassadors) of all Council of Europe contracting states that the ball got rolling. In that letter, Costa reiterated that the authority of the Strasbourg judges was necessary not only to ensure the quality of the Court's jurisprudence but also in order to gain the respect of national, 'including senior national', and CJEU judges. It is worth quoting at length:

... This aspect is also particularly important in view of the prospect of the European Union's accession to the Convention. One of the critical issues in this context will be the future relationship between the Court of Justice of the European Union and the Strasbourg Court. For that relationship to function it must be based on mutual respect. Since the entry into force of the Lisbon Treaty, appointments to the EU courts are subject to the opinion of an independent panel (Article 255 of the Treaty on the Functioning of the European Union).[29]

In PACE's draft resolution that eventually approved the idea of setting up a similar advisory panel for the ECtHR, rapporteur Renate Wohlwend expressed the view that 'this idea, modelled on the independent panel (Article 255) set up with the entry into force of the Lisbon Treaty, relates to another type of "animal" '.[30]

---

[25] Report of the Group of Wise Persons to the Committee of Ministers, M(2006)203 15 November (2006), available at <https://wcd.coe.int>, para 118, last accessed 12 June 2014.

[26] Above ch 4 s 1.

[27] Referenced in National Procedures for the Selection of Candidates for the European Court of Human Rights, Report of Committee on Legal Affairs and Human Rights, Doc 12391 (2010), available at <http://assembly.coe.int>, last accessed 12 June 2014.

[28] Letter from Mr Jean-Paul Costa, President of the European Court of Human Rights, addressed to member states' permanent representatives (ambassadors) on 9 June 2010.

[29] Ibid.

[30] National procedures for the selection of candidates for the European Court of Human Rights, Doc 12391 (2010).

Wohlwend made mention of the election of judges by the PACE which provides democratic legitimacy to the Strasbourg Court, something that 'no other international court possesses', and warned that the contracting states might view this 'hybrid creation' as inappropriate interference with their selection procedures.[31]

Despite the adaptations made in the new ECtHR Advisory Panel's institutional design (for example, unlike the 255 Panel, the Strasbourg panel does not hold interviews with the candidates, reserving this function for the PACE's Sub-Committee),[32] some of the problems hinted at by Wohlwend started to materialize in the first years of the Advisory Panel's life. For instance, there have been occasions on which the national governments have sent their list straight to the PACE's Sub-Committee without allowing time for examination of the candidatures by the panellists, or the advisory opinion of the ECtHR's Panel has not been followed by the contracting state that chose to maintain its candidate on the list and the PACE has subsequently elected that person to the Strasbourg bench.[33] Whether the power and effectiveness of the 255 Panel can be matched by that of its Strasbourg counterpart is difficult to gauge, due to the secrecy of the working methods of both panels, but also especially since the ECtHR's Advisory Panel, unlike the 255 Panel, does not report on the overall number of reviewed candidates and the portion of vetted ones. The evolving *raison d'être* of the ECtHR's Advisory Panel—one geared more toward confidentially advising the national governments at an early stage of formulating the list with candidates or more oriented toward advising the PACE's Sub-Committee—is still to be hammered out as the process unfolds.

In terms of further functional spillovers, I will acknowledge at least one explicit and three implicit ones in the functioning of the two bodies. First, the Advisory Panel has chosen, next to the fundamental criteria enshrined in Article 21.1 of the ECHR and criteria on judicial ethics elaborated by the Plenary of the Strasbourg Court in 2008, to refer in particular to the criteria elaborated in the annual reports of the 255 Panel, namely:

the candidate's legal expertise, the professional experience the candidate has acquired (characterised by both its length and nature), the suitability of the candidate to exercise the role of judge, the guarantees of independence and impartiality that the candidate presents, the linguistic abilities and suitability to work as part of a team within an international environment in which several legal traditions are represented.[34]

---

[31] Ibid.

[32] However, unlike the 255 Panel, the ECtHR's Advisory Panel has added a Supplementary Rule to its Operating Rules allowing it to use 'other sources of information' that are not limited to publicly available information, eg the Advisory Panel's judicial network or otherwise 'word-of-mouth' techniques. The Supplementary Rule can be troubling not only in view of the additional discretion that the ECtHR's Advisory Panel afforded to itself, but also from a fairness point of view. However, further evaluation goes beyond the scope of the present chapter. See 'Draft CDDH Report on the Review of the Functioning of the Advisory Panel of Experts on Candidates for Election as Judge to the European Court of Human Rights', DH-GDR (2013) R5 Addendum II.

[33] Ibid, at paras 33–9. In detail above ch 6 s 5.

[34] See Written Contribution from the Advisory Panel, Doc GT-GDR-E(2013)004REV, at p 3.

Importantly, the ECtHR's Advisory Panel 'does not in this context mention the Committee of Ministers' guidelines on the selection of candidates for the post of judge'.[35] The Steering Committee for Human Rights (CDDH) has suggested amending Ministers' Resolution CM/Res (2010)26 to reflect that the Committee of Ministers' guidelines, alongside the Convention itself, form the basis of the Panel's assessment.

Second, the CDDH also suggested that the ECtHR's Advisory Panel start issuing reports to the Committee of Ministers—this would be the equivalent of a practice first established by the 255 Panel that issues detailed annual reports for the Council of Ministers of the EU, also available on-line in an edited form.

Third, the ECtHR's Advisory Panel, acting upon the CDDH's recent recommendation to amend the ministers' resolution, may also begin transmitting the assessment of the Panel to all states parties on a confidential basis. However, unlike in the case of the 255 Panel, where the assessment is transmitted to all EU members no matter whether it is positive or negative, the CDDH's proposal is to inform the contracting states only if the Panel's opinion is negative and governments of the other Council of Europe states can trigger peer pressure to induce compliance with the Panel's advice.

Lastly, another implicit spillover worth mentioning here is the ECtHR's Advisory Panel's interpretation of the Convention's requirement for judges to possess 'the qualifications required for appointment to *high* judicial office'. The Panel has chosen to emphasize that ECtHR judges:

…can issue judgments which in effect depart from or even implicitly overrule judgments of the highest national courts…The Panel has of course to base its views on the wording of Article 21§1 of the Convention, i.e. on the expression 'high judicial office' (rather than 'highest'). This expression would seem to include judges who have held office in national supreme and constitutional courts, whereas it would seem to exclude judges of lower national first-instance courts. The provision must be given a substantive interpretation consistent with its purpose and not a purely formal one. Even in the case of candidates holding office in a highest national Court, the Panel's view is that such persons should not, for that reason alone, be automatically considered qualified to be candidates for election to the Court.[36]

In order to give such teleological interpretation to the requirement of the Convention, the Panel alludes to long experience and maturity that is unlikely to be accrued by a young candidate, since:

On the other hand, the European Court of Human Rights, by its nature, status and pan-European role assumes that its members already have, on election, all the fully developed judicial qualities that come from long experience. It would appear unlikely to find such qualities in a candidate of a relatively young age.[37]

---

[35] Draft CDDH Report (n 32), para 19.

[36] Written Contribution from the Advisory Panel GT-GDR-E(2013)004.

[37] Ibid. It is interesting to observe in this regard how much the ECtHR Advisory Panel departed from the previous practice of the PACE, when they were ready to appoint 36-year-old Ukrainian or Georgian female judges. There may be a tension between the requirement of seniority and that of gender balance. For specific detail and critical discussion see above ch 6 s 4.3.

These considerations would seem to link professional experience and age criteria to the definition of 'high' or indeed 'highest judicial office', much as in the interpretation given by the 255 Panel.[38] Since the EU Treaty's provisions are expressly distinguishing between 'high' and 'highest' judicial office[39] but the Convention's wording is limited to 'high', in light of the above-mentioned reasoning, the ECtHR's Advisory Panel has preferred not to specify an exact age range. However, in view of the occupational concerns for judges after they complete their mandates in Strasbourg, it would appear that the way in which the Advisory Panel interprets 'high judicial office' would better match the 255 Panel's description of 'highest judicial office'.

3.2. Toward soft quotas for sex equality on the CJEU's bench?

The connection, if not causality, was easier to prove in the adoption and methods of the ECtHR's Advisory Panel, which has tangibly followed, and adapted along the way, the path blazed by the 255 Panel. Conversely, a potential future spillover regarding sex equality may flow in the opposite direction: from Strasbourg to Luxembourg.

As mentioned in section 2 above, the arguments for a gender-balanced judicial bench are two-fold and interrelated: they are connected on the one hand to representativeness and the legitimacy of judgments that concern matters of gender character, and on the other to equal employment opportunities.[40] The more the ECJ adjudicates on fundamental rights cases after the adoption of a binding EU Charter of Fundamental Rights, the more the first argument gains traction. Sally Kenney quotes former ECJ judge Ninon Colneric, saying that when the ECJ struck down for the first time a positive action policy in *Kalanke*,[41] German feminists openly criticized the decision delivered by the then all-men court. In *Kalanke*, which was subsequently overruled by the ECJ in *Marshall*[42] and *Badeck*,[43] the Luxembourg Court declared a German law that introduced a tie-break clause in favour of equally qualified female candidates in sectors where women were under-represented to be incompatible with EU law. The ECJ based its reasoning on the fact that the law allowed women to be *automatically* given priority.

The *Kalanke* decision has attracted a good deal of harsh criticism.[44] Why preference can be regarded as automatic when the scheme allows for a full assessment of

---

[38] Activity Report of the Panel provided for by Article 255 of the Treaty on the Functioning of the European Union, Council Document 6509/11, 2011.

[39] Arts 253 and 254 TFEU.

[40] S Kenney, 'Equal Employment Opportunity and Representation: Extending the Frame to the Courts' (2004) 11 *Social Politics* 1.

[41] Case C-450/93 *Kalanke* [1995] ECR I-3051.

[42] Case C-409/95 *Marshall* [1997] ECR I-6363.

[43] Case C-158/97 *Badeck* [1999] ECR I-1875.

[44] For a representative sample, see A Peters, 'The Many Meanings of Equality and Positive Action in Favour of Women under European Community Law—A Conceptual Analysis' (1996) 2 *European Law Journal* 177; E Szyszczak, 'Positive Action after *Kalanke*' (1996) 59 *Modern Law Review* 876; P Kapotas, 'A Tale of Two Cities: Positive Action as "Full Equality" in Luxembourg and

the candidates' respective qualifications prior to triggering the gender tie-break is truly beyond comprehension. Kenney reinforces the example of representativeness by documenting the arguments voiced by British feminist groups who opposed the legality of the then all-male Committee of the House of Lords deciding whether a rape shield law violated a defendant's human right to a fair trial.[45] Eventually, the demand to ensure a certain gender balance on the bench in Britain for the sake of representativeness was successfully tied to the larger judicial reform underway in the country in the 2000s.

In turn, the argument based on equal opportunities has surfaced mainly in demands for the gender gap to be closed in legislatures, but it has recently also been reinvigorated in the EU, where the enhanced legal base of Article 154 TFEU enabled the tabling of a proposed Directive on improving the gender balance among non-executive directors of companies listed on stock exchanges.[46] In 2003, Norway adopted a requirement that boards of directors of publicly traded companies were to have a form of gender balance, in that 40–60 per cent of the board members were expected to be women; otherwise, companies would face sanction in the form of delisting. Spain adopted a similar statute in 2007; Belgium, Italy, and the Netherlands used a 30 per cent benchmark in 2011 when France also followed suit.[47] That same year, EU Justice Commissioner Reding encouraged companies to sign a 'Women on the Board Pledge for Europe' aiming for a target of 30 per cent female board members by 2015 and 40 per cent by 2020, through active recruitment of females as male members retired. The European Parliament passed a resolution supporting measures to improve the gender balance on corporate boards. In 2012, the European Commission came up with a slightly less ambitious version of the original proposal, requiring the member states to ensure that:

... priority shall be given to the candidate of the under-represented sex if that candidate is equally qualified... in terms of suitability, competence and professional performance, unless an objective assessment taking account of all criteria specific to the individual candidates tilts the balance in favour of the candidate of the other sex.[48]

The initiative represents an instance of the equal opportunities argument being reinforced in yet another domain of employment. Enforcement will be left largely to the member states, with the proviso that the national governments enable unsuccessful candidates to take legal action against companies that fall short of the quotas, thus empowering rejected candidates to force companies to disclose

---

Strasbourg' in K Dzehtsiarou et al (eds), *Human Rights Law in Europe: The Influence, Overlaps and Contradictions of the EU and the ECHR* (Routledge 2014).

[45] Kenney (n 39) 102.

[46] Proposal for a Directive of the European Parliament and of the Council on improving the gender balance among non-executive directors of companies listed on stock exchanges and related measures, COM (2012) 614.

[47] J Suk, 'Quotas and Consequences: A Transnational Re-evaluation' in D Hellman and S Moreau (eds), *Philosophical Foundations of Discrimination Law* (Oxford University Press 2013).

[48] Article 4(1)(3)(6). The EP approved the proposal with amendments, to which the Commission partially agreed. As of 1 May 2014, the Council has yet to consider the Commission's proposal and EP amendments on first reading.

the selection criteria used. In 2013, parliament reasoned that 'The Union institutions, bodies and agencies and the European Central Bank should lead by example as regards gender equality in decision-making, inter alia by setting objectives for a gender-balanced representation at all levels'.[49]

In the UK, litigation techniques have utilized the equal opportunities argument also in the context of judicial selection. For example, the appointment of governmental legal advisers was challenged on the ground that the position was not advertised, thereby indirectly discriminating against equally qualified female candidates who were less well connected compared to the men candidates. In the 1999 case *Coker and Osamor v Lord Chancellor's Department*[50] the lower court was not persuaded by the Lord Chancellor's defence that the long-standing practice of 'word-of-mouth' recruitment could justify the continuing lack of publicity. The law of indirect discrimination in the UK has several components: the employer must have imposed a neutral requirement or condition that fewer women than men could meet; it cannot be justifiable; and it must be to the detriment of the complainant. That all acceptable candidates were required to be personally well known to the Lord Chancellor was considered an unjustified neutral condition. In other words, the condition was seen to entrench an 'old boys' club' recruitment process.

Similarly, in 1995, Brita Sundberg-Weitman challenged the first Swedish nomination to the JECJ in Luxembourg, arguing that the Swedish system had indirect discriminatory effects. Sundberg-Weitman claimed that her PhD publications on EU law and fluency in French made her the stronger candidate. While conceding that her level of French was probably better, the District Court in Stockholm declared that she did not possess the same level of international prestige as the chosen candidate, who was a former professor of law and Dean of the Law Faculty of the University of Stockholm. Sundberg-Weitman provided statistics showing that only three out of 65 law school deans, six of 47 professors of law and six out of 41 members of the Supreme Court in Sweden by that time were female.

Both the British and the Swedish examples of litigation reveal that the equal employment opportunities argument for a gender-balanced bench has made a certain headway at both the national and the supranational levels. Moreover, recently the EU has shown a strong commitment to lead in setting examples about the importance of gender equality: both the proposed legislation for gender quotas on corporate boards discussed above, and recent calls to ensure a close to equal number of female commissioners in Jean-Claude Junker's European Commission[51] attest to that. Thus, representativeness and equal employment opportunities in judicial bodies started to be rehearsed but were rejected as arguments in the 1990s.

---

[49] European Parliament legislative resolution of 20 November 2013 on the proposal for a Directive of the European Parliament and of the Council on improving the gender balance among non-executive directors of companies listed on stock exchanges and related measures (COM(2012)0614—C7-0382/2012—2012/0299(COD)), Amendment 5.

[50] Kenney (n 39) 106–7.

[51] C Kroet, 'Call for Ten Women in the Next Commission. European Commissioners Call for Junker to Seek Gender Balance in the Next College', *European Voice*, 10 July 2014.

In the following decade, however, such arguments have successfully established gender balance as a criterion in the process of judge selection in Strasbourg, and most recently also in Belgium. I will next assess these recent developments, as well as the probability of a horizontal spillover effect related to enshrining a criterion for a gender-balanced bench in Luxembourg.

The ECtHR had the opportunity to grapple with the question of quotas for women judges in its advisory opinion from 2008.[52] In 2004, prompted by an influential NGO report,[53] the PACE decided to take active steps toward achieving a fairer balance in the gender composition of the Strasbourg Court. Resolution 1366 of the same year imposed a gender quota on the national governments, stipulating that the list of candidates should include at 'least one member of each sex'.[54] The PACE set for itself the objective 'to investigate at national and European level what obstacles currently exist to the nomination of women candidates, what measures could be taken to encourage female applicants, and to consider setting targets for achieving greater gender equality in the composition of the Court': the Sub-Committee should 'aim to include at least 40 per cent of women' and in the case of equal merit, should give preference to the candidate of the sex 'under-represented at the Court'.[55] All-female lists were still considered legitimate under PACE's Resolution 1426 of the following year (2005).[56] However, the Committee of Ministers reasoned that a contracting state might find itself unable to satisfy the merit requirements of the Convention unless it submitted an all-male candidate list. During the period of institutional impasse in 2004, the Maltese government produced an all-male list; the PACE refused to review the list, which was resubmitted unaltered in 2006 and rejected again. After extended communications, the case went to the Court's Grand Chamber.

The ECtHR found that in the interest of the proper functioning of the system, it had jurisdiction to decide the case within the framework of the advisory opinion procedure—until then only rarely used due to its alleged political implications.[57] The ECtHR analysed the provisions governing the composition of a variety of international and regional courts and found that 'only the International Criminal Court and the African Court on Human and Peoples' Rights have—non-binding—rules aimed at promoting balanced representation of the sexes in their composition'.[58] Further, the Court found that while some contracting states have legislation or action plans aimed at increasing the number of women in the public service, only three (Austria, Belgium, and Latvia) have specific provisions in their legislation ensuring egalitarian representation in their supreme and/or constitutional courts.[59] Importantly, the ECtHR did not apply its

---

[52] ECtHR Grand Chamber, *Advisory Opinion on Certain Legal Questions Concerning the Lists of Candidates Submitted with a View to the Election of Judges to the European Court of Human Rights* (12 February, 2008). For further detail, see also above ch 6 s 4.1.

[53] Limbach et al, *Judicial Independence: Law and Practice of Appointments to the European Court of Human Rights* (Interights 2003) 17.

[54] PACE Resolution 1366 (2004), modified by Resolution 1426 (2005).   [55] Ibid.

[56] Resolution 1426 (2005), modifying Resolution 1366 (2004).

[57] Above n 51, para 39.   [58] Ibid, para 34.   [59] Ibid, para 35.

consensus-based logic according to which, when faced with questions of a prec-edential nature, the Court gives a certain margin of appreciation to the national authorities when there is no clear majority or consensus in the contracting states, as strengthened by indicia of 'an international consensus' leaning in a certain direc-tion.[60] Thus, the ECtHR justified its decision not by the existence of consensus on the concrete measure (quotas for female judges on highest courts) but by the elevated status that the objective of achieving gender equality holds in contempo-rary society, as witnessed by broader measures to combat discrimination on the international and the EU levels:

...[T]he criterion in question derives from a gender-equality policy which reflects the importance of equality between the sexes in contemporary society and the role played by the prohibition of discrimination and by positive discrimination measures in attaining that objective.... [T]here is far-reaching consensus as to the need to promote gender balance within the state and in the national and international public service, including the judici-ary. [citing *inter alia*, the United Nations Convention on the Elimination of All Forms of Discrimination against Women, as well as Council of Europe and EU anti-discrimination measures...][61]

The ECtHR rejected Malta's submissions that gender balance was not among the criteria required in the Convention by clarifying that there was nothing in the Convention that could prevent the contracting parties from taking into account additional criteria such as gender balance, and that in fact the PACE has previously taken gender into account as a customary matter.[62] It distinguished, however, between criteria that were not enshrined in the Convention but 'flow implicitly' from it, such as language proficiency, which, unlike gender balance, is necessary for the work of the Court. Further, on sovereignty grounds, the ECtHR dismissed the possibility of nominating a candidate from a different nationality in order to satisfy the gender requirement. Finally, the ECtHR urged the PACE to reach a compromise decision whereby a contracting state could be relieved of the quota requirement under certain conditions:

[if] a Contracting Party has taken all the necessary and appropriate steps with a view to ensuring that the list contains a candidate of the under-represented sex, but without suc-cess, and especially where it has followed the Assembly's recommendations advocating an *open and transparent procedure involving a call for candidatures...*[63]

The linkage between the transparency of the call for applications and gender equal-ity is reminiscent of the British case discussed above. Whether the transparency

---

[60] See, among others, PJ Mahoney, 'Judicial Activism and Judicial Self-restraint in the European Court of Human Rights: Two Sides of the Same Coin' (1990) 11 *Human Rights Law Journal* 57; K Dzehtsiarou, 'Does Consensus Matter? Legitimacy of European Consensus in the Case Law of the European Court of Human Rights' (2011) *Public Law* 534; B Petkova 'Three Levels of Dialogue at the Court of Justice of the European Union and the European Court of Human Rights' in K Dzehtsiarou et al (eds) (n 46).

[61] Above n 51, para 49.   [62] Ibid, at para 45.

[63] Ibid, at para 52, emphasis added. The PACE indeed went along these lines in Resolution 1627(2008) and Resolution 1841 (2011).

of national calls (or the lack thereof) has impacted disparately on the number of female nominations to both Luxembourg and Strasbourg is an interesting but empirically unexplored question which I leave open here. However, both the various organs of the Council of Europe[64] and the 255 Panel have not hesitated to emphasize the importance of issuing public calls for candidates. As my co-authors and I have suggested elsewhere, in the case of the 255 Panel, the fact that the Greek and Swedish candidates for the GC were not nominated through an openly publicized procedure played a decisive role in the assessment of the Panel that resulted in a negative opinion for both candidates.[65] Greece and Sweden are not alone in this respect, however: our study revealed that other EU member states such as Spain and the UK do not publicize their openings for ECJ and GC judges either. Yet further empirical work might be needed to show whether the same is true for openings at the Strasbourg bench, since, at least in some cases, the national procedure followed for judicial selection of ECJ, GC, and ECtHR judges is not the same.[66]

The solution suggested by the ECtHR in its advisory opinion is largely congruent with the approach taken in the line of cases[67] that the ECJ dealt with after *Kalanke*, and also fits the framework suggested by the EU Commission in its recently proposed Directive aiming to ensure gender equality on corporate boards. In other words, both courts have insisted on having 'soft' instead of 'hard' quotas,[68] either through the insertion of 'flexibility clauses' that allow priority to be given to the female candidate 'unless reasons specific to an individual [male] candidate tilt the balance in his favour'[69] (ECJ) or through taking into account special national circumstances (ECtHR's Advisory Opinion). In light of the above considerations, so far the PACE has accepted the Belgian all-male list submitted in 2012 but rejected an all-male list previously submitted by Norway.

Since the negotiations on EU accession to the ECHR are at an advanced stage now, it could be expected that following the example of Strasbourg, the European Parliament will renew its calls[70] to ensure gender balance on the bench in Luxembourg, where the first female judge was appointed only in 1999. Out of 37 members today (28 judges and nine advocates general), there are only

---

[64] PACE Recommendation 1649 (2004) and Resolution1646 (2009), see also Committee of Ministers CM 29 March 2012.

[65] Above n 1, 462.

[66] For further discussion with respect to the ECtHR, see above ch 5 s 4.

[67] *Badeck* (n 42). See also *Abrahamsson and Anderson v Foguelqvist* [2000] ECR I-5539.

[68] In turn, Belgium has recently gone further in ensuring hard quotas for its Constitutional Court judges. On 4 April 2014, the Belgian parliament introduced a Bill that requires the constitutional court to be composed of at least a third of judges of either sex. The law will enter into force once the Constitutional Court is in fact composed of at least one third of female judges. In the meantime, the king will appoint a judge of the under-represented sex if the two preceding appointments have not increased the number of judges of the underrepresented sex: currently, only 16 per cent of Belgian constitutional judges are female. See *Loi spéciale portant modification de la loi du 6 janvier 1989 sur la Cour constitutionnelle, April 4, 2014*, Arts 12 and 38.

[69] C Barnard, 'The Principle of Equality in the Community Context: P, Grant, Kalanke and Marschall: Four Uneasy Bedfellows?' (1998) 57 *Cambridge Law Journal* 364, 366.

[70] In 1989, with the creation of the GC, then the Court of First Instance, 261 MEPs signed a declaration calling the member states to appoint women to that court: see S Kenney, *Gender and Justice: Why Women in the Judiciary Really Matter* (Routledge 2012).

seven women on the bench in Luxembourg.[71] As Article 6 of the Draft Accession Agreement reads, the European Parliament will be able to participate with the highest number of representatives allowed to a contracting party (currently 18) in the sittings of PACE whenever the Assembly exercises its functions related to the election of Strasbourg judges. The European Parliament will therefore have a significant delegation with the right to vote on judicial selection.[72] It will also have representatives at PACE's Sub-Committee, although the exact modalities of this provision still need to be worked out.[73] In any case, Parliament representatives could find themselves in the unusual situation of rejecting a potential EU all-male list or examining EU lists of candidates that contain female nominations in order to comply with the Council of Europe's soft quota requirements, whereas in the case of ECJ judicial selection, not only is parliamentarian involvement minimal,[74] but also gender criteria are inexistent.

4. Vertical Spillovers

4.1. The national counterparts of the European judicial advisory panels

In this section, I will show that when it comes to judicial selection in Europe, spillovers are commonplace both horizontally and vertically. Spillovers take place in many cases from the supranational to the national level, with respect to both substantive criteria and appointment procedures.

No uniform procedure is required for national nominations of ECJ, GC, and ECtHR judges under either EU or ECHR law. Despite this fact, several of the EU member states have adapted their appointment practices in line with the two supranational panels. The model of advisory panels, mainly composed of former and current members of the judiciary, has spread across various European states. Instrumental in the adoption of this institutional design has been the emphasis on a merit-based selection[75] and, in view of cases of executive arbitrariness, the belief

---

[71] Currently, these are judges Rosario Silva De Lapuerta, Camelia Toader, Maria Berger, Alexandra Prechal, and Küllike Jürimäe, as well as advocates general Eleanor Sharpston and Juliane Kokkot: see <http://curia.europa.eu/jcms/jcms/Jo2_7026/>, last accessed 12 June 2014.

[72] Appendix I Draft revised agreement on the accession of the European Union to the Convention for the Protection of Human Rights and Fundamental Freedoms, Strasbourg, 10 June 2013, 47_1(2013)008rev2_EN at: <http://www.coe.int/>, last accessed 12 June 2014.

[73] A Drzemczewski, 'EU Accession to the ECHR: The Negotiation Process', in V Kosta et al, *The EU Accession to the ECHR* (forthcoming, Hart 2014).

[74] One of the members of the 255 Panel is nominated by the EP. For the first nominee, see European Parliament decision of 20 January 2010 proposing the appointment of Ana de Palacio y del Valle-Iersundi to the panel set up under Art 255, P7_TA(2010)0003. It is certainly not inconceivable that in view of EU accession to the ECHR, the pressure for further involvement of the EP in the process of selecting CJEU judges may be renewed. Calls for substantive EP involvement in the process of CECJJ selection, specifically evoking the example of the PACE's involvement in the selection of ECtHR judges, were first made in the 1980s. See Kenney (n 69) 119.

[75] Activity Report of the Panel provided for by Article 255 of the Treaty on the Functioning of the European Union, Council Document 1413/12/2013 (Third Activity Report). In the part describing

that both independence and merit can be assured by instituting a stronger role for the judiciary in the selection process.[76]

The 255 Panel has been particularly influential in prompting norm spillovers in a vertical fashion. In the process of reviewing the candidatures, it insisted that the member states inform the Panel 'whether there was a public call for applications, whether national committee was set up, and if so how the national committee was made up and what it recommended'.[77] Whereas the Panel in no way formally requires the composition of an independent assessing body, its recognition that such a procedure might act in favour of the national candidate[78] has indirectly influenced several national procedures. In the years following the establishment of the 255 Panel, which was constituted in March 2010, judicial commissions for the nomination of ECJ and GC judges were set up in Finland and Bulgaria in the same year, in 2011 in the Czech Republic, and in 2012 in Croatia. All four countries introduced specific legislative reforms that set up judicial commissions to either suggest, short-list, and/or vet candidates before the respective governments could make the final selection.[79] In certain cases, such as that of Croatia, the new law makes explicit mention of the 255 Panel and the criteria set by it. In the case of Belgium, a judicial commission has also recently been instituted for nominating judges to the ECtHR.[80]

In many of the EU member states, judicial panels or commissions with varying degrees of responsibility already existed for the selection of national and, in some cases, international judges, even before the establishment of the two supranational European panels. Judicial commissions or councils with either advisory or *de facto* selection functions were in place in Poland,[81] Italy,[82] Germany, the UK, Spain, Slovakia, Slovenia, and others.[83] Some of these countries—the UK and Slovakia, for instance—have in practice engaged their existing judicial commissions or councils to examine nominations for ECJ, GC, and ECtHR judges, whereas others like Spain and Italy have not done so. At the moment of writing, Spain and Greece remain in the minority of EU states that still have an exclusively

---

the Panel's relations with the other EU institutions in view of expanding its role, the report reads: 'On 30 May 2013, Mr Sauvé and Ms Palacio [the President and EP member of the Panel] reported on the panel's work before the European Parliament's Committee on Legal Affairs. This hearing focused on an examination of the planned increase in the number of Judges of the General Court of the European Union, the procedure for appointing additional Judges and the panel's possible role in that procedure. On that occasion *it was emphasised that a model based on merit seemed appropriate in terms of achieving the smoother operation of the Union's judicial system*, whilst maintaining the Member States' prerogative in the mechanism for appointing Judges' (emphasis added).

[76] For a critique from a democratic perspective, see above ch 7.

[77] Activity Report of the Panel Provided for by Article 255 of the Treaty on the Functioning of the European Union, Council Document No 6509/11.

[78] Ibid; see also the Third Activity Report (n 74).   [79] Above n 1, 470–1.

[80] Interview with an employee at the Belgian Ministry of Justice, 10 November 2013.

[81] F Zoll, 'The System of Judicial Appointment in Poland—A Question of the Legitimacy of the Judicial Power' in Sheetreet and Forsyth (n 19).

[82] C Guarnieri and D Piana, 'Judicial Independence and the Rule of Law', in ibid.

[83] Above n 1, section III.

executive-dominated model of selection of European judges. This type of selection procedure is, however, dwindling: even countries such as Italy which do not use independent bodies to evaluate nominations of judges to the European courts have recently introduced reforms. Since 2013, it has been necessary for the Italian parliament to be apprised of the nominating procedure followed by the government; after assuming office, a judge from the ECJ or the GC might be summoned by the parliamentary committee to attend a parliamentary hearing.[84]

4.2. Setting judicial selection criteria

After having demonstrated that several national procedures have been influenced by the changes in appointments introduced in Luxembourg and Strasburg, I will now further show that spillovers are not in any way hierarchical—in other words, not only do the supranational systems influence the national ones, but the same is also true the other way around.

The 255 Panel has interpreted the EU Treaty criteria for the appointment of CJ and GC judges to mean that legal and professional experience, the ability to perform the duties of a judge, independence and impartiality, language skills, and the aptitude to work with various legal systems all form part of the assessment.[85] I touched upon the question of independence in the preceding section. Here I elaborate on the requirement of professional experience.

Although the Luxembourg bench might have shown a certain penchant for academics in the past years, in terms of the nature of professional experience, the 255 Panel has claimed it does not prioritize any particular legal career experience acquired in the course of accomplishing 'high level [legal] duties'.[86] Of particular interest for present purposes is the 'length of experience' prong in the professional experience assessment of the 255 Panel. In this regard, the Panel as a rule considers as sufficient 20 years of experience of high-level duties for judicial office at the ECJ and 12 or even 15 years of experience for judicial office at the GC.[87] As discussed above in section 3.2, the age criterion has also become popular at the ECtHR. Although the 255 Panel does not give particular examples as to which national systems it studied in order to establish the age criteria, it alludes to comparisons with the practice in place in at least some of the member states:

...With regard to length of professional experience, by analogy between the office of Judge and positions of an equivalent level in the European Civil Service, as well as *with reference to the national practices with which it is familiar*...[88]

---

[84] Legge 24 dicembre 2012, n 234, Norme generali sulla partecipazione dell'Italia alla formazione e all'attuazione della normativa e delle politiche dell'Unione europea (13G00003) Vigente al: 4-1-2013.

[85] First Activity Report (n 76).　　[86] Ibid.

[87] As discussed above in section 3.2 of this chapter, the age criterion has also gained popularity at the ECtHR.

[88] First Activity Report (n 76), emphasis added.

Since the Panel might have not assessed the procedure in place in all member states or might have adapted existing national procedures, it has preferred not to make mention of concrete jurisdictions. However, such a reference might in fact have been beneficial in order to justify the reasoning of the 255 Panel.

5. Conclusion

This chapter has shown that standards of legitimate judicial selection in Europe are not formed in isolation, but rather through influences between and across the different national and supranational levels in Europe. Subject to multiple horizontal and vertical spillovers, new norms of judicial legitimacy emerge and become entrenched from the national, to the regional, to the international levels, permeating again all the way through.

When categorizing how constitutional comparisons are made, Vicky Jackson[89] identifies three main methods: convergence, resistance, and engagement. On the one hand, absolute convergence in norms of judicial selection will be hard to imagine in the European judicial space made up of 28 national and two supranational jurisdictions. Even when the ECtHR's Advisory Panel emulated the procedure and substantive criteria set up by the 255 Panel, it did so by carefully adapting the new standard of judicial selection to the context of the Strasbourg system. Moreover, the establishment of the ECtHR's Advisory Panel was crafted in a way that attempted not to sidestep PACE's Sub-Committee's function in the process of selecting ECtHR judges. Similarly, although judicial panels on the national level resemble the two supranational ones, the membership and concrete competence of these national panels both vary. Likewise, there is a significant approximation in the formal selection criteria for judicial office, although slight differences and variations still exist.

However, if absolute convergence of norms is not a likely and perhaps not even a normatively desirable outcome of the continuous interactions between and across jurisdictions in Europe, I have attempted to demonstrate that absolute resistance to spillovers also does not score highly in the process of norm formation of legitimate judicial selection. In short, engagement with the norms introduced in sister jurisdictions and their adaptation to the particular jurisdictional setting of either national or supranational systems seems to be the model that has been preferred so far and which can be more normatively appealing than institutional resistance. Engagement with norms outside one's own jurisdiction preserves diversity and gives wiggle room for experimentation, while still demonstrating mutual comity and good faith between legal orders built upon common constitutional traditions and based on shared general principles of law. From this perspective, one could not expect that with certain automaticity, the criterion of gender equality for ECJ and

---

[89] V Jackson, 'Constitutional Comparisons: Convergence, Resistance, Engagement' (2005) 119 *Harvard Law Review* 109.

GC judges will be addressed in a manner identical to the approach adopted for the Strasbourg judges. It would however seem legitimate that, given the prominence of gender equality in contemporary democracies and the EU's pronounced commitment to serve as a leading example in ensuring gender-balanced institutions, such a criterion is at least given sufficient consideration subsidiary to that of merit and independence in the process of selecting Luxembourg judges.

11

Selection, Appointment, and Legitimacy
A Political Perspective

R. Daniel Kelemen

1. Introduction

Historically, European countries have taken a rich variety of approaches to the selection and appointment of judges.[1] The most common approaches were top-down—namely, judges were appointed by the sovereign or by a local ruler. Some approaches were bottom-up, as among early medieval Germanic peoples, when 'assemblies of freemen selected eminent persons'[2] to act as temporary judges, or in twelfth-century Italian towns such as Siena where an elected *podestà* served as the head of the judiciary, or in the context of the French Revolution, when the Jacobins briefly introduced the election of judges. Finally, some approaches were neither top-down nor bottom-up, but more horizontal—giving the legal profession or the judiciary itself a significant role in the selection of judges, often by placing restrictions on the pool of candidates from which a sovereign could select. In *ancien régime* France, judges in the *parlements* could purchase their office and pass it on to their heirs, creating the much despised *noblesse de robe*. These three approaches to judicial selection and appointment were linked to three different sources of legitimacy for the judiciary. In the top-down approaches, judges derived their legitimacy from the fact that they were appointed by the legitimate ruler. In the bottom-up approaches, judges derived their legitimacy from the fact they were—in some form—selected by members of the community. In the horizontal approaches dominated by the legal profession, legitimacy was, in principle at least, linked to the legal expertise that judges were supposed to possess. Importantly, these three bases of legitimacy were not mutually exclusive, but could be melded and merged in various ways.

In this book, we are exploring the appointment of judges to supranational courts in contemporary Europe. While many details in the selection and appointment

---

[1] See Raoul van Caenegem, *Judges, Legislators and Professors* (Cambridge University Press 1987) 145–52.
[2] Ibid, 147.

of judges have changed over the centuries, the fundamental choices and normative issues at stake remain much the same today as they were a thousand years
ago. In modern democracies, and in supranational bodies such as the EU and
Council of Europe, all three of the approaches to judicial appointment discussed
above come into play. Today, judges are typically appointed by elected leaders (the
top-down approach). However, those leaders' legitimacy (which they confer on
the appointed judges by proxy) derives from the fact they were elected by the people (the bottom-up approach). Also, leaders are generally expected or required to
appoint judges to high courts who possess professionally recognized legal expertise,
and in recent years judicial councils—collegial bodies composed of a mixture of
elected officials and member of the judiciary—play an increasingly powerful role
in the selection of judges (the horizontal approach).[3]

In contemporary democracies, the many nuanced normative questions involved
in approaching the appointment of judges boil down to a central trade-off: the
trade-off between independence and accountability. On the one hand, we want
judges to be independent.[4] Judges must be able to decide cases impartially on the
basis of the law without fear of reprisal from the parties to the case or from outside
actors, including government officials. This independence is one of the foundations
of judicial legitimacy. On the other hand, we want judges to be accountable—or,
to state it in the inverse, we worry about them being unaccountable.[5]

The tension between independence and accountability grows as judicial power
increases. European countries have experienced a dramatic increase in judicial power
in recent decades, driven by developments at both the domestic and supranational
levels. Many critics complain that the 'judicialization of politics'—particularly that
driven by the European Court of Justice (ECJ)—threatens to undermine democracy across the EU, 'substituting the decisions of unelected, unaccountable judges
for those of democratically legitimate, elected officials'.[6] Concerns about the judicialization of politics and 'government by judges' increase attention to processes of
judicial selection and appointment: if judges are to be powerful, we must pay close
attention to how they are selected. This chapter explores the relationship between
processes of judicial appointment and the legitimacy of European courts, focusing
primarily on the ECJ but including discussion of the European Court of Human
Rights (ECtHR) for comparative purposes.

The chapter advances two central arguments about the relationship between
appointment and legitimacy. First, in order for courts, including the ECJ, to maintain their legitimacy in the eyes of the public and their legitimacy in the eyes

[3] Carlo Guarnieri, 'Judicial Independence in Europe: Threat or Resource for Democracy?' (2013)
49 *Representation* 347.

[4] Georg Vanberg, 'Establishing and Maintaining Judicial Independence' in Keith Whittington,
R Daniel Kelemen, and Gregory Caldeira (eds), *The Oxford Handbook of Law & Politics* (Oxford
University Press 2008).

[5] Martin Shapiro, 'Judicial Independence: New Challenges in Established Nations' (2013) 20
Indiana Journal of Global Legal Studies 253.

[6] R Daniel Kelemen, 'Judicialisation, Democracy and European Integration' (2013) 49
Representation 295, 296.

of countervailing political branches of government, democratically elected officials must continue to play a central role in the process of judicial selection and appointment. Increasing input from judicial councils composed mostly of judges and other legal professionals is advisable insofar as it helps assure that judges possess the necessary expertise and independence. However, giving too much power to such bodies may increase the independence of judges at the expense of detaching courts from the 'democratic pedigree' that is also crucial to their legitimacy.[7] A world in which judges select judges risks becoming (and being criticized as) a modern form of *noblesse de robe*. And eventually, as Martin Shapiro argues, 'Extreme independence in the absence of effective accountability actually leads to a crisis of independence'.[8] Second, the chapter argues that even in a context where the appointment of judges becomes more politicized, this politicization need not undermine the reputation of the courts as independent and impartial arbiters of the law. Political influence over judicial appointments is a threat to independence only where that influence is concentrated in a narrow set of hands or in one period of time. If a narrow set of political actors controls judicial appointments or if political actors can rapidly 'pack' a court with their appointees, then independence is undermined. By contrast, if a variety of democratically elected bodies and officials, elected at various points in time, are involved in the process of judicial appointment on an on-going basis, this will support the court's independence, not undermine it.

The chapter focuses on appointments to the Court of Justice of the European Union (CJEU)—in particular its highest court, the ECJ[9]—and compares the process of appointment to the ECJ with the process of appointment of judges to the ECtHR. I first discuss the degree of legitimacy enjoyed by the ECJ and ECtHR, concluding that while the legitimacy of these courts is relatively high, there are reasons for concern in the current context. Second, I develop my argument concerning the importance of maintaining a strong amount of democratic input into the selection of judges and why this political influence supports rather than threatens the legitimacy of courts such as the ECJ and ECtHR.

2. Do European Courts Face a Legitimacy Crisis?

The ECJ is regularly attacked by politicians and commentators from across the political spectrum for being an 'activist' court, biased toward expanding the scope

---

[7] Christopher Eisgruber, *Constitutional Self-government* (Harvard University Press 2001).

[8] Shapiro (n 5) 264.

[9] Naming conventions for the EU's courts changed with the Lisbon Treaty. The EU's highest court is formally referred to as the Court of Justice (hereafter ECJ). The lower court, formerly known as the Court of First Instance (CFI), is now known as the General Court (GC). The EU judiciary as a whole, encompassing the ECJ, the General Court, the EU Civil Service Tribunal, and other specialized courts that the EU may establish, is known as the Court of Justice of the European Union (CJEU). This unfortunate naming convention uses the singular ('Court' in CJEU) for something that is actually a plural ('Courts').

of EU powers.[10] The ECtHR too is regularly subject to political attack. In recent years, a series of controversial ECtHR rulings—above all a judgment on prisoner voting rights—provoked public outcry, outright defiance of the ECtHR in the United Kingdom House of Commons and calls for the UK to withdraw from the European Convention on Human Rights.[11] Such episodes might lead one to conclude that European courts are facing a profound, Europe-wide legitimacy crisis. But one would be wrong. Despite attacks by critics claiming that the ECJ or ECtHR are 'activist' courts acting beyond their mandate, there is no evidence that either of these courts suffers from a widespread crisis of legitimacy in the eyes of the public or of other key compliance constituencies such as national governments or courts—at least not outside the UK.[12]

Let us begin by considering the legitimacy of the ECJ. Academic discussions of the public legitimacy of the ECJ have been heavily influenced by a set of papers published by Gibson and Caldeira in the 1990s based on surveys they had commissioned.[13] Their analysis started from the assumption that high levels of 'diffuse public support'[14] could shield a court against political attacks by raising the costs politicians would face for attempting to undermine the court or disobey its rulings.[15] Gibson and Caldeira concluded diffuse public support for the ECJ was weak and that therefore if the ECJ made unpopular decisions it might elicit a damaging political backlash. As they put it, 'the Court rests on a precarious bedrock of support...To the extent it becomes enmeshed in controversial legal disputes, its support is certainly at risk'.[16] They also argued that while levels of trust in the ECJ were high, few people were willing to accept ECJ decisions that they found objectionable.[17] More recently, Voeten[18] has noted that levels of trust in the ECJ have dropped significantly since the early 1990s, when Gibson and Caldeira conducted their research.

---

[10] Kelemen (n 6) 296.

[11] Erik Voeten, 'Public Opinion and the Legitimacy of International Courts' (2013) 14 *Theoretical Inquiries in Law* 411; Michael O'Boyle, 'The Future of the European Court of Human Rights' (2011) *German Law Journal* 1862.

[12] Voeten (n 11). On the concept of an international court's 'compliance constituencies' see Voeten (n 11); also see Alter, who uses the term 'compliance partners': Karen Alter, *The New Terrain of International Law* (Princeton University Press 2014) 53. For a perspective emphasizing threats to the legitimacy of the ECtHR, see above ch 6 s 2.

[13] Greg Caldeira and James Gibson, 'The Legitimacy of the Court of Justice in the European Union' (1995) 89 *American Political Science Review* 356; Greg Caldeira and James Gibson, 'Democracy and Legitimacy in the European Union' (1997) 49 *International Social Science Journal* 209; James Gibson and Greg Caldeira, 'The Legitimacy of Transnational Legal Institutions' (1995) 39 *American Journal of Political Science* 459; James Gibson and Greg Caldeira, 'Changes in the Legitimacy of the European Court of Justice' (1998) 28 *British Journal of Political Science* 63.

[14] Easton argues that every public institution needs a certain 'reservoir of favourable attitudes or good will' that makes the public willing to accept policy outputs to which they are opposed. David Easton, *A Systems Analysis of Political Life* (John Wiley and Sons 1965) 273.

[15] Greg Caldeira, 'Public Opinion and the US Supreme Court' (1987) 81 *American Political Science Review* 1139; Greg Caldeira and James Gibson, 'The Etiology of Public Support for the Supreme Court' (1992) 36 *American Journal of Political Science* 635.

[16] Gibson and Caldeira, 'Changes in the Legitimacy of the European Court of Justice' (n 13) 90.

[17] Gibson and Caldeira, 'The Legitimacy of Transnational Legal Institutions' (n 13) 365.

[18] Voeten (n 11) 423.

However, as I have argued in previous research,[19] Gibson and Caldeira's focus on evaluating levels of public support for the ECJ in absolute terms was misguided—instead we should evaluate support for the ECJ (or any court) in relative terms, comparing support for it with support for other political institutions. When we take this perspective, we see that on average across the EU, the ECJ is the most trusted of all the institutions of government assessed in Eurobarometer surveys, which include national governments, national parliaments, national political parties, national courts, and other EU institutions. Indeed, the ECJ is the only institution, national or supranational, that consistently has a positive net trust score.[20] Moreover, in sharp contrast to Caldeira and Gibson's expectations, trust in the ECJ remained high relative to other institutions over the course of the 1990s and 2000s despite the fact that ECJ jurisprudence spread to ever more sensitive terrain.[21] To be sure, the ECJ's good standing in public opinion in relative terms owes less to public esteem for the ECJ than it owes to public distaste for other public institutions. It is not too difficult to be the most trusted public institution when you are competing against political parties and governments that are loathed by so many of their citizens. While some scholars and much of the media seem to view the growth in ECJ power as democratically illegitimate, the public does not seem to share this sentiment.

If there is no public crisis of legitimacy, is there a crisis of judicial legitimacy in the view of the political actors upon whom the ECJ relies to be effective? Certainly there is no such crisis vis-à-vis other EU institutions, such as the Commission or European Parliament, who view the ECJ as a vital partner in promoting European integration. But what of the member state governments who must implement ECJ rulings and who, after all, appoint its judges? And what of national courts who serve as such crucial partners with the ECJ in the EU legal system?

National leaders do sometimes complain that the ECJ is an activist court, bent on expanding the scope of European law. Occasionally, governments have taken steps in intergovernmental conferences to limit the fall-out from ECJ rulings (eg the Barber Protocol to the 1992 Maastricht Treaty) or attempted to shield sensitive policy areas from ECJ influence (eg the restrictions on ECJ jurisdiction in the field of justice and home affairs put in place in Maastricht).[22] But much more common have been steps by the member state governments to expand the powers

---

[19] R Daniel Kelemen, 'The political foundations of judicial independence in the European Union' (2012) 19 *J Euro Pub Pol* 43.

[20] Net trust score is calculated as % who tend to trust minus % who tend not to trust: see Kelemen (n 19) 48. For the latest polling on trust in EU and national institutions, see European Commission, Eurobaromètre Standard 79, *L'Opinion Publique dans l'Union Européene* (2013) 90.

[21] While trust in the ECJ has declined somewhat in the years since the eruption of the Eurozone crisis, it has declined less than has trust in other EU or national institutions: European Commission (n 20).

[22] More generally, member states have not attempted to deploy political 'court curbing mechanisms' such as legislative or treaty-based override of judicial decisions, resource punishment, jurisdiction-stripping, or court-packing to rein in the ECJ. Even if they wanted to do so, they would face such a daunting set of hurdles in the EU institutional context that there is almost no chance of these mechanisms being deployed against the ECJ. See Kelemen (n 19).

of the ECJ, either by expanding the scope of fields subject to ECJ jurisdiction, by granting the ECJ new 'enforcement' powers (such as the ability to impose penalty payments on states which the granted the Court at Maastricht), or by expanding the EU judiciary itself, as with the creation of the General Court (then called the Court of First Instance) in the 1986 Single European Act—or, as is being considered now, with the proposal to add 12 judges to the General Court.

A full discussion of why member state governments have repeatedly empowered the ECJ goes beyond the scope of this paper, but two factors are worth mentioning here. First and most importantly, member state governments believe that in order for their project of political and economic integration to succeed, they need a powerful court to help them overcome collective action problems and make their commitments credible by enforcing their agreements and maintaining the rule of law within the Union.[23] Second, the Court has facilitated the acceptance of its expansive jurisprudence by engaging in what Maduro calls 'majoritarian activism'.[24] In short, the ECJ has frequently pursued legal harmonization by imposing as common EU standards norms that are favoured by the majority of member states. A court that regularly engages in this sort of majoritarian activism is unlikely to face a legitimacy crisis in the eyes of the majority of member states.

Finally, we might ask whether the ECJ suffers from a crisis of legitimacy in the eyes of the national courts who form such an integral element of the EU judicial order and upon whom the ECJ relies to send it cases via the preliminary ruling procedure and to enforce EU law. The story of how the ECJ gradually secured the support and co-operation of national courts is well known from the work of scholars such as Karen Alter, Anne Marie Slaughter, Alec Stone Sweet, Joseph Weiler, and others. The prevailing line of argument follows a form of the 'judicial empowerment thesis': in short, many national courts (in particular lower courts) saw co-operation with the ECJ (via the preliminary ruling procedure) as a means to promote judicial power at the national level vis-à-vis other branches of government (and sometimes vis-à-vis other domestic courts).

However, the story of the relationship between the ECJ and national courts did not end with their gradual acceptance of ECJ supremacy by the 1990s. Courts in Nordic member states continue to be very reluctant to use the preliminary ruling procedure,[25] and some new eastern European member states have shown similar reluctance.[26] There are still considerable tensions between the ECJ and national courts over who holds ultimate supremacy in cases of conflict between European and national law, with courts such as the German and Czech constitutional courts making decisions that seem to challenge the ECJ over supremacy and other critical

---

[23] Andrew Moravcsik, *The Choice for Europe* (Cornell University Press 1998).

[24] Miguel Maduro, *We, the Court: The European Court of Justice and the European Economic Constitution* (Hart 1998).

[25] Marlene Wind, 'The Nordics, the EU and the Reluctance Towards Supranational Judicial Review' (2010) 48 *JCMS* 1039.

[26] Michal Bobek, 'Learning to Talk: Preliminary Rulings, the Courts of the New Member States and the Court of Justice' (2010) 45 *CMLR* 1611.

doctrines.[27] Is there reason to fear that the ECJ may be losing legitimacy in the eyes of national judiciaries? Tensions between the ECJ and particular national courts remain, and may intensify in some cases. Nevertheless, it is impossible to detect any broad pattern across the EU of increased challenges from national courts to the legitimacy of the ECJ and its jurisprudence. To the contrary, the rate of preliminary rulings, the range of courts from which they originate, and the topics they cover continue to increase.

While the ECJ does not face a generalized legitimacy crisis,[28] vigilance is warranted. With the expanding scope of EU law, ECJ judgments touch on ever more sensitive policy areas, such as health, education, and taxation. ECJ rulings are regularly met by critics on the right or on the left who accuse the Court of engaging in anti-democratic judicial activism. As it treads on such controversial terrain, its decisions may spark public outcry from disaffected parties, conflict with national constitutional courts, and attempts at political reprisal. In particular, as EU law intrudes ever more on areas of core state powers associated with national sovereignty and 'constitutional identity', the ECJ may come into more intensive conflict with national constitutional courts. This is nowhere more evident than in the ECJ's on-going stand-off with the German Constitutional Court over question of *Kompetenz Kompetenz*, which may be coming to a head in light of the German Constitutional Court's pending reference for a preliminary ruling to the ECJ in the Open Market Transactions (OMT) case.[29] In this context, any discussion of reform of the process of judicial appointment must bear in mind potential impacts of such reform on the legitimacy of the ECJ in the eyes of the public and in the eyes of its other key interlocutors.

We know far less about the public legitimacy of the ECtHR, because no systematic cross-national opinion polls investigating the legitimacy of the court have been conducted.[30] Clearly, though, the legitimacy of the ECtHR varies substantially across states that are party to the convention and the court does face a crisis of public legitimacy in at least one state—the United Kingdom. As Voeten notes, controversial ECtHR rulings on prisoner voting rights and the extradition

---

[27] Arthur Dyevre, 'The German Federal Constitutional Court and European Judicial Politics' (2011) 34 *WEP* 346; Arthur Dyevre, 'Judicial Non-Compliance in a Non-Hierarchical Legal Order: Isolated Accident or Omen of Judicial Armageddon?' (2012) *Max Planck Institute for International and Comparative Law*, Working Paper; though see Michal Bobek, '*Landtová, Holubec*, and the Problem of an Uncooperative Court' (2014) 10 *EurConstLR* 54, who notes that the Czech Constitutional Court's decision in *Holubec* did not constitute the rebellion against the ECJ that many observers took it to be.

[28] For a discussion, see Joseph HH Weiler, 'Epilogue: Judging the Judges—Apology and Critique' in Maurice Adams et al (eds), *Judging Europe's Judges* (Hart 2013).

[29] Erik Jones and R Daniel Kelemen, 'The Euro Goes to Court' (2014) 56 *Survival: Global Politics and Strategy* 15; for the text of the German Court's reference, see BVerfG, 2 BvR 2728/13 vom 14.1.2014 (online at https://www.bverfg.de).

[30] Çali et al's study on the legitimacy of the ECtHR was based not on public opinion polling but on 107 interviews with politicians, lawyers, and judges from five countries: see Başak Çali, Anne Koch, and Nicola Bruch, 'The Legitimacy of the European Court of Human Rights: The View from the Ground' (2011), project report accessible online at <https://ecthrproject.files.wordpress.com/2011/04/ecthrlegitimacyreport.pdf>.

of suspected terrorists have led to a dramatic decline in public support for the ECtHR in the UK; while 71 per cent of the British public favoured the ECtHR in 1996, by 2011 only 24 per cent favoured remaining a party to the ECHR.[31] But if we step back from the tensions with the UK and consider broader trends, there are many indicators of the public legitimacy of the ECtHR. Consider first the court's surging—indeed, overwhelming—caseload.[32] The fact that, year after year, tens of thousands of citizens lodge cases with the ECtHR does not necessarily show that the Court enjoys broad support among the public at large, but it does show that the thousands filing complaints view the ECtHR as a legitimate judicial forum in which to pursue their grievances. With regard to other key interlocutors, the ECtHR is highly dependent on compliance by national governments.[33] National governments have a strong track record of respecting ECtHR rulings with regard to specific individual applicants. However, in recent years the ECtHR has started to apply its pilot judgment procedure more intensively, whereby the ECtHR considers not just the violation of an individual applicant's rights, but the underlying, systemic situation in the state giving rise to that rights violation and similar ones. The court then provides guidance to the state on remedial measures that must be taken to rectify the situation not only for the individual in the pilot judgment, but for other similarly affected individuals. A crucial test for the legitimacy of the ECtHR in the years to come will be whether states respect the pilot judgments and remedial measures suggested by the ECtHR.

3. Maintaining the Democratic Pedigree

While the ECJ and ECtHR do not currently face a crisis of legitimacy, there are reasons to be concerned about the erosion of their legitimacy in the current context. Some of the most important concerns raised recently focus on the selection and appointment of the judges who sit on these courts and the implications of these processes for judicial independence.[34] To understand why, it is useful to consider briefly the relationship between the judicialization of politics and the politicization of law.

In the course of interpreting the law, judges sometimes inevitably make the law. An extensive literature in political science and law highlights the 'countermajoritarian difficulty'[35] that ensues from this judicial law-making role: namely, in a

[31] Voeten (n 11) 418.

[32] The number of applications allocated to judicial formations of the ECtHR rose from 10,500 in 2000 to 65,900 in 2013, with a total of 99,900 pending cases before the ECtHR as of 31 December 2013: see European Court of Human Rights, Annual Report 2013 (2014) 198.

[33] By contrast, given the centrality of the preliminary ruling procedure to the EU legal system, the ECJ relies more than does the ECtHR on partnership with national courts. Çali et al's study on the legitimacy of the ECtHR focuses not on national governments but on key stakeholders (politicians, national judges, and lawyers). While they identify a number of sharp criticisms and concerns among these stakeholders, overall they find that the ECtHR enjoys 'a high level of legitimacy-credit' from them: Çali et al (n 30) 35.

[34] See above ch 6 s 2.

[35] Alexander Bickel, *The Least Dangerous Branch* (Yale University Press 1962).

democracy, how can one justify allowing unelected and unaccountable judges to overturn decisions made by elected law-makers and to sometimes make the law? One of the answers to this supposed 'difficulty' is that courts in modern democracies are not wholly unaccountable. Insofar as judges are appointed by democratically elected officials, courts have a 'democratic pedigree',[36] which provides a crucial basis for judicial legitimacy. However, the line between democratic input that can enhance judicial legitimacy and political manipulation that can undermine it may be a fine one. The judicialization of politics inevitably begets the politicization of law—including the politicization of the selection process.

As the increasing power of the European judiciary heightens political attention to the process of judicial appointment, it is understandable that advocates of judicial independence would worry about inappropriate political interference and seek to shield the appointment process from it. Therefore it is understandable that in recent years we have witnessed an effort by advocates of judicial independence to depoliticize the selection of judges in Europe. Under pressure from supranational institutions such as the Council of Europe, reforms to the process of judicial appointment in many EU member states and at the EU level itself have sought to decrease the control of elected officials over the appointment of judges and to increase the role of judicial councils dominated by judges.[37]

Concern is warranted, but efforts to depoliticize the appointment process in the name of independence could easily go too far and create a different sort of threat to judicial legitimacy. Reformers must take care to safeguard the democratic foundations of judicial legitimacy in Europe. I begin this section with some comments on the role of democratic inputs into the appointment process with respect to constitutional court judges in European states, and then explore this issue specifically in the supranational context with regard to the ECJ and the ECtHR.

The exact processes through which constitutional court judges are selected vary from country to country, but in all cases they are selected through procedures that involve some combination of democratically elected politicians.[38] Legal expertise and a reputation for independence are vital criteria in judicial selection. But we know of course that politicians will also try to select judges who share their political orientation, in the hope that their jurisprudence may reflect that orientation.

Does it compromise judicial independence if democratically elected officials seek to select judges whom they believe share their political views and who are likely to interpret the law as they (the politicians) wish it to be interpreted? Not necessarily. If a sitting government is able to rapidly pack a constitutional court

---

[36] Eisgruber (n 7).   [37] Guarnieri (n 3).

[38] For instance, in Germany, the Federal Constitutional Court is composed of 16 judges (divided into two senates), half of whom are appointed by the Bundestag and half by the Bundesrat—supported by votes of two-thirds majorities in all cases. In France, the Constitutional Council is made up of former presidents of the Republic, along with nine additional members, three of whom are appointed by the president of the Republic, three by the president of the National Assembly, and three by the president of the Senate. In Italy, the Constitutional Court is composed of 15 members: five selected by parliament, five by the president, and five by other high Italian courts. In all cases, judges are replaced on a partial, rolling basis rather than all being replaced simultaneously, and no single office holder is given complete control over appointments; see Kelemen (n 6).

with a majority of 'its' appointees, then that does in fact constitute a grave threat to judicial independence.[39] However, constitutional courts are generally designed to ensure that no single political actor that controls political power at one point in time can significantly alter the composition of the court. Constitutional courts and supranational courts in Europe are multi-member bodies, composed of 'a multitude of judges, chosen by various combinations of democratically elected officials over the span of a number of years'.[40] It is no coincidence that most judiciaries are structured such that the number of judges on a court increases as one ascends a judicial hierarchy (ie from trial, to appellate, to highest court), and that those high court judges are appointed by a variety of political actors on a time-staggered basis. This multi-member, time-staggered composition of constitutional courts is designed to reflect the input of the variety of majorities that have controlled various positions of public authority at some point in recent years. Multi-member courts may seek consensus, but they ultimately make decisions on the basis of the views of a majority (or sometimes supermajority) of their members. The decision of a majority of judges thus represents the decision of the judicial appointees of a majority of democratic majorities from recent years. Empowering the judiciary vis-à-vis a sitting parliament or executive can thus be understood as a very indirect empowerment of a collection of past majorities vis-à-vis a current legislative majority.

3.1. The Court of Justice of the EU

The structure of the ECJ also encourages a form of majoritarianism, but a different one from that built into the structure of national constitutional courts. First, a few key facts ought to be mentioned. Each EU member state appoints one judge to the ECJ for a six-year renewable term. Individual judges' decisions are shielded from scrutiny by appointing governments by the ECJ's practice of not publishing dissenting opinions, but instead issuing decisions reflecting the consensus of the ECJ. To deal with its growing caseload, the ECJ turned to hearing cases in chambers of three and five judges and in a Grand Chamber of 13 (now 15). Though they seek consensus and announce decisions in the name of the ECJ as a whole, when consensus is absent, decisions are made by a majority vote.

Could member state governments use their power over appointing ECJ judges to compromise the independence of the Court and undermine its legitimacy? This is highly unlikely. First, the introduction of the advisory panel on judicial appointments pursuant to Article 255 of the Lisbon Treaty[41] adds a safeguard

---

[39] This is why the Orbán governments' recent efforts to enlarge the Hungarian Constitutional Court and to pack it with its appointees have been so widely criticized. See for instance, Kim Scheppele, 'Hungary's Constitutional Revolution' (*New York Times*, The Conscience of a Liberal Blog, 19 December 2011) <http://krugman.blogs.nytimes.com/2011/12/19/hungarys-constitutional-revolution> accessed 27 June 2014.

[40] R Daniel Kelemen, 'Judicialisation, Democracy and European Integration' (2013) 49 *Representation* 295.

[41] Further discussed below in this section; see also above ch 1 and ch 3.

that may help screen out candidates who appear to lack independence and to have been selected to pursue a highly politicized agenda of one sort or another. Nevertheless, it is certainly possible that governments could seek to appoint judges who share their ideological orientation. If the ideological orientation or views on particular policies of a majority of member states shifted on a sustained basis, that might eventually lead to judicial appointments which would reorientate prevailing dispositions of judges on the ECJ. But such gradual judicial change as a result of changing views of the majority of democratically elected governments who appoint judges would not constitute a threat to judicial legitimacy: just the opposite, it would bolster judicial legitimacy. A Court that is totally insulated from shifts in prevailing ideological and policy orientations in society is more likely to face a legitimacy crisis than a Court whose composition gradually changes in line with such shifts. But could one or more governments quickly try to pack the ECJ with appointees who would support the government line on some issue? Court-packing of the sort that sometimes occurs in national contexts is implausible in the EU, given the great diversity of member government preferences and the role that individual governments play in the appointment of judges.

While rapid court-packing seems implausible, one could imagine some subset of states appointing judges with a particular orientation in an effort to shift the balance on the ECJ. For instance, one could imagine a handful of Eurosceptic governments appointing judges whom they hoped would rein in what they perceived as undesirable ECJ activism. However, the large size and internal structure of the court would tend to minimize the impact of a handful of such appointees.

Consider the structure of the ECJ's chamber system. The chamber system reflects a pattern (discussed above) that is found across many judicial systems, in which the number of judges sitting on a court hearing a particular case typically increases as one ascends the judicial hierarchy. In effect, the ECJ has created an internal hierarchy in which more routine cases are heard by smaller chambers of judges and more significant ones by larger chambers. Simply as a matter of logic, as one ascends this hierarchy and the size of a chamber increases, the median justice on that chamber (whose vote will determine the majority ruling) is more likely to be positioned close to the median judge of the Full Court. This structure encourages the ECJ to make 'majoritarian' rulings—ie rulings that reflect the views of judges appointed by a majority of member state governments. It also serves to constrain the ability of individual 'aberrant' judges to sway a court's decisions.[42] Given this structure, it should be no surprise that scholars such as Maduro[43] and Stone Sweet and Brunell[44] have found that the ECJ routinely engages in a pattern of 'majoritarian activism'—making rulings

[42] John Ferejohn and Larry Kramer, 'Independent Judges, Dependent Judiciary' (2002) 77 *NYU Law Rev* 962.

[43] Maduro (n 25).

[44] Alec Stone Sweet and Thomas Brunell, 'Trustee Courts and the Judicialization of International Regimes: The Politics of Majoritarian Activism in the ECTHR, the EU, and the WTO' (2013) 1 *Journal of Law and Courts* 61.

that effectively impose the will of the majority of member state governments on the minority.

If a small subset of states sent judges who were extreme Eurosceptic preference outliers to the ECJ (ie judges who interpreted the law in ways that restricted the pace and scope of European integration far more than other judges), those judges would hold views on the margins of the chambers on which they sat and be unlikely to find themselves as the median justice, in the position to sway a ruling taken on the basis of a majority vote. Moreover, as I have argued elsewhere, it seems plausible that the president of the ECJ might appoint judges to chamber strategically, 'so as to put together chambers that reflect a balance of attitudes toward European integration and that minimize the impact of outliers'.[45]

Finally, involving judges—both former CJEU judges and national high court judges—in the selection of ECJ judges through the 255 Panel introduced in the Lisbon Treaty is a salutary development. It offers a useful safeguard to screen out judges who lack the qualifications to serve on the ECJ, and it may even help screen out judges perceived to be ideological or partisan extremists of one stripe or another. As noted above, the greatest threats to the legitimacy of the ECJ are likely to stem not from public opinion, but from mounting tensions with the national judiciaries that the ECJ relies on to give effect to its judgments and, more generally, to act as an integral part of the EU judicial system. In this context, the ECJ's legitimacy in the eyes of national judiciaries may be bolstered by the fact that judges of the ECJ will all have been screened by a Panel composed primarily of senior judges from national judiciaries.[46] The involvement of high national judges in the selection of ECJ judges is likely to strengthen ties between the ECJ and national judiciaries and enhance the legitimacy of the ECJ in the eyes of national courts. Indeed, it is quite striking that today the president of the Federal Constitutional Court of Germany—the very court which has posed the most important challenges to the ECJ's assertions of supremacy—himself sits on the panel that screens nominees to the ECJ. In other words, the head of the national court that has done the most to question the bounds of the ECJ's supremacy doctrine now plays a pivotal role in selecting the judges who will sit on the ECJ. Just how the activities of the 255 Panel will affect the legitimacy of the ECJ in the long term remains to be seen. The fact that the 255 Panel has produced unfavourable opinions on 22 per cent of the new nominees for judgeships

[45] R Daniel Kelemen, 'The Political Foundations of Judicial Independence in the European Union' (2012) 19 *Journal of European Public Policy* 43.

[46] As constituted in 2010, the seven-member Panel included the vice president of the French Conseil d'Etat, a justice of the Supreme Court of the UK, the president of Supreme Court of Denmark, the president of the Hungarian Constitutional Court, an Austrian former ECJ judge, a Finnish former Court of First Instance judge, and the appointee of the European Parliament, Ana Palacio, who was a former member of the European Parliament, former Minister of Foreign Affairs in Spain, and former member of the European Commission. As of 1 March 2014, the Article 255 Panel is composed of the vice president of the French Conseil d'Etat, the president of the Finnish Supreme Court, a justice of the Supreme Court of the UK, the president of the Constitutional Court of Hungary, the president of the Federal Constitutional Court of Germany, a former judge of the ECJ, and a member of the European Parliament.

on the ECJ and GC[47] and that all nominees who received an unfavourable opinion were withdrawn already demonstrates that the Panel's work has transformed the appointment process and reduced governments' discretion in selecting judges. Importantly, the presence of the 255 Panel is likely to reduce the chances of governments attempting to appoint judges perceived to lack independence.

However, the EU should certainly not contemplate following the advice of the Council of Europe, which has suggested to members of the European Convention on Human Rights that 'The authority taking decisions on the selection and career of judges should be independent of the executive and legislative powers. With a view to guaranteeing its independence, at least half of the members of the authority should be judges chosen by their peers.'[48] The Council of Europe's advice privileges independence at the expense of accountability. It detaches the selection of judges from the input of democratically elected officials needed to legitimate judicial power.

3.2. The European Court of Human Rights

How does the process of appointing judges to the ECtHR affect the Court's legitimacy? In the case of the ECtHR, states nominate three candidates for judgeship who are then voted on by the Parliamentary Assembly of the Council of Europe (PACE), with the winning candidate securing a position on the Court. In this volume, von Bogdandy and Krenn[49] argue that from the perspective of democratic principles, the process of appointment of judges to the ECtHR is preferable to that used for the ECJ. They argue that the PACE represents citizens' interests on a transnational level and that PACE involvement in judicial selection therefore enhances the democratic legitimacy of the selection process. Moreover, they emphasize that the process of voting has stimulated deliberation within PACE over what constitutes a desirable judge at the European level. This deliberation in turn has had a number of positive effects, for instance the drive to increase the number of female judges at the ECtHR. Based on the ECtHR experience, von Bogdandy and Krenn conclude that the democratic legitimacy of the selection process for the ECJ would be enhanced by greater involvement of the European Parliament.

While I would not dispute that the process of deliberation in PACE surrounding votes on appointments to the ECtHR has yielded benefits, it is by no means clear that this process does more to enhance the legitimacy of the ECtHR than does the process currently used in the case of the ECJ. First, while PACE votes on the three candidates presented by each national government, it is widely understood that governments manage to signal which is their

---

[47] Article 255 Panel, Third Activity Report [2014] SN 1118/2014. In detail see above ch 1 s 6.1 and ch 3 s 3.
[48] Recommendation CM/Rec(2010)12 of the Committee of Ministers to member states on judges: independence, efficiency and responsibilities, para 46.
[49] Above ch 7.

preferred candidate and that that candidate almost always tops the voting. So, it is unclear how much of a check this supranational democratic control mechanism really places on governments. It would seem that the 255 Panel—which has rendered negative opinions on 22 per cent of nominees—may in fact constitute a more significant check on governments' discretion in appointing judges. More importantly, the notion that involvement of a supranational legislative body (PACE or the European Parliament) in appointment would enhance the legitimacy of judges presupposes that the legislative body in question has considerable legitimacy—which it can in effect confer on the court through the appointment process. However, as Voeten demonstrates, the legitimacy of international courts tends to reflect the legitimacy of the international institution of which it is a part.[50] In other words, if a supranational court experiences a decline in legitimacy, it is likely this would be linked to a decline in the legitimacy of the related supranational legislative body, such that the latter could hardly bolster the legitimacy of the former. Finally, as noted above, the greatest threats to the legitimacy of supranational courts are likely to come not from the public (which holds them in relatively high esteem) but from the national governments and or national courts upon whom they rely for the impact of their jurisprudence. Therefore, anchoring the selection process for judges to supranational courts with national governments and increasing the involvement of national judiciaries (as for instance through bodies such as the 255 Panel) is likely to prove more crucial for maintaining the legitimacy of the ECtHR and the ECJ than would heightening the involvement of supranational assemblies such as PACE or the European Parliament.

4. Conclusion

The ECJ and ECtHR are not suffering from the sorts of systemic crises of legitimacy—in the eyes of mass publics or key stakeholders—that their most ardent critics suggest. Nevertheless, given the growing power of these European courts, questions about their legitimacy will likely intensify, including questions about how the judges who sit on these courts are appointed. In part, this newfound focus on judicial selection and appointment reflects a broader trend across European institutions. It is perhaps no coincidence that debates surrounding the appointment of ECJ judges have become more salient just as debates surrounding the procedures for the appointment of the European Commission president have intensified. Both debates are animated by the assumption that now that supranational institutions have become more powerful than ever before, the processes through which officeholders in these institutions are selected must change. In the case of supranational executive and legislative institutions, the path of reform has generally been to render them more democratic as they become more powerful—to

---

[50] Voeten (n 11).

limit any perceived 'democratic deficit'. But with supranational courts, the concern has often been just the opposite—to limit political input, so as to safeguard independence and legitimacy. This chapter has argued that while taking steps to ensure judicial independence is warranted, maintaining the legitimacy of Europe's courts also depends on preserving a central role for democratically elected officials in the selection of Europe's judges.

12

The Legitimization Strategies of International Judges

The Case of the European Court of Human Rights

Mikael Rask Madsen

1. Introduction

The selection processes of European judges obviously have an impact on the legitimacy of European courts.[1] Yet, while the selection procedures in themselves are important to legitimize an international court, notably at the more formal level, the actual behaviour of the appointed judges undoubtedly matters more at the end of the day: that is, their ability to issue judgments that balance the development of the underlying legal frameworks of their courts with member states' support and more general socio-political evolutions in society.[2] Nevertheless, most research into the legitimacy of international courts shows very little interest in the judges of international courts and their selection; mainstream research instead remains focused on what could be termed the quasi-democratic foundations of international courts and, most often, their alleged democratic deficit.[3] This literature has generally been concerned with the normative challenges to liberal democracy implied by international courts in terms of the juridification and denationalization of politics.[4] This is linked to the critique of judicial review and constitutionalism

[1] This research was funded by the Danish National Research Foundation Grant no DNRF105 and carried out at iCourts—the Danish National Research Foundation's Centre of Excellence for International Courts, Faculty of Law, University of Copenhagen. Some of the content has appeared in a working paper: Mikael R Madsen, 'Explaining the Power of International Courts in their Context: From Legitimacy to Legitimization', 7 RSCAS Policy Paper (Courts, Social Change and Judicial Independence) 23.
[2] Cf Başak Çalı, Anne Koch, and Nicola Bruch, 'The Legitimacy of Human Rights Courts: A Grounded Interpretivist Analysis of the European Court of Human Rights' (2013) 35 *Human Rights Quarterly* 955.
[3] For a critique, see eg Andreas Follesdal, 'The Legitimacy of International Human Rights Review: The Case of the European Court of Human Rights' (2009) 40 *Journal of Social Philosophy* 595.
[4] For example Eric A Posner, *The Perils of Global Legalism* (University of Chicago Press 2009); Henry Kissinger, *Does America Need a Foreign Policy?: Toward a Diplomacy for the 21st Century* (Simon & Schuster 2002).

raised in national contexts[5] in terms of a criticism of the transfer of power away from the national parliaments and towards an (international) 'juristocracy'.

This debate is however neither new[6] nor only academic.[7] It has to a large extent concerned normative issues related to the general role of the judiciary in (liberal) political systems—the so-called counter-majoritarian difficulty.[8] Moreover, it is fuelled by a century-old fear of 'government by judges' first pronounced by French comparativist Eduard Lambert in 1921 in his study of the US legal system,[9] but now turned into the chosen rhetorical weapon against the rising power of international courts and their fellow travellers: the 'tribunalists', that is, the advocates of the virtues of international law and courts.[10] The recent British campaigns against the European Court of Human Rights (ECtHR or Court)—known as 'Strasbourg-bashing'—provide perhaps the most striking example of this growing conflict over the role and place of international courts in contemporary globalizing society. It does not, however, follow from these rhetorical hostilities that the ECtHR as such is illegitimate, as some observers tend rapidly to conclude. Neither does it follow that the Court is necessarily delegitimized by such campaigns.[11] In fact, such crises might potentially further legitimize the ECtHR in the long run, as was the case when, for example, the Thatcher government launched a scorching critique of the Strasbourg Court in the 1980s or the French supreme courts rebelled against the ECtHR in the 1990s.[12]

Generally, the evoked literature remains for the most part a normative political theoretical critique. As political philosophy, it has obvious merits and raises important questions on a more principal and abstract level. It has, however, less to offer in terms of explaining the deeper global processes against which governments delegate power to international courts in the first place and, not least, how international courts transform delegated authority into legal practices and institutional power.[13] But most importantly, as I will argue, this literature overall fails to

[5] For example Richard Bellamy, *Political Constitutionalism: A Republican Defence of the Constitutionality of Democracy* (Cambridge University Press 2007); Ran Hirschl, *Towards Juristocracy: The Origins and Consequences of the New Constitutionalism* (Harvard University Press 2004).

[6] For example Hans J Morgenthau, *Politics Among Nations: The Struggle for Power and Peace* (Alfred A. Knopf 1948); Pierre-Yves Condé, 'Des juges à La Haye. Formation d'une judiciabilité universaliste, des amis de la paix à la lutte contre l'impunité' (École Normale Supérieure de Cachan 2012).

[7] For example Robert H Bork, *Coercing Virtue: The Worldwide Rule of Judges* (AEI Press 2003).

[8] Alexander M Bickel, *The Least Dangerous Branch: The Supreme Court at the Bar of Politics* (Yale University Press 1961).

[9] Michael H Davis, 'A Government of Judges: An Historical Re-View' (1987) 35 *American Journal of Comparative Law* 559.

[10] Thomas Skouteris, 'The New Tribunalism: Strategies of (De)Legitimization in the Era of Adjudication' (2006) 17 *Finnish Yearbook of International Law* 307.

[11] Jonas Christoffersen and Mikael R Madsen, 'Postscript: Understanding the Past, Present and Future of the European Court of Human Rights' in Jonas Christoffersen and Mikael R Madsen (eds), *The European Court of Human Rights between Law and Politics* (2nd edn, Oxford University Press 2013).

[12] Mikael R Madsen, 'France, the UK and 'Boomerang' of the Internationalization of Human Rights (1945–2000)' in Simon Halliday and Patrick Schmidt (eds), *Human Rights Brought Home: Socio-Legal Perspectives on Human Rights in the National Context* (Hart Publishing 2004).

[13] Mikael R Madsen, 'Sociological Approaches to International Courts' in Karen Alter, Cesare PR Romano, and Yuval Shany (eds), *Oxford University Press Handbook of International Adjudication* (Oxford University Press 2014).

account for the flip side of the question at stake, namely how international courts develop strategies of legitimization in their interface with democratic politics as well as broader socio-political evolutions in society. While some scholars have addressed this question by setting up more or less formalistic criteria for the legitimacy of international courts, for example by focusing on questions of representativeness or notions of transparency and accountability,[14] I would argue that this only formally—and only partially—contributes to the solving of the key question in this regard. The real puzzle, when seen in the larger context of international law and politics, is how international courts remain in the game at all over time;[15] how they build and maintain authority. They have almost by definition a fairly fragile institutional set-up, legally as well as politically, and they have been the object of continuous critique of not only their practices but also even their existences. Yet twentieth-century international legal history suggests that many—if not most—of these courts continue to exist regardless of institutional fragility and criticism.[16] Thus the question is how they manage to remain powerful in what often appears to be hostile environments. Or, more specifically: what explains the successes and failures among the various international courts established since the beginning of the twentieth century in terms of legitimacy? What are their legitimization strategies?

My contention is that international courts develop ways of legitimization which are contingent on historical socio-political developments, and particularly geopolitical developments causing structural change,[17] the actual cases brought before them,[18] and the forms of support they do or do not enjoy.[19] Importantly, the argument presupposes that temporary crises and controversies are not by definition signs of defeat but instead are indicative of evolution, following, broadly speaking, the ideas of punctuational bursts and punctuated equilibria found in neo-Darwinist theories of evolution.[20] In other words, such controversies might very well serve as moments of crystallization and legitimization in which international courts develop a certain institutional robustness vis-à-vis their critics and even transform their originally more fragile roles into new, more powerful ones. Both the ECtHR

[14] Cf Mattias Kumm, 'The Legitimacy of International Law: A Constitutionalist Framework of Analysis' (2004) 15 *European Journal of International Law* 907.

[15] Karen J Alter, Laurence R Helfer, and Mikael R Madsen, 'How Context Shapes the Authority of International Courts', in *Law & Contemporary Problems*, forthcoming (2015).

[16] Suzanne Katzenstein, 'In the Shadow of Crisis: The Creation of International Courts in the Twentieth Century' (2014) 55 *Harvard Internaitonal Law Journal* 151.

[17] Mikael R Madsen, 'The Geopolitics of European Law: The ECtHR, the ECJ and the Foundation of the European Legal Field (1950–1980)' (Law and Society Annual Conference).

[18] Cf Antoine Vauchez, 'The Transnational Politics of Judicialization. *Van Gend en Loos* and the Making of EU Polity' (2010) 16 *European Law Journal* 1; Mikael R Madsen, 'Legal Diplomacy—Law, Politics and the Genesis of Postwar European Human Rights' in Stefan Ludwig Hoffmann (ed), *Human Rights in the Twentieth Century: A Critical History* (Cambridge University Press 2011); Karen Alter, *The European Court's Political Power. Selected Essays* (Oxford University Press 2009).

[19] Alter (n 17); Rachel Cichowski, 'Civil Society and the European Court of Human Rights' in Jonas Christoffersen and Mikael R Madsen (eds), *The European Court of Human Rights between Law and Politics* (Oxford University Press 2011).

[20] Cf Stephen Jay Gould, 'Episodic Change versus Gradualist Dogma' (1978) 2 *Science and Nature* 5.

and the Court of Justice of the European Union (CJEU) provide examples of such evolution and adaption.[21] However, the question of the legitimization of international courts cannot simply be reduced to their responses to government pressures, as some variants of principal–agent theory tend to suggest. As I will argue below, international courts legitimize themselves in relation to other key environments, including, most notably, the legal field and civil society.[22] It is these combined legitimization strategies that overall ensure the existence and evolution of international courts in the long run.

Invariably, a key element in these processes of legitimation is the ways in which the very judges selected to a specific international court develop the court and its jurisprudence. One of the main problems with regard to the operation of international courts is that in lieu of more formal checks and balances, they must continually act reflexively with regard to the multiple legal, political, and societal levels with which they interact. More precisely, their output—case law—must be balanced not only in terms of the political representatives of member states called before the bar, but also with changes in society. My claim is that this situation calls for more than stellar legal skills; while there is a need to know the craft of judging, there is also a distinct need for a degree of reflexivity among the appointed judges with regard to the constituencies of their court. This further puts pressure on selection processes, as the actual requirements for taking a position on the international bench are thus multiple and not necessarily the same as those typically assumed to characterize a good judge on the national plane. In this sense, the typical formal legal criteria for holding the office of international judge fail to account for the job's actual requirements and complexities.

As I will argue in this article, using the ECtHR as my empirical case, this has real consequences. More specifically, I will argue that the early ECtHR was populated by a legal–political elite of law professors who were keenly aware of how the structural challenges faced by key member states had to be considered in the development of the Court's practices. In fact, drawing on Max Weber, I argue that the rationality of the original Strasbourg Court might best be described as a form of legal diplomacy rather than formally or materially rationalized law.[23] Tracing the evolution of the Strasbourg bench, we can, against this backdrop, then identify a major shift in the composition of the Court beginning in the mid-1990s. While the old Court was fundamentally marked by elitist law professors with significant connections to both politics and legal practice, the new post-Protocol no 11 Court is increasingly losing its connectedness to politics and diplomacy. Not only are the

---

[21] Mikael R Madsen, 'The Protracted Institutionalisation of the Strasbourg Court: From Legal Diplomacy to Integrationist Jurisprudence' in Madsen and Christoffersen (n 18); Madsen (n 17); Karen Alter, *Establishing the Supremacy of European Law: The Making of an International Rule of Law in Europe* (Oxford University Press 2001); Alec Stone Sweet, 'The European Court of Justice and the Judicialization of EU Governance' 5 *Living Reviews in European Governance* (online at http://www.livingreviews.org/lreg).

[22] See also above (n 14).

[23] Madsen (n 17) and Madsen, 'The Protracted Institutionalisation of the Strasbourg Court: From Legal Diplomacy to Integrationist Jurisprudence' in Madsen and Christoffersen (n 18).

judges generally significantly younger, and correspondingly less experienced when appointed; they are also generally far more specialized in human rights. While, at first glance, this mere 'legalization' and technicalization of the ECtHR would seem a positive development of the Court, I will argue that it has in practice weakened the Court's interfaces with both politics and society, which are inevitably part of its operation. The growing criticism of the Court—notably at the advent of the Brighton Declaration[24]—in the context of the serious challenges posed by the large number of cases waiting in the docket has effectively revealed that the Court is now in a position where its increased technicalization hampers it from addressing the real political challenges ahead. And this structural weakness, I will further argue, can in large part be attributed to the new composition of the Court and, thus, the current selection processes.

To make this argument, this article proceeds in the following way: I begin with a discussion of my proposed shift in analytical perspective, from analysing the *legitimacy* of international courts (typically in more absolute normative categories) to a study of the ways in which international courts are *legitimized* by various legitimization strategies. I then provide empirical evidence of the ways in which the approach can be deployed, exemplified primarily by the case of the ECtHR. In conclusion, I very briefly restate the argument and relate it to the study of international courts more generally, and European courts in particular.

2. Overcoming the Problem of Legitimacy

While the notion of legitimacy is absolutely central to social science, it is probably also one of the most problematic and misused terms within the discipline. Possibly the best non-normative exposition of the notion is found in the seminal work of Max Weber, who demonstrated how legitimacy can take many forms—from traditional, through charismatic, to legally rational.[25] According to Weber, what makes a certain practice of power legitimate at the end of the day is the process with which the authority justifies its exercise of power and gains social acceptance. If we apply this to international courts, it follows that their legitimacy is not due to them being *representative* of society; it is due to them being *reflexive* of society.[26] Even though a court is demographically little representative—see, for example, the US Supreme Court—its practices might nevertheless reflect society and, thus, be justifiable in society.[27] In other words, the legitimacy of a given international court cannot simply be statistically deduced from the judges' representativeness of society

---

[24] Christoffersen and Madsen (n 10).

[25] Max Weber, *Wirtschaft und Gesellschaft. Grundriss der verstehenden Soziologie* (5th edn, Mohr 1980).

[26] Cf 'The Protracted Institutionalisation of the Strasbourg Court: From Legal Diplomacy to Integrationist Jurisprudence' in Madsen and Christoffersen (n 18).

[27] Madsen, 'Sociological Approaches to International Courts' in K Alter, CPR Romano, and Y Shany (eds), *Oxford University Press Handbook of International Adjudication* (Oxford University Press 2014).

and politics at large. Logically, from this it follows that even the best and most carefully thought-out procedures of (s)elections of judges, in the most extreme cases seeking to make courts representative as a sort of quasi-democratic political institution, might ultimately fail if the court's practices are not reflexive of society. Yet the profiles of a specific set of judges might at the same time very well help them gain legitimacy in specific environments, ranging from law to politics and civil society. This hinges on a sociological institutional analysis which emphasizes that perceptions of courts are mainly evaluations of courts' jurisprudence. While individual judges and their profiles contribute to the institutional rationality of the Court and thus influence its practices, they are rarely individually evaluated by the Court's publics.[28] This seems to be particularly the case with European inter- and supranational courts, as the general European public is extremely unlikely even to know the name of their own national judge.[29] The same generally goes for most of its other publics, including its legal public, where the interface is mainly trans-formed into a question of defining the law, as suggested in both Bourdieusian and Luhmannian sociologies of law.[30]

I build this argument in part on the analysis of Weber.[31] Above all, his classic essay on authority emphasizes that the legitimacy of any given institution can be derived from a number of different practices aiming at different environments (see further below). Although often overlooked in the study of international courts, which have mostly focused on international courts' interface with government prac-tices, this is perhaps particularly true for international courts. As a matter of fact, interaction between international courts and governments in a more politicized manner is the exception rather than the norm, I would argue. Instead, international courts interact most often and most directly with highly differentiated legal fields, where their interplay is generally legitimized in shared epistemologies of profes-sional legal knowledge. For the most part, this comes across as unproblematic and part of an everyday legal practice that is not all that different from what happens at the level of national courts, where the meaning of law is equally being battled out. Nevertheless, it is precisely this on-going and, in recent years, expanding[32] juridification and judicialization of international law which for the most part, via reference to the lack of democratic legitimacy of transnational legal elite net-works, is the backdrop to the political critique of juristocracy. According to this

---

[28] One exception to this might be the US Supreme Court, whose judges have increasingly been scrutinized in recent years. While the appointment of, for example, Justice Scalia, now a controversial justice, took place without much public attention, more recent appointments to the court have been significantly more politicized. Also, the analysis of patterns in judgment has become a significant research field in US political science in particular. Curiously, what is generally revealed is that judges tend to change when appointed to the bench as an effect of socialization and institutionalization.

[29] The fact that the ECJ does not publish dissent only adds to this situation of relative obscurity. On the importance of 'obscurity' to the practice of law, see Bruno Latour, *La fabrique du droit: Une ethnographie du Conseil d'État* (La Découverte 2002).

[30] Pierre Bourdieu, 'The Force of Law: Toward a Sociology of the Juridical Field' (1987) 38 *The Hastings Law Journal* 80; Niklas Luhmann, *Das Recht der Gesellschaft* (Suhrkamp 1993).

[31] See also the analysis in Çalı, Koch, and Bruch (n 1).

[32] Cesare PR Romano, 'The Proliferation of International Tribunals: Piecing Together the Puzzle' (1999) 31 *NYU Journal of International Law and Politics* 709.

critique, international judges have basically become a *de*nationalized elite who, to borrow from Huntington's analysis, basically act as the legal variant of the 'Davos men'[33]—that is, as a club of like-minded cosmopolitans (and cosmocrats) serving their own global interests. This is, however, hardly the case for international judges; in fact, international judges are probably better understood as a new 'transnational power elite'.[34] More specifically, by the notion of transnational power elites, the following are emphasized: 1) how these actors are effectively *trans*national and not *de*national, implying in this case that for the most part they have a position in both national and international fields, which also enables their practices to trespass these boundaries; 2) that they exercise a power fundamental to the existence of what is typically generally referred to as the state.[35]

As shown by a number of scholars, global elites generally play an increasingly important role in a number of fields, ranging from business[36] to development work.[37] A closer look at international legal elites, however, suggests that they do not act only on an international level and nor are they constrained to single institutional arrangements, as just suggested.[38] In this light, the critique of juristocracy generally fails due to its one-sided focus on the rather artificial dichotomy between an essentialist view of politics as the institutionalized expression of a democratic will and what might be described as international legal self-reference. This overlooks what is in practice a much more blurred boundary between international law and politics. Closely linked, it presupposes an increasingly inadequate notion of international law as an interstate contract law which very clearly defines international courts' framework and legal playing field vis-á-vis national levels of law and politics. Considering the fact that international courts have now existed for close to a century (if one uses the establishment of the Permanent Court of International Justice in 1922 as a benchmark) and in many cases have transformed themselves into something that hardly resembles their original set-up and mandate,[39] it might of course be tempting to argue for a return to a sovereign national ordering of the international. Yet that argument overlooks entirely that the very evolution of international courts

[33] Cf Samuel P Huntington, *Who are We? America's Great Debate* (Free Press 2005).

[34] Niilo Kauppi and Mikael R Madsen (eds), *Transnational Power Elites: The New Professionals of Governance, Law and Security* (Routledge 2013).

[35] For an application of the notion to, respectively, lawyers and judges, see Mikael R Madsen, 'Unpacking Legal Network Power: The Structural Construction of Transnational Legal Expert Networks' in Mar Fenwick, Steven van Uytsel, and Stefan Wrbka (eds), *Networked Governance, Transnational Business and the Law* (Springer 2013).

[36] Leslie Sklair, *The Transnational Capitalist Class* (Blackwell 2001).

[37] Jeffrey T Jackson, *The Globalizers: Development Workers in Action* (The Johns Hopkins University Press 2005).

[38] See also Yves Dezalay and Bryant Garth, *The Internationalization of Palace Wars: Lawyers, Economists, and the Contest to Transform Latin American States* (University of Chicago Press 2002); Yves Dezalay and Bryant G Garth, *Dealing in Virtue. International Commercial Arbitration and the Construction of a Transnational Legal Order* (University of Chicago Press 1996).

[39] For example Karen J Alter, 'The New International Courts: A Bird's Eye View'. Buffett Centre for International and Comparative Studies Working Paper Series No 09-001 (2009); Jonas Christoffersen and Mikael R Madsen (eds), *The European Court of Human Rights between Law and Politics* (Oxford University Press 2011); Vauchez (n 17).

is perhaps where the answer to the question of the legitimacy of international courts can be found; that is, rather than continuing the quest for a normative, and ultimately essentialist, notion of politics *v* law that, on a principal level, sets the boundaries, it might be more rewarding to inquire into what I above introduced as the real puzzle in this regard: namely, how international courts not only remain in the game but are actually proliferating.[40] As also suggested above, their ability to remain in the game is largely contingent on their legitimization strategies.

It is for these precise reasons that I will argue for a decisive shift in analytical focus. My contention is that it requires a change of focus from a more normative idea of the *legitimacy* (in terms of being *legitimate*) of international courts to a more dynamic notion of international courts' *legitimization*, and thereby a profound change of analytical perspective and framework. This, however, allows for exploration of how the idea and institutionalization of international courts has evolved over the past hundred or so years. Drawing on existing empirical studies,[41] I would argue that international courts develop legitimizing measures vis-à-vis their environments on at least three levels of external interface: the *legal* level (ie their interface with other courts in terms of eg jurisdiction and comity); the *political* level (ie their interface with national and international forms of governance in terms of eg accountability and 'boundary disputes'); and the *societal* level (ie their interface with civil society in terms of outreach, access, and legal entitlements). It is, further, my contention that these practices of legitimization are often most clearly observable in the relative clashes that international courts continuously experience at all three levels. This highlights that international courts' legitimacy is not consolidated once and for all, but is rather the product of continuous reinvestment and maintenance. This does not, of course, exclude that some courts seem to develop what Alec Stone Sweet has termed 'structural supremacy',[42] but rather points to the ways in which such power, just as any other symbolic power, has to be maintained and reproduced over time.

At the legal level, these relative clashes are generally found in the interface between national and international courts—for instance, as illustrated by the numerous disputes over the Maastricht Treaty; eg *Brunner* (1992)[43]—and now also in the form of 'jurisdictional turf wars' between international courts, as

---

[40] Cesare PR Romano, 'A Taxonomy of International Rule of Law Institutions' (2011) 2 *Journal of International Dispute Settlement* 241.

[41] For example Mikael R Madsen, 'From Cold War Instrument to Supreme European Court: The European Court of Human Rights at the Crossroads of International and National Law and Politics' (2007) 32 *Law & Social Inquiry* 13; Madsen (n 17); Alter (n 17); Alter (n 20); JHH Weiler, 'The Transformation of Europe' (1991) 100 *Yale Law Journal* 240; Antonin Cohen, '"Dix personnages majestueux en longue robe amarante": La formation de la cour de justice des communautés européennes' (2010) 60 *Revue française de science politique* 22; Vauchez (n 17); Karen J Alter, *The New Terrain of International Law: International Courts in International Politics* (Princeton University Press 2014).

[42] Alec Stone Sweet and Jud Mathews, 'Proportionality Balancing and Global Constitutionalism' (2008) 47 *Columbia Journal of Transnational Law* 73, 87.

[43] *Brunner v European Union Treaty* (2 BvR 2134/92 & 2159/92).

exemplified in such cases as *Kadi* (2005)[44] and *Bosphorus v Ireland* (2005).[45] Underlining a much-increased awareness of international courts, recent years have seen a number of controversies with regard to international courts at the political and societal levels. On the political level, these have translated into debates over the future of democracy with regard to the balance to be struck between national legislative branches and international courts—a striking example is the Danish debate over the ECJ ruling in *Metock* (2008),[46] but many others could be mentioned. At the societal level, the picture is more blurred due to the fact that international courts offer gateways for bypassing the inertia of national politics of law; thus, under certain conditions they are greatly favoured[47] while at other moments they are less interesting options, the latter exemplified by the ambiguous relationship of European trade unions with respect to European inter- and supranational courts. In all cases, these clashes underline that the place of international courts is hardly a settled one; it not only remains under scrutiny but also calls for perpetual (re)legitimization.

Hence, whereas most existing research has tended to argue that these various controversies—legal, political, and societal—are generally indicative of the weak legitimacy of international courts, I will, against the actual historical evolution of international courts, on the contrary argue that they are key to understanding the legitimization of international courts. On the legal level, they provide the 'hard cases' necessary for legal innovation and jurisprudential refinement; on the political and societal levels, they provide the continuous legitimacy tests of international courts that are crucial for further institutional and legal development. In other words, instead of insisting on the normative legal idea of international courts as autonomous legal institutions operating in a self-referential system of law and, thus, decoupling law from society and politics, my claim is that comprehending the legitimization of international courts requires an understanding of not only the response of, for example, politics and society to international courts, but also, and perhaps more crucially, how international courts themselves respond to law, politics, and society in terms of legitimating strategies. This approach allows both for an understanding of under what circumstances and at what times international courts are legitimized or delegitimized, *and* for empirical detection of how the law and institutional design of international courts is altered over time by these critical interfaces. Obviously, as stated above, the very selection of the judges is a key preliminary for this process of legitimization, as it decides the intellectual and symbolic capacities of the bench before any action takes place.

---

[44] Case T-315/01 *Kadi v Council and Commission* (2005) ECR II-3649.
[45] *Bosphorus v Ireland* App no 45036/98 (ECHR, 30 June 2005).
[46] Case C-127/08 *Metock* [2008] ECR I-6241.
[47] Cf Yves Dezalay and Mikael R Madsen, 'The Force of Law and Lawyers: Pierre Bourdieu and the Reflexive Sociology of Law' (2012) 8 *Annual Review of Law and Social Science* 433.

3. The Legitimization of International Courts: The Case of the ECtHR

The initial institutionalization and autonomization of the ECtHR provides an emblematic case for understanding these multiple dynamics of legitimization. I have analysed the evolution and transformation of the ECtHR elsewhere;[48] here I will mainly illustrate my arguments by drawing on these empirical studies and other available accounts.[49]

The drafting of the European Convention on Human Rights (ECHR) in the late 1940s was brought forward by a double socio-political legitimation: it was perceived by many as a continuation of the post-Second World War institutional build-up in which the 1948 Universal Declaration of Human Rights (UDHR) was a particular crowning moment, although brief, of the international community's effort at coming to terms with the immediate past. This overriding *illusio*[50] of the period in terms of finding international legal solutions to international political problems certainly also fuelled the initial drafting of the ECHR in the late 1940s, yet the main driver of the Convention was in practice more geopolitical; as argued elsewhere, the European Convention was above all drafted as a Cold War instrument.[51] During the actual negotiation of the ECHR, the utopian visions of universal human rights which, in the aftermath of Allied victory had enjoyed momentum at the UN and among intellectuals, were almost unequivocally substituted with a deeply westernized vocabulary of 'liberty and democracy'. In fact, the rapid drafting of the Convention reflected above all a growing fear of, on the one hand, the rising power of the national Communist parties, and, on the other, Soviet imperial expansionism into western Europe.

Andrew Moravcsik has rightly called it 'the puzzle of the European Convention' that European states opted to sign a document which so clearly removed national sovereignty in a key area of statehood and left it in the hands of international judges.[52] However, neither delegation theory nor more general principal–agent

---

[48] For example Madsen (n 41); Madsen (n 17); Madsen, 'The Protracted Institutionalisation of the Strasbourg Court: From Legal Diplomacy to Integrationist Jurisprudence' in Madsen and Christoffersen (n 18).

[49] Ed Bates, *The Evolution of the European Convention on Human Rights: From Its Inception to the Creation of a Permanent Court of Human Rights* (Oxford University Press 2010); Ed Bates, 'The Birth of the European Convention on Human Rights—and the European Court of Human Rights' in Jonas Christoffersen and Mikael R Madsen (eds), *The European Court of Human Rights between Law and Politics* (Oxford University Press 2011); Marco Duranti, 'Curbing Labour's Totalitarian Temptation: European Human Rights Law and British Postwar Politics' (2012) 3 *Humanity* 36; AW Brian Simpson, *Human Rights and the End of Empire: Britain and the Genesis of the European Convention* (Oxford University Press 2004).

[50] Pierre Bourdieu, *Le sens pratique* (Minuit 1980).

[51] For example Mikael R Madsen, 'Human Rights and the Hegemony of Ideology: European Lawyers and the Cold War Battle over International Human Rights' in Yves Dezalay and Bryant Garth (eds), *Lawyers and the Construction of Transnational Justice* (Routledge 2012); Madsen (n 16).

[52] Andrew Moravcsik, 'The Origins of Human Rights Regimes: Democratic Delegation in Postwar Europe' (2000) 54 *International Organization* 217.

theorizing provides a convincing answer to this. What is required instead is to look not only at the processes in which the Strasbourg institutions gained legitimacy, but also how they turned the Convention into something of a legal nature—and something considerably different to what could have been assumed at the moment of negotiation. A look at the actual document with a view to the *travaux préparatoires* suggests that the negotiating parties were not afraid of using the high prose of democracy and liberty, yet the document lacked a dimension of legal obligation for the member states. It was a 'Convention à la carte':[53] all the most central clauses, particularly the jurisdiction of the court and individual petition, were made optional in the original Convention. Thus, signing the document did not in fact necessarily imply a handing over of sovereignty to an uncertain supranational legal body, but rather subscribing to a political agenda of mounting importance: ensuring a free and democratic Europe. The original objective of the European Convention of 1950 was, therefore, not the development of a detailed European jurisprudence that should substantially alter national traditions of human rights, but instead the production of a document that confined the area of Free Europe; that is, the European Convention was an early form of containment politics.

Yet, for the very same reasons, the institutional development of the European system was somehow reversed and did not initially concern the carving out of a detailed jurisprudence; it rather concerned convincing the member states to accept the central optional clauses. This developed into 'a game of cat and mouse', according to Lord Lester of Herne Hill.[54] I would claim it went even further: it developed into a practice of *legal diplomacy*, in the sense that the jurisprudential developments were clearly balanced with diplomatic considerations.[55] This was above all due to the way in which the European Convention put the system in the position of having to persuade the member states of accepting its powers. Formally, for the Convention itself to be effective, ten member states had to ratify. While this was achieved by 1952 with ratification by Britain, the Federal Republic of Germany, and a series of smaller states, the real challenge—namely, to make individual petition and the court operational—remained. The clause on individual petition stipulated that six states had to accept before it was made effective with regard to the Commission. This was achieved by 1955, which meant that the procedure was made effective to the Federal Republic of Germany and a series of smaller countries. However, for the Court to start operating, eight countries had to accept; it took until 1958 for this to happen, with seven smaller states and the Federal Republic of Germany accepting its jurisdiction. What is striking is the absence of the three major European powers: France, the UK, and Italy. Conversely, this meant that both the Commission and the Court not only had to develop European

[53] Madsen (n 17).

[54] Anthony Lester, 'The European Court of Human Rights after 50 Years' in Jonas Christoffersen and Mikael R Madsen (eds), *The European Court of Human Rights between Law and Politics* (Oxford University Press 2011).

[55] See further in Madsen (n 17).

human rights but also, and as their main objectives, had to seek to convince these crucial states of the relevance and reasonableness of the Court's workings and jurisprudence, thus ensuring checks and balances of a very real nature.

This raises the question of who was appointed to take care of this rather delicate legal–diplomatic task. Formally, the Convention provided that 'The candidates shall be of high moral character and must either possess the qualifications required for appointment to high judicial office or be jurisconsults of recognised competence'.[56] Appointment was by majority vote in the Consultative Assembly of the Council of Europe, based on a list of three candidates provided by each of the member states. Based on an analysis of the candidates, both selected and not selected, it becomes apparent that the preferred socio-professional profile of the first European judges—at least among European politicians of the late 1950s—included high academic standing and exposure to international politics and law. Those favoured were not pure judges or jurists who had pursued mainly political careers, but rather jurists who could muster formal independence—thus, academics or former academics—and a sound understanding of international relations. Besides being all male and aged on average around their mid-60s, the 1959 bench comprised a highly experienced set of judges, among whom the vast majority had doctoral degrees in law but hardly any had restricted themselves to a career in academic law only. Thus, it was not a case of pure *Professorenrecht* but a continuation of a tradition in international law, dating back at least to the late nineteenth century, of perceiving international law as closely connected to international politics.[57] As part of a larger project, I have coded the social–professional backgrounds of all ECtHR judges over time; from this analysis it becomes apparent that for its first two and a half decades the Court was marked precisely by judges who not only had multiple specializations in academic law, the practice of law, and politics and policy, but in many cases had also held very high positions in many of these fields. Basically, the Court was constituted of an academic legal elite with connections to the core of law and politics in the member states.

3.1. The ECtHR in action: from legal diplomacy to progressive law

The very first jurisprudence of the Strasbourg institutions provides, in many ways, a highly illustrative case of the gradual legitimization of European human rights. The *Cyprus case*[58] before the Commission, an interstate complaint filed by Greece against the UK, imported into the system all the complexities of late colonial practices. The outcome of this case was, if anything, telling of the early Strasbourg system. As it became more and more evident during the proceedings that the UK had indeed breached the Convention, the matter was eventually solved by recourse

---

[56] ECHR Art 39(3).

[57] Cf Martti Koskenniemi, *The Gentle Civilizer of Nations: The Rise and Fall of International Law 1870–1960* (Cambridge University Press 2001).

[58] *Greece v United Kingdom* App no 176/56 (ECtHR, 14 December 1958).

to diplomacy. The case was closed with a friendly settlement—the 1959 Zurich and London agreements settlement on Cyprus—which also meant the end of the British Empire in Cyprus.[59] From the point of view of Strasbourg, however, this was a convenient solution as it thereby evaded having to pronounce violations, as well as conveying the message that it was diplomatically sound. *Lawless*, another key case,[60] was in the meantime making it to the Court as its first case. It concerned the use of detention without trial in Ireland as a response to IRA insurgency. Again, Strasbourg found a way out: according to the Court, the practice was not in compliance with Article 5 of the Convention. Yet the case did not ultimately lead to a judgment against the Irish government, as the Court interpreted Article 15 with respect to emergency situations in such a way that the Irish government was entitled to apply these measures since the 'life of the nation' was threatened. Hence, once again a conclusion was reached that calmed the member states, underlined that the ECtHR was receptive to the complexities of interior politics, and even allowed a rather large national margin of appreciation. In other words, legal diplomacy prevailed as a means for playing the double game of on the one hand affirming the Court's position as having the final say on the interpretation of the rules, while on the other finding solutions that did not alienate the member states.

The interesting finding is that legal diplomacy, as an institutionalization and legitimization strategy, generally worked.[61] It was precisely against this background of very measured legal development that, in 1966, the UK chose to accept the optional clauses on individual petition and ECtHR jurisdiction. In the following years the other key member states followed, including France and Italy, and by 1975 the Court was finally fully operational. And it did not waste much time in turning this opportunity into progressive law through a series of landmark decisions of the late 1970s which clearly signalled a shift in human rights law and discourse. In 1978, the Court came to the conclusion that the emergency interrogation measures used in Northern Ireland by the British security forces could not be justified by evoking emergency arguments (*Irish Case*);[62] soon after it pronounced that the ECHR is '[...] a living instrument... [which] must be interpreted in the light of present-day conditions... standards in the... member states' (*Tyrer Case*).[63] And to cement its position, in 1979, the Court established in the *Airey Case* that '[t]he Convention is intended to guarantee not rights that are theoretical or illusory but rights that are practical and effective'.[64]

This rather dramatic change of legal course cannot be explained as simply the fruit of the Court's legitimization in the eyes of the member states of the first decades; nor can it be explained as simply the outcome of new judges being appointed to the bench.[65] In fact, what is striking when the ECtHR judges of 1959 and 1979 are compared in terms of socio-professional profiles

---

[59] Simpson (n 49)   [60] *Lawless v Ireland* Appl no 332/57 (ECtHR 1 July 1961).
[61] Madsen (n 17).
[62] *Ireland v the United Kingdom*, App no 5310/71 (ECtHR 18 January 1978).
[63] *Tyrer v the United Kingdom*, App no 5856/72 (ECtHR 25 April 1978), para 31.
[64] *Airey v Ireland*, App no 6289/73 (ECtHR 9 October 1979), para 24.
[65] Madsen (n 16).

is resemblance, not difference. The 1979 bench contained actors with multiple qualifications and experiences, the most dominant being academia and exposure to international affairs. Overall, the picture reveals continuity. The ECtHR was still strongly male-dominated, with an average age of over 60.[66] What is striking when the data is scrutinized is that, basically, members of the same kind of international legal elite inhabited the ECtHR between 1959 and 1979. Emblematically, Pierre-Henri Teitgen, who 25 years previously was the chief drafter of the ECHR, now sat on the Court in a period marked by a series of landmark decisions. What might however explain the changing practices of a Court which is sociologically marked by continuity is that its strategic space—that is, its room to manoeuvre—was changed by broader socio-political changes during the period. This meant that legitimization strategies had to aim at a quite different set of environments, which ultimately favoured more robust human rights development.

To cut a long story short, the ECtHR generally benefited from the fact that the human rights cold war was ebbing and the major European powers had succumbed to the idea of 'Empire lost'. Due to these two closely related processes, European imperial societies were no longer the direct object of human rights activism. In western Europe, throughout the 1970s, most human rights activism was directed at non-democratic regimes outside the jurisdiction of European human rights: the Greek Colonels, Franco's Spain, and Portugal under Salazar.[67] In fact, for human rights activism in the 1970s, the real perpetrators of human rights were geographically found outside western Europe: in Latin America, South Africa, and eastern Europe. These combined circumstances also meant that by the mid-1970s, human rights once again became an interesting tool for use in the international politics of western powers.

These geopolitical changes were clearly important for the overall acceptance of the Court on the governmental level. This should, however, not overshadow that the actual jurisprudence of the ECtHR was also deeply reflective of other crucial social processes of the period. As a matter of fact, many of the key decisions concerned progressive social issues—for example, the already quoted *Tyrer* and *Airey* cases on, respectively, corporal punishment and access to divorce. In other words, the ECtHR issued some of its most important decisions by placing the question of human rights at the forefront of the evolving societal fabric of Europe; that is, dynamic interpretation was not simply teleological interpretation in respect to the *telos* of the ECHR, but in respect to European society and its evolution. While taking advantage of the geopolitical transformations of international human rights in the context of the Cold War détente to improve its overall institutional position, the ECtHR distilled its notion of 'present-day [social] conditions' to legitimize progressive European human rights law. This strategy had important ramifications

[66] To this point only one woman, the Dane Helga Petersen, had been on the Court. See also above ch 10 s 3.2.
[67] Greece withdrew from the European system between 1970 and 1975, whilst Portugal and Spain only joined the system in, respectively, 1977 and 1978 after their transitions to democracy.

in terms of legitimacy. It challenged the former hegemony of the 'principals' on the Court by changing the ways in which the Court legitimized its practices. Rather than relying on governments, the Court increasingly legitimizes its practices in social issues and sentiments beyond the control of governments. This reorientation also meant that the initial dominance of diplomacy and public international law perceptions of the Convention were contested by a new social political interest in European human rights law as a tool for reforming national democracies.[68]

This brings us once again back to the role of the actors. The general push for human rights of the late 1970s cannot alone explain why the ECtHR went this far in turning structural opportunity into legal practice. While the many mobilizations in favour of human rights at the time had an overall legitimizing effect and, importantly, created actual cases, one should not overlook the legitimization already acquired by the initial judicial restraint of the ECtHR. This is not simply to argue that legal diplomacy opened the door for progressive jurisprudence, however, but to underline that these are two sides of the same coin, albeit occurring at two different moments in the Court's development. In both cases, this particular evolution was primarily made possible by legal–political reflexivity of the small legal elite inhabiting the Court during the first 20 years or so, who implicitly understood when to hold back and when to push for European human rights. Hence, while geopolitics was in turn a limitation and then an opening, these actors managed to strike at the very moment when human rights were most in demand and most viable.

3.2. The second transformation of the ECtHR

The Court's subsequent development throughout the 1980s only confirmed the importance of this diversification of legitimacy, as the ECtHR effectively constructed itself a role as the quasi-Supreme Court of human rights in Europe. Basically, it developed from something of a Cold War political compromise into a genuine court with *de facto* supreme jurisdiction over human rights in Europe.[69] With this has also followed gradual growth in its caseload. In its first decade of operation, 1959–69, the Court delivered some ten judgments; this number climbed steadily in the three subsequent decades, and reached some 800 cases in total in the 1990s. However, the real effect of the end of the Cold War was not to be seen until after 1998, when the ECtHR transformed from a non-permanent, more traditional international court into, in the wake of Protocol no 11, a permanent international court operating out of a striking glass and steel palace on the brink of the River Ill. Just as the combined structural effects of increased European integration

---

[68] For details, see Mikael R Madsen, 'France, the United Kingdom and the "Boomerang" of the Internationalisation of Human Rights (1945–2000)', in Simon Halliday and Patrick Smith (eds), *The Domestication of Human Rights* (Hart 2004); Mikael R Madsen, 'L'Emergence d'un champ des droits de l'homme dans les pays européens: enjeux professionnels et stratégies d'Etat au carrefour du droit et de la politique (France, Grande-Bretagne et pays scandinaves, 1945–2000)' (l'École des hautes études en sciences sociales 2005).

[69] Madsen (n 49).

and détente politics provided a unique window to develop the ECtHR to a whole new level in the late 1970s, the subsequent transformation of the European map following the fall of the Berlin Wall only underlined the contingency of the Court in these broader structural transformations.

Generally, the post-Cold War geopolitical transformation of Europe had a very significant effect on the structures of the European human rights legal field in many ways similar to those addressed above: the ECtHR was suddenly forced to deal with what were eventually termed 'endemic' and 'structural and systemic problems' of human rights violations in the new member states. Moreover, it forced the whole system to adjust to the fact that it was now the highest legal authority with regard to protecting the human rights of some 800 million Europeans from 47 different countries—some of which markedly differed in their views on human rights and the rule of law. What was effectively in the making in the period beginning around 1990 was a European mega-Court of human rights—with a corresponding mega-load of cases.[70]

The new ECHR system post-1998 had, however, been on its way for some time. The original proposals for what eventually became Protocol no 11 were tabled in the mid-1980s and mainly concerned an attempt at rationalizing the system; that is, getting rid of the two-tier system of Court and Commission.[71] The idea of rationalizing the system from within was an almost emblematic reaction towards the ECHR system practically until the Brighton Declaration (2012). In fact, every single new Protocol has been an attempt to rationalize the system in order to deal with the challenges facing it—yet suggestions of somehow limiting the system or even discussing a reorientation of the system have generally had a hard time being heard at the political level.[72] Rationalization and effectiveness became instead the credo for a set of reforms which only to a limited extent actually solved the problems faced by the Court. Certainly, the caseload kept growing, at a point almost exponentially, during this period until it eventually began to drop in 2012.[73]

There is generally consensus in the literature that the single greatest challenge to the ECtHR at the moment is the massive case (over)load of the ECHR system which has accumulated over the past 10–15 years as a result of both the specific institutional set-up post-Protocol no 11 (particularly the closing down of the Commission) and the significant expansion of membership of the ECtHR.[74] The question is, however, whether broader socio-political structural change might provide another, and perhaps better, explanation of the challenges currently faced by the Court. If we address the current transformation in the light of geopolitical

---

[70] Christoffersen and Madsen (n 10).

[71] Robert Harmsen, 'The Reform of the Convention System: Institutional Restructuring and the (Geo-)Politics of Human Rights' in Jonas Christoffersen and Mikael R Madsen (eds), *The European Court of Human Rights between Law and Politics* (Oxford University Press 2011).

[72] Ibid; Robert Harmsen, 'The European Convention on Human Rights after Enlargement' (2001) 5 *The International Journal of Human Rights* 18.

[73] In June 2012 a staggering 144,150 applications were pending before a judicial formation: this is actually a reduction of some 5 per cent since the beginning of 2012.

[74] For example Steven Greer and Luzius Wildhaber, 'Revisiting the Debate about 'Constitutionalising' the European Court of Human Rights' (2012) 12 *Human Rights Law Review* 655.

change, it becomes more apparent why—at least until the Brighton Declaration (2012)—it was practically impossible to seriously reform the ECtHR. The west's relative victory in the Cold War for many translated into an almost blind belief in human rights and rule of law as the best measures for furthering and spreading democracy. With the eastern bloc soon joining the (western) European human rights flagship—the ECHR system—many saw allowing the Court to get somewhat swamped in cases as a necessary price to pay for solving eastern Europe's problems. In other words, the doxa of the post-Cold War for at least a decade and a half dictated more human rights rather than less—even the EU felt compelled to create its own human rights charter and proper constitutional structures.[75] And there was a belief across the foreign services of most western European states that this was the right way to go. Thereby the 'Washington Consensus' became the Brussels/Strasbourg consensus.

It is in fact only very recently—post-Brighton—that rationalization has come to imply possible limitations in access, greater subsidiarity, and a generally more restrained role for the Court. More specifically, there has been growing frustration with the ECtHR in Russia in particular since around 2005, but it is only very recently that an actual majority of member states, including western European states and notably the UK, have turned to more radical measures of reform. At the structural level, this is above all illustrative of an initial disintegration of the post-Cold War consensus on human rights. It is an uncertain development which is only starting to unfold, but it relates to a much larger geopolitical restructuring in which western universals are declining and new forms of economic realism are gaining foothold, thus trumping democratic liberalism. I will not attempt to analyse these correlations here but will simply make the argument that, just as geopolitical changes previously changed the playing field of the ECtHR, they are likely to do so again. More precisely, what we are observing is a reorientation of some of the key constituencies: the UK increasingly favouring extra-European interests; Russia reclaiming a kind of exceptionalism with regard to Europe in combination with attempts at regaining international power. My claim is that, just as in previous periods, all this is impacting the ECtHR's strategic space and therefore also its legitimization strategies.

The real paradox is, however, that this has occurred precisely at the moment in which the ECtHR have stepped out of relative international obscurity to be integrated at the heart of the legal (and political) systems of European states, a process furthered by the Convention's implementation into national law since the early 1990s. Basically, at the very moment at which the ECtHR seem to have accomplished most of its legal objectives and become truly embedded in European law and society,[76] it is facing a significant political crisis, as witnessed during the

---

[75] Ian Manners, 'Normative Power Europe: A Contradiction in Terms?' (2002) 40 *Journal of Common Market Studies* 23; Mikael R Madsen, 'The Power of Legal Knowledge in the Reform of Fundamental Law: The Case of the European Charter of Fundamental Rights' in Antoine Vauchez and Bruno de Witte (eds), *The European Legal Field* (Hart Publishing 2013).

[76] Laurence R Helfer, 'Redesigning the European Court of Human Rights: Embeddedness as a Deep Structural Principle of the European Human Rights Regime' (2008) 9 *European Journal of International Law* 125.

Brighton proceedings.[77] Without attempting to predict the future, it is clear that a certain rebalancing is currently in process.[78] While the immediate functionalist answer to the problem would inevitably be a call for renewed 'legal diplomacy', this seems in practice not to be such an obvious turn if we look more closely at the current Strasbourg bench. More precisely, even if legal diplomacy could perhaps solve some of the immediate problems faced by the Court, it is questionable whether the necessary staff are available to engage in such a practice and legitimization strategy.

4. Conclusion: Implications for Judicial Selection to the ECtHR

I have generally argued that the balancing of the ECtHR with its environments is key for its legitimacy, as this is the main way in which it can justify its practices. I have moreover related this to the actual intellectual and professional capabilities of the Court. Consequently, a key question with regard to the current situation of the ECtHR and its ability to respond to the on-going transformations is the configuration of the existing bench. In this regard the Court has changed very significantly. The current profile of the Strasbourg bench is fundamentally different from the original cast of judges, which largely consisted of high-profile jurists with contacts in multiple legal and political milieux, as detailed above; that is, the current bench does simply not have the social and political capital that enabled the original incarnation of the Court to move fairly easily between law and politics and, by doing so, legitimize the institution. Second, the current institutional set-up does not allow for more intermediate legal solutions. The closing down of the Commission effectively caused a loss of balance in the entire system with regard to the more diplomatic role of the Court[79] which remains unsolved. Basically, the combined effects of a more judicialized ECtHR in terms of both institutional set-up and agency (as I will detail right below) do not easily allow for a return to a more reflexive and adaptive approach. This is probably the single greatest problem for the ECtHR right now in light of the large caseload, the changing socio-political configurations in which it acts, and the general critique of it raised by a number of constituencies (mainly governments and agents of the legal systems of the member states).

With regard to the contemporary selection of judges, the schism basically relates to the fact that recruitment patterns in recent years have favoured judges with mainly legal capital at the expense of other relevant capital, notably exposure to

---

[77] Spyridon Flogaitis, Tom Zwart, and Julie Fraser (eds), *The European Court Of Human Rights And Its Discontents: Turning Criticism into Strength* (Edward Elgar 2013).
[78] Christoffersen and Madsen (n 10); Laurence Helfer, 'The Burdens and Benefits of Brighton' 1 *ESIL Reflections* (online at http://esil-sedi.eu/node/138); Greer and Wildhaber (n 73).
[79] Lester (n 53).

the politics of international law. If we look at the sociological configuration of the current ECtHR, the first main difference between it and the former Court consisting of a well-connected legal–academic elite is that it lacks access to constituencies outside law. This process was influenced by the arrival of increasing numbers of eastern European judges coming from environments where 'political capital' often meant the *wrong kind* of political capital. This is closely linked, generally speaking, to a general disqualification of the older elites of the legal field in many of these countries. In practice, this implied that younger candidates were favoured, as they did not carry the potentially toxic baggage of their older colleagues who had navigated the Communist state and, often, made some compromises along the way. More generally, the average age of the members of the bench is now around 51–2 years (compared to mid-60s in the 1959 Court)[80], including a number of judges— mainly, but not exclusively, from eastern Europe—in their 30s. Their younger age, inevitably, implies shorter careers prior to appointment and thereby, naturally, less time for connecting to multiple constituencies. As described by David Kosař in this volume, this appointment pattern of young Eastern European judges has caused an abundance of critique mainly with regard to their—assumed—lack of experience.[81] However, by 'experience', most authors mean legal experience with human rights and experience with judging.

This, however, misses the real picture. The real empirical situation of the Court is that, although the current bench is younger and cannot boast the illustrious careers enjoyed by some of the judges in its earlier incarnations (for example Cassin, Rolin, Teitgen, etc), it is probably almost entirely wrong to accuse them of lacking legal expertise in human rights. As a matter of fact, in most cases the grandees of the earlier court had close to no experience of international human rights—partly because the subject did not yet exist as a specialized legal field, partly because the member states preferred such candidates. Some countries even consciously sought to appoint judges with no expertise in human rights with the goal of avoiding the court becoming a militant human rights court.[82] The current selection practices are, I would argue, instead negatively influenced by two broader and interconnected processes:

(1) the judicialization of the Court post-Protocol no 11;

(2) the specialization of European human rights law.

As to the former, judicialization, it seems generally positive that the Court is developing strictly court-like features, notably independence, in a moment of great transformation and uncertainty. Yet the downside to this, as already noted, is the limitation of its strategic room for manoeuvre. As to the latter, the specialization

---

[80] As a matter of fact, a number of the selected judges in 1958–9 would not have been eligible for the current Court, as they were simply too old (over 64) at the time of appointment. Further on the age limit see above ch 6 s 4.3.

[81] See above ch 6 s 4.3. and s 5.

[82] Mikael R Madsen, *La genèse de l'Europe des droits de l'homme: Enjeux juridiques et stratégies d'Etat (France, Grande-Bretagne et pays scandinaves, 1945-1970)* (Presses universitaires de Strasbourg 2010).

of European human rights through systematization and doctrine development at numerous law schools, specialized research centres, and law offices has in itself transformed human rights from a highly uncertain and, for many, mainly political enterprise into a more professional legal practice, one that can be taught and learned and documented on CVs. The negative consequence of this is that the field is much less interesting to leading lawyers and, ultimately more importantly, it has produced the illusion that human rights can somehow be tamed in terms of law; that is, the socio-political complexity has been reduced by the legal field following the logic prescribed by Luhmannian sociology of law.[83]

Both these processes are evocative of what Max Weber would have described as a process of routinization.[84] Paradoxically, these two processes generally result in the ECtHR increasing its legal capabilities (when compared to the earlier Court). Basically, it is coming of age as a 'real' court based on legal rationalization and not legal diplomacy. Many would, of course, argue that this is generally a good thing; such an analysis however overlooks that it is an international court we are dealing with, and it is as such situated differently with regard to the other branches of government: the 'checks' are mainly informal—'Strasbourg-bashing' in the media for instance—but most often have to be assumed by the judges, and that requires the ability to reflect upon them in the legal practice. Success as an international court very often requires a dose of diplomacy, and that is somehow lost in Strasbourg now. That being said, the solution obviously cannot be a return to a different era. Yet the Court, and those appointed its judges, will have to take far more seriously that an international court like the ECtHR cannot simply treat the inherently politicized nature of human rights with a judicial-bureaucratic solution. The current procedures for attracting new judges do not seem to strike a good balance between specialized law and an appreciation of the inherently political nature of human rights. What is needed is an institutional overhaul that takes seriously the fact that the caseload of the ECHR system is not in sync with the solutions offered. The pilot procedure is an example of the Court seeking to go beyond mere judging and to take part in policy-making, but it also reveals the obvious limitations of the current Court in finally following through. Ultimately, the selection of judges can only be improved if it is accepted that the Court is in practice undertaking a multitude of tasks, from repeat cases that perhaps would be better dealt with by a specialized institution/commission on, for instance, prison conditions, to supreme court-like judging in the grand chamber. The basic problem is that the right candidates for these two tasks are rarely the same. Right now, the selection process produces a Court that is not fit for either of these tasks.

---

[83] Niklas Luhmann, *Grundrechte als Institution: ein Beitrag zur politischen Soziologie* (Duncker & Humblot 1974) and Luhmann (n 29).

[84] Weber (n 24).

Epilogue

Searching for the European Hercules

Michal Bobek

1. Hercules. Or Hermes? Or was it Pallas Athena?

Who is a good European judge?[1] It is fascinating to realize that after years of operation of several European selection panels and an entire volume dedicated to the study of the same phenomenon, we are not much closer to a comprehensive definition of the European judicial virtues.[2] We are given some basic, minimalist contours of the person we are looking for: she must be independent, speak foreign languages (preferably some French), and possess a decent knowledge of EU law or the law of the European Convention. However, with regard to the definition of her personality, nature, or character, arguably far more important characteristics of a good judge than technical knowledge of the law in a foreign language, we remain in the dark. Is it indeed (Euro)Hercules we are looking for? Or should it rather be Jupiter? Or a bit of a Hermes?[3] Or, as far as gods have a gender, a Pallas Athena? Is it not odd to have lengthy discussions about *how* to select Europe's judges without setting out first *who* we are supposed to find? To passionately argue about how to get best to an unknown destination?

Even if perhaps odd at first sight, the absence of a positive definition of criteria relating to the desired personality or character of European judges is not that surprising for two reasons. First, the recent changes in the ways Europe's judges are to be selected have been *procedure-driven* (ie 'this is the process nominations ought to follow in the future'), not *substance-driven* (ie 'these are the types of candidates we ought to be looking for, these are the personal qualities they must have'). Elaborate procedures have been put in place without it being clearly stated what exactly they

---

[1] I am indebted to Henri de Waele, Pavlína Hubková, and David Kosař for their critical comments on the draft of this chapter, as well as to Mitchel de S-O-L'E Lasser for stimulating discussions on the issues raised therein. The usual disclaimer, however, fully applies.

[2] For the exception confirming the rule, see above ch 4 s 3.

[3] See, for further elaboration of Dworkin's figure of the judge Hercules, F Ost, 'Jupiter, Hercule, Hermès: Trois modèles du juge' in F Ost, *Dire le droit, faire justice* (Bruylant 2007) 33–60.

are supposed to lead to, what the desired final 'product' is. The gradual substantive changes that are likely to come with the changes in the process are a sort of procedural by-product, procedure spilling over into substance.

Second, providing any comprehensive list of European judicial virtues never was and perhaps never should have been the aim of the recent reforms. The mandate was only to provide a common European echelon of minimal, functional requirements, within which the member states are free to realize their preferences. This is, in a way, an example of the traditional European 'minimal harmonization', with all its (dis)advantages. Additionally, a degree of internal diversity in terms of backgrounds, experience, even personalities is always healthy for a high court. Even more so for a European court, in which different national ideas about who is a good judge meet. Thus, what we have is in fact an approximately known (or approximately unknown) destination. We have an idea of a region we want to arrive at, and a whole list of regions where we certainly do not want to land, but little notion of the specific places we want to visit.

There is no doubt that soon, elaborate theories will start being formulated concerning the new selection procedures for the European courts, suggesting new modes of governance, the rise of the European 'juristocracy', the empowerment of this agent and the disempowerment of that principle, and so on. In the first four years of the operation of these new mechanisms, the reality has been perhaps more modest and sober. The new bodies have been just finding their place, the new procedures being tested and calibrated, with a new institutional balance being sought. It would thus be premature to outline grand theories or designs at this stage, also in view of the yet unclear trajectory of the entire process.

This Epilogue will therefore limit itself to rather pragmatic and functional observations concerning a selection of themes that recurred throughout a number of chapters in this volume. First, section 2 will carry out a comparative assessment of the overall performance of the judicial expert panels in the EU and the ECHR. It will discuss why, after the first few years of its operation, the 255 Panel became widely regarded as a success story in terms of guaranteeing a greater quality of Union courts' appointees, whereas the Committee of Ministers' Advisory Panel was less so. Section 3 will critically revisit the selection criteria coined by the 255 Panel, in particular with regard to how far they can be said to follow the Treaties. In section 4, a theme that is problematic in both European systems and has been tackled throughout the volume will be revisited: the lack of transparency and control of the operation and output of the expert panels and, by implication, the overall European judicial selection process. Sections 5 and 6 deal with the more sociological questions: what type of European judges are the new criteria and procedures likely to generate? It will be suggested that so far, no deeper imprint of the professional background of the selectors may be detected on the type of selectees chosen. Rather to the contrary: open competitions with demanding requirements that are genuinely being tested are likely to attract different kinds of candidates from those perhaps originally wished for. Section 7 concludes with reflection as to whether or not having a working language of a court which is no longer so widely spoken might not in itself operate as an obstacle in attracting top judicial candidates.

2. The 255 Panel and the Advisory Panel: A Comparison

Most of the discussions in this volume—as well as, in fact, in the following sections of this Epilogue—focus chiefly on the operation and impact of the 255 Panel within the EU. Such focus was not entirely intentional. It emerges nonetheless rather naturally when exploring the (visible) innovations in the selection of Europe's judges. Generally, the 255 Panel is seen as the success story, whereas the Committee of Ministers' Advisory Panel is perceived as lagging behind.

Before plunging into discussion of key differences between the two systems that might account for the varying degree of success of each of them, a preliminary issue of comparability arises. A number of chapters in this volume have carried out comparisons, implicitly or explicitly, between the two international systems. The comparisons of the two regimes emerged spontaneously, often in subtext, assuming that both are international organizations, both have supranational courts, and in both organizations questions of the quality of judicial appointments recently arose, together with a desire to carry out some reforms in this regard.

When looking more specifically, however, at the 255 Panel and the Advisory Panel, it can be claimed that these two are institutionally different creatures. They both operate in distinct institutional environments. Jumping then to the conclusion that the Advisory Panel is a 'failure' since it has not been able to deliver the same results as the 255 Panel is unfair and incorrect. The Advisory Panel has never been given the same standing, tools, and powers to start with. Put metaphorically, it would be like castigating a 7-year-old boy for not being able to jump as high as his 16-year-old brother.

This is a valid objection, but only to a certain extent. It relates to the choice of a comparator. A sound comparison can be made if carried out on the level of stated aims and goals that are the same in both systems. The point of comparison (or *tertium comparationis*) is not the mere institutional (dis)similarity, but the (in)efficiency in achieving largely the same goals both systems set for themselves. This then becomes a comparative assessment of two different institutional designs, which have both introduced institutional changes at roughly the same time with a similar goal: to strengthen the quality and professionalism of their judges, and thus to enhance the authority and legitimacy of their respective courts. What is therefore being evaluated is not how each of the panels resemble each other, but how far they are able to realize the third, independent value within their respective institutional settings. In other words, even if one system is established under the clear influence and inspiration of another,[4] its quality shall not be comparatively evaluated by how far and how faithfully it resembles the original 'donor', but by whether and how far it is able to achieve the aims in the name of which it has been put in place and perhaps adapted within the 'recipient'.[5] Thus, the yardstick for

---

[4] As was the Advisory Panel under the apparent lead of the then newly born 255 Panel. See above ch 5 s 3.2 and ch 10 s 3.1.

[5] Further M Bobek, *Comparative Reasoning in European Supreme Courts* (Oxford University Press 2013) 245–8.

comparing the 255 Panel and the Advisory Panel is not how far the Advisory Panel resembles the 255 Panel, but to what extent each of the panels is able to realize the goal in the name of which they have been introduced within their respective environments.

2.1. C(z)ecking the limits

When looking at the position of the respective expert panels within their organizations, it is clear that the 255 Panel has brought about a new institutional balance within the EU. In a nutshell, the 255 Panel is now running the show, certainly on the European level. Irrespective of what the formal value of the 255 Panel's opinions is supposed to be, the Panel has gained an effective power of veto over national nominations. As has already been identified above in a number of chapters,[6] the hidden beauty of institutional design lies in the 'common accord' that Art 253 TFEU (or 254 TFEU for the General Court) requires. If an appointment can be made only by unanimity among all the member states' governments, this *de facto* applies also to overturning a negative opinion of the 255 Panel.

To overturn the negative opinion of the 255 Panel appears extremely unlikely, essentially for two reasons. First, potential reversal of the 255 Panel's opinion in one case would open the door for the mutual challenging of other candidates in other future cases. As this was not something governments of the member states were keen to engage in in the past, when they were themselves running the show, it is even less likely to occur once it would entail going against the expert opinion of their own panel at the same time—unless, of course, there was an instance of the 255 Panel issuing an egregious opinion that could simply not be accepted by the member states. However, such a singular case might not be perceived by the member states as re-opening the Pandora's box of starting to assess themselves the qualities of a candidate, but rather as the necessity of showing the 255 Panel its proper place. Second, however, even if there was, following a singular case, at least some willingness among some member states to overturn the negative opinion of the 255 Panel and appoint a candidate notwithstanding the Panel's veto, one or two single 'dissenters' among the member states are enough to block the appointment. In such a case, it could be expected that strategic alliances between key members of the 255 Panel and their national governments might be formed.

In sum, the 255 Panel filled up the empty merit-related decision-making space on the European level, and made the best use of it. Conversely, as has also been shown above,[7] the position of the Advisory Panel within the Council of Europe has been developing in a much more questionable way. True, shrouded in the mists of complete confidentiality, nobody is able to tell what the Advisory Panel is genuinely doing, how many candidatures it has evaluated, and how. It nonetheless appears that its opinions have been either disregarded or not even requested by the individual contracting parties, not to speak of the Parliamentary Assembly

---

[6] Above ch 1 s 5 or ch 3 s 3.   [7] Above ch 5 s 3.3.

(PACE). This has even led to its president's open expression of frustration voiced in the Committee of Ministers.[8]

An example might be given in order to illustrate this perceived contrast. The Czech Republic has recently gained the reputation of an institutional 'beta-tester' who does not hesitate to check the limits of the system of judicial nominations to the European courts. What might have caused nightmares for the officials and diplomats involved may be greeted with pure scholarly joy by the institutional and constitutional European lawyers. In an almost laboratory-style parallel experiment, the Czech Republic has recently made questionable nominations to both European courts, thus putting both systems to the test simultaneously.

In 2012, with the Czech judge at the European Court of Human Rights (ECtHR) retiring, the Czech Republic submitted a list of three candidates. One of the candidates on the list was apparently declared unsuitable by the Advisory Panel and later not recommended by the PACE Sub-Committee. He was nonetheless eventually elected by the PACE.[9] Conversely, in case of another questionable Czech candidate, who was nominated to the GC in 2013, the 225 Panel issued a negative opinion. The candidate was in fact a member of the Czech government at that time. He was nominated by the government in disregard of a recommendation made by the national selection panel that was, according to the selection rules, binding on the government. In spite of the unfavourable opinion issued by the 255 Panel, the Czech government wished to maintain and submit his nomination to the governments of the member states anyway, perhaps hoping for a similar 'override' to that achieved with respect to the ECtHR nomination the year before. Rumour has it that the governments' representatives did not discuss the issue fully when it came before them for the first time in the summer of 2013. Soon afterwards, the Czech government maintaining the proposal was toppled and the succeeding 'caretaker' administration withdrew the nomination in favour of the already sitting Czech judge, who was in fact the original nominee selected on the national level by the selection panel, before the government intervened.

2.2. The differences: institutional design, communication, allocation of responsibility

The narrative emerging from the Czech example is that the EU system and in particular the 255 Panel have been successful in maintaining the standards and the professional reputation of the Court of Justice of the European Union's (CJEU) judges, whereas the Council of Europe system failed with respect to the ECtHR.[10] When looking more closely at the differences between the two bodies and their institutional embedment, there are three sets of issues that might account for this.

First, it is apparent that on the institutional plane, the Advisory Panel was born as a 'weak baby' in the shadow of a bigger sibling. Already on the symbolic plane, in contrast to the 255 Panel, the Advisory Panel does not feature in the European

---

[8] Ibid. See also ch 6 s 5.　　　[9] For details above ch 6 s 5.　　　[10] Ibid.

Convention. It has no 'primary' law status. More practically, however, within the Council of Europe system, the Parliamentary Assembly and its Sub-Committee is the older sibling that has always been keen to assert its key role in the selection of judges to the ECtHR. Thus, when the Committee of Ministers came up with the idea of an expert panel, the wings of that panel were clipped before it could fly: no hearings of candidates; no public reporting of the results, only a sort of semi-secret reporting, and this to just the one contracting party that made the nominations in question, not even to other contracting parties; and something of a wall between the Advisory Panel and the PACE.[11] What emerges is a weak institutional actor that has understandable difficulties in finding any reasonable space for its already narrow mandate. In sum, the institutional house of the Council of Europe is already a bit too full for a newcomer.

Second, the 'communication and marketing skills' of the Advisory Panel could be improved. Naturally, the operating rules have sworn the members of the Advisory Panel to confidentiality.[12] However, there is still quite some leeway for a confidential body to communicate and, on the whole, present its purpose, operation, and activities while remaining within the bounds of its mandate and operating rules. The proactive and communicative approach of the 255 Panel and its members might indeed be an example in this regard. Confidentiality with respect to individual decisions and its reasons does not necessarily mean overall secrecy as to its aims and work, as the regular activity reports of the 255 Panel show. For example, reporting only to the contracting party concerned about the candidates it proposed does not preclude calling in an exceptional meeting with representatives of all contracting parties when one contracting party is not respecting the opinion of the Panel, pursuant to Rule (ix) of the Operating Rules. Equally, a weak institutional player failing to find much authority and support internally might perhaps logically search for external support and alliances. It could proactively engage with the professional and academic community, talking and discussing its work in general terms with interested public and professionals.

Instead, the Advisory Panel has shrouded itself in secrecy, recently joined by confidential frustration.[13] It is therefore hardly surprising that the European academic community voices limited enthusiasm for the secret work of a secret panel.[14] However, it is fair to admit that every body works within certain organizational and institutional settings. Those prevailing within the Council of Europe generally appear to be permeated by a spirit of exacerbated confidentiality, which may eventually undermine all the goodwill present. This apparently does not render

---

[11] In greater detail see above ch 5 s 3.2 and ch 6 s 5. See also NP Engel, 'More Transparency and Governmental Loyalty for Maintaining Professional Quality in the Election of Judges to the European Court of Human Rights' (2008) 32 *Human Rights Law Journal* 448, 449.

[12] In detail above ch 9 s 2.   [13] Further above ch 5 s 3.3.

[14] With a notable exception in the form of the contribution by NP Engel (n 11), originally published in German in the *EuGRZ* 2012 at p 486. This contribution presents, however, a different kind of puzzle: if a great deal of information discussed in that article is confidential and cannot be normally disclosed, from where can one privileged academic author obtain it? With tongue in cheek, if there is anything that the academic community likes even less than secrecy, it is *selective* secrecy.

internal institutional communication easier, perhaps also partly due to the fact that the Advisory Panel might be perceived by other Council of Europe institutions as being more inclined to follow the lead of the 255 Panel than the Council of Europe's political institutions.[15]

The question marks over confidentiality apply, however, not only to the Committee of Ministers and its Advisory Panel, but also to the PACE and its Sub-Committee. For instance, a critical observer may harbour some doubts about the quality and openness of the democratic process in the PACE if a member of the Assembly wishing to discuss in the plenary a report by the PACE's Sub-Committee that all the members of PACE have received is silenced on the basis of confidentiality. No debate is allowed to take place, and then the apparently unsuitable candidate is elected.[16] This is odd, to say the least. How can something be kept confidential from those who received it? Why would it be that a report of the PACE's own Sub-Committee might not be discussed or commented upon in full assembly? Provided that there were public present on the gallery or in the room of the Assembly, they could be asked to leave the room on grounds of confidentiality, but this is hardly a reason for silencing the democratic debate on a key issue that is to be decided upon by the Assembly.

Partially connected to the previously discussed first point is the third one, which might be considered the most important for the institutional design of the selection procedure to the ECtHR: it is the overall problem of diluted, unclear responsibility. Within the Council of Europe, a significant number of actors are involved: the PACE with its Sub-Committee, the Committee of Ministers with its Advisory Panel. To this European level is added the national one, typically with more actors involved as well: the national selection committee; the national parliament; the national government. Within such settings—coupled with the fact of the three candidates being nominated at national level but the election itself taking place on the European level—*collective responsibility* may quickly turn into *collective irresponsibility*. As in the saying about too many cooks, eventually no one may feel directly responsible for the broth prepared. The national level blames the European level for electing the weakest possible candidate of the three presented; the European level replies that if the candidate was weak, why was s/he proposed at all? All of the actors are then likely to turn against the expert panel which was to blame for not weeding out the unfit candidate.

Perhaps the right recipe here should not enhance the complexity in terms of procedures, bodies, and conditions, but simplify it. Clear responsibility ought to be allocated for the final outcome horizontally (within the Council of Europe institutions) as well as vertically (between the Council of Europe and the contracting parties). A contrast with the EU procedure is illuminating in this regard: the

---

[15] By embracing the conditions set out in the 255 Panel reports and perhaps slightly neglecting the Council of Europe's own criteria and requirements. Further above ch 6 s 4, as well as ch 5 s 3.2 and ch 10 s 3.1.

[16] Above ch 6 s 5, mentioning the incident in the plenary when Lord Tomlinson wanted to quote from the Sub-Committee's recommendation regarding the qualification of the Czech candidate.

responsibility rests clearly with the member states that are obliged to produce one single (and hopefully the best) candidate. The EU level, represented formally by the governments of the member states but in reality by the 255 Panel, is just a negative veto player. It can block, but it cannot choose. Thus, in the end, it is only these two actors, one for each of the levels, that share the credit or blame for a particular appointment.

In contrast to the three problematic spots identified, there is one that tends to be invoked sometimes as the reason for questionable ECtHR appointments, but which has advisedly not been included here: the election of judges *per se*.[17] It could be argued that a system in which judges are elected by politicians (members of parliament) following the political preferences of the latter will always be flawed, by definition. Such an argument is based, however, on a rather exclusionary vision of technocratic judicial legitimacy, in which 'expertise' shall be the only criterion for selection and appointment. At the same time, it also strikingly idealizes the 'expert' comitology type of decision-making, which is believed to be devoid of such flaws.[18] There may, however, also be compromise solutions. A political election can, for example, take place within a pool of equally qualified candidates.[19] Such effort for compromise between the two types of legitimacy perhaps lay originally at the root of the idea of the PACE selecting from a list of three candidates submitted by a contracting party. Since this model, although generating 'mishaps' in some cases, functions well in others, it cannot be discarded as being by definition 'dysfunctional'.

In sum, there are considerable differences between the two systems examined, the EU and the Council of Europe. They explain why, even if two actors declare that they wish to do the same, they may eventually end up not doing the same. On the whole, it is intriguing to see that the choice of both international organizations in terms of how to select their judges appears to be out of sync with their prevailing self-presentation and the political narrative. On the one hand there is the European Union, which has been claiming, certainly since the Treaty of Maastricht, that it is something more than just an international organization.[20] It is to be the Union of peoples, aspiring towards some sort of statehood, and wishing correspondingly to build up its democratic legitimacy, participation, transparency. Yet with and within all these statements and narratives, the model chosen for selecting or rather confirming judges for the European courts remains the good old 'comitology', reminiscent of a classic international organization. On the other hand, there is the Council of Europe which, in spite of being an advanced political international organization, has not been aspiring to similar democracy-driven statehood claims. Yet internally, it appears to be doing more in terms of seeking democratic

---

[17] Notably above ch 3 s 3.   [18] Further on this below, s 7 of this Epilogue.
[19] Further above, Prologue s 3.2 and ch 11 s 3.
[20] The factual big question whether it indeed is can be left open at this stage. The focus here is on the prevailing narrative. Critically see eg B de Witte 'The European Union as an International Legal Experiment' in JHH Weiler and G de Búrca (eds), *The Worlds of European Constitutionalism* (Cambridge University Press 2012).

legitimacy for its judges.[21] Thus, in both organizations, the internally chosen way of selecting judges does not entirely correspond with the prevailing narrative and self-presentation of the organization.

2.3. The future: crystallizing conventions or oblivion?

Finally, having outlined the key differences in the design and operation of the two panels, where do the institutional dynamics appear to lead each of the panels? With regard to selections to the CJEU, unless the 255 Panel commits a egregious mistake, its future looks bright. If not challenged by the member states in the near future, the so far positional strength derived from the fact that, with 28 states, nobody is able to drum up unanimity in order to 'overrule' the opinion of the Panel, might soon crystallize into a convention that 'the 255 Panel is to be followed'. The case able to derail this development would indeed have to be a single, strong incident. It would have to upset the majority of the member states. Conversely, repetitive 'smaller' incidents, by which the 255 Panel upsets primarily just one given member state whose candidate was vetoed, do not pose such a threat. Quite to the contrary: provided that more and more member states see their candidates rejected for reasons that can be adequately explained, they all buy into the system by the logic of *schadenfroh* equality—'since I had to suffer the slight of my candidate being rejected and had to come up with a new one, so you shall too'.

On the other hand, there is no doubt that within the EU, member states remain in charge of the composition of the 255 Panel. Although the appointment of its members follows the proposal made by the president of the CJEU, it is conceivable that the member states could make their preferences known to the CJEU president, ultimately by rejecting the list of names proposed, and forcing the president to come up with different candidates. It remains to be seen whether a second convention might eventually crystallize with regard to the composition of the 255 Panel, namely that its majority is formed by high-ranking senior judges from the member states. So far, in appointing the second 255 Panel, the member states have shown satisfaction in this regard. If eventually both these conventions are fortified, entailing that the opinion of the 255 Panel composed predominantly of senior national judges is considered binding on the member states, then one can indeed talk of 'a germ of a council of judiciary within the Union'[22]—and quite a powerful one, in fact.

The future of the Committee of Ministers' Advisory Panel looks less clear. With the Committee of Ministers apparently not ready to police and enforce the opinions of its own advisory body vis-à-vis its members, and with the PACE jealously guarding its prerogatives and territory, thus preventing much 'external' growth, the Advisory Panel finds itself in a precarious position. Moreover, it would appear

---

[21] Again, with what real success is a question which can be left open here. See the debate above, in particular in ch 7 s 3 and ch 11 s 3.2.

[22] As suggested by President Sauvé above ch 3 s 3.

that most recently, the PACE has sought to re-assert its leading role in screening candidates for the ECtHR by upgrading its Sub-Committee on the Election
of Judges to the European Court of Human Rights into a permanent and full
committee.[23]

The latter fact does not in any way directly impinge upon the operation of
the Advisory Panel. It could be interpreted as the PACE being independently
concerned with the quality of the judicial candidates and, as the report accompanying the resolution states, having the desire to 'strengthen the Assembly's
decision-making process in this area, give it greater importance and improve the
Assembly's political visibility'.[24] However, a less charitable interpretation of the
same step might focus more on the last turn of phrase in the statement quoted.
The resolution is more of a signal seeking to re-assert who is in charge horizontally
within the Council of Europe in terms of judicial selections. Since, apart from the
increased number of members, the new permanent committee has not gained any
more powers than its predecessor in the form of a sub-committee, the desire for
improvement of the PACE's 'political visibility' might indeed be the genuine driving force in this regard.

In sum, the search for a new balance between the democratic and the technocratic within the Council of Europe's judicial selections following the insertion
of the new Advisory Panel might eventually be resolved by a re-affirmation of the
political element. On the whole, however, this victory might be quite short-lived,
unless serious attention starts being given also to the professional quality of the
candidates by the political bodies in charge.

3. The 'More Precisely Explained' Criteria

The criteria coined by the 255 Panel and establishing the minimal, functional
requirements that a candidate for European judicial office should fulfil are,[25]
in a way, a true success story in terms of their dissemination. Originally elaborated by the Civil Service Tribunal (CST) Selection Committee, they were later
taken over by the 255 Panel.[26] From there, they made their way horizontally to

---

[23] See 'Evaluation of the implementation of the reform of the Parliamentary Assembly', Resolution
2002 (2014), and in particular 'Appendix—Terms of reference of the Committee on the Election of
Judges to the European Court of Human Rights', together with the accompanying Report 'Evaluation
of the implementation of the reform of the Parliamentary Assembly' of 6 June 2014, Doc 13528,
points 89–91.

[24] 'Evaluation of the implementation of the reform of the Parliamentary Assembly', ibid, point 89.

[25] These are: 1) candidate's legal expertise, demonstrating a real capacity for analysis and reflection
upon the conditions and mechanisms of the application of EU law; 2) adequate professional experience at the appropriate level of at least 20 years for appointment to the Court of Justice, and at least
12–15 years for appointment to the General Court; 3) possessing the general ability to perform the
duties of a judge; 4) guarantees of independence and impartiality; 5) knowledge of languages; 6) aptitude for working as part of a team in an international environment in which several legal systems are
represented. In detail above ch 1, s 4.1.

[26] Above ch 4 s 1.

Strasbourg—perhaps to the slight embarrassment of the Council of Europe's institutions, which previously devised their own criteria—but saw the Advisory Panel choosing to rely more on the wisdom of its EU counterpart than on the guidance of the Council of Europe's own institutions.[27] Finally, by the joint force of both systems, the criteria spilled over onto at least some national levels. There they function as *de facto* additional criteria to the national ones, since member states realized, in particular in relation to EU selections, that candidates not meeting these criteria are likely to be rejected.

3.1. Progress by stealth?

Taking into account how the criteria were created, the official position put forward in the reports of the 255 Panel[28] and also endorsed in the writings of the esteemed president of the Panel,[29] namely that the 255 Panel did nothing else but 'more clearly and precisely explain' the *exhaustive* conditions of Art 253 TFEU (or Art 254 TFEU with respect to the GC), is not entirely convincing. This is not to say that the criteria are illogical or outrageous; the suggestion is a different one. Hiding the fact that the 255 Panel created new criteria that are not contained in the Treaties (or took over the criteria created by the CST Committee) behind the narrative of an obvious 'immaculate materialization' of the six requirements from the Treaties themselves rather highlights the (perceived or real) lack of authority the 255 Panel had for doing so. In a way, it is like a magician who needs to prepare for a new trick that is to be carried out with his left hand, but instead of remaining silent about it and performing a diversion trick with his legs in the meantime, the magician keeps loudly repeating to the audience: 'do not look at my left hand, there is nothing to be seen.' Naturally, this will only fix the gaze of everybody in the room on the left hand.

To provide perhaps the most obvious example in this regard: the 255 Panel stated that for candidates for the office of judge or advocate general of the Court of Justice, 'less than twenty years' experience of high-level duties' would be unlikely to be deemed sufficient in terms of the required professional experience.[30] In Art 253 TFEU, however, the only Treaty-based requirement that could relate to the length of practice of a judicial candidate to the Court of Justice[31] is a cross-reference back to national law which states that in order to be eligible for appointment to

---

[27] Above n 14.

[28] First report of 17 February 2011 (No 6509/11); Second report of 22 January 2013 (No 5091/13); Third report of 13 December 2013 (No SN 1118/2014). All three reports are accessible online at <http://curia.europa.eu>.

[29] '*Ces critères* [those of Art 253 and 254 TFEU—author's note] *sont exhaustifs, mais le comité a néanmoins estimé nécessaire, afin d'exercer pleinement sa mission, **de les expliciter et de les préciser** au travers de six éléments qu'il apprécie lors de l'examen de chaque candidature.*' In J-M Sauvé, 'Le rôle du comité 255 dans le sélection du juge de l'Union', in A Rosas, E Levits, and Y Bot (eds), *The Court of Justice and the Construction of Europe: Analyses and Perspectives on Sixty Years of Case-law—La Cour de Justice et la Construction de l'Europe: Analyses et Perspectives de Soixante Ans de Jurisprudence* (Asser Press/Springer 2013) 111 (highlighting added by the author).

[30] Third Activity Report (n 28) 18.

[31] Leaving aside the somewhat amorphous category of 'jurisconsults of recognised competence'.

the Court of Justice, the candidates must 'possess the qualifications required for appointment to the highest judicial offices *in their respective* countries'.[32]

It remains unclear what precisely are supposed to be 'high-level duties'. The 255 Panel reports are silent on this issue. However, if one were to logically assume that it implies reaching at least a certain position within the respective career ladder (academic, judicial, civil service), since one is unlikely to assume 'high-level' duties immediately upon graduating from university, then what we are looking at is a *de facto* imposed requirement of candidates being 50 years of age or often even older. Such a requirement can, however, be inferred neither from Art 253 TFEU nor from a comparative study of the practice in the member states, with perhaps the exception of England and Wales.[33] More importantly, Art 253 TFEU makes a clear cross-reference to the appointment conditions, including length of practice, of the *particular* member state that makes the *particular* nomination. In other words, the diversity in requirements that might exist in different member states is foreseen and provided for. For example, if member state A allows any qualified lawyer who has at least ten years of (general) legal practice to be appointed to the national supreme court, then that person is by virtue of Art 253 TFEU eligible also for appointment to the Court of Justice. Similarly, if for example member state B has a provision stating that full ('habilitated' or 'agrégé' or whatever the local equivalent might be) professors of law in public universities are eligible to sit at the highest national courts, then such a professor is also eligible for an appointment to the Court of Justice, even if she might be quite junior.

The newly created requirement of 20 years' high-level practice for *all* candidates thus takes away the Treaty-based diversity by attempting to impose the same standard on everybody. This is certainly no mere 'clear and precise explanation' of the conditions inherent in the Treaty. This is a new requirement which goes beyond what the Treaties say, as well as beyond the previous state practice.

This is not to say that the need for an overall increase in the length of practice for appointees to the European courts could not be argued for.[34] It is rather to substantiate the previously made point, namely that the 255 Panel has in fact created new conditions without, as has been repeatedly pointed out in this volume,[35] there having been any debate about them. The changes have not been carried out democratically, or at least following broader discussions, but rather by stealth, by a confidential panel that is apparently not even ready to acknowledge that fact.

It ought, however, also to be admitted that, first, the length of practice requirement set by the 255 Panel goes the furthest in terms of novelty. The other criteria[36]

---

[32] Highlighted by the author. Interestingly, in Art 254 TFEU, which is applicable to the GC, the cross-reference to national laws is dropped, as well as the category of 'jurisconsults of recognized competence': 'The members of the General Court shall be chosen from persons whose independence is beyond doubt and who possess the ability required for appointment to high judicial office.'

[33] See the (limited in scope, but illustrative) comparative review by T Dumbrovský, B Petkova, and M Van der Sluis, 'Judicial Appointments: The Article 255 TFEU Advisory Panel and Selection Procedures in the Member States' (2014) 51 *Common Market Law Review* 460, 476–79. More generally see eg J Bell, *Judiciaries within Europe* (Cambridge University Press 2006).

[34] For the argument in its favour in the ECtHR context, see above ch 6 s 4.3.

[35] Notably above in ch 7.   [36] Above n 25.

can indeed be more plausibly presented as a mere confirmation of what has always been required, or perhaps rather what should have been required if there had been anybody who was able to verify it on the European level before the establishment of the 255 Panel. Second, the 255 Panel underlines its relative flexibility with respect to individual criteria, stressing that it carries out an *overall* assessment of the candidates. Thus, a moderate lack in one of the six criteria required may be compensated by strength in another. Specifically with respect to the length of professional experience requirement, the 255 Panel stated and its recent practice confirms that the presumption of unsuitability because of short practice can be 'overridden where a candidate demonstrates exceptional expertise'.[37]

If some criteria set by the 255 Panel can be said to be 'overdeveloped', there are others that could in turn to be seen as 'underdeveloped' or neglected.[38] First, on the face of the criteria established, there is no differentiation between the office of the judge at the Court of Justice on the one hand and judge at the GC on the other. The only visible difference is the 'discount' in terms of years of previous high-level practice required—20 years for the Court of Justice and just 12–15 for the GC. However, an argument could be made that there is a deeper, *functional* difference between the two jurisdictions that requires a slightly different skill-set for the respective judicial nominees.[39] GC judges are in fact trial judges, who should ideally have some trial practice on either side of the bar. The ability to establish facts and to question parties and solid 'judicial management' of a case are perhaps more important for a GC judge, maybe even more relevant than a long list of academic publications. Should such functional differentiation not be reflected in the minimal requirements for the GC, which, in contrast to the (perhaps more academically-minded) Court of Justice, ought to encompass some element of past practical legal experience?

Second, the 255 Panel criteria make no distinction at all between the offices of judge and advocate general at the Court of Justice. Again, should candidates for both of these offices meet the same set of requirements? If the original French inspiration for establishing the office of the advocate general in the Court of Justice present back in the 1950s[40] is (still?) to be taken into account, then the profile of an advocate general (*commissaire du gouvernement/rapporteur public*) would correspond rather to a brilliant junior lawyer. The virtues sought in such a type of advocate general are dynamic, critical, but constructive thinking, and the potential not only to analyse but also to challenge with a fresh mind. In such a model, what is being generated is a fruitful tension and co-operation between the more junior

---

[37] Third Activity Report (n 28) 18.

[38] See also Dumbrovský, Petkova, and Van der Sluis (n 33) 464–6 and 481–2.

[39] In addition to the more formal argument that the Treaty itself distinguishes between appointments to the Court of Justice and the GC by the slightly different wording in Art 253 TFEU (ECJ) as opposed to Art 254 TFEU (GC).

[40] Generally see N Burrows and Rosa Greaves, *The Advocate General and EC Law* (Oxford University Press 2007) or Le Clément-Wilz, *La fonction de l'avocat général près la Cour de justice* (Bruylant 2011).

advocates general and the more senior, by definition rather conservative judges.[41] However, if at the Court of Justice candidates for both of these offices are supposed to meet exactly the same set of criteria, what is then the 'added value' of advocates general? Why should there be a 'fourth in the court' if it appears to be another copy of the judges?[42]

Third, perhaps the least problematic in practical terms but still with the potential to agitate some Treaty 'purists', is the fact that in the 255 Panel reports, 'jurisconsults of recognised competence' ceased to be a self-standing category. In Art 253 TFEU, 'jurisconsults of recognised competence' are a free-standing category of candidates eligible to appointment to the Court of Justice, provided that they are at the same time persons 'whose independence is beyond doubts'. In the 255 Panel reports, however, the six requirements[43] are apparently applicable to all candidates indistinctively. There is thus in fact only one type of candidate, which is at the same time nonetheless quite open in terms of professional background (accommodating former judges, civil servants, or academics). It could be theoretically mooted that 'jurisconsults of recognised competence' ought to be a full-fledged category of its own and that, following the Treaty, there should be a distinct set of requirements for this particular category. However, insistence on such formal differentiation appears to be redundant, provided that the one common set of requirements is genuinely open to all professional backgrounds.

In sum, the absence of further internal differentiation within the criteria so far employed by the 255 Panel is understandable from the point of view of their origin: the CST Committee selects only one 'type' of judges for the CST Tribunal. There was thus no need for further internal differentiation among the individual categories when the CST Committee elaborated its original set of criteria. With respect to appointments to the Court of Justice and the General Court, however, there are more types of judicial office and a more diverse (and explicitly differentiated) Treaty background which ought to be taken perhaps into account. With the 255 Panel in its second mandate, the time might be ripe to revisit the original criteria and begin to differentiate between the individual categories in a more nuanced way.

On the whole, however, there is no doubt that having and enforcing at least some minimalist criteria for appointment to European courts represents progress in terms of ensuring basic quality of the appointees. However, as most of these

---

[41] As has been traditionally the case in the Conseil d'Etat, where the *commissaires du gouvernement* (today *rapporteurs public*) were recruited from the ranks of *maîtres des requêtes*, who belong to the more junior members of the staff. After having served as a *commissaire du gouvernement*, the person is likely to go on and become a *conseiller d'État*, ie in a sense a 'full' judge in the judicial section of the Conseil d'Etat. On the internal 'taxonomy' of the Conseil d'Etat in English see eg N Brown and J Bell, *French Administrative Law* (5th edn, Clarendon 1998), in particular 49, 90, and 104–6 or in general B Latour, *The Making of Law: An Ethnography of the Conseil d'État* (Polity 2010).

[42] See M Bobek, 'A Fourth in the Court: Why Are There Advocates-General in the Court of Justice?' 14 *Cambridge Yearbook of European Legal Studies* 529 (2012), discussing the challenges and evolution regarding the office of the advocate general at the Court of Justice in recent years.

[43] Above n 25, cross-reference to n 25.

processes take place behind closed doors, without any discussion or without any control or review, they represent a sort of Janus-faced progress by stealth.

3.2. A comparative inspiration?

In Europe, there has traditionally been diversity in the ways the highest judges are selected and appointed in the member states. The procedural and institutional differences are rooted in a deeper differentiation as to the vision of judicial authority and organization of judicial systems.[44] Such differentiated visions account for the different types of selection procedures, which in turn generate different types of judicial legitimacy.[45]

The traditional divide, by now nonetheless somewhat blurred in a number of countries, is between the continental and the common law traditions. The continental tradition was said to breed judges–officials, whose bureaucratic authority is rooted in the technical knowledge of the law. Their merit is knowledge-based, tested in mandarin-styled examinations early in their careers. Once they enter the judicial profession, their advancement is primarily linked to the amount of years spent in the service. Knowledge is not likely to be tested again. Conversely, in the common law systems, merit was said to be derived primarily from experience, from previously demonstrated expertise and integrity in another legal profession. Consequently, it was the more senior candidates who would be selected for judicial office. However, such senior candidates are unlikely to be tested as to their knowledge of the law at the point of entry into the judiciary. After all, they have already demonstrated their competence and it is precisely because of that they are being selected for judicial office.

Which of these two traditions should the selection of European judges rather follow? Is there any comparative inspiration detectable on the European plane? In fact, the criteria chosen together with the procedural practice carried out on the two levels, European and national, represent a sort of a mixture. On the one hand, it would appear that there is more of the common law inspiration present, certainly if focusing on the element of finding established senior experts who enjoy an excellent reputation in their home countries, and ideally Europe-wide. Thus, specifically, the required 20 years of high-level experience could be said to be a sort of a common law element that has few parallels on the continent. On the other hand, the selection procedures as currently organized insist on testing candidates and conducting interviews relating also to technical knowledge of the law, legal expertise, and language skills. These are extensively tested, in some cases even twice, on the national and European levels. This has the flavour, even if done in the

---

[44] MR Damaška, *The Faces of Justice and State Authority; A Comparative Approach to the Legal Process* (Yale University Press 1986) 16, but going back already, in a way, to Max Weber, *Economy and Society* (University of California Press 1963) 784–801.

[45] Further eg JP Dawson, *The Oracles of the Law* (University of Michigan Law School 1968), chapter 1; J Krynen, *L'Etat de justice France, XIIIe–XXe siècle. Tome II: L'emprise contemporaine des juges* (Gallimard 2012).

most respectful and sensible way, of a more continental element of testing judicial trainees as to whether or not they have mastered their codes.

On the more positive side, achieving a synthesis of both systems might be presented as the eventual coming together of both traditions in Europe. On the less positive side, the piling up of various conditions and criteria originating from different systems in order to satisfy everybody involved might eventually create a hardly digestible *Eintopf*. If anything might be inferred from the (largely ideal) models outlined in this section, it is that when selecting judges, one can either extensively test the more junior candidates, or diplomatically select, because of their previous achievements, the more senior candidates. As will be discussed in greater detail below in section 6, a 'comparative synthesis' amounting to (extensively) testing of senior candidates is, just as an *Eintopf*, bound to attract only a narrow set of dedicated connoisseurs.

4. The Remaining Thorn: Transparency and Control

The one reproach voiced in a number of chapters in this volume that stands out in the otherwise rather positive appraisals of the expert panels is the lack of transparency and absence of any control or review. The transparency-related reservations were voiced with respect to three distinct yet interrelated levels.

First, there is the systemic, separation-of-powers-driven critique of confidentiality, challenging the *de facto* law-making powers exercised by these panels. It is concerned with the setting of criteria and standards that are later to be applied by such panels. It suggests that the 'playing field' of expert panels ought to be demarcated by other, democratically legitimized actors. It is contrary to democratic principles, including also the principle of transparency and representation, that the criteria are elaborated by the panels themselves, additionally in a secretive and confidential manner.[46]

The second, other transparency-related objections are also systemic, but more functional in their focus. By operating in a secretive way, without the outside world knowing why a certain candidate was rejected and another was approved, a confidential expert panel is unable to fulfil its key pedagogical function. It cannot provide any guidance to the general public as to who is a good European judge. How then could potential candidates, as well as the public, understand and predict the decisions of the panel if they have no idea as to their content and reasons?[47]

---

[46] In particular above ch 7.

[47] In particular above ch 9. The medieval practice of keeping the reasons for judicial decisions secret, as was the case in for example the *Parlement de Paris* in the fourteenth century, might provide an intriguing parallel in this regard. All that was communicated to the public was the result of the decision of the court; the reasons for arriving at the given decision were seen as a part of the judicial deliberations, which were to be kept confidential. A similar type of judicial decision-making was, however, not able to provide any guidance in future cases. Thus, the rise of the case law as a distinct source of law was only possible later, when judicial decisions started to be properly published and accessible. Further see eg Dawson (n 45) 286–7; P Godding, 'Jurisprudence et motivation des sentence, du

Third, there is the level of individual cases and the exclusion of arbitrary or unjust decisions therein. What differs here from the second type of objection is the focus on the individual candidates and fairness in their cases. The actors involved remain the same; their order just becomes reversed. The primary interest is that one of the individual candidate who wishes to know the reasons for a decision that concerns her. There is, however, also the right of the public to know what and why was decided, thereby exercising indirect control in individual cases. It is for the same reason that European legal systems would generally insist on any decision of the public power, but in particular judicial decisions, to be announced publicly and in full, unless there is a compelling and clearly stated reason for excluding the public in the particular case.

Explicitness about what type of transparency is being aimed for is essential for discussion of the appropriate remedies. The first set of objections might in fact be satisfied if the rules and criteria followed by the respective expert panel were adopted by an institution endowed with democratic legitimacy. It is at the same time, however, more flexible on confidentiality of individual cases. The second set of concerns requires the disclosure of individual decisions but, with a bit of goodwill and trust, might also be satisfied with the intermediary solution currently offered by the 255 Panel: the publication of a general, anonymized annual report. This intermediary solution is able to provide some guidance in the future, but it fails to guarantee control in individual cases. It is only the third level or set of transparency concerns that demands the full disclosure of individual decisions, perhaps even coupled with the possibility of (judicial) review of an individual decision.

In discussing the appropriate level of transparency and control that ought to be exercised vis-à-vis the expert panels, two visions of their role collide. The first one, frequently academic and coming from the outside, is driven by a particular normative idea of what a procedure for selection to a European court should look like. The second, typically represented by the 'insiders', practitioners, and officials, tends to be more pragmatic. The latter vision would stress the existence of *legal* constraints (the panels were endowed with a certain mandate and must stick to it) as well as *pragmatic* constraints (protecting the reputation of the candidates and thus the operation of the system). In discussions, proponents of the former position tend to over-reach, suggesting considerable alterations that the mechanisms of expert panels might find difficult to accommodate. Conversely, the 'insiders' may be tempted to under-reach, and to hide behind legal or even legalistic arguments of the given mandate.

Starting with the pragmatic constraints, it is true that a number of these might not live up to closer critical scrutiny.[48] In particular, the argument that confidentiality is there to protect the candidate's reputation may appear convincing at first

---

moyen âge à la fin du 18e siècle' in Ch Perelman and P Foriers (eds), *La motivation des décisions de justice* (Bruylant 1978) 37–67.

[48] In detail above ch 9, suggesting that the current confidentiality policy of the panels appears more effective in protecting the panels' operation from public scrutiny than the candidates.

sight, but it encounters difficulties in reality. As pointed out in the Prologue,[49] not knowing the reasons why a particular candidate was rejected, while nevertheless knowing that she was unsuccessful, is bound to give rise to speculation and gossip, which in turn might be more harmful to the candidate in question than the (diplomatically put) truth. The aforementioned example of the questionable Czech nomination to the GC in 2013 might provide an illustration in this regard.[50] After the 255 Panel issued a negative opinion concerning the Czech candidate for the GC, Mr Mlsna, who was back then a minister of the Czech Government, was attacked by the opposition in Prague. Then leader of the opposition, today's prime minister, Mr Sobotka, denounced the unsuccessful candidate as a 'ridiculous figure' and suggested that he should step down from the government[51] since he had been rejected by the EU. The implicit message in such statements was that the candidate was a poor lawyer who was unfit for the job, as now 'certified' by the EU. It is clear that the opposition of the day was misusing the information void that emerged after the candidate was rejected, without the reasons for his rejection being known. But since the content of the opinion was confidential, and nobody knew why precisely Mr Mlsna had in fact been rejected, who could publicly contradict the opposition?

Similarly, a number of other, seemingly functional arguments relating to the necessary confidentiality of the expert panels' operation may be questioned.[52] Thus, the perhaps less exciting, but in fact more solid arguments in favour of confidentiality, are those of a legal(istic) nature based on the letter of the current mandate given to both expert panels by their creators. In the legal texts establishing both panels, considerable stress is indeed placed on the confidentiality of the operation and the output of the panels.[53] At the same time, however, there is some leeway within the rather rudimentary operating rules of both panels. Whatever the exact issue may be in these discussions, it is true that at the end of the day the operating rules of both panels can be changed with relative ease, being but a simple decision or resolution of the respective bodies that adopted them.

Last, apart from the functional or legal arguments, there are powerful symbolic considerations. Three of them may be highlighted. First, there is a certain justificatory narrative that accompanied the birth of the expert panels. It pictured knowledgeable experts who would bring the light of rational quality decision-making

---

[49] Above, Prologue s 2 and 3.5.

[50] Above s 2.1 of this Epilogue and also above ch 6 s 5.

[51] This was widely reported by all major Czech newspapers as well as television channels. See for example the article 'Ministra Mlsnu odmítl Soudní dvůr EU. Zesměšnil se, ať odejde, říká ČSSD' [Minister Mlsna rejected by the Court of Justice of the EU. He ridiculed himself, he should leave, says the Czech Social Democratic Party] of 10 May 2013, online at <http://zpravy.idnes.cz>, or the Czech TV entry 'Sobotka: Ministr Mlsna se stává definitivně směšnou figurou' [Sobotka: Minister Mlsna definitely became a ridiculous figure] of 10 May 2013, online at <http://www.ceskatelevize.cz/ct24/domaci/226479-sobotka-ministr-mlsna-se-stava-definitivne-smesnou-figurou>, both last accessed 31 July 2014.

[52] However, as was already pointed out above, in Prologue s 3.5, there is a lack of reliable empirical data in this regard.

[53] Further above ch 1 s 4.1 and ch 9 s 2.

into the dark corridors of shabby political deals, disguised behind the veil of state sovereignty. Such a narrative, if it is to be believed and to provide on-going legitimacy for these expert bodies, brings with it an implied promise of a different operation, a different style, and also a different level of transparency and control than those uncontrolled and unprincipled diplomats could ever provide. This picture naturally exaggerates a bit. There is, however, a grain of truth in it. One narrative and legitimizing story cannot be split up out of convenience, it cannot be selectively dropped with regards to some of its elements and kept being invoked for the rest.

Second, the current European (non-)transparency may not be regarded with overwhelming enthusiasm at the level of the member states. Both European systems—more so the ECHR, but to some extent also the EU—require members when selecting candidate(s) at the national level to be transparent, to hold open calls, and to report and justify the outcomes of the national selections at the European level.[54] Some states might start asking why the same requirements are not applicable to the European selections as well.

Third, there is the overall symbolism of the judicial office and function. The process being discussed here is selection of judges to the European courts. It involves identification of the ultimate guardians of rule of law in Europe, the selection of persons who are likely to preach to other actors across Europe about what is right or wrong, what is correct and what is not. What message does it send and with what legitimacy does it equip the incumbents of the office if they are selected in confidential hearings with secret results, on the basis of criteria that 'materialized' out of thin air that nobody else approved, and without any possibility of review? What sort of legitimacy does this bestow for subsequently judging others on their compliance with the rule of law, or perhaps even transparency?

In sum, the otherwise beautiful rose that is expert panels in the European judicial selections carries with it an unpleasant thorn. The thorn is called lack of transparency on a number of levels. The very existence of the thorn may be contested, just as the existence of the rose itself, in fact. It might be suggested that all the transparency-related critique is mistaken, since what is being analysed is in fact no free-standing plant, no rose, but a sort of mistletoe. It cannot therefore be analysed on its own, against a normative ideal of how judicial selections to the European courts should look like, but only in combination and in symbiosis with its host and principal, the Council and the Committee of Ministers, respectively.

This is certainly true. One cannot expect a rose to start growing from the top of an oak. On the other hand, the transparency-related reservations voiced in this volume aim primarily at the system as such and its respective legislative frameworks, not at the plants growing in their shadows, whether they are to be classified as roses or as mistletoe. It is, however, clear that the issues of transparency and control have remained somewhat underdeveloped in the institutional design of

---

[54] Further above ch 1 s 3 (with regard to the EU); ch 5, ss 3 and 4 (on the ECHR); and generally ch 10 s 4.

the new expert panels, endangering their standing and possible further evolution. They ought therefore to be revisited at the first opportune occasion.

5. Thou Shalt be Made in (Whose?) Image

Two intriguing issues concerning the social and professional background of judges of the European courts, present and past, were discussed in the previous chapters. The first was the change in the professional backgrounds of judges at both courts over time, coupled with questions regarding how such a fact altered the judicial mentality, and correspondingly also the legitimacy of those courts. Second, the question of connection between the composition of the selection panels and the preferred or chosen composition of the bench arose. In other words: how far are the current selectors or confirmers able to leave a personal imprint in terms of composition of the respective bench? Both issues will be examined in turn in this section.

5.1. Of esteemed legal diplomats and technocratic human-rightist greenhorns

As far as the diachronic examination of the professional background of judges at the Court of Justice was concerned, the picture painted[55] was diverse: the original, diplomatic, and perhaps more political composition of the first Court of Justice was gradually altered by the incoming judges (often crossbred with academics) and by the subsequent tide of civil servants, European and national. There are thus various ebbs and tides over the years, but the composition appears to be quite mixed, with legal academia, the judiciary, and the European and national civil service being the traditional sources of recruitment for the Court of Justice.

With respect to the ECtHR, the evolution outlined[56] was more one-directional: from the fraternity of esteemed legal diplomats in the pre-1998 ECtHR to more technocratic, human rights-focused 'youngsters' of today. The former ECtHR's judges had multiple forms of social capital, experience, and previous exposure to international affairs that allowed them to better interact with domestic and international constituencies. The ECtHR judges of today are said to be, with a bit of exaggeration, rather 'human rights yuppies'. With human rights developing into a field in its own right, links with other fields, both legal and non-legal, have been severed.[57] Such 'one-dimensional' appointees lack the general international law *gravitas* of their predecessors and are no longer so able to tackle political problems through legal diplomacy.

---

[55] Above ch 2 and also ch 1 s 1.   [56] Above ch 12 s 3.
[57] See with regard to the knowledge of national law and public international law also above ch 6 s 4.4. and 4.5.

Upon reading such harmonious accounts of the good old bygone days, the sceptical alarm of a critical reader is bound to start ringing. First, did such an ideal ECtHR really ever exist? Or is this just a narrative—a powerful but still idealized narrative, a nostalgia for an ideal court one had wished for, conjured up on the basis of a few big names that remain so when looking back, while nonchalantly neglecting the perhaps less stellar rest? Second, even if it did exist at least to some extent, since nobody asked Cassin, Rolin, or Teitgen to dispose of tens of thousands of cases every year, they actually could be legal diplomats, swirling with ease and time on their hands between national academia, international academia, and international organizations, with just occasional trips to a non-permanent court in Strasbourg to impart some wisdom. It is perhaps safe to guess that under such conditions, a number of current ECtHR judges would have no objection to engaging in such a type of legal diplomacy as well.

Third, if the sceptical reader is a lawyer, she might wonder what precisely 'legal diplomacy' entails, and whether it is an appropriate activity for a judge at all. At the level of social interaction, does it mean rubbing shoulders with national stakeholders at various venues or social occasions? It is certainly important for a judge to be visible, to engage socially. But too much 'legal diplomacy' might be at odds with judicial impartiality and independence. At the level of decision-making and case law, it is certainly important for a judge to be diplomatic in the sense of being tactful, considerate, and sensitive in her decision-making and reasoning. It is, however, certainly a judicial vice to be 'diplomatic' in the sense of 'open to negotiation' in individual cases, orienting the decision and its reasons on the anticipated reactions of the parties. Such 'legal diplomacy' generates unprincipled and unpredictable decisions,[58] made *ad hoc* and depending on the party in front of the court. In the eyes (at least) of lawyers, traditionally fond of consistency and coherence in terms of case law of a court and impartiality and independence as to its judges, such a kind of 'legal diplomacy' lacks any type of legitimizing effect.

It is perhaps in particular the last point that best reveals the nature of the ideological divide between the pre-1998 and the post-1998 ECtHR. Before the entry into force of the Protocol no 11, the ECtHR was indeed a diplomatic rather than judicial body. Greater participation of 'legal diplomats' was therefore understandable. However, once the ECtHR was functionally shaped into a court, with all the attributes of such, 'legal diplomacy', whatever the notion precisely entails, inevitably started to dissipate. If a court wishes to be perceived as a genuine court, an impartial and independent institution, 'legal diplomacy' is likely to undermine

---

[58] To mention just one illustrative example from the case law of the ECtHR that might leave a curious reader puzzled in terms of potential legal diplomacy involved: the European Convention, the 'living instrument' interpreted in the light of present-day conditions, meant in 1978 that subjecting a schoolboy to three strokes of the birch amounted to degrading punishment within the meaning of Art 3 of the Convention—*Tyrer v UK*, App No 5856/72 (ECtHR 25 April 1978). However, in 1993, giving another schoolboy three whacks on the bottom through his shorts with a rubber-soled gym shoe was not (or was no longer?) a violation of the same provision—*Costello-Roberts v UK*, App No 13134/87 (ECtHR 25 March 1993).

its credit rather than strengthening it, certainly within the professional circles of lawyers.

This can be said to be more broadly a trait common to the evolution of both European courts. With their transformation in the past two decades,[59] both courts have been gliding more towards professionalism and independence as their key legitimizing elements. This corresponds to the broader narrative that they are no longer just 'international' courts, but 'supranational' or 'European' courts. In a way, the legitimizing narrative that is sought is no longer the international–diplomatic one, but much closer to the more traditional national judicial one. The picture solicited is no longer that of a skilled international diplomat who knows all the people and corridors, but that of a learned highest national or constitutional court judge, perhaps slightly more reserved and detached. That is also why today, vener-able diplomatic personalities of the past might not be even considered eligible for European judicial office.[60]

In sum, the 'legal diplomacy' narrative, if embraced, provides explanations for the past patterns and (non)reception of European laws in the member states. A return to legal diplomacy is, however, not a recipe for the European courts of today. In the logic of the evolution of the European courts, it would represent a step backwards.

5.2. The panels: senior judges preferred?

It has been convincingly argued that the professional backgrounds of judges mat-ter.[61] Selectors' preferences for certain type(s) of professional backgrounds are bound to push the thusly composed court in a specific direction. This may hold the key for a meta-evolution of the institution: is the Court of Justice to be the constitutional court of the EU, or rather the ultimate interpreter of secondary, technical legislation?[62] Is the ECtHR to be more of a constitutional, human rights court for Europe, or is its international law element to be strengthened?[63] The choice between the two (or more) directions for each of the courts requires a differ-ent skill-set from the judicial candidates. Understandably, it would be slightly out of place to develop grand constitutional theories in a rudimentary trademark case. Conversely, a trademark specialist becoming a judge at the Court of Justice might

---

[59] Above. Prologue s 1.

[60] See above ch 1 s 1 (setting out the quite diverse backgrounds of the first appointees to the Court of Justice). Generally see also eg A Cohen, 'Sous la robe du juge. Le recrutement social de la Cour' in P Mbongo and A Vauchez (eds), *Dans la fabrique du droit européen: scenes, acteurs et publics de la Cour de justice des Commuatés europeénnes* (Bruylant 2009); N Brown and T Kennedy, *The Court of Justice of the European Communities* (5th edn, Sweet & Maxwell 2000) 58–63.

[61] Above ch 2. For the ECtHR, see notably Erik Voeten, 'The Politics of International Judicial Appointments: Evidence from the European Court of Human Rights' (2007) *International Organization* 669.

[62] Above ch 2 s 7.

[63] See above ch 6 s 4.5 with respect to the debate between the ECtHR as the 'constitutional' or the 'international' court.

be slightly puzzled and/or uninterested if asked to meditate on the concept of the national constitutional identity of the member states.

There will be no attempt to address these grand normative questions here. The focus of this section will be much more modest: to what extent can the object of this study, the expert panels, in fact influence the selection of candidates with certain professional backgrounds?[64] First, however, what is in fact the favoured profile? With clear or even dominant majorities of senior national judges in both expert panels, the 255 Panel and the Advisory Panel, can it be said that there would now be a clear preference for senior national judges to be appointed to the European bench? Is the ideal Euro-Hercules a 50-plus-year-old judge from a national supreme or constitutional court, fond of Europe, at least with some knowledge of French and a keen interest in EU or ECHR law? Is there any correlation between the chosen selectors and the criteria they have established and applied?[65]

There are two criteria that come particularly to the fore in this regard: professional background and age. As far as past professional experience is concerned, the 255 Panel has stated on several occasions[66] and also confirmed by its past practice that it does not favour any specific professional profile of candidates. In the past, the 255 Panel was ready to approve academics, civil servants, and also judges. Conversely, the grapevine has it that the 255 Panel did not hesitate to reject a senior national judge who nonetheless demonstrated no convincing knowledge of and past experience in EU law. Suggestions of judicial fraternities co-opting new members to the European courts in their own image, preferably from the ranks of senior national judiciaries, are therefore not warranted so far, certainly not with respect to the professional background element.

With regard to the criterion of age, articulated in terms of length of professional experience, the picture becomes more blurred. The 255 Panel has already rejected several younger candidates, apparently in and around their mid-thirties. However, as much as can be ascertained from the outside, neither of these nominally 'age-related' rejections occurred as part of a clear-cut case in which the length of practice would have been *the only* question mark in the case of an otherwise stellar candidate. The problem appeared to be the age/length of professional experience *in combination with* other factors relating to a lack of guaranteed independence and impartiality as perceived by the Panel (ie the candidate was essentially a political rather than merit-based nomination made by a national government of the day—or in one case a sitting minister of the government who virtually nominated himself), or age in combination with a lack of convincing expertise in EU law. At the same time, the 255 Panel showed itself ready to approve of younger

---

[64] Leaving aside the already discussed issue of whether it has in fact any legitimacy and mandate for doing so, ie whether expert panels should be entitled to make any such choice (see in particular above ch 7).

[65] See eg above ch 1 s 2.3, warning against the members of the panel wittingly or unwittingly composing a court in their own image. See also Dumbrovský, Petkova, and Van der Sluis (n 33) 482, voicing 'self-replication concerns'.

[66] Third Activity Report (n 28) 18.

candidates with non-judicial backgrounds, who, being in their early 40s, could not be considered to have 20 years' experience of 'high-level duties'.

Thus, even if composed in a rather distinct way as regards their own professional background, there is so far no evidence that the dominant senior judicial element within the 255 Panel would be imposing its own particular preferences in the selection process. It allows for the necessary professional diversity on the bench. Moreover, in terms of the past compositions of the Court of Justice, pushing for greater numbers of national judges would constitute quite a rupture with previous practice. Traditionally, the Court of Justice has arguably been a distinctly 'academic' court.[67] Even today, it is composed of high-profile experts with chiefly academic, not necessarily judicial, professional backgrounds. Within the present 37 members of the Court of Justice (28 judges and nine advocates general), 11 mention in their official online biographies at least some judicial experience in national ordinary courts prior to their appointment. A further three members of the Court of Justice, although having primarily academic professional backgrounds, have had judicial experience from national constitutional courts. The majority of current members have, however, no prior judicial experience. They have either an academic or a civil service (including diplomatic) background, or frequently both.

The distinctly 'academic' flavour in the composition of the Court of Justice can be justified both functionally as well as culturally, naturally provided that it does not lead to the Court of Justice losing touch with the reality of national judicial function(s).[68] *Functionally*, the more abstract law-making carried out by the Court of Justice in particular within the preliminary rulings procedure calls for analytical minds able to rise above a single case and a national judicial routine, able to see the bigger European picture. A similar mindset can certainly come from both sides: from the side of a theorizing practitioner as well from a practically minded academic. *Culturally* and historically, insisting on a higher court composed of (mainly or wholly) senior judges, believed to be the only persons competent to understand the business of judging, is a reflection of one particular legal tradition within the Union. Conversely, other legal traditions in Europe are much more open towards higher courts being composed also of academics. Moreover, using a historical parallel, is the preliminary ruling procedure at the end of the day all that much different from the seventeenth or eighteenth-century practice of *Aktenversendung*, by which any German court could have requested a legal opinion on a complex case from a *Spruchkollegium* of esteemed law professors?[69]

---

[67] Further above ch 2 s 6.

[68] See generally M Bobek, 'Of Feasibility and Silent Elephants: The Legitimacy of the Court of Justice through the Eyes of National Courts' in M Adams et al (eds), *Judging Europe's Judges: The Legitimacy of the Case Law of the European Court of Justice* (Hart 2013) 197, 227–9. More critically see PJ Wattel, 'Köbler, CILFIT and Welthgrove: We Can't Go On Meeting Like This' (2004) 41 *CMLRev* 177.

[69] See eg S Vogenauer, 'An Empire of Light? Learning and Lawmaking in the History of German Law' (2005) 64 *CLJ* 481, 486; RC van Caenegem, *Judges, Legislators and Professors: Chapters in European Legal History* (Cambridge University Press 1987) 64–5.

Finally, looking at the professional backgrounds of the selectors themselves, a discernible tendency towards appointing high-ranking senior national judges can be observed. In the second embodiment of the 255 Panel, the presence of such judges has even increased from four to five.[70] Composing the 255 Panel in this way was a choice exercised by the president of the CJEU and confirmed by the Council. Art 255 TFEU provides for three different sets of candidates from which members of the 255 Panel might be drawn: 'members of national supreme courts' is just one such option, alongside 'former members of the Court of Justice and the General Court' and 'lawyers of recognised competence'. Thus, it would have been equally plausible to compose the seven-member Panel from former judges of Union courts together with stronger representation of the European Parliament and other lawyers of recognized competence put forward by other Union institutions. Such composition of the 255 Panel would, however, follow a different logic, perhaps inspired more by a vision of horizontal institutional balance/separation of powers among the EU institutions, similarly to the selection of judges on the national levels.

The president of the CJEU decided nonetheless to go down a different path, which, in the EU of today, can only be applauded. In times of a crisis of confidence in the European institutions, additional (democratic) legitimacy may only come from the national level.[71] Thus, putting national judges at the centre of the European game has been a wise move that may only increase the legitimacy of the European courts within what is arguably their most important constituency: national judges. In the eyes of some national judiciaries, the previous system might have appeared too political, government-driven, and determined in some member states without any representative involvement of the national judiciary in the nomination process. In sum, judges might feel that eventually they have found some footing on the European level as well, counterbalancing the previous governmental and diplomatic monopoly.

6. The Paradox of Success? Open Competitions, Fewer Candidates?

If there is one point on which all contributors to this volume agree, then it is the praiseworthiness of the introduction of clear selection criteria for candidates to the European courts, and the importance of their respect and reasonable enforcement. This is natural. Hardly anybody would object to the principled point of having transparent criteria, and their enforcement and policing.

It could be expected that once a selection process becomes clearer and more open, there are bound to be more candidates. No more secretive 'taps on the shoulder' for the select few, but an open competition which everybody can enter. This

---

[70] For the exact composition of the respective panels, see above ch 1 s 2.1.
[71] Above ch 11 s 3.2.

expectation, however, appears not to hold entirely, at least not with regard to those candidates primarily solicited. Heretical as it sounds, the more transparent and rigorously enforced the (current) selection criteria become, the fewer candidates seem likely to apply. This is the result of two factors that have come together for the first time since the establishment of the expert panels: a particular set of criteria and the open selection procedure.

First, the criteria that have been formulated by the 255 Panel point to a particular type of candidate: senior lawyers, preferably practitioners, ideally judges, between 50 and 65 years of age;[72] proficient in foreign languages, with French strongly advised; skilled in international environments and with very good knowledge of EU/ECHR law, if possible to be proven by a publication record in the field. If such candidates may be in short supply in the 'older' member states, in the 'newer' Europe, ie the member states that joined the EU in 2004, 2007, or 2013, they are very rare. Certainly, as the regular reports of the 255 Panel indicate[73]—and there is no reason to doubt that the Advisory Panel would act differently in this regard—assessment of whether these criteria are fully met is conducted with some flexibility. Individual criteria may be, to some extent, compensated. On the other hand, not so many individuals, especially those in senior positions in the member states, might be tempted to try to test how far such compensation is in fact really possible.

Second, the already not so substantial reservoir of 'fully' eligible candidates might be further put off by the prospect of being tested like schoolboys in the process of ascertaining whether or not they actually meet all these criteria. To be asked about their knowledge of EU or ECHR law by a selection panel twice, on the national as well as the European level? To sit regular language examinations in French, grappling with irregular verbs and the *subjonctif*?[74] It is not only the senior judicial candidates who might find the very thought of this problematic. Moreover, on the national level, if the candidate is a senior national judge, she is likely to be examined by a panel composed of civil servants or politicians (minister of justice, minister of foreign affairs, or their deputies), who are likely to be parties to cases she hears, or by other senior judges or court presidents, who are likely to be colleagues or even inferior judicial officials.

All in all, it is quite understandable that a senior candidate of certain stature, who is likely to have sat her last examination some 20 or more years ago, will hardly be tempted by such prospects. To be precise: the core of the problem is not the (non-)disclosure of the results of such an examination, but the mere fact of having to undergo such an examination.[75]

---

[72] The upper age limit is applicable to the candidatures to the ECtHR only—see above ch 6 s 4.3.

[73] Above n 27.

[74] As appears to be the practice in some of the member states, like the recent selection to the ECtHR in the UK (above ch 5 s 4.3) or CJEU selection in Bulgaria (Dumbrovský, Petkova, and Van der Sluis, n 33, 478) and perhaps also other states in which the candidates sit regular French language tests.

[75] The transparency/publicity issues discussed above in s 4 of this Epilogue are thus secondary to the primary problem of having to go through such type of examination. It might be even suggested

The combination of these two factors creates a paradox. The stated criteria and the profile of the candidates desired are out of sync with the procedure that is supposed to lead to their identification. Put differently: the preferred type of candidate has been pushed out of the game by the procedure. This has two consequences. First, the typical profile of candidates who are 'ready to give it a go' in terms of subjecting themselves to the lengthy dual selection procedure is more likely to be that of younger, academic or civil service candidates, who are perhaps more comfortable with the idea of being repetitively grilled on their skills and knowledge. Supreme Court Law Lords or professors–judges from the *Bundesverfassungsgericht* are unlikely to be prepared to sit French language tests or be examined as to their knowledge of the latest European case law on European Monetary Union. Second, the overall numbers of candidates applying may not be that high. This is naturally very country-dependent, but with regard to the ECtHR selections, more and more member states, in particular smaller ones, face genuine difficulties in coming up with a list of three good candidates.[76] Also with regard to the CJEU—where the problem is less visible, since only one candidate will reach the European level—the turnout in national competitions is not high, in particular in the newer member states.[77]

The current combination of high demand and thorough testing has created a bit of a deadlock. The candidates that Europe apparently wants seem not to be ready to apply under such conditions, and the candidates that are ready to apply are not that much wanted by Europe. In a way, the already discussed European *Eintopf* in terms of elaboration of criteria[78] backfires: common law-based merit and experience selection is difficult to reconcile with the vision of the more continental mandarin-styled *councours (sur titres)*, multiplied by two levels. This leads to the expert panels, national as well as European, being presented with a dilemma: either they re-affirm their vision and then face the absence of good candidates, or they are bound to resort to considerable flexibility in terms of application of their criteria. Reasonable evaluation flexibility is to be welcomed. If there is, however, too much of it, the credibility of the original set of criteria will suffer. On the other hand, it may eventually lead to a sensible re-evaluation of the original criteria.

that once somebody is in fact ready to be subject to such type of examinations, she might have less problems with her results, as well as those of the other candidates, being publicly known.

[76] See eg above, the situation with respect to the Czech Republic, ch 6 s 5. Further, for example, Slovakia saw its list twice rejected in 2013, and has not yet been able to come up with a third one.

[77] In the newer member states, it is in particular the 'length of practice requirement' that may appear problematic. Twenty years of high-level duties experience essentially means that only lawyers who graduated and started working before 1989 in these countries are eligible. Within this set of candidates, however, international experience, the knowledge of languages, and other skills that could hardly be obtained behind the Iron Curtain are likely to be lacking. Thus, if all of the conditions announced by the 255 Panel (above n 25) were to be met, there would hardly be any candidates at all. See in this respect also the discussion in J Malenovský, *L'indépendance des juges internationaux* (Recueil des cours de l'Académie de droit international de la Haye, Martinus Nijhoff 2011) 186–7.

[78] Above s 3.2.

In sum, the profile of the ideal judicial candidate announced by the expert panels is out of sync with the procedures that are supposed to lead to finding one. In other words, substantive calls for senior judicial Hercules are answered, because of the procedure that comes with them, instead by the junior Hermes. This is not to say that Hermes might not be a suitable choice. It is rather to suggest that, in spite of popular beliefs, the impact of the expert panels might not be that strong in terms of preference for candidates with certain professional backgrounds. The effect might be even precisely the opposite: to put off especially the type of candidates desired in terms of background and seniority.

7. Coda (Française)

How to attract top candidates to the European courts? A number of important suggestions have been made at various points of this volume with regard to this recurring question, ranging from smaller fixes to greater changes. As far as could be detected, the suggestions made were rather in a positive tone: some elements of procedure or substance needed to be fixed here or there. However, in spite of the general and omnipresent 'crisis-talk', none of the chapters in this volume suggested that finding excellent candidates for the European courts would be *per se* impossible, since from the 'no Demos' in Europe follows 'no Eros' for the European courts, and therefore being a judge at a national supreme or constitutional court or an esteemed law professor will always be considered to be a better job. The more plausible explanations for the occasional lack of suitable candidates were identified on the more pragmatic and practical side of the process, or in the dissonance between the criteria established and the process leading to the selection, as discussed in previous sections of this Epilogue.

The positive overall assessment of the operation of the expert panels in European judicial selections, in particular as far as the 255 Panel is concerned, should nonetheless not be stretched too far. There has certainly been an improvement contrasted with the situation several years ago. It might be criticized as a rather pragmatic progress by stealth, focused on the technocratic outcome and not on the democratic process, but it is clearly an improvement in terms of ensuring the quality of judicial appointees. This should, however, not lull the observer into believing that all is now fine with regard to the judicial appointments to the European courts.

On the one hand, there are persisting problems that were present before the establishment of the expert panels, and that these panels could, for obvious reasons, not remedy structurally. The notable example in this category is the problem of (non)renewal of the mandates of outgoing European judges. Today the problem is limited to the EU Courts, since the European Convention wisely opted to prolong the mandate of the ECtHR judges but make it non-renewable.[79] Within the

---

[79] Art 2 of Additional Protocol no 14 to the European Convention that entered into force in June 2010 introduced a nine-year non-renewable mandate for the ECtHR judges.

EU system, however, the relatively short and renewable six-year mandate poses an on-going problem in at least two dimensions.

First, the erratic policy of the non-renewal of mandates for the outgoing CST judges, as embraced so far by the Council, is difficult to explain and justify.[80] It destabilizes this jurisdiction and should be reconsidered, at least to some extent. It is certainly not suggested that the CST judges ought to remain on the court for decades. A sensible compromise could be for instance achieved by, as a rule, renewing sitting judges only once, provided that they are not blatantly underperforming.

Second, the relatively short and renewable six-year mandate poses even a greater problem with regard to the Court of Justice and the GC. Sitting judges (or advocates general from member states with permanent advocates general) who wish to be renewed are forced to 'campaign' for their renewal, at least in the form of keeping their links with the domestic 'constituencies' alive, in order to prevent being ousted by new candidates with better political connections formed back home during the course of the former's time away. This situation remains alarming in terms of the judicial independence of EU judges.[81] There certainly is an internal differentiation in the practices of member states, with at least some member states feeling bound by the convention that a sitting judge wishing to continue ought to have her term renewed.

The establishment of the 255 Panel could not have solved this problem. Only a Treaty revision similar to the changes made under the European Convention system can do so, by prolonging the mandate and making it non-renewable. In the meantime, however, the 255 Panel can alleviate the problem by diplomatically endorsing the convention with respect to all member states that as a rule, well-performing judges are to be renewed. In fact, the Panel's practice can be said to already move in that direction. In its reports, the 255 Panel stated that although it conducts review of candidates for a renewal of a term of office, this is a 'light' review. As the 255 Panel noted, although issuing a negative opinion in the case of a sitting judge or advocate general 'cannot be completely ruled out, it nevertheless remains a largely theoretical option'.[82]

On the other hand, in addition to such types of persisting problems, the overall enchantment with the new European procedures and the corresponding institutional optimism should not cloud the fact that on the whole, the key stage of the selections remains at national level and subject to sometimes quite different standards. Moreover, even if, following the European lead and inspiration, at the national level selection committees with judges and other experts as members are established, it may not necessarily mean that the old, bad times of politicking and

---

[80] In particular above ch 4 s 2.2.

[81] Above ch 8 s 4.4. See also eg Malenovský (n 77) 189–202 or JHH Weiler, 'Epilogue: Judging the Judges – Apology and Critique' in Adams et al (n 68) 251–2.

[82] Third Activity Report (n 28) 12. There is no doubt that issuing a negative opinion with regard to an already sitting judge would represent a slight 'earthquake' in terms of the institutional authority of the respective court, which could be even translated into *ex post* challenges made to the previous decisions issued by the judge in question (or by the formation she sat in).

wheeling and dealing have disappeared. Judicial bodies and judges are not immune to politicking. As the disturbing example of judicial (self-) administration in the form of councils of judiciary in central and eastern Europe demonstrates,[83] absent deeper cultural changes in terms of mentality and practices, the same patterns of behaviour that previously happened in the political arena may be reproduced within judicial bodies as well. From this angle the belief that, if run by judges and other experts, the national selections will be free of politicking appears to be somewhat naïve, certainly in the less mature environments in some member states. This, however, provides the 255 Panel with another opportunity. Again, it is not capable of solving the potential problem on the national level, but it may substantially contribute to diminishing it by rigorously insisting on the open and fair procedure aspect of the national selections.[84]

Finally, in all the meditations present in this volume as to how to attract the best candidates to the European courts, one particular issue is conspicuous by its absence. It is, however, quite important in terms of the best candidates being likely to apply for the European bench. It thus deserves to be mentioned at least at the very end of the volume. It is the elephant in the room called French, certainly with regard to the Court of Justice of the EU today.[85] In terms of foreign languages and their knowledge, the enlarged Europe of 2014 looks very different from the Europe of the 1950s. Stated in a non-diplomatic nutshell: anyone engaged with anything foreign in Europe today is likely to speak English, as well as perhaps other foreign languages. French, however, might not be among these other languages. In today's Europe, it might be German, especially in central and eastern Europe; it might increasingly be Spanish; or it may be another language.[86]

Naturally, this has implications for judicial selections to European courts, where *all* Europeans are supposed to come together and to decide cases. It may not appear that obvious from a Brussels or Luxembourg perspective, but finding excellent lawyers who speak good French is increasingly difficult in the north of Europe, in central and eastern Europe, but also in south-east Europe. Sometimes, with a bit of exaggeration, the national selection bodies are not searching for the best possible candidates, but for lawyers who happen to speak some French and are ready to be tested on it.

The continuous choice of French as the internal working language of Court of Justice of the EU may be seen as a source of *dual* institutional *isolation*. The first type, less important but also visible today, is horizontal. Within the Union

---

[83] Further M Bobek and D Kosař, 'Global Solutions, Local Damages: A Critical Study in Judicial Councils in Central and Eastern Europe', 15 (7) *German Law Journal* 171 (2014).

[84] As a rule, the 255 Panel requires from the member states information on the national selection procedure that took place and a statement of reasons why a certain candidate was selected—see Third Activity Report (n 28) 14.

[85] The specific bilingual regime of the ECtHR may create different sorts of problems, which were discussed above in ch 6 s 4.2.

[86] Cf eg the data in European Commission, *Europeans and their Languages* (Special Eurobarometer 386, European Commission 2012) 19–22, indicating that English is the universally used first foreign language and German and French would be the second most widely used foreign languages, with Spanish learning increasing. Other statistics, which are naturally heavily dependent on the way the data are gathered, place German as the second foreign language within the EU today.

institutions), only the CJEU uses French as its only internal working language; the other EU institutions have effectively switched to English.[87] The second type, much more important, is vertical, placing the CJEU at a distance from the majority of the member states. *Linguistic* domination[88] spills over into *intellectual* domination, which leads to ideas, notions, or solutions from outside the Francophone legal family not being genuinely represented within the institution, and not being systematically translated into its cases.[89] This in turn may lead to a certain institutional alienation, as the solutions eventually adopted and chosen are not truly comparatively elaborated on a Europe-wide plane, but have been more one-sidedly copied from within the internally dominant system.

There is no need to enter into debates on the virtues of French as the language of the CJEU here.[90] In the context of this Epilogue, the language point was made simply to state a perhaps obvious but, for diplomatic reasons, neglected fact: the use of French as the one working language within the CJEU backfires in the selection process itself and influences the number of potential candidates likely to apply. Furthermore, with the number of people learning French as their (first) foreign language apparently not increasing,[91] the situation is not likely to improve in the future.

[87] The other institutions of the Union have been apparently increasingly using English as their *de facto* working language since the 2004 enlargement. An illustration of the shift might be provided by statistics of the Commission's DG for Translation that reveal in what languages these institutions draft their documents. Whereas in 1997, 45.4 per cent of texts translated by the DG for Translation were originally drafted in English and 40.4 per cent in French (the remaining 14.2 per cent were in other languages), in 2008 72.5 per cent of texts were drafted in English and only 11.8 per cent in French (with the remaining 15.7 per cent drafted in other languages, in particular German and Dutch)— see Information Booklet *Translating for a Multilingual Community* (Luxembourg, Office for Official Publications 2009) 6. Absent newer statistics, it is safe to assume that this trend has progressed even further since 2008, making English the dominant language in all institutions other than the CJEU.

[88] French being the only working language within the CJEU has as one other important consequence the dominance of French native speakers among the Court's legal secretaries. See eg S Gervasoni, 'Des référendaires et de la magistrature communautaire' in *Etat souverain dans le monde d'aujourd'hui: Mélanges en l'honneur de Jean-Pierre Puissochet* (Pedone, 2008) 105. Moreover, a number of the legal secretaries who do not hold French or Belgian nationality did at least receive a part of their legal education in French.

[89] Cf eg the intriguing statistics in H Bouthinon-Dumas and A Masson, 'Quelles sont les revues juridiques qui comptent à la Cour de justice de l'Union européenne?'[2013] *RTDeur* 781 that confirm the strong influence of French legal journals on the thinking of the CJEU. For example, the most widely read law journal at the CJEU outside the field of EU law is *AJDA* (*L'actualité juridique Droit administratif*). This might be understandable from the point of view of the linguistic composition of the staff of the CJEU, but it is quite striking in terms of representativeness of the broader academic and professional discourse extant in Europe today. It might also be seen as an indirect hint at the dominance of French administrative law thinking on the articulation of the standards of judicial review in the EU courts.

[90] The reasons why French ought to be kept as a working language of the CJEU are essentially of two types: linguistic–cultural and pragmatic–operational. The former suggestions relate to French being traditionally *the* language of EU law, unique and irreplaceable for its precision of expression. The latter ones focus on the fact that with all the CJEU's translation machinery being set at and structured around French, together with the fact that finding English translators may be more difficult, the language-switching costs for the CJEU would be too high and would also involve a number of practical problems.

[91] Above n 86, 19 and 22.

Select Bibliography

Alexander, L and Sherwin, E, *The Rule of Rules: Morality, Rules and the Dilemmas of Law* (Duke University 2001)

Alter, K, *Establishing the Supremacy of European Law: The Making of an International Rule of Law in Europe* (Oxford University Press 2001)

Alter, K, *The European Court's Political Power* (Oxford University Press 2009)

Alter, K, 'The New International Courts: A Bird's Eye View' (2009) Buffett Centre for International and Comparative Studies Working Paper Series No. 09-001

Alter, K, *The New Terrain of International Law* (Princeton University Press 2014)

Arnull, A, *The European Union and Its Court of Justice* (Oxford University Press 2006)

Avril, P and Gicquel, J, *Le Conseil constitutionnel* (Montchrestien 2005)

Balandier, M, *Le Conseil supérieur de la magistrature—De la révision constitutionnelle du 27 Juillet 1993 aux enjeux actuels* (Editions Le Manuscrit 2006)

Bates, E, *The Evolution of the European Convention on Human Rights: From Its Inception to the Creation of a Permanent Court of Human Rights* (Oxford University Press 2010)

Bates, E, 'The Birth of the European Convention on Human Rights—and the European Court of Human Rights' in J Christoffersen and M Rask Madsen (eds), *The European Court of Human Rights between Law and Politics* (Oxford University Press 2011)

Baum, L, *Judges and Their Audiences: A Perspective on Judicial Behavior* (Princeton University Press 2006)

Bell, J, *Judiciaries within Europe: A Comparative Review* (Cambridge University Press 2006)

Bellamy, R, *Political Constitutionalism: A Republican Defence of the Constitutionality of Democracy* (Cambridge University Press 2007)

Benvenisti, E and Downs, G, 'Prospects for the Increased Independence of International Tribunals' (2011) 12 German Law Journal 1057

Bernier, A, 'Constructing and Legitimating: Transnational Jurist Networks and the Making of a Constitutional Practice of European Law, 1950–70' (2012) 21 Contemporary European History 399

Besson, S, 'European Human Rights, Supranational Judicial Review and Democracy. Thinking Outside the Judicial Box' in P Popelier, C Van de Heyning, and P Van Nuffel (eds), *Human Rights Protection in the European Legal Order: The Interaction Between the European and the National Courts* (Intersentia 2011)

Bickel, A, *The Least Dangerous Branch* (Yale University Press 1962)

Bobek, M, 'Learning to Talk: Preliminary Rulings, the Courts of the New Member States and the Court of Justice' (2010) 45 Common Market Law Review 1611

Bobek, M, *Comparative Reasoning in European Supreme Courts* (Oxford University Press 2013)

Bobek, M, 'Of Feasibility and Silent Elephants: The Legitimacy of the Court of Justice through the Eyes of National Courts' in M Adams et al (eds), *Judging Europe's Judges: the Legitimacy of the Case Law of the European Court of Justice* (Hart 2013)

Bobek, M, '*Landtová, Holubec*, and the Problem of an Uncooperative Court: Implications for the Preliminary Rulings Procedure' (2014) 10 European Constitutional Law Review 54

Bobek, M, 'Legal Reasoning of the Court of Justice of the EU' (2014) 39 European Law Review 418

Boerger-De Smedt, A, 'La Cour de justice dans les négociations du traité de Paris instituant la CECA' (2008) 14 Journal of European Integration History 7

Bork, R, *Coercing Virtue: The Worldwide Rule of Judges* (AEI Press 2003)

Bossuyt, M, 'Should the Strasbourg Court Exercise More Self-restraint? On the Extension of the Jurisdiction of the European Court of Human Rights to Social Security Regulations' (2007) 28 Human Rights Law Journal 321

Bossuyt, M, 'Judges on Thin Ice: The European Court of Human Rights and the Treatment of Asylum Seekers' (2010) 3 Inter-American and European Human Rights Journal 3

Bourdieu, P, *Le sens pratique* (Minuit 1980)

Bourdieu, P, 'The Force of Law: Toward a Sociology of the Juridical Field' (1987) 38 The Hastings Law Journal 80

Brown, N and Kennedy, T, *The Court of Justice of the European Communities* (5th edn, Sweet & Maxwell 2000)

Buergenthal, T, 'Proliferation of International Courts and Tribunals: Is It Good or Bad?' (2001) 14 Leiden Journal of International Law 267

Bühlmann, M and Kunz, R, 'Confidence in the Judiciary: Comparing the Independence and Legitimacy of Judicial Systems' (2011) 34 West European Politics 317

Burbank, S, 'Judicial Independence, Judicial Accountability, and Interbranch Relations' (2007) 95 The Georgetown Law Journal 909

Çali, B, Koch, A, and Bruch, N, 'The Social Legitimacy of Human Rights Courts: A Grounded Interpretivist Theory of the Elite Accounts of the Legitimacy of the European Court of Human Rights' (2013) 35 Human Rights Quarterly 955

Çali, B, Koch, A, and Bruch, N, 'The Legitimacy of Human Rights Courts: A Grounded Interpretivist Analysis of the European Court of Human Rights' (2013) 35 Human Rights Quarterly 955

Caflisch, L, 'Independence and Impartiality of Judges: The European Court of Human Rights' (2003) 2 The Law and Practice of International Courts and Tribunals 169

Caldeira, G, 'Public Opinion and the US Supreme Court' (1987) 81 American Political Science Review 1139

Caldeira, G, 'The Etiology of Public Support for the Supreme Court' (1992) 36 American Journal of Political Science 635

Caldeira, G, 'The Legitimacy of the Court of Justice in the European Union' (1995) 89 The American Political Science Review 356

Caldeira, G, and Gibson, J, 'Democracy and Legitimacy in the European Union' (1997) 49 International Social Science Journal 209

Cardwell, M, *Milk Quotas: European Community and United Kingdom Law* (Oxford University Press 1996)

Carrubba, C, Gabel, M, and Hankla, C, 'Judicial Behavior under Political Constraints: Evidence from the European Court of Justice' (2008) 102 American Political Science Review 435

Cartier, S and Hoss, C, 'The Role of Registries and Legal Secretariats in International Judicial Institutions' in C Romano, K Alter, and Y Shany (eds), *Oxford Handbook of International Adjudication* (Oxford University Press 2013)

Chalmers, D, 'The Positioning of EU Judicial Politics within the United Kingdom' (2000) 23 West European Politics 169

Chalmers, D, 'The Reference Points of EU Judicial Politics' (2012) 19 Journal of European Public Policy 25

Chalmers, D, *European Union Law* (3rd edn, Cambridge University Press 2014)

Chalmers, D and Barroso, L, 'What Van Gend en Loos Stands For' (2014) 12 International Journal of Constitutional Law 105

Chalmers, D and Chaves, M, 'EU Law-Making and the State of Democratic Agency' in O Cramme and S Hobolt (eds), *Democratic Politics in a European Union under Stress* (Oxford University Press 2014)

Choi, S and Gulati, M, 'A Tournament of Judges?' (2004) 92 California Law Review 299

Christoffersen, J and Rask Madsen, M (eds), *The European Court of Human Rights between Law and Politics* (2nd edn, Oxford University Press 2013)

Cohen, A, ' "Ten Majestic Figures in Long Amaranth Robes": The Formation of the Court of Justice of the European Communities' in A Vauchez and B de Witte (eds), *Lawyering Europe* (Hart Publishing 2013)

Cohen-Jonathan, G, 'La reconnaissance par la France du droit de recours individuel devant la Commission européenne des Droits de l'Homme' (1981) 27 Annuaire français du droit international 269

Colin, J-P, *Le gouvernement des juges dans les communautés européennes* (Pichon et Durand-Auzias 1966)

Costa, J-P, 'On the Legitimacy of the European Court of Human Rights' Judgments' (2011) 7 European Constitutional Law Review 173

Crawford, J and McIntyre, J, 'The Independence and Impartiality of the "International Judiciary" ' in S Shetreet and C Forsyth (eds), *The Culture of Judicial Independence* (Martinus Nijhoff Publishers 2012)

Davies, B, *Resisting the European Court of Justice: West Germany's Confrontation with European Law, 1949–1979* (Cambridge University Press 2012)

Davis, M, 'A Government of Judges: An Historical Re-View' (1987) 35 The American Journal of Comparative Law 559

Dashwood, A and Johnston, A (eds), *The Future of the Judicial System of the European Union* (Hart Publishing 2001)

Dawson, JP, *The Oracles of the Law* (University of Michigan Law School 1968)

Dehousse, R, *The European Court of Justice. The Politics of Judicial Integration* (Macmillan 1998)

Dezalay, Y and Garth, B, *Dealing in Virtue. International Commercial Arbitration and the Construction of a Transnational Legal Order* (University of Chicago Press 1996)

Dezalay, Y and Garth, B, *The Internationalization of Palace Wars: Lawyers, Economists, and the Contest to Transform Latin American States* (University of Chicago Press 2002)

Drezemczewski, A, 'Election of Judges to the Strasbourg Court: An Overview' [2010] European Human Rights Law Review 377

Drezemczewski, A, 'L'élection du juge de l'Union européenne à la Cour européenne des droits de l'homme' [2013] Revue trimestrielle des droits de l'homme 551

Dumbrovský, T, Petkova, B, and Van der Sluis, M, 'Judicial Appointments: the Article 255 TFEU Advisory Panel and Selection Procedures in the Member States' (2014) 51 Common Market Law Review 455

Dzehtsiarou, K, 'Does Consensus Matter? Legitimacy of European Consensus in the Case Law of the European Court of Human Rights' (2011) 10 Public Law 534

Elek, J and Rottman, D, 'Improving Judicial-Performance Evaluation: Countering Bias and Exploring New Methods' (2013) 49 Court Review 140

Engel, NP, 'More Transparency and Governmental Loyalty for Maintaining Professional Quality in the Election of Judges to the European Court of Human Rights' (2008) 32 Human Rights Law Journal 448

Engel, NP, 'Mehr Tansparenz für die Wahrung professionneller Qualität bei den Richter-Wahlen zum EGMR' (2012) 39 Europäische Grundrechte-Zeitschrift 486

Eriksen, E, *The Unfinished Democratization of Europe* (Oxford University Press 2009)

Ferejohn, J and Kramer, L, 'Independent Judges, Dependent Judiciary: Institutionalizing Judicial Restraint' (2002) 77 New York University Law Review 962

Fiss, O, 'The Right Degree of Independence' in I Stozky (ed), *Transition to Democracy in Latin America: The Role of the Judiciary* (Westview Press 1993)

Flauss, J-F, 'Radioscopie de l'élection de la nouvelle Cour européenne des droits de l'homme' [1998] Revue trimestrielle des droits de l'homme 435

Flauss, J-F, 'Le renouvellement triennal de la Cour européenne des droits de l'homme' [2001] Revue trimestrielle des droits de l'homme 693

Flauss, J-F, 'Brèves observations sur le second renouvellement triennal de la Cour européenne des droits de l'homme' [2005] Revue trimestrielle des droits de l'homme 5

Flauss, J-F, 'Les élections de juges à la Cour européenne des droits de l'homme (2005–2008)' [2008] Revue trimestrielle des droits de l'homme 713

Flogaitis, S, Zwart, T, and Fraser, J (eds), *The European Court of Human Rights and Its Discontents* (Edward Elgar Publishing 2013)

Follesdal, A, 'The Legitimacy of International Human Rights Review: The Case of the European Court of Human Rights' (2009) 40 Journal of Social Philosophy 595

Follesdal, A, Schaffer, J, and Ulfstein, G (eds), *The Legitimacy of International Human Rights Regimes* (Cambridge University Press 2013)

Fyrnys, M, 'Expanding Competences by Judicial Lawmaking. The Pilot Judgment Procedure of the European Court of Human Rights' in A von Bogdandy and I Venzke (eds), *International Judicial Lawmaking* (Springer 2012)

Garoupa, N and Ginsburg, T, 'Judicial Audiences and Reputation: Perspectives from Comparative Law' (2009) 47 Columbia Journal of Transnationational Law 451

Garoupa, N and Ginsburg, T, 'The Comparative Law and Economics of Judicial Councils' (2009) 27 Berkeley Journal of International Law 52

Garzón Clariana, G, 'Le rôle du Parlement européen dans le développement de la Cour de justice' in Ninon Colneric et al (eds), *Une communauté de droit. Festschrift für Gil Carlos Rodríguez Iglesias* (BWV 2003)

Geyh, C, 'Judicial Election Reconsidered: A Plea for Radical Moderation' (2012) 35 Harvard Journal of Law and Public Policy 623

Gibson, J and Caldeira, G, 'The Legitimacy of Transnational Legal Institutions' (1995) 39 American Journal of Political Science 459

Gibson, J and Caldeira, G, 'Changes in the Legitimacy of the European Court of Justice' (1998) 28 British Journal of Political Science 63

Gibson, J, Caldeira, G, and Baird, V, 'On the Legitimacy of National High Courts' (1998) 92 American Political Science Review 343

Ginsburg, T, 'Political Constraints on International Courts' in C Romano, K Alter, and Y Shany (eds), *The Oxford Handbook of International Adjudication* (Oxford University Press 2014)

Grabenwarter, C and Pabel, K, *Europäische Menschenrechtskonvention* (5th edn, Beck 2012)

Greer, S, *The European Convention on Human Rights: Achievements, Problems and Prospects* (Cambridge University Press 2006)

Greer, S, 'What's Wrong with the European Convention on Human Rights?' (2008) 30 Human Rights Quarterly 701

Greer, S and Wildhaber, L, 'Revisiting the Debate about 'constitutionalising' the European Court of Human Rights' (2012) 12 Human Rights Law Review 655

Guarnieri, C, 'Judicial Independence in Europe: Threat or Resource for Democracy?' (2013) 49 Representation 347

Guarnieri, C and Piana, D, 'Judicial Independence and the Rule of Law' in S Sheetreet and C Forsyth (eds), *The Culture of Judicial Independence. Conceptual Foundations and Practical Challenges* (Martinus Nijhoff 2012)

Habermas, J, *Der gespaltene Westen* (Suhrkamp 2004)

Habermas, J, 'Konstitutionalisierung des Völkerrechts und die Legitimationsprobleme einer verfaßten Weltgesellschaft' in *Philosophische Texte Band 4. Politische Theorie* (Suhrkamp 2009)

Habermas, J, 'The Crisis of the European Union in the Light of a Constitutionalization of International Law' (2012) 23 European Journal of International Law 335

Harmsen, R, 'The European Convention on Human Rights after Enlargement' (2001) 5 The International Journal of Human Rights 18

Harmsen, R, 'The Reform of the Convention System: Institutional Restructuring and the (Geo-)Politics of Human Rights' in J Christoffersen and M Rask Madsen (eds), *The European Court of Human Rights between Law and Politics* (Oxford University Press 2011)

Hedigan, J, 'The Election of Judges to the European Court of Human Rights' in M Kohen (ed), *Promoting Justice, Human Rights and Conflict Resolution Through International Law. Liber amicorum Lucius Caflisch* (Brill 2007)

Helfer, L, 'Redesigning the European Court of Human Rights: Embeddedness as a Deep Structural Principle of the European Human Rights Regime' (2008) 9 European Journal of International Law 125

Helfer, L and Slaughter, AM, 'Toward a Theory of Effective Supranational Adjudication' (1997) 107 Yale Law Journal 273

Helfer, L and Slaughter, AM, 'Why States Create International Tribunals: A Response to Professors Posner and Yoo' (2005) 3 California Law Review 899

Helfer, L, Slaughter, AM, and Voeten, E, 'International Courts as Agents of Legal Change: Evidence from LGBT Rights in Europe' (2014) 68 International Organization 77

Hirschl, R, *Towards Juristocracy: The Origins and Consequences of the New Constitutionalism* (Harvard University Press 2004)

Jacob, M, 'Precedents: Lawmaking Through International Adjudication' (2011) 12 German Law Journal 1005

Jacob, M, *Precedents and Case-Based Reasoning in the European Court of Justice: Unfinished Business* (Cambridge University Press 2014)

Jackson, V, 'Constitutional Comparisons: Convergence, Resistance, Engagement' (2005) 119 Harvard Law Review 109

Jackson, V, 'Judicial Independence: Structure, Context, Attitude' in Anja Seibert-Fohr (ed), *Judicial Independence in Transition* (Springer 2012)

Jestaedt, M et al, *Das entgrenzte Gericht* (Suhrkamp 2011)

Jones, E and Kelemen, D, 'The Euro Goes to Court' (2014) 56 Survival: Global Politics and Strategy 15

Karpenstein, U, 'Article 253 TFEU' in E Grabitz, M Hilf, and M Nettesheim (eds), *Das Recht der Europäischen Union* (Beck 2013)

Katzenstein, S, 'In the Shadow of Crisis: The Creation of International Courts in the Twentieth Century' (2014) 55 Harvard International Law Journal 151

Kauppi, N and Madsen, MR (eds), *Transnational Power Elites: The New Professionals of Governance, Law and Security* (Routledge 2013)

Keohane, R, Moravcsik, A, and Slaughter, AM, 'Legalized Dispute Resolution: Interstate and Transnational' (2000) 54 International Organization 457

Kelemen, D, *Eurolegalism: The Transformation of Law and Regulation in the European Union* (Harvard University Press 2011)

Kelemen, D, 'The Political Foundations of Judicial Independence in the European Union' (2012) 19 Journal of European Public Policy 43

Kelemen, D, 'Judicialisation, Democracy and European Integration' (2013) 49 Representation 295

Kennedy, T, 'Thirteen Russians! The Composition of the European Court of Justice', in AIL Campbell and M Voyatzi (eds), *Legal Reasoning and Judicial Interpretation of European Law. Essays in Honour of Lord Mackenzie-Stuart* (Trenton Publishing 1996)

Kenney, S, 'The Members of the Court of Justice of the European Communities' (1998) 5 Columbia Journal of European Law 101

Kenney, S, 'Breaking the Silence: Gender Mainstreaming and the Composition of the European Court of Justice' (2002) 10 Feminist Legal Studies 262

Kenney, S, 'Equal Employment Opportunity and Representation: Extending the Frame to the Courts' (2004) 11 Social Politics 1

Kenney, S, *Gender and Justice: Why Women in the Judiciary Really Matter* (Routledge 2012)

Kohler-Koch, B and Rittberger, B (eds), *Debating the Democratic Legitimacy of the European Union* (Rowman & Littlefield Publishers 2007)

Kosař, D, 'The Least Accountable Branch (review essay)' (2013) 11 International Journal of Constitutional Law 234

Kosař, D, 'Policing Separation of Powers: A New Role for the European Court of Human Rights?' (2012) 8 European Constitutional Law Review 33

Koskenniemi, M, *The Gentle Civilizer of Nations: The Rise and Fall of International Law 1870–1960* (Cambridge University Press 2001)

Krüger, HC, 'Procédure de sélection des juges de la nouvelle Cour européenne des droits de l'homme' (1996) 8 Revue universelle des droits de l'homme 113

Krynen, J, *L'Etat de justice France, XIIIe–XXe siècle. Tome II: L'emprise contemporaine des juges* (Gallimard 2012)

Kuijer, M, 'Voting Behaviour and National Bias in the European Court of Human Rights and the International Court of Justice' (1997) 10 Leiden Journal of International Law 49

Latour, B, *La fabrique du droit: Une ethnographie du Conseil d'État* (La Découverte 2002)

Lester, A, 'The European Court of Human Rights after 50 Years' in J Christoffersen and MR Madsen (eds), *The European Court of Human Rights between Law and Politics* (Oxford University Press 2011)

Limbach, J et al, *Judicial Independence: Law and Practice of Appointments to the European Court of Human Rights* (Interlights 2003)

Lord Lester, A, 'Universality v. Subsidiarity: A Reply?' (1998) 1 European Human Rights Law Review 73

Loucaides, L, 'Reflections of a Former European Court of Human Rights Judge on his Experiences as a Judge' [2010] Roma Rights Journal 61

Louis, J-V, 'La nomination des juges de la Cour de justice' (2013) 48 Cahiers de droit européen 567

Luhmann, N, *Grundrechte als Institution: ein Beitrag zur politischen Soziologie* (Duncker & Humblot 1974)

Luhmann, N, *Das Recht der Gesellschaft* (Suhrkamp 1993)

Mackenzie, R and Sands, P, 'Judicial Selection for International Courts: Towards Common Principles and Practices' in Kate Malleson and Peter H Russell (eds), *Appointing Judges in an Age of Judicial Power: Critical Perspectives from around the World* (University of Toronto Press 2006)

Mackenzie, R and Sands, P, 'International Courts and Tribunals and the Independence of the International Judge' (2003) 44 Harvard International Law Journal 27

Mackenzie, R et al, *Selecting International Judges: Principle, Process, and Politics* (Oxford University Press 2010)

Madsen, MR, 'France, the UK and "Boomerang" of the Internationalization of Human Rights (1945–2000)' in S Halliday and P Schmidt (eds), *Human Rights Brought Home: Socio-Legal Perspectives on Human Rights in the National Context* (Hart Publishing 2004)

Madsen, MR, 'From Cold War Instrument to Supreme European Court: The European Court of Human Rights at the Crossroads of International and National Law and Politics' (2007) 32 Law & Social Inquiry 13

Madsen, MR, *La genèse de l'Europe des droits de l'homme: Enjeux juridiques et stratégies d'Etat (France, Grande-Bretagne et pays scandinaves, 1945-1970)* (Presses universitaires de Strasbourg 2010)

Madsen, MR, 'Legal Diplomacy—Law, Politics and the Genesis of Postwar European Human Rights' in SL Hoffmann (ed), *Human Rights in the Twentieth Century: A Critical History* (Cambridge University Press 2011)

Madsen, MR, 'Human Rights and the Hegemony of Ideology: European Lawyers and the Cold War Battle over International Human Rights' in Y Dezalay and B Garth (eds), *Lawyers and the Construction of Transnational Justice* (Routledge 2012)

Madsen, MR, 'Sociological Approaches to International Courts' in K Alter, CPR Romano, and Y Shany (eds), *Oxford University Press Handbook of International Adjudication* (Oxford University Press 2014)

Mahoney, P, 'Judicial Activism and Judicial Self-restraint in the European Court of Human Rights: Two Sides of the Same Coin' (1990) 11 Human Rights Law Journal 57

Mahoney, P, 'The International Judiciary—Independence and Accountability' (2008) 7 Law and Practice of International Courts and Tribunals 313

Majone, G, *Dilemmas of European Integration. The Ambiguities and Pitfalls of Integration by Stealth* (Oxford University Press 2005)

Malenovský, J, 'L'indépendance des juges internationaux' in *Recueil des cours de l'Académie de droit international de la Haye* (Martinus Nijhoff 2011)

Malleson, K, 'Parliamentary Scrutiny of Supreme Court Nominees: A View from the United Kingdom' (2007) 44 Osgoode Hall Law Journal 557

Malleson, K and Russell, P (eds), *Appointing Judges in an Age of Judicial Power* (University of Toronto Press 2006)

Mancini, F and Keeling, D, 'Democracy and the European Court of Justice' (1994) 57 Modern Law Review 175

Mbongo, P and Vauchez, A (eds), *Dans la fabrique du droit européen: scenes, acteurs et publics de la Cour de justice des Communautés europeénnes* (Bruylant 2009)

Milner, D, 'Protocols no. 15 and 16 to the European Convention on Human Rights in the Context of the Perennial Process of Reform: A Long and Winding Road' (2014) 17 Zeitschrift für Europarechtliche Studien 19

Möllers, C, *The Three Branches: A Comparative Model of Separation of Powers* (Oxford University Press 2013)

Moravcsik, A, *The Choice for Europe* (Cornell University Press 1998)

Moravcsik, A, 'The Origins of Human Rights Regimes: Democratic Delegation in Post-war Europe' (2000) 54 International Organization 217

Myjer, E, 'Are Judges of the European Court of Human Rights so Qualified that they are in No Need of Initial and In-Service Training? A "Straatsburgse Myj/mering" (Myjer's Musings from Strasbourg) for L Zwaak' in Y Haeck et al (eds), *The Realisation of Human Rights: When Theory Meets Practice: Studies in Honour of Leo Zwak* (Intersentia 2014)

O'Boyle, M, 'The Future of the European Court of Human Rights' (2011) 12 German Law Journal 1862

Ost, F, *Dire le droit, faire justice* (Bruylant 2007)

Passos, R, 'Le système juridictionnel de l'Union' in G Amato, H Bribosia and B de Witte (eds), *Genèse et destine de la Constitution européenne* (Bruylant 2007)

Paynter, S, and Kearney, R, 'Who Watches the Watchmen? Evaluating Judicial Performance in the American States' (2010) 41 Administration and Society 923

Penner, J, 'Legal Reasoning and the Authority of Law' in S Paulson et al (eds) *Rights, Culture, and the Law: Themes from the Legal and Political Philosophy of Joseph Raz* (Oxford University Press 2003)

Pernice, I et al, *A Democratic Solution to the Crisis. Reform Steps towards a Democratically Based Economic and Financial Constitution for Europe* (Nomos 2012)

Pescatore, P, *The Law of Integration* (Springer 1974)

Petkova, B, 'Three Levels of Dialogue at the Court of Justice of the European Union and the European Court of Human Rights' in K Dzehtsiarou et al (eds) *Human Rights Law in Europe: The Influence, Overlaps and Contradictions of the EU and the ECHR* (Routledge 2014)

Posner, E, *The Perils of Global Legalism* (University of Chicago Press 2009)

Posner, E and Yoo, J, 'Judicial Independence in International Tribunals' (2005) 93 California Law Review 1

Rasmussen, M, 'Revolutionizing European Law: A History of the Van Gend en Loos judgment' (2014) 12 International Journal of Constitutional Law 136

Rasmussen, M, 'The Origins of a Legal Revolution: The Early History of the European Court of Justice' (2008) 14 Journal of European Integration History 77

Resnik, J, '"Naturally" without Gender: Women, Jurisdiction, and the Federal Courts' (1991) 66 New York University Law Review 1682

Rodriguez Iglesias, G, 'The Judge Confronts Himself as Judge' in R Badinter and S Breyer (eds), *Judges in Contemporary Democracy. An International Conversation* (New York University Press 2004)

Romano, C, 'A Taxonomy of International Rule of Law Institutions' (2011) 2 Journal of International Dispute Settlement 241

Romano, C, 'The Proliferation of International Tribunals: Piecing Together the Puzzle' (1999) 31 New York University Journal of International Law and Politics 709

Ross, W, 'The Ratings Game: Factors that Influence Judicial Reputation' (1996) 79 Marquette Law Review 401

Ruiz, B and Rubio-Marín, R, 'The Gender of Representation: On Democracy, Equality, and Parity' (2008) 6 International Journal of Constitutional Law 287

Russell, P and O'Brien, D (eds), *Judicial Independence in the Age of Democracy: Critical Perspectives from Around the World* (University Press of Virginia 2001)

Sajó, A, 'An All-European Conversation: Promoting a Common Understanding of European Human Rights', in S Flogaitis, T Zwart, and J Fraser (eds), *The European Court of Human Rights and its Discontents* (Edward Elgar Publishing 2013)

Sankari, S, *European Court of Justice Legal Reasoning in Context* (Europa Law Publishing 2013)

Sauvé, J-M, 'Le rôle du comité 255 dans le sélection du juge de l'Union', in A Rosas, E Levits, and Y Bot (eds), *The Court of Justice and the Construction of Europe: Analyses and Perspectives on Sixty Years of Case-law—La Cour de Justice et la Construction de l'Europe: Analyses et Perspectives de Soixante Ans de Jurisprudence* (Asser Press/Springer 2013)

Schaiko, G, Lemmens, P, and Lemmens, K, 'Belgium' in J Gerards and J Fleuren (eds), *Implementation of the European Convention on Human Rights and of the Judgments of the ECtHR in National Case Law. A Comparative Analysis* (Intersentia 2014)

Schepel, H and Wesseling, R, 'The Legal Community: Judges, Lawyers, Officials and Clerks in the Writing of Europe' (1997) 3 European Law Journal 165

Schermers, H, 'Election of Judges to the European Court of Human Rights' (1998) 23 European Law Review 568

Schönberger, C, 'Höchstrichterliche Rechtsfindung und Auslegung gerichtlicher Entsch eidungen' in G Lienbacher et al (eds), *Grundsatzfragen der Rechtsetzung und Rechtsfindung. Veröffentlichungen der Vereinigung der Deutschen Staatsrechtslehrer* (De Gruyter 2012)

Sevón, L, 'La procédure de sélection des membres du TFPUE' in '*Le TFPUE 2005-2010: Actes du colloque organisé à l'occasion du 5ème anniversaire du TFP*', Special issue (2011) 20 Revue universelle des droits de l'homme, 1-3

Shapiro, M, *Courts. A Comparative and Political Analysis* (University of Chicago Press 1981)

Shapiro, M, 'Judicial Independence: New Challenges in Established Nations' (2013) 20 Indiana Journal of Global Legal Studies 253

Shany, Y, 'No Longer a Weak Department of Power? Reflections on the Emergence of a New International Judiciary' (2009) 20 European Journal of International Law 73

Shany, Y, *Assessing the Effectiveness of International Courts* (Oxford University Press 2014)

Sheetreet, S, *Judges on Trial: A Study of the Appointment and Accountability of the English Judiciary* (North Holland Publishing Company 1976)

Sheetreet, S, 'The Normative Cycle of Shaping Judicial Independence in Domestic and International Law: The Mutual Impact of National and International Jurisprudence and Contemporary Practical and Conceptual Challenges' (2008) 10 Chicago Journal of International Law 299

Sheetreet, S, 'Creating a Culture of Judicial Independence: The Practical Challenge and the Conceptual and Constitutional Infrastructure' in S Sheetreet and C Forsyth (eds), *The Culture of Judicial Independence. Conceptual Foundations and Practical Challenges* (Martinus Nijhoff 2012)

Shelton, D, 'Legal Norms to Promote the Independence and Accountability of International Tribunals' (2003) 2 The Law and Practice of International Courts and Tribunals 27

Siegel, R, 'From Colorblindness To Antibalkanization: An Emerging Ground of Decision in Race Equality Cases' (2011) 120 Yale Law Review 1278

Simpson, B, *Human Rights and the End of Empire: Britain and the Genesis of the European Convention* (Oxford University Press 2004)

Skouteris, T, 'The New Tribunalism: Strategies of (De)Legitimization in the Era of Adjudication' (2006) 17 Finnish Yearbook of International Law 307

Slaughter, A-M, *A New World Order* (Princeton University Press 2004)

Slaughter, A-M et al (eds) *The European Courts & National Courts: Doctrine and Jurisprudence* (Hart 1998)

Solanke, I, 'Independence and Diversity in the European Court of Justice' (2009) 15 Columbia Journal of European Law 91

Stein, E, 'Lawyers, Judges and the Making of a Transnational Constitution' (1981) 75 American Journal of International Law 1

Steinberg, R, 'Judicial Lawmaking at the WTO: Discursive, Constitutional, and Political Constraints' (2004) 98 The American Journal of International Law 247

Stone Sweet, A, 'Sur la constitutionnalisation de la Convention Européenne des Droits de l'Homme: Cinquante ans après son installation, la Cour Européene des Droits de l'Homme conçue comme une cour constitutionelle' (2009) 80 Revue trimestrielle des droits de l'homme 923

Stone Sweet, A, 'The European Court of Justice and the Judicialization of EU Governance' (2010) 5 Living Reviews in European Governance

Stone Sweet, A, 'Trustee Courts and the Judicialization of International Regimes: The Politics of Majoritarian Activism in the ECTHR, the EU, and the WTO' (2013) 1 Journal of Law and Courts 61

Stone Sweet, A and Brunell, T, 'The European Court of Justice, State Noncompliance, and the Politics of Override' (2012) 106 American Political Science Review 204

Stone Sweet, A and Mathews, J, 'Proportionality Balancing and Global Constitutionalism' (2008) 47 Columbia Journal of Transnational Law 73

Tarr, G, *Without Fear or Favor: Judicial Independence and Judicial Accountability in the States* (Stanford University Press 2012)

Terris, D, Romano, C, and Swigart, L, *The International Judge: An Introduction to the Men and Women Who Decide the World's Cases* (Brandeis University Press 2007)

Toniatti, R, 'L'indipendenza dei giudici sovranazionali ed internazionali' (2010) IV Diritto Pubblico Comparato ed Europeo 1733

Vajić, N, 'Some Remarks Linked to the Independence of International Judges and the Observance of Ethical Rules in the European Court of Human Rights' in C Hohmann-Dennhardt et al (eds), *Grundrechte und Solidarität: Durchsetzung und Verfahren Festschrift für Renate Jaeger* (NP Engel Verlag 2010)

Vanberg, G, 'Establishing and Maintaining Judicial Independence' in K Whittington, RD Kelemen, and Gregory Caldeira (eds), *The Oxford Handbook of Law & Politics* (Oxford University Press 2008)

van Caenegem, R, *Judges, Legislators and Professors* (Cambridge University Press 1987)

van der Woude, M, 'Het Gerecht van de Europese Unie—Een bestuursrechter onder druk' (2013) 87 Nederlands Juristen Blad 14

Vauchez, A, 'The Transnational Politics of Judicialization. Van Gend en Loos and the Making of EU Polity' (2010) 16 European Law Journal 1

Vauchez, A and de Witte, B (eds) *Lawyering Europe: European Law as a Transnational Social Field* (Hart 2014)

Vesterdorf, B, 'La nomination des juges de la Cour de Justice de l'Union européenne' (2012) 47 Cahiers de droit européen 610

Voßkuhle, A, *Rechtsschutz gegen den Richter: Zur Integration der Dritten Gewalt in das verfassungsrechtliche Kontrollsystem vor dem Hintergrund des Art. 19 Abs. 4 GG* (Beck 1993)

Voßkuhle, A, and Sydow, G, 'Die demokratische Legitimation des Richters' (2002) 57 Juristenzeitung 673

Voeten, E, 'Does a Professional Judiciary Induce More Compliance? Evidence from the European Court of Human Rights', 2012, online at <ssrn.com/abstract=2029786>

Voeten, E, 'The Politics of International Judicial Appointments: Evidence from the European Court of Human Rights' (2007) 61 International Organization 669

Voeten, E, 'The Impartiality of International Judges: Evidence from the European Court of Human Rights' (2008) 102 American Political Science Review 417

Voeten, E, 'The Politics of International Judicial Appointments' (2008–9) 9 Chicago Journal of International Law 387

Voeten, E, 'Politics, Judicial Behaviour, and Institutional Design', in J Christoffersen and M Rask Madsen (eds), *The European Court of Human Rights between Law and Politics* (Oxford University Press 2011)

Voeten, E, 'Public Opinion and the Legitimacy of International Courts' (2013) 14 Theoretical Inquiries in Law 411

von Bogdandy, A and Venzke, I, 'In Whose Name? An Investigation of International Courts' Public Authority and Its Democratic Justification' (2012) 23 European Journal of International Law 7

von Bogdandy, A and Venzke, I, 'On the Functions of International Courts: An Appraisal in Light of their Burgeoning Public Authority' (2013) 26 Leiden Journal of International Law 49

von Bogdandy, A and Venzke, I, *In wessen Namen? Internationale Gerichte in Zeiten globalen Regierens* (Suhrkamp 2014)

von Danwitz, T, 'Funktionsbedingungen der Rechtsprechung des Europäischen Gerichtshofes' (2008) 43 Europarecht 769

Wagner, R and Pembridge, L, 'Is the Federal Circuit Succeeding? An Empirical Assessment of Judicial Performance' (2004) 152 University of Pennsylvania Law Review 1105

Weber, M, *Wirtschaft und Gesellschaft. Grundriss der verstehenden Soziologie* (5th edn, Mohr 1980)

Weiler, J, 'The Transformation of Europe' (1991) 100 Yale Law Journal 2403

Weiler, J, 'Epilogue: Judging the Judges—Apology and Critique' in Maurice Adams et al (eds), *Judging Europe's Judges* (Hart 2013).

Wheeler, R, 'Judicial Independence in the United States of America', in A Seibert-Fohr (ed), *Judicial Independence in Transition* (Springer 2012)

Wildhaber, L, 'A Constitutional Future for the European Court of Human Rights?' (2002) 23 Human Rights Law Journal 161

Wind, M, 'The Nordics, the EU and the Reluctance Towards Supranational Judicial Review' (2010) 48 Journal of Common Market Studies 1039

Wind, M, 'When Parliament Comes First—The Danish Concept of Democracy Meets the European Union' (2009) 27 Nordisk Tidsskrift For Menneskerettigheter 272

Wood, M, 'The Selection of Candidates for International Judicial Office: Recent Practice' in TM Ndiaye and R Wolfrum (eds), *Law of the Sea, Environmental Law and Settlement of Disputes* (Koninklijke Brill 2007)

Zimmermann, D, *The Independence of International Courts* (Nomos 2014)

Zoll, F, 'The System of Judicial Appointment in Poland—A Question of the Legitimacy of the Judicial Power' in S Sheetreet and C Forsyth (eds), *The Culture of Judicial Independence. Conceptual Foundations and Practical Challenges* (Martinus Nijhoff 2012)

Zwart, T, 'More Human Rights than Court: Why the Legitimacy of the EurCourtHR is in Need of Repair and How It Can be Done' in S Flogaitis, T Zwart, and J Fraser (eds), *The European Court of Human Rights and its Discontents* (Edward Elgar Publishing 2013)

Index